Valor and Vulnerability

Valor and Vulnerability

Pastoral Explorations of Intimacy, Grief, and Resilience among Boys and Men

Edited by
ROBERT C. DYKSTRA
& RYAN LAMOTHE

PICKWICK *Publications* · Eugene, Oregon

VALOR AND VULNERABILITY
Pastoral Explorations of Intimacy, Grief, and Resilience among Boys and Men

Copyright © 2025 Wipf and Stock Publishers. All rights reserved. Except for brief quotations in critical publications or reviews, no part of this book may be reproduced in any manner without prior written permission from the publisher. Write: Permissions, Wipf and Stock Publishers, 199 W. 8th Ave., Suite 3, Eugene, OR 97401.

Pickwick Publications
An Imprint of Wipf and Stock Publishers
199 W. 8th Ave., Suite 3
Eugene, OR 97401
www.wipfandstock.com

PAPERBACK ISBN: 979-8-3852-0911-8
HARDCOVER ISBN: 979-8-3852-0912-5
EBOOK ISBN: 979-8-3852-0913-2

Cataloguing-in-Publication data:

Names: Dykstra, Robert C., editor. | LaMothe, Ryan, editor.

Title: Valor and vulnerability: pastoral explorations of intimacy, grief, and resilience among boys and men / edited by Robert C. Dykstra and Ryan LaMothe.

Description: Eugene, OR: Pickwick Publications, 2025. | Includes bibliographical references and index.

Identifiers: ISBN 979-8-3852-0911-8 (print). | ISBN 979-8-3852-0912-5 (print). | ISBN 979-8-3852-0913-2 (epub).

Subjects: LSCH: Boys. | Teenage boys. | Pastoral care.

Classification: BV4450 V15 2024 (print). | BV4450 (epub).

Scripture quotations marked (CEV) are from the Contemporary English Version Copyright © 1991, 1992, 1995 by American Bible Society. Used by Permission.

Scripture quotations marked (KJV) are from the King James Version or Authorized Version (1611), which is in the public domain.

Scripture quotations marked (NIV) are taken from The Holy Bible, New International Version® NIV® Copyright © 1973, 1978, 1984, 2011 by Biblica, Inc. Used with permission. All rights reserved worldwide.

Scripture quotations marked (NRSV) are taken from the New Revised Standard Version Bible © 1989 Division of Christian Education of the National Council of the Churches of Christ in the United States of America. Used by permission. All rights reserved worldwide.

The editors wish to express appreciation to Springer Publications for permission to use material from works previously published in *Pastoral Psychology*: Robert C. Dykstra, "Therapeutic Imagination and the Mystical Moment: Transforming Entrenched Boyhood Grief," 69 (2020) 331–51; Nathan Carlin, "A Psychoanalytic Reading of *A Monster Calls*: Biblical Congruencies and Theological Implications," 66 (2017) 759–77; Craig A. Rubano, "Opening Doors to Resilience and a Gender-Diverse Pastoral Theology," 71 (2022) 769–87; Danjuma G. Gibson, "When Empathy Is Not Enough: A Reflection on the Self-Experience of Black Boys in Public Spaces," 67 (2018) 611–26; Jaco J. Hamman, "The Organ of Tactility: Fantasy, Image, and Male Masturbation," 67 (2018) 627–53; Rubén Arjona, "You Are My Friends: Pastoral Care With Young Mexican Men," 67 (2018) 589–610; Ryan LaMothe, "Men, Warriorism, and Mourning: The Development of Unconventional Warriors," 66 (2017) 819–36; Adam Tietje and Joshua Morris, "Moral Injury: Care and Politics," initially published as "Shifting the Pastoral Theology Conversation on Moral Injury: The Personal Is Political for Soldiers and Veterans, Too," 72 (2023) 863–80; Hyon-Uk Shin, "An Eriksonian Psycho-Social Response to Confucius on the Development of Virtue in Boys and Men," 67 (2018) 673–688; Phil C. Zylla, "Aspects of Men's Sorrow: Reflection on Phenomenological Writings About Grief," 66 (2017) 837–54. The editors offer grateful thanks to the Estate of Philip Guston and the Guston Foundation for permission to use Philip Guston's *Locker Room (Navy Pre-Flight Training)*; 1943; watercolor and ink on paper; 30 x 40 in.; private collection; artwork © The Estate of Philip Guston; image courtesy of the Guston Foundation and Hauser & Wirth. Kind thanks to W. W. Norton & Company, Inc., for permission to use excerpts from chapter 5 of *Narrative Therapy in Wonderland: Connecting with Children's Imaginative Know-How* by David Marsten, David Epston, and Laurie Markham, © 2016 by David Marsten, David Epston, and Laurie Markham.

In memory of Donald Capps
and with gratitude for our friends in the Philadelphia Group for
Pastoral Theology with Boys and Men

Contents

List of Contributors | xi

Acknowledgments | xv

Introduction | xvii

1   Therapeutic Imagination and the Mystical Moment: Transforming Entrenched Boyhood Grief | 1
ROBERT C. DYKSTRA

2   A Psychoanalytic Reading of *A Monster Calls*: Biblical Congruencies and Theological Implications | 30
NATHAN CARLIN

3   Opening Doors to Resilience and a Gender-Diverse Pastoral Theology | 56
CRAIG A. RUBANO

4   No Greater Love: The Light of Beauford Delaney in the Life of James Baldwin | 80
JAY-PAUL HINDS

5   When Empathy is Not Enough: A Reflection on the Self-Experience of Black Boys in Public Spaces | 98
DANJUMA G. GIBSON

6   The Organ of Tactility: Fantasy, Image, and Male Masturbation | 120
JACO J. HAMMAN

7   You Are My Friends: Pastoral Care with
    Young Mexican Men | 158
    RUBÉN ARJONA

8   Men, Warriorism, and Mourning:
    The Development of Unconventional Warriors | 188
    RYAN LAMOTHE

9   Moral Injury: Care and Politics | 212
    ADAM TIETJE AND JOSHUA MORRIS

10 William James's Depression, Vocational Despair,
    and Self-Murder | 236
    REGGIE ABRAHAM

11 An Eriksonian Psycho-Social Response to Confucius
    on the Development of Virtue in Boys and Men | 260
    HYON-UK SHIN

12 Aspects of Men's Sorrow: Reflection on
    Phenomenological Writings About Grief | 281
    PHIL C. ZYLLA

Index | 305

Contributors

REGGIE ABRAHAM is Assistant Professor of Pastoral Care and Chaplaincy at United Theological Seminary in Dayton, Ohio. He also serves as the Director of Christian Education for the Ebenezer Mission in India, where he has oversight for two seminaries and three Bible schools. In addition to congregational ministry leadership, he has nearly a decade of experience in prison ministry at Rikers Island Correctional Facility in Jamaica, New York, and completed clinical pastoral education training in hospice and Level 1 trauma centers in Pennsylvania and Illinois. His teaching and research interests include the psychology of religion, William James studies, and pastoral encounters with world religions.

RUBÉN ARJONA is Assistant Professor of Pastoral Care at Union Presbyterian Seminary in Richmond, Virginia. He was born and raised in Mexico City, where he was ordained as a Presbyterian minister and served several congregations and seminaries. His research includes the intersections of pastoral care and liberation theologies, the pastoral care of men, the care of couples and families, and Erik H. Erikson's psychosocial theory.

NATHAN CARLIN is Director of the McGovern Center for Humanities and Ethics and Samuel Karff Professor at The University of Texas Health Science Center at Houston. He is the author of nine books, including most recently core texts for medical humanities. These include *Medical Humanities: An Introduction*, *Teaching Health Humanities*, *Contemporary Physician-Authors: Exploring the Insights of Doctors Who Write*, and *Pathographies of Mental Illness*. He lives in Houston, Texas.

ROBERT C. DYKSTRA is Charlotte W. Newcombe Professor of Pastoral Theology at Princeton Theological Seminary and co-organizer of scholarly conferences of the Group for New Directions in Pastoral Theology and the Philadelphia Group for Pastoral Theology with Boys and Men. His books include *Losers, Loners, and Rebels: The Spiritual Struggles of Boys* and *The Faith and Friendships of Teenage Boys*, both co-authored with Allan Hugh

Cole Jr. and Donald Capps, and most recently *Finding Ourselves Lost: Ministry in the Age of Overwhelm*.

DANJUMA G. GIBSON is Professor of Pastoral Theology, Care, and Counseling and Director of the Master of Arts Program in Clinical Mental Health Counseling at Calvin Theological Seminary. A licensed psychotherapist in private practice, his current research explores the intersection of urbanism, Black religious experience, socioeconomics, and psychoanalytic thought. His most recent book, *Through the Eyes of Titans: Finding Courage to Redeem the Soul of a Nation*, engages psychohistory and psychobiography to reimagine leadership, self-care, and love in the 21st century.

JACO J. HAMMAN is Professor of Religion, Psychology, and Culture at Vanderbilt University School of Divinity. A past chaplain and psychotherapist, his research explores play, leadership, the care of men, technology, and aspects of human flourishing. Recent books include *The Essence of Leadership: Maintaining Emotional Independence in Situations Requiring Change* (co-authored with Derek W. Anderson), *Pastoral Virtues for Artificial Intelligence: Care and the Algorithms That Guide Our Lives*, and *Just Traveling: God, Leaving Home, and a Spirituality for the Road*. He lives in Nashville, where he co-founded Our Place Nashville, a nonprofit that places adults with developmental disabilities in Friendship Houses alongside graduate students and displaced elderly persons.

JAY-PAUL HINDS is Associate Professor of Pastoral Theology at Princeton Theological Seminary. He earned his master of divinity and master of theology from Princeton Theological Seminary and his PhD from Emory University along with a certificate in psychoanalytic studies from the Emory University Psychoanalytic Institute. His academic interests include the psychology of religion, object relations theory, pastoral theology, Black psychology, critical pedagogy, and the psycho-spiritual development of African American men. His work has been published in the *Journal of Religion and Health* and *Pastoral Psychology*. His recent book is *A Gift Grows in the Ghetto: Reimagining the Spiritual Lives of Black Men*.

RYAN LAMOTHE is Professor of Pastoral Care and Counseling at Saint Meinrad Seminary and School of Theology. Past president of the Society for Pastoral Theology, he has authored numerous books and articles in the areas of political pastoral theology, psychoanalysis, and psychology of religion. His most recent monographs are *Care of Souls, Care of Polis: Toward a Political Pastoral Theology*, *The Coming Jesus and the Anthropocene*, *Pastoral Care in the Anthropocene Age*, and *A Political Psychoanalysis for*

CONTRIBUTORS

the Anthropocene Age. LaMothe graduated from West Point and is a former U.S. Army Airborne Ranger. He lives in Louisville, Kentucky, with his wife Cindy and Grace the cat.

JOSHUA MORRIS is Assistant Professor of Practical Theology at Union Presbyterian Seminary in Charlotte, North Carolina. He is the author of *Moral Injury Among Returning Veterans: From "Thank You for Your Service" to a Liberative Solidarity* and numerous articles in *Pastoral Psychology*, *Journal of Pastoral Theology*, and *Reflective Practice*. He is an ordained minister with the United Church of Christ and a board-certified chaplain through the Association of Professional Chaplains. He serves as an army chaplain in the U.S. Army Reserve.

CRAIG A. RUBANO is a minister with the Unitarian Universalist Association of Congregations. A summa cum laude graduate of Yale College, he earned a master's degree in English and comparative literature from Columbia University and a master of divinity, master of theology, and PhD in pastoral theology from Princeton Theological Seminary. His articles have focused on practices of grief, along with explorations of resilience and alliance among and with gender-creative persons of all ages, the focus of his recent book *Emerging as Affirmative Pastoral Caregivers Beyond Gender Binaries: Gender Creative Promise*.

HYON-UK SHIN is Adjunct Professor of Pastoral Care and Counseling at Seoul Women's University and founder of Jacob's Well Institute of Psychoanalysis and Psychotherapy in Seoul, South Korea. After completing his PhD in pastoral theology at Princeton Theological Seminary, he trained at the William Alanson White Institute in New York and is a full member of the International Psychoanalytical Association and the American Psychoanalytic Association. He is the author of *Vulnerability and Courage: A Pastoral Theology of Poverty and the Alienated Self* and several articles in the areas of pastoral theology, psychoanalysis, and the psychology of religion. He lives in Seoul with his wife Jeong-Eun and their daughter Claire.

ADAM TIETJE is editor for the *U.S. Army Chaplain Corps Journal* and a ThD candidate in theology and ethics at Duke Divinity School. He is the author of *Toward a Pastoral Theology of Holy Saturday: Providing Spiritual Care for War Wounded Souls* and articles in *Pastoral Psychology*, the *Journal of Church and State*, and *Pro Ecclesia*. Tietje is an ordained minister with the United Church of Christ. He is U.S. Army Ranger qualified and a chaplain in the U.S. Army Reserve.

PHIL C. ZYLLA is Professor of Pastoral Theology and J. Gordon and Margaret Warnock Jones Chair in Church and Ministry at McMaster Divinity College in Hamilton, Ontario. He is the author of *Virtue as Consent to Being: A Pastoral Theological Perspective on Jonathan Edwards* and *The Roots of Sorrow: A Pastoral Theology of Suffering*. His current research focuses on Christian spirituality and congregational studies. He lives in Ancaster, Ontario, with his wife Melodie.

Acknowledgments

We want to thank K. C. Hanson, editor-in-chief at Wipf and Stock, for his many expressions of generosity and kindness to us, along with the entire Pickwick Publications team for their support, including Matthew Wimer, managing editor; George Callihan, editorial administrator; K. C. Hanson for copyediting; marketing director James Stock; Jonathan Hill for typesetting; and Shannon Carter for designing the cover. We are grateful as well to Tiffany Wang and Emily Larson at Hauser & Wirth and to the Philip Guston Foundation for their help obtaining permission to use Guston's artwork on the cover.

We are indebted to Lewis Rambo, former editor of *Pastoral Psychology*, and to Kirk Bingaman, the journal's current editor, for their steadfast support for our own pastoral and scholarly pursuits and for those of other authors whose works are represented here. Kathy McKay deserves a special shoutout for her keen skills as the journal's copyeditor and for her fastidious additional assistance in support of this book.

We also wish to thank Princeton Theological Seminary, including President Jonathan Walton and Dean John Bowlin, for their significant support for this project. With unceasing good cheer, our research assistant Dongho Han, a doctoral student in pastoral theology at Princeton Seminary, has offered inimitable attention to countless details involved in preparing both the manuscript and the book's index. In addition, we offer profound gratitude to executive director Nancy J. Taylor, Lorraine Brown, and the entire staff of the Presbyterian Historical Society in Philadelphia for their consummate hospitality to the Philadelphia Group for Pastoral Theology with Boys and Men.

We offer this book in memory of our beloved friend and colleague Donald Capps (1939–2015) and as a tribute to the many scholars who have participated in the Philadelphia Group over the years. William James (1958), in his essay "What Makes a Life Significant," observes that "certain persons do exist with an enormous capacity for friendship and for taking delight in other people's lives; and . . . such persons know more of truth than if their hearts were not so big" (p. 171).[1] Donald Capps, it strikes us, was just such a person; he had an immense capacity for friendship with us and with many. Friendship and kindness, he believed, are the path to a more expansive truth, a premise that grounds our work and has given us pause and delight in the Philadelphia Group for Pastoral Theology with Boys and Men.

---

1. W. James (1958), *Talks to teachers on psychology: And to students on some of life's ideals*, Norton (original work published 1899).

Introduction

Life is precarious, full of peril and opportunity. Disasters natural and human, oppression, disease, and death afflict individuals, families, and communities. There is no escaping an existential precarity that prompts within us divergent responses, from opportunistic exploitation and despair to courageous perseverance and compassion. Theologies, in one sense, are stories depicting human vulnerability and sometimes valiant, sometimes sinister prospects for meeting its challenges. These stories serve to help us understand, survive, and flourish amid life's challenges and limits. As in other epic narratives, one finds in theological stories heroes and villains, victims and victimizers, rebels and rulers, peacemakers and warriors, creators and destroyers, those who persevere and those who fall.

Pastoral theologians have long sought to understand and assuage the fallout from these experiences of precarity within and among persons and communities (see Clebsch & Jaekle, 1994; Doehring, 2015; Dykstra, 2005; Holifield, 1983; Scheib, 2016). Beginning in the 1930s, Anton Boisen, one of the founding figures of the clinical pastoral education movement, strove to educate ministers in pastoral responses to those suffering from mental illness (Holifield, 1983, pp. 104–105). In the latter half of the twentieth century, the works of Archie Smith (1982), Larry Kent Graham (1992), Bonnie J. Miller-McLemore (1995), and many other pastoral theologians broadened Boisen's initial focus to consider the complexities of caring for children (Lester, 1985), older women (Scheib, 2004), the traumatized (Poling, 2002), the ostracized (Marshall, 1997), and those who grieve (Kelley, 2010). More recently, pastoral theologians have tackled how macro systems such as classism, neoliberal capitalism, and postcolonialism are implicated in the suffering of persons, societies, other species, and the Earth (Helsel, 2015; Johnson, 2016; LaMothe, 2017, 2018, 2023, 2024; McCarroll, 2020; Miller-McLemore, 2022; Pihkala, 2016a, 2016b, 2018a, 2018b; Rogers-Vaughn, 2016). We attempt in this book to further these pastoral theological traditions and trajectories by focusing on the valor and vulnerability of boys and men.

INTRODUCTION

The origin of our project dates to the spring of 2015 and a conversation over lunch shared by Donald Capps and Robert Dykstra, colleagues in pastoral theology at Princeton Theological Seminary. Impressed and aided in their seminary courses by rich edited volumes on nuances of pastoral care around concerns specific to women—books shaped over several years by prominent women pastoral theologians who had collaborated in shared conference conversations (Glaz & Moessner, 1990; Miller-McLemore & Gill-Austern, 1999; Moessner, 1996; Stevenson-Moessner & Snorton, 2009)—Donald and Robert began to wonder whether similar possible benefits might accrue from a focus by male pastoral theologians on contemporary struggles of boys and men. A vision for an academic conference began to take shape that included the conviction that diverse scholars, from doctoral students to faculty of every rank, would have a place at the table.

Nathan Carlin, a pastoral theologian who teaches medical humanities at the University of Texas Medical School at Houston, agreed to help Robert in scoping out a meeting site in the Old City Historic District of Philadelphia. After briefly pounding the cobblestone pavement surrounding Independence Hall one morning, they were welcomed with an astounding degree of hospitality by the staff of the Presbyterian Historical Society, which provided an ideal space for a conference. Invitations were sent to about twenty pastoral theologians in the United States, Canada, and South Korea for a gathering slated for late May of 2016. Those invited were asked to prepare a paper reflecting on any topic of significance to them related to the expansive theme of pastoral theology with boys and men. A full hour of discussion time was promised for each participant's paper along with prospects for deepening friendships through shared laughter over meals. The organizers were buoyed in their hope that conference papers could reach a much wider audience when Lewis Rambo, at that time editor of *Pastoral Psychology*, signaled his willingness to publish them, after peer review, in the journal. Within days, an impressive group of scholars accepted the invitation to attend.

Sadly, Donald Capps would not be among those present at that initial gathering. He died in the aftermath of a car accident in Princeton in August of 2015. Those who had agreed to attend the conference and who knew Professor Capps personally were surveyed following his death and unanimously indicated a desire to proceed. We met as planned the following May. Our shared grief over the loss of a treasured friend and colleague, vigorous conversations around dynamic conference papers, and genuine gratitude over deepening connections among participants at levels both personal and professional led to a widespread sense that what had been conceived as a one-off gathering should recur the following year. As we write this

INTRODUCTION   xix

introduction in 2024, what unofficially has become known as the Philadelphia Group for Pastoral Theology with Boys and Men has met annually, apart from two pandemic years, with a steady influx of new players.

It is hard to capture the degree of intimacy, vulnerability, creativity, intellectual stimulation, and pastoral concern for boys, men, and one another we have experienced in and among this group over time. As co-editors of this volume, we have been impressed by the expansive array of topics, and the depth of efforts at once introspective and academic to address them, that conference participants have pursued in their desire to enhance pastoral approaches to and with those who identify as boys and men. Our primary challenge has been having to choose among what is by now an extensive pool of remarkable essays presented at these conferences over the years. We trust that the present collection will not only heighten the pastoral sensitivity of seminary students, ministers, chaplains, and other readers to complex contemporary plights of boys and men, including quandaries we ourselves confront, but will also hint at the rich satisfactions we have gained as pastoral theologians in common pursuit of addressing these plights.

A BRIEF SYNOPSIS OF THE CHAPTERS

The book consists of twelve chapters written by thirteen scholars. The chapters are ordered to reflect development through the life cycle, moving from dilemmas of grief, sexuality, and gender and racial identity concerns in boyhood, adolescence, and young adulthood to a culminating focus on men's grief in midlife and beyond. Each chapter may be read independently of the others, enabling readers to enter the book at any point of specific personal interest.

In chapter 1, "Therapeutic Imagination and the Mystical Moment: Transforming Entrenched Boyhood Grief," Robert C. Dykstra draws from psychology of religion on the nature of conversion and from pastoral counseling theory on methodizing mystical experiences to explore a previously published case of the rapid transformation of a 10-year-old boy's entrenched grief by means of narrative therapy. Dykstra includes additional reflections on the case derived from a personal interview with the boy's therapist.

Nathan Carlin offers a deep dive into Patrick Ness's (2011) *A Monster Calls*—an award-winning novel and more recent powerful film about a 13-year-old boy whose mother is dying of cancer—in chapter 2, "A Psychoanalytic Reading of *A Monster Calls*: Biblical Congruencies and Theological Implications." Carlin draws on Freud's (2001) *On Dreams* to interpret several scenes from the novel interspersed with lessons from the life of Jesus.

He presses readers to take to heart the complexity of the emotional lives of adolescents and to endeavor to transform their ambivalence into paradoxical truth.

In chapter 3, "Opening Doors to Resilience and a Gender-Diverse Pastoral Theology," Craig A. Rubano attends to young people who migrate away from prescribed gender strictures and into a realm of what psychologist Diane Ehrensaft has coined "gender creativity." Surveying cultural pathologies that subject gender-nonconforming persons to high risk for developing psychosocial adversities that threaten health, safety, and life itself, Rubano envisions a pastoral theology that would open doors to genuine dialogue primed to enhance the resilience of gender-creative individuals.

Jay-Paul Hinds examines the friendship between artists Beauford Delaney and James Baldwin in chapter 4, "No Greater Love: The Light of Beauford Delaney in the Life of James Baldwin." Even in his later years, long after having stepped as an adolescent through Delaney's "unusual door," Baldwin lauded Delaney as the first person who taught him what it means to be an artist. Hinds finds that Delaney's art opened Baldwin's eyes to the transformational power of light and that their friendship allowed Baldwin, during a very dark time in his life, to see not only the world but himself anew.

In chapter 5, "When Empathy Is Not Enough: A Reflection on the Experience of Black Boys in Public Spaces," Danjuma G. Gibson builds on interviews with Black boys in Chicago to ask how they might experience themselves in life-giving ways when negative images and stereotypes denigrate their humanity. Gibson introduces here concepts of "group-level racial delusion"—a societal splitting that inflicts disproportionate violence on Black boys in public spaces—and of "demonic transference," which occurs just prior to the imposition of emotional or physical harm.

Jaco J. Hamman explores the impact of Internet pornography and the interplay of fantasy and image in chapter 6, "The Organ of Tactility: Fantasy, Image, and Male Masturbation." Drawing from several histories of masturbation—British psychoanalyst Brett Kahr on sexual fantasy, philosopher Michael Taussig's concept of "the eye as the organ of tactility," and the case of a 17-year-old boy—Hamman suggests that the use of fantasy, a form of nonvisual sexual arousal, can serve as an alternative to the "tyranny of the eye" and offer relief from compulsive masturbation.

Rubén Arjona, in chapter 7, "You Are My Friends: Pastoral Care With Young Mexican Men," discusses the significance of friendship in counseling young men. Drawing on a case of a Mexican minister and his young parishioner as well as on the friendship motif in the Gospel of John, Arjona maintains that ministers can effectively offer counsel with young Mexican

INTRODUCTION

men who are both parishioners and friends despite the power differential and imperfect mutuality between them.

In chapter 8, "Men, Warriorism, and Mourning: The Development of Unconventional Warriors," Ryan LaMothe considers the interrelation of the warrior ethos, warriorism, and mourning. Drawing from psychology of religion, from Nathan Carlin's discussion of religious mourning, and from the life of Marine Corps Major General Smedley Butler, LaMothe wrestles with how a young man might move from warriorism—an uncritical acceptance of the warrior ethos—to becoming an unconventional warrior capable of critiquing the government he serves.

Adam Tietje and Joshua Morris extend LaMothe's call for "unconventional warriorism" in their work in chapter 9, "Moral Injury: Care and Politics." After reviewing historical and current work in pastoral theology on moral injury among soldiers and finding its depoliticized approach wanting, Tietje and Morris assert that a liberative trajectory can provide the basis for a more robust political pastoral theology and for reinvigorated conceptual categories and resources for pastoral care with veterans.

In chapter 10, "William James's Depression, Vocational Despair, and Self-Murder," Reggie Abraham traces a period of late adolescence and early adulthood in which the great American psychologist and philosopher William James experienced vocational despair. Although a grandson of one of the richest men in America, James was assailed by doubts about his ability to make a living and find a path to personal success. Abraham implicates in part James's mother, Mary Walsh James, in what William James indirectly describes as a "self-murder" that steered him from pursuing the visual arts to graduate studies in the sciences—a murder nonetheless key, Abraham posits, to contributions James made to American intellectual life.

Hyon-Uk Shin offers "An Eriksonian Psycho-Social Response to Confucius on the Development of Virtue in Boys and Men" in chapter 11. Shin notes that for over 600 years Confucius has influenced the formation of Korean males, emphasizing values of benevolence, righteousness, propriety, wisdom, and sincerity. Shin conjectures that relational and emotional vulnerability in Confucius's own boyhood may have contributed to the heightened Confucian emphasis on cognition, will, rites, rules, and decency over the value of human emotion. He proposes the work of Erik H. Erikson, which proffers that robust emotion enriches cognition and strengthens the will, as a complement to Confucian teachings to help Korean men embrace a richer complexity of self.

Finally, in chapter 12, "Aspects of Men's Sorrow: Reflection on Phenomenological Writings on Grief," Phil C. Zylla draws on Max van Manen's discussion of "phenomenological writing," along with recent scholarship on men's grief, to explore C. S. Lewis's (1963) *A Grief Observed*, Nicholas Wolterstorff's (1987) *Lament for a Son*, and Henri Nouwen's (1980, 1982) *In Memoriam* and *A Letter of Consolation*. In considering these well-known autobiographical works, Zylla underscores existential experiences of men mourning the loss of a loved one and offers strategies for the eventual transformation of men's grief into solace.

ON VALOR AND VULNERABILITY

It is a fact for all living beings that life is precarious, and the climate crisis has heightened our awareness of this existential reality. As in any crisis, responses range from feats of compassion and valor to acts of nihilistic despair and mendacity, the latter revealing a desperate fear and rejection of vulnerability whether by an individual or group. Feats of valorous compassion, by contrast, necessarily accept and allow for vulnerability and fear, while also embracing the categorical command to care for one another and, in this climate crisis, to care for other species and the Earth. We often forget that the courage to recognize and accept vulnerability emerges from our caring and faithful relations with each other.

We find this unsettling connection between valor and vulnerability in the stark watercolor entitled *Locker Room (Navy Pre-Flight Training)* by artist Philip Guston (1943) depicted on the cover of this book. In this piece, Guston (1913–1980)—described recently as one of the "most important, powerful, and influential American painters of the last 100 years" (Saltz, 2020) and who from his earliest works in adolescence bore witness to ravages of racism and antisemitism in American life—captures valiant aspiring U.S. Navy pilots, about to be commissioned to combat German atrocities in World War II, in a moment of intentional proximity and tenderness (see "The Air Training Program," 1944). Valor and vulnerability—the stakes for boys and men are sometimes tragically, sometimes triumphantly high. Our gatherings of the Philadelphia Group to reflect on the experiences of boys and men have brought home to us again and again, as we trust the pages that follow will corroborate for readers, the significance of friendship, faith, and care in our responding to precarity together.

REFERENCES

The air training program: In two years it has produced the world's greatest air army. (1944, February). *Fortune*, 29(2). 147–152+. https://www.fulltable.com/vts/f/fortune/pg.htm

INTRODUCTION

Clebsch, W., & Jaekle, C. (1994). *Pastoral care in historical perspective*. Aronson.
Doehring, C. (2015). *The practice of pastoral care*. Westminster John Knox.
Dykstra, R. C. (2005). *Images of pastoral care: Classic readings*. Chalice.
Freud, S. (2001). On dreams. In J. Strachey (Ed. & Trans.), *The standard edition of the complete psychological works of Sigmund Freud* (Vol. 5, pp. 629–686). Vintage. (Original work published 1901).
Glaz, M., & Moessner, J. S. (1990). *Women in travail and transition: A new pastoral care*. Fortress.
Graham, L. K. (1992). *Care of persons, care of worlds: A psychosystems approach*. Abingdon.
Guston, P. (1943). *Locker room (Navy pre-flight training)* [Watercolor and ink]. Private collection.
Helsel, P. B. (2015). *Pastoral power beyond psychology's imagination*. Palgrave.
Holifield, E. B. (1983). *A history of pastoral care in America*. Abingdon.
Johnson, C. C. (2016). *Race, religion, and resilience in the Neoliberal Age*. Palgrave Macmillan.
Kelley, M. (2010). *Grief: Contemporary theory and the practice of ministry*. Fortress.
LaMothe, R. (2017). *Care of souls, care of polis: Toward a political pastoral theology*. Cascade.
LaMothe, R. (2018). *Pastoral reflections on global citizenship: Framing the political in terms of care, faith, and community*. Lexington.
LaMothe, R. (2023). *Pastoral care in the Anthropocene Age: Facing a dire future now*. Lexington.
LaMothe, R. (2024). *The coming Jesus and the Anthropocene*. Cascade.
Lester, A. D. (1985). *Pastoral care with children in crisis*. Westminster John Knox.
Lewis, C. S. (1963). *A grief observed*. Seabury.
Marshall, J. L. (1997). *Counseling lesbian partners*. Westminster John Knox.
McCarroll, P. (2020). Listening for the cries of the Earth: Practical theology in the Anthropocene. *International Journal of Practical Theology, 24*, 29–46.
Miller-McLemore, B. J. (1995). *Also a mother: Work and family as a theological dilemma*. Abingdon.
Miller-McLemore, B. J. (2022). Climate violence and Earth justice. *International Journal of Practical Theology, 26*(2), 329–366.
Miller-McLemore, B. J., & Gill-Austern, B. L. (1999). *Feminist and womanist pastoral theology*. Abingdon.
Moessner, J. S. (1996). *Through the eyes of women: Insights for pastoral care*. Fortress.
Ness, P. (2011). *A monster calls*. Candlewick.
Nouwen, H. J. M. (1980). *In memoriam*. Ave Maria.
Nouwen, H. J. M. (1982). *A letter of consolation*. HarperCollins.
Pihkala, P. (2016a). The pastoral challenge of the eco-reformation: Environmental anxiety and Lutheran eco-reformation. *Dialog: A Journal of Theology, 55*, 131–40.
Pihkala, P. (2016b). Rediscovery of early twentieth-century ecotheology. *Open Theology, 2*, 268–285.
Pihkala, P. (2018a). Death, the environment, and theology. *Dialog, 57*, 287–94.
Pihkala, P. (2018b). Eco-anxiety, tragedy, and hope: Psychological and spiritual dimensions of climate change. *Zygon, 53*, 545–69.
Poling, J. N. (2002/2012). *Render unto God: Economic vulnerability, family violence, and pastoral theology*. Wipf & Stock.

Rogers-Vaughn, B. (2016). *Caring for souls in a neoliberal age*. Palgrave.

Saltz, J. (2020, October 1). 4 museums decided this work shouldn't be shown. They're both right and wrong. Fear postponed a Philip Guston retrospective. *New York Magazine*. https://www.vulture.com/2020/10/museums-decided-philip-gustons-work-shouldnt-be-seen-why.html.

Scheib, K. D. (2004). *Challenging invisibility: Practices of care with older women*. Chalice.

Scheib, K. D. (2016). *Pastoral care: Telling the stories of our lives*. Abingdon.

Smith, A. (1982). *The relational self: Ethics and therapy from a Black church perspective*. Abingdon.

Stevenson-Moessner, J., & Snorton, T. (2009). *Women out of order: Risking change and creating care in a multicultural world*. Fortress.

Wolterstorff, N. (1987). *Lament for a son*. Eerdmans.

1

Therapeutic Imagination and the Mystical Moment

Transforming Entrenched Boyhood Grief

ROBERT C. DYKSTRA

This chapter builds on a personal interview conducted with narrative therapist David Marsten concerning an extended case study of Marsten's work over several sessions with a young boy and his father (see Marsten et al. 2016). I offer here reflections on Marsten's interventions in conjunction with thoughts of psychologist William James (1902/1982, pp. 189–258) on the nature of religious conversion, the focus of two lectures (IX and X) that conclude the first of two sets of James's 1901–1902 Gifford Lectures and were subsequently published as *The Varieties of Religious Experience: A Study in Human Nature*. Only subtle references to religious language and experience appear in Marsten's case report, which precludes describing what transpired with the boy and his father as a "conversion" experience. But there are a number of evident parallels between its depiction of a rapid and stable transformation of the boy's entrenched grief and his father's hapless response, on the one hand, and of James's understanding of the nature of conversion, on the other.

These parallels, in turn, lend support to pastoral theologian Donald Capps's (1999) claim that certain therapeutic strategies entail a kind of intentional methodizing or operationalizing of mystical, or conversion-like, encounters. For Capps, such practices take the mystical moment, often identified as an encounter with the divine, "out of the realm of the occasional, transcendental experience and [relocate] it in a routine, systematic attention to the problems of ordinary living" (pp. 42–43), not unlike what religious leaders attempt to facilitate through liturgical and sacramental practices. Marsten's imaginative engagement with the boy and his father serves as an impressive model of this therapeutic regularizing of the transcendent.

GIFTS DERIVED FROM CONFRONTING DEATH

In the chapter entitled "The Therapist's Imagination Lends Inspiration" in *Narrative Therapy in Wonderland: Connecting with Children's Imaginative Know-How* (Marsten et al. 2016), Marsten recounts his therapy sessions with 10-year-old Danny and his father, Alex. Alex phoned Marsten, worried about his son's "laziness" and "constant fears." The boy had been living with his father in Los Angeles following the tragic death four years earlier of Danny's mother, with whom he had previously lived in a city 100 miles away. Since then, the father explained, all Danny "'does is sit around and read his books or watch TV. If we go out, I have to drag him along'" (p. 96). Danny was also awakening most nights from nightmares, afraid that someone was breaking into the house or hiding under his bed.

Marsten, a licensed clinical social worker who directs an affordable psychotherapy clinic in Central Los Angeles, noted as he hung up the phone with Alex that his "thoughts drifted to memories of young people who had been prematurely confronted by the death of a parent. In each instance, one or more special gifts appeared" (p. 96). Might Danny's nightmares and anxieties suggest evidence of an especially sensitive imagination? If so, Marsten wondered, might it be enlisted toward more positive ends in the therapy process?

THE FIRST SESSION: DANNY IN THE LION'S DEN

Alex arrived the next day at Marsten's office with Danny lagging behind and carrying a book. Marsten asked about it. The boy silently showed him *A Series of Unfortunate Events, Book the Ninth: The Carnivorous Carnival* by Lemony Snicket (2002), the pen name of author Daniel Handler. The cover illustration reminded Marsten of the biblical "Daniel in the lion's den and [was] enough to give anyone distressing dreams" (p. 97). Danny said that the books in this series were his favorites and asked whether Marsten had read them. Marsten confessed he had not but proceeded to inquire about them in some detail, wondering to himself whether their protagonists, the Baudelaire children, might offer some clues for engaging whatever problems Danny was facing. Marsten was determined to find out, first in doing his homework after this initial session by reading the books.

A Series of Unfortunate Events, eventually spanning 13 volumes published between 1999 and 2006 and today translated into dozens of languages with sales of over 60 million copies, is also a recent successful Netflix television series. It depicts the lives of the three orphaned Baudelaire children, each of whom has unusual talents—Violet, age 14 as the series begins, a world-class inventor; her brother Klaus, age 12, an avid researcher; and their infant sister Sunny, whose sharp teeth can bite through almost anything. As the story opens, the wealthy Baudelaire parents have died and their mansion destroyed in a suspicious fire. A sinister distant relative, Count Olaf, along with his lover, Esmé Gigi Genevieve Squalor, appear in the children's lives ostensibly as guardians but actually intending to rob them of their parents' fortune, which the children are due to inherit on coming of age. As Marsten quickly learned in his post-session research, "Literature has rarely produced, through the ages, two more menacing characters, with their designs on the Baudelaire inheritance, not to mention plans for the orphans' premature demise" (pp. 97–98). The dangers faced by the Baudelaire children were extreme, but "their talents for problem solving and escaping deadly traps with ingenuity and courage were, by now, legendary to their readership" (Marsten et al. 2016, p. 97).

Danny first wanted Marsten to know that no adults in the Baudelaire children's lives were in any sense competent in caring for or protecting them. Count Olaf, Danny explained, was "like the worst person you could ever meet" (p. 98). But Danny held vast sympathy and respect for Violet, Klaus, and Sunny in their heroic capacities to survive. Marsten noted to himself that Danny's world, like that of the Baudelaires, had been upended in the aftermath of his mother's sudden death and his subsequent migration to a city where, apart from his father, he knew no one. Beyond this, Marsten reports, "Father and son had not found their way into each other's hearts. To Alex, Danny was a riddle. He was 'baffled by him'" (p. 98). Danny's energy emerged only in discussing the Baudelaire children, not when talking about himself. Thus, the therapist's "own imagination began to come alive" in pondering what sustained Danny's interest through nine whole books in the series. *Why hadn't Danny stopped after books three or four?* Marsten wondered aloud. "Danny rolled his eyes. It was clear [his therapist] had a lot to learn" (p. 101).

While Danny appeared to appreciate Marsten's initial tracking with the basic plotline of the stories, he withdrew and asked if he could go to the bathroom when Marsten followed with a question—"*Is there a special kind of link between you and the Baudelaires?*"—that, evidenced by Danny's response, proved too direct for a first interview. Marsten realized that this question had been "an ill-conceived attempt to connect real and imagined worlds. A sturdier bridge would be needed" (p. 102). When Danny returned, Marsten tried again:

> **DM:** Is there something in particular about the Baudelaires that interests you, Danny?
>
> **Danny:** I don't know. I just like them and the way they can get out of anything. And they're smarter than the grownups. (He looks up as he says this, seeming to wonder if DM can take it. Not all adults are enthusiastic about being upstaged.)
>
> **DM:** Is that right? Do they live in an upside-down world where kids are smarter? Because in this world, don't we treat adults as smarter than kids and knowing what kids need? In the world of Violet, Klaus, and Sunny, is it the kids who know what kids need? (Attempting to support a worldview in which young people, and perhaps by extension Danny, might know best.)
>
> **Danny:** Yeah. (Smiling.)
>
> **DM:** Is that one of the best things about the books?
>
> **Danny:** Yeah. (He seems pleased with how the conversation is proceeding.)
>
> **DM:** Is there something special about kids' knowledge? Can kids' ideas fit into kids' lives better than adult ideas some of the time? (DM hopes this will be a more suitable connection.)
>
> **Danny:** Yep! (Stated with obvious pleasure. Danny seems to move toward a more explicit understanding of young people as knowledgeable, an understanding that may have only been implicitly appreciated previously.)
>
> **DM:** Do you relate with your mind to the way that Violet uses her mind? (Attempting, once again, to bridge the two worlds.)
>
> **Danny:** What?
>
> **DM:** Let me try that again. Can you use your mind to understand the way Violet uses her mind?
>
> **Danny:** I guess so. (He seems hesitant, a possible indication of how foreign Danny's own skills are to him at this point. Or perhaps the question still needs revising.)
>
> **DM:** Do you like putting your mind to work or giving your mind a good workout, the way Violet does? (Finally getting the question into better shape).
>
> **Danny:** Sometimes. (pp. 103–104)

ALWAYS ASK ABOUT THE BOOK

I initially may have been drawn to Marsten's case and the plight of Danny and Alex in part because my own children were avid readers of the many volumes of *A Series of Unfortunate Events*. They managed to convince me if not to read the books, then at least to watch all 25 episodes of the television series. I had come to know much about the Baudelaire orphans' woes before encountering Marsten's account.

An additional and more powerful draw for me, however, may have been my experience of anxiety as a boy not much older than Danny around the threat of my own mother's premature death. When I was 13, she was diagnosed, at age 40, with breast cancer just months after her own mother's death from the same disease. I assumed (as did my mother) that she, too, would succumb to it, but throughout the course of her illness no adult asked about my fears. Although my mother ultimately did survive an arduous treatment regimen and lived for many more years, I found myself identifying with the boy Danny's great loss of his mother and his subsequent isolation. We shared in common not only the early loss, or threatened loss, of our mothers but also the incapacity of our fathers or others to help us navigate the peril.

But my continuing resonance with Marsten's case of Danny and Alex—I have found myself dabbing away occasional tears in the reading—suggests an even deeper personal identification with their exchanges. In my later adolescent years, I was enveloped by attentive pastoral care from the minister of the local Presbyterian congregation in which I had been raised, a man who would become something of a second father to me. Through numerous consequential conversations with him in my youth and beyond, I experienced a sense of release from shame that derived from being recognized, heard, and accepted by a sage outsider. Nothing has been more urgent in my subsequent vocation as a minister and pastoral theologian than to attempt to pass along to others this sense, as further consideration of Marsten's work with Danny will show, of the power of attentive conversation for allaying childhood wounds. The grace I derived as a young person from recognition by a gifted observer—a sense of acceptance I continue to covet and rely on even today—fuels my visceral connection to Marsten's conversations with Danny and his father. I recognize how much is at stake, for them but also for me, in this encounter.

It thus comes as no surprise to me that Danny first wants Marsten to know that no adults in the Baudelaire orphans' lives were capable of aiding them in their quandary, given that over the previous four years no one has helped Danny in his. This, as noted, is for Danny "one of the best things about the books." In his words, "I just like [the Baudelaires] and the way they can get out of anything. And they're smarter than the grownups" (Marsten et al. 2016, p. 104). Marsten recognizes in this claim Danny's implicit, if preconscious, challenge posed not only to his father but to Marsten himself as therapist. Danny in effect dares them to help him. Marsten intuits that his capacity to reach the boy will depend on somehow surreptitiously enlisting "kids"—cue the Baudelaire orphans—to guide the way. He attempts, in his words, "to support a worldview in which young people, and perhaps by extension Danny, might know best" (p. 104). He appears to sense from the outset that the boy may be using the books not merely as escapist entertainment but as potential guides by which to navigate the menacing peril not just of his mother's but of his own threatened premature demise.

Marsten thus tracks with strategic interest Danny's understanding of the book series. (Note to counselors: *Always ask about the book. What is it that energizes this particular counselee? How might you become interested in what interests him or her?*) Marsten then tries, with mixed success across several attempts, to bridge the fictional and actual worlds in which Danny lives. Through this process, Marsten learns that Danny's experience has convinced him that children know what they need better than adults do. As impressive, he helps Danny to name aloud and consider, no doubt for the first time, that the boy's inventive mind, not unlike that of Violet Baudelaire, aids in his own heroic capacity to survive. In taking to heart *the one peculiar topic of conversation that energizes Danny*, Marsten exhibits not only a generosity of spirit and therapeutic savvy but also great respect for the boy's own ingenuity around how best to survive his debilitating inertia of grief. Marsten embraces the possibility that sometimes it actually is "kids who know what kids need" (p. 103). He finds in Danny not a "lazy" and "anxious" boy, as his father had described him, but someone, in prematurely confronting the death of a parent, bequeathed the gift "of an especially sensitive imagination" (Marsten et al. 2016, pp. 96–97).

But how might his therapist shepherd Danny's rich imagination to more healing ends? To Marsten's credit, he is willing to do his homework in order to find out.

A CONVERSATION WITH DAVID MARSTEN

On August 3, 2019, I enjoyed a 90-minute phone conversation with David Marsten in which we talked at some length about his work with Danny and Alex in particular but also about his own personal entry into and understanding of narrative therapy more generally. I learned that Alex was in his mid-40s at the time of their sessions and had a slight accent that led Marsten to believe Alex may have immigrated to the United States sometime between the ages of 12 and 14. I also learned that Alex had been estranged from his wife since Danny was three or four years old. Prior to her death, Alex had had contact with Danny only once every few months. I asked whether any new crisis had precipitated Alex's contacting Marsten some four years after his ex-wife's death. "No," he said, "it was just his growing frustration over Danny's numbness."

I also asked about the book. Noting that *Book the Ninth* of *A Series of Unfortunate Events* had been published in 2002, I wondered if it was around then that Marsten had met with Alex and Danny. No, he said, he saw them in 2009 and 2010, after Danny would have had access to the entire series. At the time of my conversation with Marsten, Danny would have been around 20 years old and, Marsten had heard, was a college student still living with his father in Los Angeles. Marsten's immediate interest in Danny's "resonance and solidarity in relation to the Baudelaires" in the book series mirrored Marsten's own broader interests in narrative therapy, which also involves, he said, "protagonists and antagonists, plot twists and surprises."

WILLIAM JAMES AND THE DIVIDED SELF

At the time of his meeting with Marsten, Danny had been living a paralyzing half-life of grief for nearly half his life. Unable to connect with his father or establish friendships with other children, he embodied a number of characteristics of what psychologist William James (1902/1982), the progenitor of modern pastoral theology, calls the "sick soul." James devotes several early lectures in *The Varieties of Religious Experience* to considering two contrasting but concurrent dispositions or temperaments in individuals, one the *healthy-minded* and the other the *sick soul*. These defining traits or prevailing aspects of an individual's nature, according to James, in turn reflect—or lead to—differing forms of personal religious experience.

Healthy-minded individuals readily "throw off the burden of the consciousness of evil" (p. 133), their religious life reflecting an optimistic attitude of freedom, happiness, positive thinking, and belief in the natural goodness of creation—though often at the expense of acknowledging more threatening or sinister aspects of living, including the reality of inevitable death. Those who align temperamentally with the *sick soul*, by contrast, express—James quotes Martin Luther here—a "holy desperation" (p. 129) born of a sense of wrongness, pain, fear, or helplessness at the very core of their being (p. 136). Such individuals become "in [their] own person,"

James says, "the prey of a pathological melancholy" (p. 145). Spirit wars with flesh (p. 169), the divided self finding hope of unification if not through stoic resignation or suicide then through an experience, whether gradual or sudden, of redemption or "second birth" felt to emanate from an external, often divine, source:

> The happiness that comes, when any does come . . . , is not the simple ignorance of ill, but something vastly more complex, including natural evil as one of its elements, but finding natural evil no such stumbling-block and terror because it now sees it swallowed up in supernatural good. The process is one of redemption, not of mere reversion to natural health, and the sufferer, when saved, is saved by what seems to him a second birth, a deeper kind of conscious being than he could enjoy before. (pp. 156–157)

For James, the "completest religions" are those, including Christianity, that consider and seek to deliver individuals from these more troubling elements of human experience, including trepidations concerning death (p. 165). "Help! Help!" becomes, he says, "the core of the religious problem," and "deliverance must come in as strong a form as the complaint" (p. 162).

Though Marsten's account of his work with Danny and Alex offers scant data by which to assess their natural temperaments or religious experiences—and on inquiring in our phone conversation, Marsten told me he was unaware of the family's religious background—we do know that Danny has been ensconced in acute grief that has morphed over years into a chronic melancholy that mirrors something of James's depiction of the sick soul. By day, Danny evinces one form of pathological melancholy that James (1902/1982) characterizes as a "passive joylessness and dreariness, discouragement, [and] dejection" (p. 145), wherein Danny reads a lot and watches TV but resists leaving the house. By night, he experiences anguishing nightmares and threats that James would recognize as another, more active, form of melancholic depression but one that is cloaked in self-loathing, exasperation, "suspicion, anxiety, trepidation, [or] fear" (p. 147). For four years Danny oscillates between debilitating worlds of numbing apathy by day and raw terror by night. He inhabits a sort of limbo or purgatory in which he is unable to return to the mother and community he loved but is powerless to move forward without them.

The sick soul signifies, for James, a divided self yearning for unification, though in Danny's case, we might presume, a divide manifesting less an inborn heterogeneous disposition or temperament—though this too is possible—than the traumatic fallout of his mother's death (and perhaps, in

THERAPEUTIC IMAGINATION AND THE MYSTICAL MOMENT

addition, of his parents' earlier separation and divorce). Whatever its original source, this internal struggle presses for resolution. James (1902/1982) says:

> Now in all of us, however constituted, but to a degree the greater in proportion as we are intense and sensitive and subject to diversified temptations... does the normal evolution of character chiefly consist in the straightening out and unifying of the inner self. The higher and the lower feelings, the useful and the erring impulses, begin by being a comparative chaos within us—they must end by forming a stable system of functions in right subordination. Unhappiness is apt to characterize the period of order-making and struggle. (p. 170)

In persons religiously inclined or of "tender conscience," James notes, this "unhappiness will take the form of moral remorse and compunction, of feeling inwardly vile and wrong, and of standing in false relations to the author of one's being and appointer of one's spiritual fate," a "religious melancholy and 'conviction of sin'" that in the history of Protestant Christianity drive individuals to conversion experiences (pp. 170–171).

But James recognizes that a specifically religious resolution of the divided self is not inevitable; instead, he says, "Religion is only one out of many ways of reaching unity; and the process of remedying inner incompleteness and reducing inner discord is a general psychological process, which may take place with any sort of mental material, and need not necessarily assume the religious form" (p. 175). In addition, he notes that unification of the self is a process unique to each individual:

> It may come gradually, or it may occur abruptly; it may come through altered feelings, or through altered powers of action; or it may come through new intellectual insights, or through experiences which we shall later have to designate as "mystical." However it come, it brings a characteristic sort of relief; and never such extreme relief as when it is cast into the religious mould. (p. 175)

Again, though Marsten did not explicitly explore Alex and Danny's religious understandings, he told me that he is always ready in therapy "to listen for faith, and not just respect it but pursue it actively. We have to rely on what people bring." Despite in this case not knowing for certain, it requires no great stretch of the imagination to perceive, with Marsten, that Danny is a seeker of "tender conscience," likely enlisting *A Series of Unfortunate Events* as a collection of sacred texts by which to attempt to transcend his divided self. While Danny's unification of self will come, as we consider next, only loosely swathed in religious imagery or idiom, it does occur quite abruptly and by means of a combination, in James's terms, of altered feelings, actions, intellectual insights, and poignant experiences that border on the mystical.

THE SECOND SESSION: A SACRED EPISTLE

A week after their first session, Marsten met with Danny and his father for a second time and continued to probe the workings of Danny's mind. Alex noted that Danny had "'the ability to focus in on something if he cares about it'" (Marsten et al. 2016, p. 108) and that there were two nights in the previous week when Danny had been able to conquer his fears and sleep through the night. Marsten asked whether Danny's talent for focusing his mind had contributed to defeating Fear on those two nights. Danny was unsure.

Finding Danny still straining to answer more usual interview questions, Marsten (2016) decided that an infusion of something new was needed (p. 108). Just then, a noise caught their attention. They saw an envelope sail through the mail slot in the therapist's door. Marsten retrieved it and found it was addressed to Danny. The boy slowly examined and opened it, then read it first silently and finally, a second time, aloud:

> *Dear Danny:*
>
> *Your current plight—a word used here to mean a challenging circumstance someone is facing—has come to my attention. Given that I am unable to visit you at this time—as it will be no surprise to you that we currently have our hands full, to say the least, with none other than Count Olaf—I immediately decided to put pen to paper and write to you. I hope to have more time to write in the future, but for now, just a quick note of support and appreciation. I have felt very lucky to have a mind that works in my favor and helps me deal with plights in my own life, not to mention the importance of being able to come to the aid of my brother, Klaus, and sister, Sunny, both of whom are very dear to me. Though I have only recently learned about you, I have an early hunch and wonder if I am right. Are we—you and I that is—like-minded? Have you ever put your mind to something and found that your very own thinking provided the answers you were looking for? If so, isn't it a wonderful feeling? I made the exciting discovery some time ago that I had the kind of mind that could be put to good use for all sorts of things. But I'd be interested to know more about you, Danny. Have you ever thought back to early signs of your mind trying to tell you something clever or brave? Is there a*

favorite story about you that your mother or grandparents used to love to tell whenever the whole family got together?

That's all I can say for now. I hear heavy footsteps on the staircase and they're getting louder. Unless I'm mistaken, they are the footsteps of YOU KNOW WHO! Wish me luck, and the same to you (of course, if I'm right about you, we both have a little more than luck going for us, don't you think?) Keeping you in mind,
Violet B. (p. 109)

Marsten reports that after Danny finished reading the letter, he looked to the therapist with "equal parts astonishment and suspicion and asked if he had written it." Marsten said he had not. Alex, too, denied it. However suspicious, Danny appeared all "too willing to suspend disbelief. Maybe this was the wake-up call he needed, the one his imagination had been waiting for. Danny had been stalled for some time in a liminal space, having been wrenched from the world he knew, without having yet achieved a sense of arrival at a new destination" (p. 110).

Conversation then turned to events that had led four years earlier to the death of Danny's mother, who was hit as a pedestrian by a speeding car driven by a drunk driver. Alex mentioned that Danny had shown no emotion over her death then or since. Danny added, "Everyone was crying at the funeral but me" (p. 114). "It's like he's numb," Alex said.

DM: Do the Baudelaires talk much about the loss of their parents?

Danny: Not that much. (He seems wary.)

DM: Do you have a hunch about why that is?

Danny: It's not easy to talk about.

DM: Do you think their parents would understand anyway, how much they are missed, even if Violet and Klaus don't say much? (Calling the Baudelaires to share in Danny's experience.)

Danny: Yeah.

DM: What would their parents understand?

Danny: That they miss them.

DM: What about your mom? Do you think your mother would understand, even though you didn't show much outwardly? (Perhaps the Baudelaires will once again offer passage.)

Danny: I don't know. She's not here. (He states this lifelessly.)

DM: Do you believe your mother is watching over you? (Trying to engage Danny's imagination or perhaps his faith.)

Danny: I don't know.

DM: If she were, would she be surprised about the numbness you've lived with these last 4 years? (Posed subjunctively as speculation.)

Danny: No. (He pauses, seeming to consider the question.)

DM: Did your mother know you best? Would she understand what this numbness is all about? (Attempting to establish an alliance between mother and son that would begin to unriddle Danny. One's sense of identity is often made vivid with the benefit of an audience to one's experience. Lost loved ones can be called upon on such occasions . . .)

Danny: Yes. (His tone is serious.)

DM: What would she know? What would she understand about how numbness took hold? (Here Danny is being relied upon to help them, and perhaps himself, reach some understanding.)

Danny: That it was hard. (His voice is thick with emotion. Danny seems to be moving toward a position of knowing. Perhaps he is becoming more known to himself through his mother's eyes.)

DM: Are you talking about your mother's passing? Is that what was so hard on you?

Danny: M-hm. (He is choked up.)

DM: Do people feel deep loss especially when they have felt deep love? (Danny is being acknowledged for an experience of numbness that is profound rather than being mistaken as unfeeling or heartless.)

Danny: Yeah. (Holding his breath.)

DM: (To Alex) Did Danny and his mother love each other deeply? (Inviting Alex to bear witness to this developing account.)

Alex: They had a good relationship. They were very close.

DM: Was she a good mother to Danny?

Alex: She was. She was very involved in his life. She was devoted to him. (Alex is invited to contribute to the story under development.)

DM: (To Alex) And was Danny a good son to his mother?

Alex: Yes, I think so. (Danny looks up.)

DM: Danny, is it possible that the numbness that came into your life was proof of your deep love for your mother?

Danny: Yeah. (There appears to be relief in his tone, as tears begin rolling down his cheeks.)

DM: Do you think your mother knows and understands this even now, from where she is?

Danny: Yes.... (pp. 114–116)

Reflecting on this moving exchange, Marsten notes that by enlisting Danny's mother "as a trusted aide and consultant," Danny is empowered to see his experience through her eyes in a richer light and meaning (p. 116). In my conversation with Marsten, I asked whether Danny had shed any tears at all in the previous four years. "No," he said, "these had been the first. My question landed in an experience-near way, and I was fortunate that it did. Maybe Danny moved from feeling ashamed for not having cried to a new meaning for his numbness."

TAKING TO HEART THE MIND

Even before this invocation of Danny's mother as co-therapist, however, the session is jolted by a mysterious visitation of an entirely different sort, the arrival of a letter addressed to Danny from none other than fellow protagonist and inspirational guide in the struggle for survival Violet Baudelaire. It would be hard to overstate the therapeutic virtuosity that prompted such an intervention or the power of its reception and impact—in this case occasioning tears and insights long dormant in Danny. Marsten told me he regularly makes use of such letters in his work with children but also sometimes creates video depictions of child clients' predicaments and resources by means of animated characters he finds online. Creating such a letter or video presentation, he said, can take hours of his time between sessions, especially early in the therapy process, but the children are uniformly fascinated by this labor of love. That Danny, at a pivotal stage as a 10-year-old in which emerging adolescent suspicion vies with established childhood credulity, so readily suspends disbelief and accepts support from Violet's letter speaks not only to the depths of his chaos but to the efficacy of its claims. Her letter is, for Danny, a lightning bolt out of the blue, manna from heaven, holy writ and revelation to a boy clinging to the Baudelaires for life support and salvation.

Striking throughout are the letter's many references to the *mind*. For someone whose emotional range has been constrained by grief, this attention to the healing power not just of feelings but of thoughts and insights offers Danny an alternative path to hope. Violet tells him that she feels "very lucky to have a *mind* that works in [her] favor" and has only "recently *learned about*" him. She reveals an "*early hunch*" that she and Danny are "*like-minded*" and wonders if he has "ever put [his] *mind* to something and found that [his] *very own thinking* provided the answers [he was] looking for." She expresses gratitude for "the exciting discovery... that [she] had the kind of *mind* that could be put to good use for all sorts of things" and asks whether Danny has "ever *thought back* to early signs of [his] *mind* trying to tell [him] something *clever* or *brave*." She affirms that Danny has "*more than luck* going for [him]" and closes her letter with "Keeping you in *mind*" (Marsten et al. 2016, p. 109, emphasis added).

This steady drumbeat underscoring the healing power of the mind supports James's (1902/1982) view that "remedying inner incompleteness and reducing inner discord," though often an overtly religious quest, is nonetheless at base a *psychological* process, one that engages the *mind*. As such, the divided self's unification comes not only through altered feelings but also at times through "altered powers of action," through "new intellectual insights, or through experiences [we] designate as 'mystical'" (p. 175). Violet's letter to Danny, while not neglecting the role of feelings (she mentions, for example, that she *feels lucky* to have a mind that makes *exciting* discoveries and wonders whether Danny has ever *felt* not only clever but *brave*), offers him alternative restorative options from James's menu, especially, as noted, that of drawing from his *intellect* or *mind*.

In our conversation, Marsten offered thoughtful reflections on this connection between *mind* and *feeling* in the therapy process: "Children are capable of solving their problems," he told me,

> but you have to determine their *interest* in solving them. Narrative conversations can be really heartfelt, but they're not conversations about *feelings* but about *ethics* and *power*—how power distributes itself between therapist and client and the power of a problem narrative over a person. People must be allowed to be difficult, to be oppositional, to be crummy if they so choose. People are *allowed*. If a young person decides *This is how I want to be right now*, I'm not going to usurp her own authority. Instead, I'll turn to the parents and ask, "How will you learn to live with this?" We have to search for *desire* [to change] on the part of the young person. It's up to me to try a dozen ways to get at her desire so that the work can shift and continue. Multiplicity is always present in a narrative approach. There is no one story of a person's life. Rather than trying to simplify children's problems and telling them to let go and move on, if we can help them see the seriousness of the problem they're dealing with,

> they can reclaim their own stature. Danny appeared to move from feeling *ashamed* for not having cried to a new *meaning* for his numbness.

Marsten's comments underscore James's claim that transformation stems from manifold roots, including intellectual insights as well as emotional engagement and even mystical experiences.

Violet Baudelaire's letter appears to engage Danny at these multiple levels, and its impact is immediate. Its arrival—Marsten told me he timed it to arrive 20 minutes into the session—allows the therapist to move deftly from Danny's observation that the Baudelaire children rarely mention their parents' deaths because "it's not easy to talk about" to getting Danny to affirm that the Baudelaire parents would understand this difficulty and know how much their children miss them to acknowledging that Danny's own mother, who knows him best, would likewise understand his numbness and how it "took hold" (pp. 114–116). Then, enlisting both the spirit of Danny's mother—invoking Danny's imagination and, Marsten notes, possibly his *faith*—and his father's actual presence, Marsten accesses Danny's *emotions*, here for the very first time in the four years since his mother's death, by talking about their mutual *understanding*. Marsten engages Danny's *feelings*, in other words, by having him talk about what he and his mother (and father) *know*, that is, by probing their *minds*:

> **DM:** Did your mother know you best? Would she understand what this numbness is all about? . . .
>
> **Danny:** Yes. (His tone is serious.)
>
> **DM:** What would she know? What would she understand about how numbness took hold? . . .
>
> **Danny:** That it was hard. (His voice is thick with emotion. Danny seems to be moving toward a position of knowing. Perhaps he is becoming more known to himself through his mother's eyes.)
>
> **DM:** Are you talking about your mother's passing? Is that what was so hard on you?
>
> **Danny:** M-hm. (He is choked up.)

Thus, we find ourselves caught up in the seeming paradox of a heart-rending conversation about emotional numbness flooded with cathartic release:

> **DM:** Danny, is it possible that the numbness that came into your life was proof of your deep love for your mother?

> **Danny:** Yeah. (There appears to be relief in his tone, as tears begin rolling down his cheeks.)

Then, for a second time, Marsten underscores this transformative moment with a benedictory summons of Danny's mother in heaven:

> **DM:** Do you think your mother knows and understands this even now, from where she is?
> **Danny:** Yes. (pp. 114–116)

THERAPEUTIC TRANSFORMATION AND RELIGIOUS CONVERSION

A number of factors in this remarkable series of exchanges strike me as consistent with William James's reflections on the nature of religious conversion. Danny, as a 10-year-old confronting grave life circumstances beyond his years, approaches the developmental span of early adolescence that James (1902/1982) and others have noted is highly conducive to conversion experiences (pp. 198–199). Although their conversation touches only covertly on religious themes, Marsten notes that on the arrival of the mysterious letter from Violet Baudelaire, Danny seems all too willing, in an act equally necessary to an experience of faith, to "suspend disbelief." That her letter precipitates an almost immediate and, as we shall see, enduring transformation of Danny's entrenched grief likewise reflects a recurring focus of James (1902/1982) on the sometimes sudden and often stable nature of conversion (see pp. 193–194, 230–242, 258). Moreover, when Marsten, "trying to engage Danny's imagination or perhaps his faith," inquires as to whether Danny believes his mother is "watching over" him in an afterlife, Danny's initial uncertainty ("I don't know. She's not here") shifts moments later to a firmer *yes*, accompanied by tears, when asked whether his "mother knows and understands" that his numbness "was proof of his deep love for [her]." One need not conflate therapeutic transformation and religious conversion, nor describe what transpires with Danny (or with his father or therapist) as a conversion experience, to find instructive an exploration of these and other parallels between them.

Experiences of religious conversion are the focus of two lectures (IX and X) that conclude the first of the two sets of James's (1902/1982) Gifford Lectures. Earlier in the lecture series, James offers his working—if, in his understanding, "arbitrary"—definition of *religion*, namely, "*the feelings, acts, and experiences of individual men in their solitude, so far as they apprehend themselves to stand in relation to whatever they may consider the divine"* (p. 31, emphasis in original).

His purpose throughout the series becomes, then, one of examining self-reports of those "most accomplished in the religious life and best able to give an intelligible account of their ideas and motives" (p. 3). In an axiom later appropriated by—and often wrongly attributed to—Anton Boisen (1936, pp. 10-11, 89-90), founder of the clinical pastoral education movement, James (1902/1982) expresses his intent in *Varieties* to focus on "human documents," that is, on the lived experiences not just of esteemed religious pioneers but also of ordinary persons who "lie along the beaten highway":

> The *documents humains* which we shall find most instructive need not then be sought for in the haunts of special erudition— they lie along the beaten highway; and this circumstance, which flows so naturally from the character of our problem, suits admirably also your lecturer's lack of special theological learning. (p. 3)

James's (1902/1982) two lectures on conversion, then, follow directly from his earlier ones on the sick soul and divided self. Conversion becomes, for him, "the process, gradual or sudden, by which a self hitherto divided, and consciously wrong inferior and unhappy, becomes unified and consciously right superior and happy, in consequence of its firmer hold on religious realities" (p. 189). This definition underscores how James views conversion phenomena as much through a psychological as a religious lens. He notes that among new converts there is surprisingly little focus on transformation of immorality or debauchery; nor do they attend much to intricate twists and turns of theological doctrine (p. 211). Conversion is more often experienced instead as dramatic release from a *subjective sense of enervating melancholy*. As James notes, "There is little doctrinal theology in such an experience, which starts with the absolute need of a higher helper, and ends with the sense that he has helped us" (p. 203). Conversion is "*a process of struggling away from sin rather than of striving 'toward righteousness'*" (p. 209, emphasis in original). A sense of "brooding, depression, [and] morbid introspection," particularly in the struggling adolescent, is exchanged for "a happy relief and objectivity, as the confidence in self gets greater through the adjustment of the faculties to the wider outlook" (p. 199).

James draws this understanding of conversion from the psychological theory of *association*, which suggests that a person's "ideas, aims, and objects form diverse internal groups and systems, relatively independent of one another. Each 'aim' which [an individual] follows awakens a certain specific kind of interested excitement, and gathers a certain group of ideas together in subordination to it as its associates" (p. 193). When one aim or group of ideas captures a person's interest, "all the ideas connected with other groups may be excluded from the mental field" (p. 193). It is generally unremarkable when these various aims alternate back and forth from the center to the periphery of one's conscious attention. Emotionally charged or, in James's term, "hot" central aims are displaced on occasion by formerly "cold" ones moving in from the margins.

But in the divided self these alternating aims engage in open warfare. Such an individual, according to James, internally experiences "great oscillation in the emotional interest, and the hot places may shift before one almost as rapidly as the sparks that run through burnt-up paper" (p. 196). In these circumstances, "whenever one aim grows so stable as to expel definitely its previous rivals from the individual's life, we tend to speak of the phenomenon, and perhaps to wonder at it, as a 'transformation'" (p. 194). And when "the focus of excitement and heat . . . come to lie permanently within a certain system" and "the change be a religious one, we call it a *conversion*" (p. 196, emphasis in original). "To say that a man is converted," James concludes, means "that religious ideas, previously peripheral in his consciousness, now take a central place, and that religious aims form the habitual centre of his energy" (p. 196).

James accounts for the sudden or seemingly instantaneous nature of more dramatic transformations or conversions by focusing on the power of the subconscious mind (p. 207). He offers the illustration of our trying to remember a forgotten name, first by

> working for it, by mentally running over the places, persons, and things with which the word was connected. But sometimes this effort fails; you feel then as if the harder you tried the less hope there would be, as though the name were *jammed*, and pressure in its direction only kept it all the more from rising. And then the opposite expedient often succeeds. Give up the effort entirely; think of something altogether different, and in half an hour the lost name comes sauntering into your mind, as Emerson says, as carelessly as if it had never been invited. Some hidden process was started in you by the effort, which went on after the effort ceased, and made the result come as if it came spontaneously. (p. 205)

This process, James continues, is also evident in the athlete "'who sometimes awakens suddenly to an understanding of the fine points of the game . . . , when all at once the game plays itself through him,'" or in the musician whose "pleasure in the technique of the art entirely falls away, and in some moment of inspiration... becomes the instrument through which the music flows" (p. 206). The pattern common to these moments involves first doing all in one's power to achieve the desired end but then ultimately yielding by relaxing or surrendering the will and leaving the "very last step" to input from other forces "without the help of [one's own] activity"; in this, one gives "one's self over to the new life" (pp. 208, 210).

Some individuals more than others, James points out, possess a particularly rich subconscious life. Their "motives habitually ripen in silence," but then, when they surface, appear as instantaneous transformations both difficult to explain and often attributed to divine intercession (pp. 198, 216). Citing Janet, Breuer, Freud, and others, James recognizes that investigation of these subconscious fields of awareness is "the most important step forward that has occurred in psychology since I have been a student of that science" and sheds "light on many phenomena of religious biography" (pp. 233–234), particularly conversion experiences (p. 236). Individuals predisposed to sudden conversion tend to be "suggestible," exhibit a "pronounced emotional sensitivity," and show a propensity for other subconscious automatisms such as "hypnagogic hallucinations, odd impulses, [or] religious dreams" (pp. 240–241).

While this kind of psychological musing on conversion experiences could be perceived as threatening by some individuals with religious leanings, James (1902/1982) finds no great cause for alarm:

> Psychology and religion are thus in perfect harmony up to this point, since both admit that there are forces seemingly outside of the conscious individual that bring redemption to this life. Nevertheless psychology, defining these forces as 'subconscious,' and speaking of their effects as due to 'incubation,' or 'cerebration,' implies that they do not transcend the individual's personality; and herein she diverges from Christian theology, which insists that they are direct supernatural operations of the Deity. (p. 211)

But James, while respecting this divergence between the disciplines, proceeds to chip away at it:

> If you, being orthodox Christians, ask me as a psychologist whether the reference of a phenomenon to a subliminal self does not exclude the notion of the direct presence of the Deity altogether, I have to say frankly that as a psychologist I do not see why it necessarily should... *If there be* higher spiritual agencies that can directly touch us, the psychological condition of

their doing so *might be* our possession of a subconscious region which alone should yield access to them. The hubbub of the waking life might close a door which in the dreamy Subliminal might remain ajar or open. (p. 242, emphasis in original)

More important to James than speculation on the *source* of transformational experiences is consideration of their impressive *fruits*—often an enduring "sense of higher control" or of an infusion of grace and, if not usually a complete waning of melancholy, then at least a greater sense of being able to live with it in hope (pp. 243–244). Newly converted persons experience a change in *feelings*, losing their previous sense of worry and gaining a new desire to live "even though the outer conditions should remain the same"; they notice a change in *thinking*, welcoming "truths not known before" as revelations in which "the mysteries of life become lucid" though not always easy to describe; and they discover a change in *seeing*, whereby objects in the surrounding world gain new luminosity as transformed individuals really do come to "see the light" (pp. 248, 251).

If, as James notes, "'Help! Help!'" is "the real core of the religious problem" and "deliverance must come in as strong a form as the complaint," then as we return again to the case of Danny and Alex, one can imagine characterizing their cry for help as at least in some sense a religious one. Marsten's interventions, in turn, strike me as of a form worthy of the complaint. Chief among these interventions early on, as we have seen, is the arrival of an epistle that Danny finds both mystical and revelatory and to which he quickly "surrenders" by "suspending disbelief." The many volumes of *A Series of Unfortunate Events* that he has devoured for tacit guidance through entrenched melancholy suddenly now speak to him and his circumstances in a much more direct way, a word from on high no longer intended for a general audience but instead targeted and personal. The grace of Violet's letter washes over him.

In taking seriously Danny's deep interest in the book series and the plight of the Baudelaire orphans, Marsten reflects something of James's convictions about the individualized nature both of religion ("*the feelings, acts, and experiences of individual men in their solitude*") and of therapeutic transformation or religious conversion ("*a self hitherto divided and consciously wrong . . . becomes unified and . . . happy*"). A letter from Violet Baudelaire would elicit indifference from any of Marsten's other clients but speaks volumes to Danny in his struggle. Beyond this personalized letter, however, we find Marsten invoking a whole community of saints as witnesses to, and support for, Danny, including not only Violet but also the Baudelaire parents, then Danny's mother in heaven, followed by his father

THERAPEUTIC IMAGINATION AND THE MYSTICAL MOMENT

Alex there in the therapy room, and finally, of course, Marsten himself. In relying on this larger cloud of witnesses, Marsten's work may suggest a measured corrective to James's emphasis on the individualized nature of religious experience and transformation.

The rapidity of Danny's transformation in this second therapy session—he sheds tears for the first time in four years—tracks with James's exposition of the psychological theory of association and the work of subconscious mental processes. It is easy to imagine Danny as a boy of "tender conscience" and "pronounced emotional sensitivity," someone both open to and familiar with incursions from the margins of consciousness and whose "motives habitually ripen in silence." His rich imagination catches him up in novels of terror and redemption by day and conjures nightmares of bad guys breaking in by night. He has spent four years quietly processing devastating losses, drawing reflexively on the book series and, no doubt, on other meaningful objects in seeking his path. The gears of difficult emotional work have long been grinding under the surface. The new revelations in these initial therapy sessions—of the power in problem-solving of using one's *mind* or of numbness as a sign of *great love*—and the empathic support generated by Violet's letter and the ensuing conversation with Marsten and his father are enough to produce a tipping point that leads Danny to tears and transformation. While in one sense not much has changed for him—his mother and former community remain no longer present—yet in another, as we turn to consider next, all things have become new.

THE THIRD SESSION: INVOKING MOTHER, RE-JOINING FATHER

A second letter, this one also addressed to Danny, arrived through the mail slot of Marsten's door at the beginning of their third session. Danny was delighted to open it, once again first reading it to himself and then aloud to his father and therapist:

> *Dear Danny,*
> *I was in the middle of reading a book on reptiles this morning when Violet came rushing in and interrupted me. I tried to make clear to her that I was busy and did not wish to be disturbed. I am sure you know how absorbed—the word is used here to describe the pleasure that can be felt in losing oneself in a riveting text—and contented one can become while engaged in a gripping story. This was just such a story, specifically one about poisonous snakes that are common to the Americas. Would it interest you*

> to know, Danny, that there are 32 species of rattlesnake? But that is beside the point. Violet insisted that we speak right then and there. She rarely interrupts me without good reason. As a result, I have learned to trust her in such instances, so I closed my book and gave her my full attention. When she told me your story and how you suffered the loss of your mother, I was really moved. Of course, there is no avoiding the sadness I feel over the loss of my parents and I know Violet and Sunny suffer, too . . . especially Violet. Sunny is still very young. I have imagined both my parents watching over me from heaven, and sometimes I am convinced that this is absolutely the case. Sometimes they are closest to me in the moments before I fall asleep and also in my dreams. I think of those experiences as the most special, holding bits of magic, at which times anything is possible. Have you found ways of reconnecting with your mother, Danny? It is a most wonderful feeling. At times I cry and cry over the loss, but Mr. Snicket doesn't say too much about that in the book series. This is in keeping with my request for a degree of privacy. Violet knows better than anyone how I have struggled with the loss. I have turned to her many times for comfort. It is sometimes a great mystery to me how to face the loss of my parents and, at the same time, still hold them close in my heart.
>
> I want to thank you for your interest in our sad story and for sticking with us through book nine. My thoughts are with you, Danny.
>
> In sympathy and friendship,
> Klaus B. (p. 117)

Marsten comments that in Klaus's joining "Danny in the saddest of all human experiences," Danny's imagination was summoned to see his mother and feel her love. The letters and conversations enabled both what Marsten calls a "performance of meaning" and a connection to those persons—fictional (the Baudelaire orphans), living (Marsten and Danny's father), and in heaven (Danny's mother)—who could serve as witnesses to this performance (p. 118).

Marsten next focuses on Alex in an attempt to strengthen the father-son bond. Recall that earlier Marsten (2016) had noted that "father and son had not found their way into each other's hearts" (p. 98). Now, in session three, Alex confesses that he is coming to realize just how much Danny has been through, something previously harder for him to consider amid their day-to-day frustrations:

> **Alex:** ... I've always known he's been through a lot, but I feel more aware in a way. In a way it makes sense that he's had such a hard time. I guess I kept thinking that he should be over it by now.
>
> **DM:** And now?
>
> **Alex:** Now, I think he's doing pretty good considering... (pp. 122–123)

Alex says he has noticed recently that he and Danny have been spending more time together—watching television or preparing dinner.

> **DM:** [To Danny] With what you've been through, would you agree with your dad that you're doing pretty good or doing your best?
>
> **Danny:** Yeah, because I've been through a lot, and after my mom died, I just didn't care about anything and was just kind of in shock. I just missed her and didn't want to move, and I didn't really care about anything, school or anything...
>
> **DM:** For somebody who knows deep love and is capable of giving it and receiving it, is it even more important to be able to care again?
>
> **Danny:** Yeah.
>
> **DM:** Can you explain why, Danny? Do you feel like you know something about love and caring and what's important about it?
>
> **Danny:** Because if you don't care about people or if they don't care about you, then what's the point?
>
> **DM:** Yeah, that makes sense. And this has come back to you, this awareness?
>
> **Danny:** Yeah. (pp. 123–124)

Danny knows that he has returned to loving and caring about life, he tells Marsten, because he has started to spend more time with his father, and their time together has been important to him.

> **DM:** Alex, did you know that Danny's been caring more about caring, in a way, and that he's bringing caring back into his life and relationship with you?
>
> **Alex:** Yes and no. As I said, he's been hanging around more, but I didn't know he's been thinking about it or really caring about it. (Alex seems surprised.)

DM: (To Alex) How is it affecting you to know this? What would it mean to you to see your son caring about you and about his life again?

Alex: It would mean everything to me. (He is clearly moved.)

DM: Do you think the two of you just might make good partners in caring?

Alex: I'm sure we will. We're gonna be okay. (He looks at Danny tenderly.)

Danny: Yeah! (There is unmistakable warmth between them.)

METHODIZING THE MYSTICAL MOMENT

In an imaginative but little-known article entitled "From Mystical Moment to Therapeutic Method: Connections between Psychology of Religion and Pastoral Counseling," Donald Capps (1999) proposes an innovative pastoral theological methodology inspired by *Six Degrees of Separation*, a film positing "that we could discover a connection between ourselves and any other living person if we could identify the five individuals who would constitute the intervening links" (p. 24).

Capps acknowledges that given its interdisciplinary nature, pastoral theology traditionally has shown preference for just *one* degree of separation between theorists in whatever fields it engages, where, in the familiar correlational model, "for example, the pastoral theologian creates a 'dialogue' between representatives of two disciplines (e.g., Ricoeur for theology and Kohut for psychology)" (p. 24). One degree of separation intuitively tends to feel "like a much stronger link" than the six degrees Capps puts forward in his essay. But he notes that, on the other hand,

> in the large majority of cases, the "dialogue" does not occur in the real world. The theologian and the psychologist do not actually carry on an enduring conversation such as occurs, for example, in a marital relationship. Rather, the "dialogue" is constructed by a third person (the pastoral theologian) who on the basis of reading the writings of the "dialogue" partners makes connections between them that they had not made themselves. (pp. 24–25)

As is the case with the "one degree" or "dialogue" model, where the pastoral theologian *reads* and then seeks to adjudicate works of authors from divergent disciplines, Capps's six degrees of separation approach is likewise based on *reading*, but with a big difference. In the latter case the theorists involved "are related by virtue of the fact that *they have read the work of the individual who immediately precedes them* in the transmission process," making the connection between them *less* contrived than in an approach where a "dialogue" is created by a third party who serves as moderator (p. 25, emphasis added).

Seeking for his purposes to demonstrate connections between psychology of religion and pastoral counseling, Capps traces through six generations of theorists the transmission of a specific desire "to articulate the methodological implications of mystical experience for their respective fields" and especially to consider various possibilities for generating or "methodizing the mystical moment" through rather ordinary human means (p. 25). He acknowledges in this quest "the dangers of idolatry—of mistaking the methods for the real thing"—but points out that "this desire to 'methodize' experience is not very different from efforts in religion to routinize the experience of the transcendent through liturgical and sacramental practices" (p. 25).

In his pursuit of six degrees of transmission, then, Capps initially focuses on Benjamin P. Blood, who described himself as an "idle, indifferent, and amateur fraud" (p. 27) and, in a crank pamphlet self-published in 1874, claimed to have experienced a mystical revelation of "the genius of being" by breathing nitrous oxide gas. Blood would have been lost to history were it not for William James, to whom Capps turns for his second degree of transmission. James read Blood's pamphlet (and, like Blood, experimented with nitrous oxide) and, in *Varieties* and other writings, referenced his curious ideas about experiences of transcendence. Most intriguing to James were Blood's assertions that, in James's words, "We may all grasp the secret of being if we only intoxicate ourselves often with laughing-gas" and that, quoting Blood, "The disease of Metaphysics vanishes in the fading of the question and not in the coming of an answer" (James 1992, p. 984, as quoted in Capps 1999, p. 27).

Capps builds on this latter claim in particular by turning next in the transmission process to careful consideration of works of Ludwig Wittgenstein. Wittgenstein looked to James's *Varieties* not only for consolation in his personal struggles with melancholy, often to the point of suicidal ideation—what made James such a "good philosopher," Wittgenstein once said, was that "he was a real human being" (Monk 1990, p. 478, as quoted in Capps 1999, p. 29)—but also for a viable sparring partner for Wittgenstein's philosophical skepticism concerning whether "there is correspondence between our language and our emotions" (Capps 1999, p. 29). "There are things," Wittgenstein writes in the *Tractatus*, "that cannot be put into words.

They make themselves manifest. They are what is mystical," and "What we cannot speak about we must pass over in silence" (Wittgenstein 1961, propositions 6.522 and 7, as quoted in Capps 1999, pp. 31–32, emphasis in original). Capps suggests that in the *Tractatus* Wittgenstein was seeking "a more 'systemized method' than laughing gas or alcohol for routinizing the experience of mystical oneness—the reconciliation of opposites" (p. 28).

Prospects for making such a method accessible to ordinary (i.e., non-mystical) persons, Capps continues, emerge in their reading of Wittgenstein by psychotherapists Paul Watzlawick and Steve de Shazer, who represent the fourth and fifth degrees of separation in Capps's schema. Watzlawick, a therapist and noted author at the Mental Research Institute (MRI) in Palo Alto, arduously applied Wittgenstein's reflections on "language games" and the multiplicity of meaning in language to therapeutic problem-solving in counseling relationships. There at MRI Watzlawick, in turn, taught and influenced Steve de Shazer, another Wittgenstein enthusiast who in his own books additionally drew from Watzlawick in conceptualizing and practicing solution-focused therapy at the Brief Family Therapy Center in Milwaukee (Capps 1999, pp. 34–41).

Watzlawick and his colleagues, mirroring Wittgenstein's skepticism concerning connections of language to emotion, "do not take for granted that the counselee already knows what her problem is when she comes for counseling. In fact, they are likely to help her reformulate the problem so that it becomes amenable to a solution" (Capps 1999, p. 35). Here, the therapist seeks to help counselees step outside their usual frames of reference so that the solution becomes "either self-evident or the problem is no longer a problem." Reminiscent of Blood's original claim that "the disease of Metaphysics vanishes in the fading of the question and not in the coming of an answer," Watzlawick and colleagues attempt in therapy to offer, Capps (1999) suggests, "a methodized form of the mystical moment, i.e., of viewing the [problematic] situation '*sub specie aeterni*'" (p. 36).

To a degree greater even than for Watzlawick, de Shazer is uninterested in identifying "'emotional states' that lie behind" the counselee's construal of the problem or even in hearing descriptions of the problem at all. Instead, he focuses from the outset of the therapeutic process on co-creating with clients various ways to imagine or identify "what would constitute a 'solution,' i.e., what would the counselee view as a satisfactory achievement or accomplishment such that therapy would no longer be required" (Capps 1999, pp. 38–39). For de Shazer, too, as Wittgenstein puts it, "The solution of the problem of life is seen in the vanishing of the problem" (Capps 1999, p. 40).

Finally, in the sixth degree of transmission, we come to Capps himself, who in a number of his own books and articles on principles of reframing (Capps 1990, 1998) serves to appropriate for pastoral care and counseling the works of both Watzlawick and de Shazer. Again, Capps (1999) claims that one shared purpose or context among these otherwise divergent theorists across six degrees of separation—and particularly evident in the therapeutic methods of Watzlawick and de Shazer—is that of taking the mystical or transformational moment "out of the realm of the occasional, transcendental experience and [relocating] it in a routine, systematic attention to the problems of ordinary living" (pp. 42–43). In addition, Capps hopes to "argue for a 'degrees of separation' method for doing pastoral theology"—one, he concludes, "perhaps illustrative of what William James . . . describes as the '*strung-along* and flowing reality which we finite beings swim in'" (p. 43, emphasis in original).

This cursory summary cannot do justice to the intricacies of Capps's argument, though it may hint at how appealing I find his proposal of a new "six degrees of separation" approach for pastoral theology. But I touch here on his plea for the therapeutic conjuring of mystical moments because I find in Marsten's work with Danny and Alex—particularly in the dispatching of letters from the Baudelaire children—a vivid expression of its transformational power. Marsten's capacity to conjure down-to-earth mystical experiences may well stem from the fact that he, too, studied at MRI in the early 1990s—in his case, I learned, with John Weakland and especially Jeffrey Zimmerman (see, e.g., Zimmerman 2018; Zimmerman and Dickerson 1996) rather than with Watzlawick. It was at MRI that Marsten first encountered what he told me is the "fire in the belly for cultural critique" that motivates narrative therapy and that soon thereafter led him to establish his own practice in the "diverse, gritty, challenging neighborhood of Central L.A."

It is easy to imagine Marsten's work being caught up into the "degrees of separation" web spun by Capps, especially as we notice how the Baudelaires' letters mysteriously bridge or mediate for Danny (and indeed for Alex, Marsten, and us readers) the real and imagined worlds in which he and we live. Their letters reveal how near, one could say, is the kingdom of God. They bring good news. They remind Danny that he is not alone. They give him permission to cry. They precipitate a rapid transformation in which he exchanges perpetual and foreboding subconscious ruminations for a conscious luminosity, a newfound appeal in relating to his father, and a capacity once again to care:

DM: (To Danny) With what you've been through, would you agree with your dad that you're doing pretty good or doing your best?

Danny: Yeah, because I've been through a lot, and after my mom died I just didn't care about anything and was just kind of in shock. I just missed her and didn't want to move, and I didn't really care about anything, school or anything . . .

DM: For somebody who knows deep love and is capable of giving it and receiving it, is it even more important to be able to care again?

Danny: Yeah.

DM: Can you explain why, Danny? Do you feel like you know something about love and caring and what's important about it?

Danny: Because if you don't care about people or if they don't care about you, then what's the point? (pp. 123–124)

Even in this brief exchange, we find evidence of meaningful changes in the way Danny *feels*, the way he *thinks*, and the way he *sees*, characteristics noted in James's consideration of religious conversion and psychological transformation. Danny, at long last, is going to be okay, and being okay amid great loss is plenty and good. In session three, Marsten proceeds to ask Alex, *What would it mean to you to see your son caring about you and about his life again?* We bystanders, by way of identification, echo and amplify the father's tender reply: *It would mean everything to me.*

CONCLUDING SESSIONS: LEARNING ABOUT CARING

Marsten met with Alex and Danny three more times in the ensuing six months. He notes that Danny continued to stick with his commitment to caring about his life, even when, on occasion, Fear reappeared in the middle of the night. At those times, Alex came to trust his son and allowed him to find safety in his father's bed. At their last session, Marsten reports, "One last letter floated through the mail slot in the door. Danny jumped up to retrieve it, familiar with the routine by now. He opened it without hesitation and read its contents, grinning from ear to ear. He showed the letter first to his father," then to Marsten. In either Violet's or Klaus's handwriting and with six symmetrical indentations at the bottom—a sure sign of razor-sharp teeth—it read:

> *Grrox!*—Most likely meaning, "Danny, thanks for teaching me so much about caring." Sunny. (p. 126)

REFERENCES

Boisen, A. (1936). *The exploration of the inner world: A study of mental disorder and religious experience*. Harper & Brothers.

Capps, D. (1990). *Reframing: A new method in pastoral care*. Fortress.

Capps, D. (1998). *Living stories: Pastoral counseling in congregational context*. Fortress.

Capps, D. (1999). From mystical moment to therapeutic method: Connections between psychology of religion and pastoral counseling. *Pastoral Psychology, 48*(1), 23–44.

James, W. (1902/1982). *The varieties of religious experience: A study in human nature*. Penguin.

James, W. (1992). The sentiment of rationality. In G. E. Myers (Ed.), *William James: Writings 1878–1899* (pp. 950–985). Library of America.

Marsten, D., Epston, D., & Markham, L. (2016). *Narrative therapy in wonderland: Connecting with children's imaginative know-how*. Norton.

Monk, R. (1990). *Ludwig Wittgenstein: The duty of genius*. Penguin.

Snicket, L. (2002). *A series of unfortunate events, book the ninth: The carnivorous carnival*. HarperCollins.

Wittgenstein, L. (1961). *Tractatus logico-philosophicus* (D. F. Pears & B. F. McGuinness, Trans.). Routledge.

Zimmerman, J. (2018). *Neuro-narrative therapy: New possibilities for emotion-filled conversations*. Norton.

Zimmerman, J. L., & Dickerson, V. G. (1996). *If problems talked: Narrative therapy in action*. Guilford.

2

A Psychoanalytic Reading of *A Monster Calls*

Biblical Congruencies and Theological Implications

NATHAN CARLIN

INTRODUCTION

In *Wishes Don't Make Things Come True*, Fred Rogers (1987)—one of the most well-known and influential Presbyterian ministers of the twentieth century, largely on account of his creating the television show *Mister Rogers' Neighborhood*—offers a story for children to help them learn about feelings. Rogers, who took classes in child psychology at the University of Pittsburgh (Lewis 2003), writes in the preface of the book a note to parents: "Pretending can be a big help to children as they work to understand more about feelings, but grownups sometimes need to clarify for children just where pretend stops and reality begins" (Rogers 1987, p. i). Noting that his book is one in a series of books on feelings, he continues:

> Some of those feelings are happy ones and some aren't—jealousy and anger, for instance. Strong feelings can be hard to talk about, but pretending about them can make it easier. We hope that these stories will help you talk about feelings in *your* family. Though the stories are only make-believe, the feelings are real, and children need to know that having feelings of all kinds is a very real part of what makes us human beings. (p. i)

As a direct message to children, Rogers explains that "wishes *don't* make things come true, even though sometimes it may seem like they do" (p. 2). Rogers then proceeds to teach this message in narrative form.

Wishes Don't Make Things Come True

Wishes Don't Make Things Come True begins in Paris, France, where Grandpère is excited about the imminent visit of his granddaughter, Collette, whose beautiful photograph he has on display. X the Owl looks with admiration at the photograph of Collette and remarks to Henrietta just how pretty Collette is. Henrietta was filled with jealousy.

Henrietta very much wanted to be noticed to be pretty like Collette. So she went home and dressed up. When her friends stopped by and saw her dressed up, they did in fact comment on how pretty she looked. Henrietta was so pleased. Her friends then went to meet Collette, inviting Henrietta to go with them, but Henrietta stayed behind, saying that she'd meet them all later.

When Henrietta went to meet them, to her great dismay her outfit and her hair got messed up along the way because it was windy. At the castle, the location of the party, a picture of Collette (the one that Henrietta had seen earlier) was on display outside. Henrietta looked at it with envy and said that she wished that the picture would just fall over. Right then, a wind blew and the picture *did* fall over! Henrietta felt guilty for seeming to make this happen, even though an adult nearby heard her wish, saw what happened, and explained to her that her wish did not make the picture fall down, that wishes don't make things come true. Still, in shame and in fear of doing more damage, Henrietta ran home.

Meanwhile, the king welcomed Collette to the castle. Collette suggested to the king that she'd like to throw a party for the whole neighborhood, hosted at the castle. The king thought that this was a great idea. So Collette went back to Grandpère's house to make party hats for everyone.

After making the hats, Collette asked Daniel to distribute them and to invite everyone to come to the party. He did. But when Daniel went to Henrietta's house to invite her, she indicated that she did not want to go because she was afraid of her negative feelings, fearing that she might cause something else bad to happen, something even worse than making Collette's picture fall down. Daniel responded by saying, as had been explained to Henrietta, that wishes don't make bad things happen. To argue his point, he noted that Henrietta could neither wish the castle to fall down nor a tree to fall down—only big winds could do that. This line of reasoning seemed compelling to Henrietta, but it still did not inspire her to go to the party.

Just then Grandpère showed up and asked Henrietta to be a special friend to Collette, explaining that Henrietta knew everyone and that she was, therefore, the perfect person for this much-needed task. Henrietta, after seeing the truth in Grandpère's words, and now feeling warmly affirmed and genuinely needed, accepted the offer. Grandpère said: "Oh, Henrietta, my thanks to you for making my wish come true!" (p. 26). Everyone came to the party and had a great time. Concluding the book with another direct message to children, Rogers writes: "*People* can make things happen, but *wishes* don't make things happen" (p. 29).

The Focus of This Chapter: "Taking Teenagers Seriously as Complex Beings"

This chapter, like *Wishes Don't Make Things Come True* (Rogers 1987), is about feelings but, unlike Rogers's book, I address an older audience: middle-school-aged children (grades 6–8, or ages 11–13). Here I explore feelings, which become more complex as children grow, by focusing on a recent book for this age group: Patrick Ness's (2011) *A Monster Calls*, a story about a 13-year-old boy whose mother is dying of cancer.

A Monster Calls, a work of fiction, is based on an idea by Siobhan Dowd, author of a number of young adult books (Dowd 2008a, 2008b). The book has won a number of awards and has received considerable accolades, including the Carnegie Medal and the Kate Greenaway Medal. It recently has been made into a movie.

Ness wrote the book because Dowd died of breast cancer at the age of 47 before she could complete the book (O'Donoghue 2012). Both Ness and Dowd, who never met, worked (and Ness still works) with the same editor: Denise Johnstone-Burt. After Dowd's death, Johnstone-Burt asked Ness if he would write the book (see Bruder 2011, October 14; Ness and Kay 2012, June 14).

Ness was given total autonomy with regard to writing the story. The idea and the notes he received were only to be a springboard: "I wouldn't have taken it on if I didn't have complete freedom to go wherever I needed to go with it" (Ness and Kay 2012, June 14). He adds, "I wasn't trying to guess what she might have written, I was merely following the same process she would have followed, which is a different thing" (Ness and Kay 2012, June 14). Ness also noted that what he and Dowd had in common was "a kind of wanting the emotional truth for our readers, of wanting teenagers to be taken seriously, as complex beings" (Ness and Kay 2012, June 14). It is this sentiment from Ness, along with his raw talent as a writer, that makes *A Monster Calls* a compelling source worthy of our attention as pastoral theologians; my suggestion is that we can become better caregivers to this demographic by reading books such as this one.

As is somewhat predictable with books dealing with death or grief, *A Monster Calls* has been read in light of Elisabeth Kübler-Ross's (1969/1997) stages of death and dying (see Day 2012), despite the fact that Kübler-Ross's model has been criticized heavily in recent decades for not having an empirical basis and for popularizing an inaccurate depiction of grief processes (O'Rourke 2010). Yet the influence of Kübler-Ross's model continues. In this chapter I offer an alternative reading of the novel, specifically by employing a psychoanalytic reading of the novel in light of Sigmund Freud's (1901/2001c) essay "On Dreams."[1] My reading is also theological, though to a lesser extent than it is psychological, in that I draw from the life of Jesus. I argue that reading *A Monster Calls* this way can shed light on the experiences of teenagers who are struggling to come to terms with feelings of ambivalence due to a parent's illness.

Part one offers an overview of the novel. Part two offers a summary of Freud's (1901/2001c) "On Dreams." And part three uses psychoanalytic insights (along with biblical congruencies) to interpret the novel, focusing on three stories that are told by a monster in the book. Thus, my treatment of these stories of the monster in part one is brief, as they receive extended consideration in part three. The chapter closes with an affirmation of God as One who has a wider range of experience than we do and can therefore embrace us more lovingly than we can accept ourselves.[2]

PART ONE: PLOT SUMMARY

The book, set in present-day England, begins on a Sunday in October with a monster showing up at 12:07 a.m. to visit 13-year-old Conor O'Malley. The following is a paraphrase of the book. Conor, who had been experiencing a recurring nightmare, thought that this encounter with this monster was just a variation of his recurring nightmare, which involved his mother being pulled over a cliff by a monster. So when Conor heard the monster call his

---

1. The history of psychoanalysis is long and complex, and many theorists after Freud could be used to interpret this novel fruitfully. I encourage such post-Freudian readings. My psychoanalytic interpretation is one among many possibilities.

2. For a critique of the language of acceptance, see Donald Capps's (1993, p. 91) *The Depleted Self*.

name, he panicked. Then, looking out his window, Conor saw the monster in his yard looking back at him (pp. 1–8).

The monster outside was a talking yew tree. It was not the monster from Conor's recurring nightmare. It shook the house, but Conor remained unafraid. Instead, he was disappointed. He was more afraid of his recurring nightmare. Then the giant yew tree monster[3] roared, shattering glass and wood and cracking the walls. Still, Conor remained unafraid. The monster was confused by the boy's lack of fear (pp. 8–9).

In the morning, the house was in perfect shape: no cracks, no shattered glass. So Conor knew that it had all been a dream. But the floor was covered with leaves *from a yew tree*. The leaves just blew in through the window, he told himself. As Conor was about to leave for school, his mother called from upstairs. She had been sleeping still, exhausted from her latest round of chemotherapy. She informed him that his grandmother would be coming to stay with them to help out while she was going through her next treatment (pp. 10–17).

At school, three boys—Harry, Anton, and Sully—had been bullying Conor. During one such episode another classmate, Lily, stuck up for Conor, though Conor did not want her help because he considered Lily an ex-friend for breaking the news at school about his mother's cancer. In English class Conor was learning about life writing. His teacher told them that they should write about their lives. Conor recalled his parents' divorce, which had happened six years ago, along with his father moving to the United States to be with his new wife, Stephanie (pp. 18–27).

That night at 12:07 Conor got up to look out the window, and he found the monster waiting for him. He asked the monster what it wanted, but the monster replied, "*It is not what I want from you, Conor O'Malley,*" but "*it is what you want from me*" (p. 30). Confused, Conor said that he didn't want anything from the monster. He asked the monster *what* it was but the monster responded that he[4] was a *who*. The monster told Conor that he would tell him three stories and that after that Conor would be required to tell him a fourth. Conor, still not afraid, poked fun at the idea of storytelling. But the monster replied that stories are the wildest things and added that Conor's story must contain the truth, *Conor's personal truth*. Somehow the monster knew about Conor's recurring nightmare. *Now* Conor *was* afraid (pp. 28–37).

---

3. In this paper I use "the monster," "the yew tree monster," and "the yew tree" interchangeably, sometimes for the sake of variety and other times to be consistent with this variation in names in *A Monster Calls*.

4. The monster is not given a gender in the book.

Conor woke up in bed. He knew that he was dreaming, just like before, but when he got up he discovered that, all over the floor, there were poisonous red yew tree berries. He looked and saw that the window was closed. Was he dreaming? Was the monster real? Now he was not so sure (p. 37).

The next day Conor's grandmother came to visit. She wanted to talk to Conor about what would happen after Conor's mother died, but Conor would have none of it. While she was talking, he looked out of the kitchen window and saw the monster in broad daylight—the monster was real!—as his grandmother was telling Conor that he needed to talk with his mother about Conor moving in with her. That night the nightmare returned. He looked at the clock: 12:07. He went to look outside. The monster was waiting for him. Conor mentioned to the monster that when he had seen him earlier during the day, he had wondered if the monster had come to help him, and he added that he was disappointed that all the monster had to offer was stories. But the monster said, "Stories are wild creatures," adding, "When you let them loose, who knows what havoc they might wreak?" (p. 51). The monster then went on to tell him the first story, which involved a wicked queen, a prince, and his bride. Conor was confused by the story (pp. 38–64).

The next day Conor saw Lily, and they got into an argument. Conor was still angry at Lily for telling the other children at school that his mother had cancer. Other children treated Conor as though *he* had cancer. After school, Conor's grandmother told him that his mother was going back to the hospital and also that the treatment was not working. She told him that his father would be visiting them as well, which greatly surprised him. Later, Conor asked his mother why she was going back to the hospital. She told him that she was going to be okay. But Conor pressed her, wanting the truth. She just hugged him without saying anything (pp. 66–78).

At his grandma's house, Conor didn't feel welcome. It was filled with antiques. When his father arrived, Conor smiled. Conor said that he would like to come live with his father in the United States, that he did not want to live with his grandmother, but his father said that there was no room for him there, though he did invite Conor to visit at Christmas. Conor still felt unwanted (pp. 80–90).

Sometime later Conor was in his grandmother's house alone. He looked at the clock and held onto the hands of it, until he realized he had broken it. He was scared because he realized that it was very expensive. The monster, somehow able to be in the room with him, said, "As destruction goes . . . this is all remarkably pitiful" (p. 95).

Unsure if he was awake or sleeping, he asked the monster why he had come. The monster said that he had come to tell him the second tale, a tale about a man who thought only of himself. Conor thought of his father when the monster said this. This tale involved a parson, his two daughters, and an apothecary. The story ended with the monster destroying a house, and Conor joined in the destruction. But when Conor woke he discovered that he was in his grandmother's house and that he had destroyed her sitting room. The monster was nowhere to be found. Conor had destroyed many of his grandmother's precious belongings. Was the monster a hallucination instead of a dream? The question is unresolved at this point in the novel (pp. 98–114).

Conor didn't understand what had happened. Just then his grandmother returned. When she saw the mess, she groaned and screamed. She didn't look at Conor. She just stared blankly and then went to her room and wept. Conor worked through the night, trying to clean up the mess (pp. 115–119).

The next day Conor came down for breakfast and his father made him eggs. His father told him that Conor's mother had taken a turn for the worse. He did not discipline him for destroying the room. He said that they were all going to pretend that this had never happened because of Conor's mother's health. Conor seemed disappointed that he wasn't going to be punished (pp. 122–124).

At school, everyone kept their distance. After school, Conor went to see his mother. She explained that the treatments weren't working but that there was one more treatment that they were going to try, a medication made from a yew tree. Is *this*, he wondered, why the monster came to visit him? Did the monster come to save his mother? (pp. 125–130).

Down the hall, Conor saw his father and his grandmother fighting, and his grandmother stormed off. When Conor asked what was going on, his father said that he had to fly back to the United States because his daughter was sick (with, in all likelihood, nothing serious) but that he would come back within two weeks. His father took him for a walk and explained that his mother's medication was not going to work. Conor refused to believe him. He just *knew* that *this* was why the monster had visited him, to save his mother (pp. 131–135).

Later, at 12:07, Conor asked the monster if he could heal his mother. The monster said that such matters were not up to him but that, if she could be healed, the yew tree would do it, but he also asked Conor if he knew why he had called him. Conor did not admit to calling the monster, though he added that if he did call the monster, it was for his mother. The monster disputed this (pp. 136–141).

The next day, Conor didn't want to go to school but his grandmother made him go. Everyone was still ignoring him except Harry, Anton, and Sully. But then Harry thought of the worst thing that he could do; he held out his hand, shook hands with Conor, and said goodbye, adding that he no longer saw Conor. They all walked away. It was 12:06. When it turned 12:07, the monster appeared, to tell him the third tale. This story was unlike the others in that Conor was awake. The story was about an invisible man who forced others to see him by means of violence. As the monster told this story, Conor inflicted a beating on Harry. Conor, just as in his grandmother's house, was not aware of what he had done (pp. 142–152).

Conor hit Harry so hard that he put him in the hospital. Harry's parents threatened to sue, but the school told them that Harry was bullying Conor, so they backed down for fear of damaging Harry's record. Conor was told that the rules of the school dictated that he should be expelled and, to Conor's surprise, he felt *relief*. He was grateful for the punishment. But then the punishment was taken away because of all that he had been going through with his mother. He went back to class and, although everyone saw him now, he felt more alone than ever (pp. 153–158).

Days passed. His grandmother would not talk to him. No one at school would talk with him. His mother was too tired to talk. When his father called, Conor would not have anything to say. The monster even stopped visiting. Every time he slept, he had the nightmare (pp. 159–161).

At school, Lily handed him a note that stated that she was sorry, that she missed him, and that she saw him. Deeply moved, Conor wanted to say something to Lily, but just as he was about to do so Conor was taken from class to the hospital. He was afraid. He never had been taken from school before; he knew that this was bad. When he went into his mother's room, she was sitting up, looking as though she was getting better. The yew tree worked, he thought! But then he saw his mother's eyes, that she was sad. She told him that the treatment wasn't working (pp. 162–165).

Conor asked what the next treatment was, but she replied that there would be no more treatments and that she was sorry. Angry, Conor accused his mother of lying. She replied: "I think, deep in your heart, you've always known" (p. 167). She added, "It's okay to that you're angry, sweetheart," and "You be as angry as you need to be. . . . Don't let anyone tell you otherwise. Not your grandma, not your dad, no one. And if you need to break things, then by God, you break them good and hard" (p. 167). She continued: "And if, one day . . . you look back and you feel bad for being so angry, if you feel bad for being *so* angry at me that you couldn't even speak to me, then you have to know, Conor, you have to know that it was *okay*. It was okay. That I *knew*. I *know*, okay? I know everything you need to tell me without you having to say it out loud. All right?" (p. 167). Conor nodded. His mother drifted off to sleep.

Conor demanded to go back to his house, and his grandmother complied. She said she'd leave him there for an hour. Conor then went outside, making his way to the tree. He called to it for it to wake up. He kicked it and kicked it, but nothing happened. Then the monster appeared. Conor shouted at the monster, complaining that the medicine did not work. "*I said if she could be healed, the yew tree would do it*," the monster replied (p. 171). Conor attacked the tree. He wanted to know why the monster had come, if not to heal his mother. Yet again the monster replied, as he had before, that Conor was the one who had called him, that he had come not to heal her but rather to heal him. Conor, breaking down, asked for the monster to help him. The monster replied that now it was time for the fourth tale (pp. 168–172).

Conor found himself in a dark forest with his mother farther ahead of him, dangerously close to a cliff. Conor yelled to her that she needed to get away from the cliff, but she didn't move. Conor ran to her, telling her that she needed to run. Conor heard a noise from over the cliff. It was a monster—the *real* monster, not the yew tree monster—and Conor kept running but he knew he couldn't get there in time. Two giant hands from over the cliff grabbed his mother. Conor ran and, just in time, grabbed her hands. This is where Conor's nightmare always began (pp. 179–186).

His mother yelled for help, asking Conor not to let go. The nightmare monster pulled harder. Conor looked back at the yew tree monster, asking for help, but he did nothing. Conor grew weak. Then the yew tree monster demanded that Conor speak the truth, to tell the fourth tale. Conor refused. His mother fell. Although Conor usually woke up at this point in the nightmare, this time he did not. He stood there with the yew tree monster, who said that Conor still needed to speak the truth. But Conor just wanted out of the nightmare. But the yew tree monster demanded that Conor speak the truth. Conor said that he didn't know it (pp. 179–186).

Then Conor realized that he *did* know the truth. The yew tree monster then said: "*You could have held on for longer . . . but you let her fall. You loosened your grip and let the nightmare take her*" (p. 187). The yew tree monster then said that Conor wanted her to fall. Conor yelled "No!" The yew tree monster demanded that he speak the truth, and Conor again refused, saying that it would kill him if he did. The yew tree monster replied that it would kill him if he did not. He demanded to know why Conor let his mother go. Then Conor spoke the truth: "I can't stand knowing that she'll go! I just want it to be over! I want it to be *finished!*" (p. 188). Then fire overtook the world. Conor was pleased, because Conor knew that he was a monster who needed to be punished.

When Conor awoke, he was lying in the grass beside his house. He was disappointed at being alive. The yew tree monster was still there. Conor said to him that he knew that his mother was not going to make it and that he could not stand the waiting. Conor began crying, heavily. The yew tree monster said: "*And a part of you wished it would just end . . . even if it meant losing her*" (p. 190). Conor nodded. But Conor added, "I didn't *mean* it, though . . . I didn't mean to let her go! And now it's for real! Now she's going to die and it's my fault!" (p. 190). "*And that,*" the yew tree monster said, "*is not the truth at all*" (p. 190).

The yew tree monster continued, "*You were merely wishing for the end of pain . . . your own pain. An end to how it isolated you. It is the most human wish of all*" (p. 191). Conor said that he didn't mean it but the yew tree said that he did mean it and also that he didn't mean it. "How can both be true?" Conor asked (p. 191). The yew tree monster replied, "*Because humans are complicated beasts,*" and added:

> *Your mind will contradict itself a hundred times each day. You wanted her to go at the same time you were desperate for me to save her. Your mind will believe comforting lies while also knowing the painful truths that make those lies necessary. And your mind will punish you for believing both.* (p. 191)

Conor wanted to know how to fight these competing forces, and the yew tree said, "*By speaking the truth*" (p. 191). The yew tree then told Conor why he came walking—to heal Conor. He added that it is actions, more than thoughts, that matter. Conor then asked the yew tree monster what he should do. The yew tree monster told him to speak the truth.

After taking a nap, Conor awoke to his grandmother's voice. She rushed him back to the hospital. When they arrived at the hospital, they found Conor's mother, sleeping. Conor's grandmother grabbed her hand and kissed it. She awoke. She reached for Conor and he took her hand. The yew tree monster told him to tell her the truth. Conor knew that the yew tree monster had come for this exact moment. And Conor told his truth:

> "I don't want you to go," he said, the tears dropping from his eyes, slowly at first, then spilling like a river.
> "I know, my love," his mother said in her heavy voice. "I know."
> He could feel the monster, holding him up and letting him stand there.
> "I don't want you to go," he said again. (p. 204)

"And that," Ness writes, "was all that he needed to say" (p. 204). Conor held his mother, tightly, and by "doing so, he could finally let her go" (p. 205).

PART TWO: ON DREAMS

In 1901, Freud published "On Dreams" (Freud 1901/2001c), a summary of the major insights in *The Interpretation of Dreams* (Freud 1900/2001a). He begins the essay by noting that during the prescientific era, the general public had no feeling of difficulty in explaining dreams because they were believed to be of divine origin, but today (i.e., Freud's day) dreams require a new explanation because we are living in an age of science. Medical writers, he continues, tend to think that dreams are random and meaningless, but Freud's clinical experience leads him to conclude otherwise. If dreams are not from the gods, and if they are not random and meaningless, how are we to understand them?

By following the free associations of his patients and by examining his own dreams, Freud discovered that the meaning of a dream can be determined, to a great extent, by following a certain interpretive method. For Freud, the key to understanding dreams is to understand them as wishes. He gives this example:

> One day a girl of three and a quarter made a trip across a lake. The voyage was evidently not long enough for her, for she cried when she had to get off the boat. . . . [The next day] she reported that during the night she had been for a trip on the lake: she had been continuing her interrupted voyage [in her sleep during a dream]. (Freud 1901/2001c, p. 644)

These kinds of dreams, which children often have (and adults sometimes do as well), can be seen as fulfilled wishes in the present. In this sense, dreams help children and adults keep sleeping. If, for example, one is hungry before going to bed, one may dream about food so as not to wake from hunger. Dreams preserve sleep.

But not all dreams are understood as easily as this. Many dreams are strange. This is because the wish that is being expressed in the dream is disguised. Why? This disguising is due to the fact that the wish is unacceptable to the dreamer, often because the wish is sexual or aggressive in nature.

This insight—that many dreams consist of wishes that are disguised—led Freud to postulate that dreams consist of two kinds of content: manifest content and latent content. The manifest content of a dream is the dream as we remember it when we wake up, but the latent content of the dream is the source of the dream, and there is a mental process (what Freud called the dream-work) that converts the latent content of dreams into the manifest content of dreams.

The dream-work has four ways of converting the latent content of dreams into the manifest content of dreams. The first is *condensation*. Here, various elements of a dream are compressed into a single construction. For condensation to work there "must be one or more *common elements* in all the components . . . [and] the common element in them then stands out clearly in the composite picture, while contradictory details more or less wipe one another out" (p. 649). Freud adds: "This method of production also explains to some extent the varying degrees of characteristic vagueness shown by so many elements in the content of dreams" (p. 649). He also notes,

> There are many sorts of ways in which figures of this kind can be put together. I may build up a figure by giving it the features of two people; or I may give it the *form* of one person but think of it in the dream as having the *name* of another person; or I may have a visual picture of one person, but put it in a situation which is appropriate to another. (p. 651)

Freud adds that the dream-work often represents contrary ideas by the same composite structure and also that single elements of any given dream are "overdetermined"; that is, they do not have one single cause or one single meaning.

The second way that the dream-work has of converting the latent content of dreams into the manifest content of dreams is by means of *displacement*. Displacement in dreams occurs when "*psychical intensity passes over from the thoughts and ideas to which it properly belongs on to others which in our judgement have no claim to any such emphasis*" (p. 654, emphasis in original). If a person were to dream of assassinating the king, for example, this might be an example of a wish to murder one's own father. The mechanism of displacement also explains why dreams can be so convoluted: "The more obscure and confused a dream appears to be, the greater the share in its construction which may be attributed to the factor of displacement" (p. 655).

The third way is by means of *pictorial arrangement* or *visual symbols*—or symbolization. This is a milder form of distortion than displacement. Visually, dreams

> reproduce *logical connection* by *approximation in time and space*. . . . Dreams carry this method of reproduction down to details; and often when they show us two elements in the

> dream-content close together, this indicates that there is some especially intimate connection between what corresponds to them among the dream-thoughts. Incidentally, it is to be observed that all dreams produced during a single night will be found on analysis to be derived from the same circle of thoughts. (p. 661, emphasis in original)

Freud adds that although the concept of "no" does not seem to exist in dreams, opposition is often represented by means of reversals.

The fourth way that the dream-work has of converting the latent content of dreams into the manifest content of dreams is by means of *secondary revision*. After a dream has already been constructed, the process of secondary revision adds some degree of intelligibility to the dream. Just as our minds often seek to find meaning and order for our perceptions in waking life, they do the same while we are asleep. But this ordering of the whole is a way of obscuring the meaning of the parts.

Dreams undergo these various forms of distortion because such dreams are derived from repressed material, which is unconscious. When one is sleeping, one's critical agency (pp. 676–677) is weakened, thus allowing repressed material, in disguised form, to come to consciousness. This is why, in part, we forget our dreams shortly after we wake—our critical agencies are fully functioning again.

Freud observes that there are three types of dreams: (1) dreams derived from unrepressed material that are not disguised and are easily understandable (as in the dream of the little girl mentioned above who wanted to continue her voyage), (2) dreams derived from repressed material that are disguised by means of the four processes of dream-work discussed above, and (3) dreams derived from repressed material that is insufficiently disguised. This third type of dreams explains anxiety dreams. In such cases, the repressed wish is too close to becoming fully conscious, so one wakes up instead of expressing the wish in the dream. Conor's waking up from the recurring nightmare illustrates this nicely.

PART THREE: PSYCHOANALYTIC INTERPRETATION

A Monster Calls seems to be magical realism. For much of the novel, it's not clear whether the yew tree monster is real and, if so, whether he will save Conor's mother. Yew trees are common in England and they are found in many cemeteries there. Thus, yew trees can be symbolic of death. The fact that some chemotherapies are made from yew trees is an intriguing feature of the book—yew trees also can be symbolic of life. Trees standing for life and death, of course, have deep resonances in the Western psyche (see Genesis 2) and also have a kind of spiritual dimension to them.

In terms of psychoanalytic interpretation, perhaps the place to begin is by simply observing the sexual nature of the yew tree. It is phallic, as most trees are, but its wiry branches also resemble pubic hair. So the fact that this tree is visiting Conor at age 13, around the average age of puberty for boys, is suggestive. Sexuality, which perhaps has been latent for Conor for some years, is becoming manifest again.

The plot of *A Monster Calls*, as noted, centers on four stories, three that the monster tells and one that Conor must tell. Two of the three stories that the monster tells seem to occur in Conor's sleep as dreams (the second story is ambiguous in this regard). In what follows, I use Freud's writing on dreams, interspersed with lessons from the life of Jesus, to interpret the three stories of the monster. It is through these dreams that Ness, I suggest, takes the emotional lives of teenagers seriously.

Relatedly, the yew tree monster's demand for Conor to speak his personal truth is akin to the talking cure of psychoanalysis as well as to pastoral theologian Donald Capps's interpretation of this saying of Jesus: "I am the way, the truth, and the life" (John 14:6 NRSV). Reflecting on this passage, Capps writes, "'The truth' is the middle term between 'the way' and 'the life,' as if to suggest that finding's one way and experiencing life depend on realizing the truth about oneself" (as quoted in Carlin 2014, p. 44, n. 87). This is precisely what the yew tree monster demands of Conor. That is, he must realize the truth about himself in order to find his way to experience life.

The First Story

The first story told by the monster, as noted in part one, occurred after Conor's grandmother had come to visit to help take care of Conor's mother and Conor while Conor's mother received another round of chemotherapy. The monster came to visit at 12:07 and told the following story (see pp. 52–64).

Once upon a time there was a town with a king who was wise on account of his suffering. The king's wife had given birth to four sons, but all of them died during various battles fought on behalf of the kingdom. Only one male heir remained, the king's infant grandson. Then the king's wife died, as did the mother of the king's grandson (i.e., the king's daughter-in-law). So, the king decided to remarry. He married a young princess.

As time passed, the young prince grew into a young man, and the king grew ill. Some suspected that the king's wife was poisoning him. Rumor had it that she was not young at all, that she was a witch who used magic to make herself appear to be young. Then the king died.

So, the king's wife became the queen, assuming the throne before the king's grandson, serving as regent in his place until he turned 18. She seemed to be a good queen. Meanwhile, the prince fell in love. Although most approved of this match, the queen did not, as she wanted to marry the prince so as to remain in power. But the prince refused to marry his stepmother. Instead, he ran away with his beloved, vowing to return on his 18th birthday to free the kingdom from the queen.

One night the prince and his beloved slept together under a yew tree, and when the prince awoke his beloved was dead. The prince ran back toward the village and told the townsfolk that the queen had killed his bride-to-be. Enraged, the villagers stormed the queen's castle, and the monster (the yew tree) marched with them. When the villagers were about to burn the queen alive, the yew tree monster picked the queen up and took her to safety, to a village far away, where she lived happily ever after.

Conor was furious. He wanted the *queen* to be punished for killing the prince's bride. But the monster told Conor that the queen did not kill the prince's bride, even though the prince *said* that the queen did. The monster then told Conor that the *prince* killed his bride. Conor was baffled. The monster added that the prince himself had told the monster that the prince had done so, for the good of the kingdom, because the queen really was a witch and because the prince knew that he needed the help of the villagers in order to overthrow the queen. The prince reasoned that the only way to overthrow the queen was to murder his bride and frame the queen, thus stirring the anger of the villagers. So the queen was indeed a witch, but she was not a murderer. Conor asked what happened to the prince who became the king, whether he ever got caught. The king lived happily ever after, too, the monster said.

Conor, further upset and more confused, wondered what the lesson of this story was supposed to be. The monster said that in life there is neither always a good guy nor always a bad guy, that most people are a mix of both. Conor greatly disliked the story. But the monster said it was nevertheless *true*. Identifying the witch in his story with his grandmother, Conor asked the monster how the monster was going to save Conor from her. The monster replied that it was not her from whom Conor needed saving.

Interpretation of the First Story

The Oedipal resonances in this story are readily apparent. A (step)mother wishing to marry a (step)son is a reversal of the universal wish of a son wanting to marry his mother, taking the place of his father and using violence if necessary in order to do so. *Symbols*—e.g., a king, a queen—are being used as disguising mechanisms of the dream-work. Also, according to the dynamics of the dream-work, the murderous desire of the son in this story is *displaced*; the prince kills his bride, not the father (who is already dead) or his (step)mother. The fact that the queen can be seen as standing for various persons in Conor's psychic life—his father, his grandmother—suggests that *condensation* is at work here as well.

Also, the queen seems to stand for Conor's grandmother: Just as the queen wishes to marry the prince, so does Conor's grandmother want Conor to move in with her. The yew tree monster in the dream does indeed save Conor (the prince) from this fate, though not by killing the queen (his conscious wish to be free from his grandmother) but by saving her, removing her from the situation. The prince also gets away with killing his bride. This is unacceptable to Conor's conscious mind, but, to his unconscious mind, this is very healing. Why? This is because the prince's bride seems to stand for Conor's mother; Conor wishes to kill her and not be punished, just like the prince. He wants to be forgiven for wanting his mother to die.

As with most dreams, various principles of dream interpretation are at work, and there is not just one wish that is being expressed—that is, the dream is *overdetermined*. In sum, here are some of Conor's apparent sexual and aggressive wishes:

1. the Oedipal wish to have his mother sexually (symbolized in the action in the dream of the prince sleeping with his bride); and
2. the wish to kill the father in order to have one's mother (symbolized in the action in the dream of the prince's plot to kill the queen) and Conor's wish to kill his mother (symbolized in the action in the dream of the prince murdering his bride).

Some of the wishes are contradictory but this is not a problem for the dream-work. Indeed, the dream-work is attempting to express ambivalence—opposites—so contradiction is the rule, not the exception, in dream interpretation. For Conor, who is suffering from profound ambivalence (that is, he is holding mutually exclusive wishes, with no rational way of resolving them), the dream frees him from this ambivalence by expressing it in disguised form, in the form of paradox: the wicked queen is saved, not punished, by the yew tree monster.

And if this wicked queen might be saved, isn't there hope for Conor as well? Jesus, who was, according to the gospels, so often criticized for spending time with sinners and tax collectors, is reported to have said: "For the Son of Man came to seek and to save the lost" (Luke 19:10 NIV). Like Jesus, the yew tree monster unexpectedly saved a sinner, the wicked queen who was lost, and also Conor. Relatedly, in *The Parables of Jesus and the Problems of the World* Richard Ford (2016) insightfully observes that modern interpretations of the parables of Jesus tend to be restricted in that they assume that "the dominant parable character somehow represents God" (p. 3). The upshot is:

> On the one hand are those who are "all-good"—that is, commanding, authoritative, generous, and compassionate (the landowners, the slave masters, the rich man, the father). On the other hand are those who are "all-bad"—that is, murderous, cowardly, unforgiving, envious, dishonest, profligate, and ungrateful (the tenants, the slaves, the laborers, the manager, the sons). If listeners discover in the superior character a figure for God, thus giving him not only all the respect but also all the work, they can position themselves to have no work of their own to do. From such a vantage point, these narratives are no longer encountered as surprising or even puzzling. (p. 2)

Ford notes, however, that the parables can be read assuming the opposite—that the dominant parable character should *not* be assumed to represent God—and that Jesus, speaking as a peasant primarily to peasants, told these stories to expose "the endless corruption in human hierarchies" (p. 151). Parables, Ford is arguing and Ness would agree, are wild things, and we ought not to domesticate them. But my main point here is that the first parable told by the yew tree monster is a fresh reminder that the dominant character in the parables of Jesus should not be assumed to be simply good, for human beings indeed are complicated beasts. The prince is not an unambiguous hero, and if Conor is the prince, this parable is inviting him to look more deeply into his own heart, for the parables in *A Monster Calls*, in contrast to typical, modern interpretations of the parables of Jesus, *are* surprising and puzzling, especially to Conor.

The Second Story

The second story, as noted above, occurs after Conor's mother is about to go through another treatment, just after Conor's father had come to visit from the United States. When Conor broke the clock in his grandmother's house, the monster told this story (see pp. 99–114).

One hundred and fifty years ago, Great Britain industrialized. The monster and Conor gazed into the past together at an old village. In the village there was the Apothecary (a pharmacist) who practiced the old ways of medicine, using herbs and bark and leaves and berries. The Apothecary charged a lot for his remedies; he was greedy. But it became harder for the Apothecary to find his materials for healing as factories spread and towns became cities, about which the Apothecary was bitter. Also, the townsfolk began to seek more modern therapies as science progressed, which embittered the Apothecary even further.

In the village there also lived a parson who had two daughters. On the grounds of the parsonage, there was a yew tree—it was the monster—and the Apothecary wanted the yew tree to make healing concoctions from it. But the parson would not allow the Apothecary to have it. The parson, being enlightened and modern and scientific, preached against the old, superstitious ways of the Apothecary.

Then one day the daughters of the parson became ill. Modern medicine could not heal them, and the parson's prayers went unanswered as well. So the parson turned to the Apothecary. But the Apothecary would not help, not because the parson preached sermons against him, and not because the parson had previously refused to give up the yew tree, but because the parson was turning his back on his own beliefs. Both of the parson's daughters died.

The yew tree then stepped in. "Good!" Conor shouted. But it tore *the parson's* house apart, *not* the Apothecary's. Conor, in disbelief, yelled that the Apothecary was the bad guy. The monster, however, disagreed, explaining that the parson should have let the yew tree be cut down when the Apothecary first asked. But Conor countered and said that the Apothecary was greedy. The monster replied, "*He was greedy and rude and bitter, but he was still a healer. The parson, though, what was he? He was nothing. Belief is half of all healing*" (p. 109).

Conor was furious as he and the monster looked through time at the monster destroying the parson's house. The monster invited Conor to join in the destruction. He did. But when Conor woke, he discovered that he had destroyed his grandmother's sitting room, as noted.

Interpretation of the Second Story

The second story continues with the themes of ambivalence and paradox. In this story, as noted, a parson loses his faith, and for this reason his daughters are allowed to die; the parson is even punished by the yew tree monster for losing his faith.

In this dream, the parson seems to stand for Conor. Conor believes that his mother can be healed, but he also *doesn't* believe because part of him knows the truth, that his mother cannot be healed. And for this half-belief—for this lack of faith—he is punished in his dreams. The dream in this sense expresses his doubt and also fulfills his wish to be punished.

It is worth noting that at the time of writing "On Dreams," Freud had not yet conceived of the mind in terms of the id, the ego, and the superego, but in a footnote in a revision of *The Interpretation of Dreams*, which was added in 1930, Freud suggests that punishment dreams can be seen as "fulfillments of the wishes of the superego" (Freud 1900/2001a, p. 476, n. 2). Thus, Conor's wish to be punished can be seen as deriving from his superego; the yew tree monster fulfills this wish for Conor, among other wishes.

As with the first dream, the second dream is *overdetermined*. The Apothecary also can be seen as Conor, though at a younger age of development, in that the Apothecary practices the old ways of medicine, of "magic," we might say, just like Conor once believed in magic and monsters as a boy. But as a teenager, Conor has given up—or is trying to give up, or is being forced to give up—the ways of boyhood on his way to becoming an adult. He is halfway between boyhood and manhood. He knows that only children believe in monsters, but he is not quite ready to give them up. If the wishes of the first story were primarily sexual, the wishes of the second story are primarily aggressive. The wishes of both stories are unacceptable to Conor's conscious mind. In both of these dreams (assuming these stories were dreams that Conor had), Conor's emotional ambivalences were transformed into paradoxical truths about life, taught by the monster, which lends credence to the idea that the monster is a kind of moral or spiritual teacher.

In a creative reading of the parable of the prodigal son (Luke 15:11–32), Mary Ann Tolbert (1979) offers a psychoanalytic reading in which she suggests that the two sons in the parable—the prodigal who runs away and the elder son who remains at home—represent two selves within the father. The parable, then, is not simply about forgiveness. Rather, the parable is "expressing the longing of the human heart for wholeness, for a reintegration of the conflicting elements of life" (p. 101). She observes:

> We can begin to see at this point some of the parable's appeal to people throughout the centuries. The wish to restore a unity, a harmony among the conflicting elements of one's life is an almost universal desire. Seen from this perspective the parable speaks to our deepest desire for reconciliation. (p. 101)

She continues

> The parable presents us with three characters . . . [who] are present in the psyche of every individual. The voice inside us which demands the fulfilling of every desire, the breaking of every taboo [i.e., the id/the prodigal son], is pitted against the often equally strong voice of harsh judgement on those desires [i.e., the superego/the elder brother]. Both voices are infantile; they are the cries of children; the desires are often beyond what reality could possibly fulfill, and the judgement is often stronger and harsher than the present situation at all requires. Mediating between these two voices is the one who attempts to bring unity and harmony [i.e., the ego/the father]. The wish for unity that the parable embodies, then, repeats and represents the desire for wholeness, the resolution of conflicts within the psyche of every individual. (pp. 101–102)

The congruencies between the yew tree monster's second parable and the parable of the prodigal son, as interpreted by Tolbert (1979), are striking, for both as expressions of wishes are attempting to deal with the conflicts between the id and the superego. Conor wishes to be free (an expression of the id), but he also is punishing himself for this desire (an expression of the superego), and the experience of this parable is helping Conor, like the father in the parable of the prodigal son, to resolve his ambivalence.

The Third Story

The third story, as noted, occurred while Conor's mother was undergoing her final treatment, one that used chemotherapy from yew trees. At school, Harry's bullying of Conor reached a new level, which was psychological. Harry bullied Conor by acting as though Conor were invisible. The monster went on to tell this story while Conor was awake but in an altered state of consciousness (see pp. 146–152).

The monster said that *"there was once an invisible man who had grown tired of being unseen"* (p. 146). As the monster told Conor this story, Conor walked toward Harry. Conor yelled for Harry, but Harry did not turn around. When Conor grabbed him, Harry acted as though Sully were the one grabbing him. The monster then said that the invisible man made others see him. And with the monster's strength, Conor threw Harry across the cafeteria. Harry got up, wiping blood from his forehead. Harry said that he wasn't afraid of Conor and continued taunting him. Harry then said that he did not see Conor. But Conor, with the help of the monster, *made* Harry see him with an amazing show of force. When Conor was dragged away, he denied having hit Harry, saying that the monster did it. But the whole cafeteria had seen Conor do it.

Interpretation of the Third Story

The third story, as noted, is not a dream. It is an alternated state of consciousness, perhaps a hallucination, which, Freud argued, also can be interpreted with psychoanalytic principles, as the key to understanding both dreams and psychoses is that they both are wish fulfillments (Freud 1900/2001a, p. 91). It seems as though Conor had a kind of temporary and slight psychotic break because the pressures he was facing—his mother's dying, struggles with his grandmother, disappointment with his father, and bullying from Harry and others—were too much. Harry pushed Conor too far and so Conor poured out his rage on him. So, psychologically, the hallucination can be read as providing a release for Conor's aggression, pure and simple. But what is striking about this display is that several people commented on how surprised they were that *one* boy caused such pain. This little detail invites the reader to consider that Conor's expression of aggression might be more complex than it appears.

As I reflected on this episode, I recalled an observation made by Freud (1917/2001b) in "Mourning and Melancholia" in which Freud made the point that the depressed person's self-hatred to outside observers seems unjustified because it is too excessive—it seems exaggerated—leading Freud to suggest that the hatred toward the self in states of melancholia is so extreme because it involves not only grief at losing an object (e.g., the loss of a lover) but also an attack on the object that was lost. In melancholia, Freud argued that the lost object becomes internalized and that extreme states of melancholia reflect both a sadness over having lost the object and an aggression toward it. Similarly, it occurred to me that perhaps Conor's extreme display of aggression is not simply an attack on Harry, though it surely is this, but also an externalization of the self-hatred that Conor feels toward himself. Since Conor was not able to satisfy his desire for punishment, this desire became externalized in the form of punishing Harry. This line of thought is consistent with psychoanalytic writing on the death instinct that views aggressive behavior as a protective measure against suicide (see, e.g., Jentzen et al. 1994).

I also recalled Capps's (2000) discussion of Jesus causing a disturbance in the temple, an episode that is found in all four canonical gospels (Matt 21:12–13; Mark 11:15–19; Luke 19:45–48; and John 2:13–25). Capps notes that there are two main schools of thought on these passages on the disturbance. One school of thought interprets Jesus as *cleansing* the temple, whereas another school of thought interprets Jesus as *destroying* the temple. Capps sides with the cleansing tradition because he views the temple as symbolically representing mother and that Jesus, by causing this disturbance in the temple, was cleansing the body of his mother, Mary, who had conceived Jesus illegitimately, Capps argues, quite likely due to rape. Thus, this cleansing of the temple by Jesus was an act to purify his mother's body (Capps 2000, pp. 256–257; also see Carlin 2014, pp. 24–25). Capps's discussion of this disturbance occurred to me because it seems to me that Conor's disruption in the cafeteria could be viewed similarly. The cafeteria, as a source of food, has maternal resonances, and because the cafeteria is where much of the bullying in middle school occurs (rather than in, say, a science class), it seems likely that this was the very place in which Harry or others called Conor's mother "baldy," making the cafeteria, like the temple, the emotionally charged venue where mother's body could be cleansed via violence. Jesus, who was not "seen" by religious authorities to be legitimate, made himself to be seen in the temple, as did Conor, who was not "seen" by social authorities (i.e., Harry as a popular kid), in the cafeteria.

CONCLUSION

In "Mothers and Fairy Tales," a chapter in *On Balance*, a collection of essays by contemporary psychoanalyst Adam Phillips, Phillips (2010) considers the fairy tale "Jack and the Beanstalk" from a psychoanalytic perspective. In doing so, he notes that the problem with most psychoanalytic readings of fairy tales is that

> when the militant psychoanalyst interprets fairy tales we usually end up with a list of the forbidden or unacceptable desires that story has managed more or less artfully to disguise. As though the fairy tale—however frightening or gruesome—is the good-manners version and the psychoanalytic interpretation is the bad-manners version. What has been revealed, supposedly, is why the child, unbeknown to himself, likes the story: because it

enacts, it dramatizes, his most enticing and forbidden wishes in a pleasurable way. (p. 292)

Phillips adds that, if so, psychoanalytic readings of stories still do not replace the stories themselves, for knowing about the Oedipus complex is no substitute for reading *Hamlet*. Why? This is because "the story goes on working because it can't be explained away" (p. 292). With regard to psychoanalytic readings of literature, he concludes, "the question is: what, if anything, has a psychoanalytic interpretation got to add to this? Not, what is the story really about, but what does it make you go on thinking about, or wanting to say" (p. 292). *A Monster Calls* is, as I have argued, a story about ambivalence—Conor wants his mother to live, *and* he wants her to die—and what Ness offers is a beautiful representation of the depth and complexity of this ambivalence. My psychoanalytic reading makes explicit this depth and complexity. But, to answer Phillips, what does a psychoanalytic reading of *A Monster Calls* make us go on thinking about and wanting to say?

A Monster Calls makes me want to say, as psychoanalysis has always held (and Christianity, too), that we are strangers to ourselves, that we see "through a glass darkly" (1 Cor 13:12 KJV). *A Monster Calls* makes me want to say that it seems to me as though our confusion about ourselves grows as we grow, that we understand ourselves both more—and *less*—as we age. *A Monster Calls* makes me want to go on thinking about the healing nature of paradox, religious and secular.

The point that we understand ourselves both more and less as we age can be observed by comparing *Wishes Don't Make Things Come True* (Rogers 1987) and *A Monster Calls* (Ness 2011). In *Wishes Don't Make Things Come True*, a story for young children, Henrietta is afraid that she knocked over the picture of Collette simply by wishing it to fall over, and Henrietta further fears that she could do something worse simply by wishing it. But adults in *Wishes Don't Make Things Come True* have a wider experience of the world, and they eventually convince Henrietta to give up this magical thinking, for which she was punishing herself. Henrietta's emotional ambivalences, like the little girl in Freud's (1901/2001c) "On Dreams" who wished to go on sailing, are undisguised and on the surface.

In *A Monster Calls*, a book for teenagers, Conor's wish for his mother's death (though terrifying to him) is completely understandable to adults, especially to his mother. She understood that Conor was living in limbo (see Capps and Carlin 2010), waiting for her to die. And she knew everything Conor wanted to say but could not because she had a wider context of human experience that relativized Conor's wish. She embraced Conor completely and without reservation. She could do this for Conor easily, but it took a lot of emotional work for Conor first to know himself and then even more emotional work for him to accept himself. Conor was more confused than even he knew, much more so than Henrietta, because he was older and more complex than she. The upshot in comparing these two stories is this: *As we grow, our wishes become more complicated and so, too, do our mechanisms for disguising our wishes, which means that, paradoxically, just when we learn more about ourselves, we discover later that we know less, because we are now more complex, with deeper ambivalences, known only partially to ourselves.* We find ourselves lost (Dykstra 2010).

Reading *A Monster Calls* through the lens of psychoanalysis provides opportunities for a rich analysis, more so than others readings, such as Kübler-Ross's stages of death and dying or grief and grieving, because it seems to me that Conor's acceptance of his mother's death—the final scene of *A Monster Calls*—will not resolve his grief. Conor's grief will be lifelong. Also, I have my own ambivalence about acceptance as a category or goal, the final stage of Kübler-Ross's model, for various reasons. I wonder whether we can accept death and also whether we can accept ourselves. As adults, we, like Conor's mother, often can embrace those younger than we are for who they are, but can we accept ourselves? Can we, I wonder, ever really accept ourselves for any substantial amount of time? My guess is that we cannot.

I also believe that, theologically speaking, it is only God who can accept us—embrace us—for God has a wider range of experience that relativizes our own. If we are able to think differently about ourselves at all, it seems to me that stories—religious ones, like the story of Jesus, or secular ones, like this story about Conor—are vital in this regard in that stories help us to work through our emotional ambivalences, converting them into paradoxical truths. Stories are able to do this because they, like dreams, are mechanisms of expression for our unconscious, both at the individual level and at the level of the group. Of course, parents, parental figures, pastors, therapists, and friends also can provide us with some of the acceptance that we need at various points in our lives, helping us to get our stories about ourselves straight, but because of my fundamental belief regarding our basic incapacity to accept ourselves, it would be no wonder to me if it sometimes took a monster to scare us into thinking differently about ourselves, if only for a little while. And what is the gospel, after all, other than the most sacred of stories that helps us think differently about ourselves? That is why we need to hear the old, old story—the story of God's embracing of us, which far surpasses our feeble attempts of self-acceptance—so often, in all of the ways in which it is proclaimed. And parables, both old and new, can help all of us, young and old, transform emotional ambivalence into paradoxical truth on our own terrifying journeys of getting to know ourselves.

REFERENCES

Bruder, J. (2011). It takes a monster to learn how to grieve. *The New York Times*. http://www.nytimes.com/2011/10/16/books/review/it-takes-a-monster-to-learn-how-to-grieve.html?_r=0.

Capps, D. (1993). *The depleted self: Sin in a narcissistic age*. Fortress.

Capps, D. (2000). *Jesus: A psychological biography*. Chalice.

Capps, D., & Carlin, N. (2010). *Living in limbo: Life in the midst of uncertainty*. Cascade.

Carlin, N. (2014). *Religious mourning: Reversals and restorations in psychological portraits of religious leaders*. Wipf & Stock.

Day, G. (2012). Good grief: Bereavement literature for young adults and *A monster calls*. *Medical Humanities, 38*, 115–119.

Dowd, S. (2008a). *Blog child*. Fickling.

Dowd, S. (2008b). *The London eye mystery*. Fickling.

Dykstra, R. (2010). Finding ourselves lost. *Pastoral Psychology, 59*(6), 737–746.

Ford, R. (2016). *The parables of Jesus and the problems of the world: How ancient narratives comprehend modern malaise*. Cascade.

Freud, S. (2001a). The interpretation of dreams. In J. Strachey (Ed.), *The standard edition of the complete psychological works of Sigmund Freud* (Vols. 4 & 5). Vintage. (Original work published 1900).

Freud, S. (2001b). Mourning and melancholia. In J. Strachey (Ed. & Trans.), *The standard edition of the complete psychological works of Sigmund Freud* (Vol. 14, pp. 237–260). Vintage. (Original work published 1917).

Freud, S. (2001c). On dreams. In J. Strachey (Ed. & Trans.), *The standard edition of the complete psychological works of Sigmund Freud* (Vol. 5, pp. 629–686). Vintage. (Original work published 1901).

Jentzen, J., Palermo, G., Johnson, L. T., Ho, K. C., Stormo, K. A., & Teggatz, J. (1994). Destructive hostility: The Jeffrey Dahmer case: A psychiatric and forensic study of a serial killer. *The American Journal of Forensic Medicine and Pathology, 15*(4), 283–294.

Kübler-Ross, E. (1997). *On death and dying*. Scribner. (Original work published 1969).

Lewis, D. (2003). Fred Rogers, host of "Mister Rogers' Neighborhood," dies at 74. *The New York Times*. http://www.nytimes.com/learning/teachers/featured_articles/20030228friday.html.

Ness, P. (2011). *A monster calls*. Candlewick.

Ness, P., & Kay, J. (2012). How we made *A monster calls*. *The Guardian*. http://www.theguardian.com/childrens-books-site/2012/jun/14/a-monster-calls-patrick-ness-jim-kay/.

O'Donoghue, O. (2012). *A monster calls* (book review). *The Lancet Oncology, 13*(5), 458.

O'Rourke, M. (2010). Good grief: Is there a better way to be bereaved? *The New Yorker*. http://www.newyorker.com/magazine/2010/02/01/good-grief/.

Phillips, A. (2010). Mothers and fairy tales. In *On balance* (pp. 288–307). Farrar, Straus & Giroux.

Rogers, F. (1987). *Wishes don't make things come true*. Random House.
Tolbert, M. (1979). *Perspectives on the parables: An approach to multiple interpretations*. Fortress.

3

Opening Doors to Resilience and a Gender-Diverse Pastoral Theology

CRAIG A. RUBANO

ALL TOGETHER

Demographic statistics, though imperfect (as they rely on self-reporting), indicate that 1.7% of all persons in the United States begin life "in between" sexes, another 0.6% identify as transgender, and 3.5% consistently identify as gay, lesbian, and/or bisexual (Flores et al., 2016). Thus, the group of people that veers away from the normative strictures of gender's component continua of anatomical sex, gender identity, gender expression, and attraction[1] conservatively totals over 6% of humanity. Separating out by age, the number of persons falling under the LGBTQ+[2] umbrella escalates relative to the youth of respondents. In a 2015 polling of the U.S. population, asked "how they would identify on the Kinsey Scale—a six-point rating spanning from 'exclusively homosexual' to 'exclusively heterosexual'—about *a third of millennials* pointed somewhere in the 'non-binary' middle, compared to about 8% of people over the age of 45" (Steinmetz, 2016, emphasis added).

---

1. For a useful description and discussion of these four continua of gender, see Sam Killermann, *A Guide to Gender: The Social Justice Advocate's Handbook*, 2nd ed. (Impetus, 2017).

2. The LGBTQ+ acronym represents persons who identify as lesbian, gay, or bisexual and/or transgender and/ or queer, thus covering both affectional/sexual orientations and gender identities; the plus sign (+) at the end proactively includes other nonheteronormative and/or nonbinary identities not covered by the previous initials.

And in a 2017 GLAAD[3] Accelerating Acceptance survey of 2,037 U.S. adults, a stunning 20% of 18–34-year-olds identified as "LGBTQ" (with 12% of 35–51-year-olds, 7% of 52–71-year-olds, and 5% of persons 72 years old and older so identifying), perhaps a testament to the broadness of "Q" as a categorical option (GLAAD, 2017; Gonella, 2017). Compare any of these figures to, say, the world population of Jewish persons at 0.2%, and one begins to get a sense of the number of individuals living well outside of normatively prescribed gender strictures.

Overall, the complexity of gender means that there is no standard way to approach members of variously defined groups of people who differ in their gender components and in the degree to which they stretch cultural norms.[4] Most persons need to be coaxed into conversation on gender diversity, and finding places of shared experience, even shared anxiety, can help invite interlocutors to the table. In any given opportunity for relationship, one might not arrive at anyone's idea of an adequate "understanding" of another person's gender complexities, but if some degree of awareness can be inculcated, one is on the path toward being able to affirm and welcome an expansiveness both in another and in oneself and to live into those possibilities in mutually accountable community.

The field of pastoral theology is a place of synthetic critical inquiry, a meta-analysis, drawing from theology but also from cognate disciplines such as psychology, sociology, and anthropology, as well as the worlds of cultural identity and political activism, in order to provide resources for the practitioners of pastoral care and counseling, usually ministers in places of engagement with suffering persons in settings such as churches, hospitals, the military, and outpatient clinics. In a vital collection of historical pastoral theology documents, *Images of Pastoral Care: Classic Readings*, editor Dykstra (2005) introduces the work of Bonnie J. Miller-McLemore by describing the field as one that "joins persons across all barriers of cultural location and difference," quoting the latter on a central lesson that pastoral theology

---

3. GLAAD, the name of a monitoring organization that tries to ensure equitable LGBTQ+ media coverage, was an acronym for Gay and Lesbian Alliance against Defamation until 2013, when the organization removed the acronym's explanation so as to be more inclusive of "B," "T," and "Q" concerns; see https://www.glaad.org/.

4. In fact, there is a subgenre of transgender publications of "do-it-yourself" gender workbooks for persons of all ages to get perspective on the contours of their gender components; see Kate Bornstein, *My New Gender Workbook: A Step-By-Step Guide to Achieving World Peace through Gender Anarchy and Sex Positivity*, 2nd ed. (Routledge, 2013); Rylan Jay Testa, Deborah Coolhart, and Jayme Peta, *The Gender Quest Workbook: A Guide for Teens and Young Adults Exploring Gender Identity* (Instant Help Books, 2015); and Dara Hoffman-Fox, *You and Your Gender Identity: A Guide to Discovery* (Skyhorse, 2017).

learns again and again: "[W]e must hear the voices of the marginalized from within their own contexts" (p. 4). As such, pastoral theology is an apt field with which to engage in the kinds of compassionate dialogue, welcome, affirmation, and cooperation across gender binaries I advocate here.

As a cisgender man,[5] I have felt drawn in my congregational work to the stories of gender-creative people,[6] young and old alike. Being in relationship with them has compelled me to find ways to move forward in welcoming and affirming them, in learning from their example, and in embracing mutually enriching and promising gender complexities. My interest in fostering gender-creative promise was initially inspired by the gender-variant children in my ministerial care, which led me to the pioneering work of Diane Ehrensaft with younger persons living into their true gender selves. She writes,

> For so many years, in trying to make a more equitable and accepting world, we have focused on teaching tolerance. Now it is time to teach *resilience*—the inner strength and centered sense of self and community that is never a given but rather *a communal accomplishment*. (Ehrensaft, 2018, p. vii; emphases added)

I seek to enhance this communal accomplishment of resilience through a gender-creative deployment of pastoral theology as a field, taking into account benefits derivable from religious affiliation. Gender-creative resilience is certainly necessary in U.S. culture as currently constituted.

THE 2015 U.S. TRANSGENDER SURVEY

The largest survey to date (*U.S. Transgender Survey*; see James et al., 2015) examining the lived experiences of transgender people in the United States was conducted in the summer of 2015 by the National Center for

---

5. "Cis" is a Latin prefix for "on this side of." "Cisgender," then, serves as a description of non-transgender persons ("trans" is a Latin prefix meaning "on the other side of") to indicate persons whose sex assigned at birth coincides with their true and lived gender identity.

6. Psychologist and preeminent expert in treating gender-diverse youth and their families Diane Ehrensaft designates "gender creative" as an umbrella term more encompassing even than "transgender," although all terminology regarding gender is constantly and necessarily in flux. See Diane Ehrensaft, *Gender Born, Gender Made: Raising Healthy Gender-Nonconforming Children* (The Experiment, 2011) and *The Gender Creative Child: Pathways for Nurturing and Supporting Children Who Live Outside Gender Boxes* (The Experiment, 2016). See also Craig A. Rubano, "Where Do the Mermaids Stand? Toward a 'Gender-Creative' Pastoral Sensibility," *Pastoral Psychology* 65, no. 6 (December 2016), https://doi.org/10.1007/s11089-015-0680-2.

Transgender Equality, surveying anonymous online entries from nearly 28,000 "transgender" respondents.[7] Overall, in the year preceding the survey, 46% of respondents had been verbally harassed and 9% physically attacked over their transgender identities; 10% had been sexually assaulted, with 47% having been sexually assaulted at some point in their lives (James et al., 2015, p. 5; see also pp. 139-146). "Severe economic hardship and instability" were seen across the transgender sample, with 29% living in poverty (compared to 12% of the U.S. population), 15% unemployed (three times the U.S. rate), and 30% having experienced being unhoused in their lifetimes (James et al., 2015, p. 5).

This level of violence and instability understandably leads to "harmful effects on physical and mental health," with 40% of respondents having attempted suicide (nine times the U.S. rate) and 23% not seeking needed healthcare because of fear of being mistreated or harassed in health provider care environments (33% had already experienced negative treatment, including outright refusal of service in some cases) (James et al., 2015, p. 5; see also pp. 92-129). All of the statistics showed "the compounding impact of other forms of discrimination," a severe intersectional[8] skewing of experienced hardship among transgender populations of color, among undocumented respondents, and among respondents with disabilities (James et al., 2015, p. 6).[9] The study's executive summary headings are dire in their implications, beginning with "pervasive mistreatment and violence" (James et al., 2015, p. 4; see also pp. 197-211), and the survey's full-text report makes it evident that transgender and gender-nonconforming persons experience hardships in nearly every juncture: family life, identity documentation, health care, schooling, income levels, employment and the

---

7. Respondents were comprised of adults (18 and over) from all 50 states, the District of Columbia, and various U.S. territories and military bases around the world.

8. "Intersectionality" refers to the way the oppressive impact of multiple marginalized identities adds up to more than a sum of each identity's effects. The term emerges from the work of Crenshaw (1989) on the experiences of African American women: "Because the intersectional experience is greater than the sum of racism and sexism, any analysis that does not take *intersectionality* into account cannot sufficiently address the particular manner in which Black women are subordinated" (p. 140). For a pastoral theology perspective on intersectionality, see Nancy J. Ramsay, "Intersectionality: A Model for Addressing the Complexity of Oppression and Privilege," *Pastoral Psychology* 63, no. 4 (August 2014).

9. There is an extensive literature documenting the disproportionate ways that societal transphobic opprobrium is refracted and intensified along intersectional lines of marginalization; see especially David Valentine, *Imagining Transgender: An Ethnography of a Category* (Duke University Press, 2007); C. Riley Snorton, *Black on Both Sides: A Racial History of Trans Identity* (University of Minnesota Press, 2017); and b. binaoham, *Decolonizing Trans/Gender 101* (Biyuti, 2014).

workplace, a prevalent sex work/underground economy, military, housing, police interaction, experience of harassment and violence, places of public accommodation, restrooms, civic participatory life—and faith communities (see James et al., 2015, p. iv).

The growing emergence of gender-creative people as an identifiable population was evident in this study, with the number of respondents to the survey more than four times that of the previous such survey conducted in 2008–2009 (James et al., 2015, p. 6).[10] Additionally, the diversity within the transgender community was evident, with nonbinary persons (not exclusively male or female, of no gender, of other gender, or of more than one gender) representing over a third (35%) of the sample (p. 7; see also pp. 43–63).[11] Of great positive significance, there was evidence of experienced support for those who were "out" to their immediate families (60%), co-workers (68%), and classmates (56%) (p. 7; see also pp. 64–76).

Of significance for this chapter, 63% of respondents reported that they had a spiritual or religious identity (James et al., 2015, pp. 76–77), 21% of whom identified as Christian (pp. 54–55). Of the 66% of respondents who reported having been a part of a faith community at some point in their lives, 39% had left due to fear of being rejected and 19% had left because of enacted rejection (pp. 77–78). However, of the latter, 42% had found new, welcoming communities; inherent in that reported felt sense of welcome were a specific acceptance of them by religious community leaders and/or members (94%) and being told that their religion or faith itself accepted them (80%) (p. 78). The positive takeaway is the high level of resilience transgender persons employed in the face of rejection. In an essay on the state of "transgender people in the United States," minister and theologian Tanis (2018), referencing the James et al., (2015) study, writes,

> While the rejection of nearly 1 in 5 of those who were religiously active is appalling, these numbers also show that transgender people are often able to locate affirming communities where they are receiving positive messages about both their gender identity and their faith. (p. 158)

Tanis continues with the sobering truth that "much of the [overall cultural] energy opposing transgender rights comes from religious groups and individuals, particularly Christians" (p. 158).

---

10. The previous report (*The National Transgender Discrimination Survey*) was issued in 2011 (Grant et al., 2011).

11. In the 2011 report, participants did not use the term "nonbinary"; 14%, however, identified as "gender non-conforming" (Grant et al., 2011, p. 24).

It is clear from many studies that gender-creative children, adolescents, and adults are at "risk for developing a downward cascade of psychosocial adversities including depressive symptoms, low life satisfaction, self-harm, isolation, homelessness, incarceration, posttraumatic stress, and suicide ideation and attempts" (Hidalgo et al., 2013, p. 286). In response to this need, Diane Ehrensaft, along with seven other psychotherapists representing four sites nationwide specializing in gender variance in children, issued a 2013 state of the field report in the journal *Human Development*. Their gender-affirmative model has five major premises:

> (a) gender variations are not disorders; (b) gender presentations are diverse and varied across cultures, therefore requiring our cultural sensitivity; (c) to the best of our knowledge at present, gender involves an interweaving of biology, development and socialization, and culture and context, with all three bearing on any individual's gender self; (d) gender may be fluid, and is not binary, both at a particular time and if and when it changes within an individual across time; (e) if there is pathology, it more stems from cultural reactions (e.g., transphobia, homophobia, sexism) rather than from within the child. (Hidalgo et al., 2013, p. 158)

These basic contentions of a gender-affirmative model of psychotherapeutic intervention are a good place to start for any affirmative pastoral stance toward gender variance. If pastoral caregivers can understand more fully the variations and diversities present in the gender-creative population and more fully appreciate the interwoven nature of the components of gender creativity, then at the very least they can cease to be a part of the cultural opprobrium that is the true pathology at work in the lives of transgender and gender-nonconforming persons. Even better, pastoral ministry as a whole can be enhanced by affirming a vision of God's creation that includes lives beyond gender binaries, allowing caregivers and care receivers to move toward embodying mutual, affirmative co-curation of God's love.

GENDER-CREATIVE RESILIENCE

Psychologist Anneliese A. Singh is Associate Dean for Diversity, Equity, and Inclusion; Associate Professor at the University of Georgia's Department of Counseling and Human Development; and co-founder of the Georgia Safe Schools Coalition and Trans Resilience Project, an initiative that works to combat intersectional oppressions in Georgia public schools. In a series of articles and in an accessible workbook for navigating sexual orientation and gender, Singh reports back from transgender persons, having listened to and compiled their strategies for resilience in the face of oppression (Singh et al., 2011).[12] Singh is the foremost expert on transgender and gender-nonconforming resilience, having written over 100 peer-reviewed journal articles, chapters, and media publications as well as coediting with lore m. dickey the influential collection *Affirmative Counseling and Psychological Practice with Transgender and Gender Nonconforming Clients* (Singh & dickey, 2017). For a general definition of resilience, Singh cites the work of child development specialist Ann S. Masten, who describes resilience as a network of "the 'ordinary magic' that you can use to bounce back from hard times" (Singh, 2018, p. 1). In an interview, Masten states that the engines of resilience are

> the basic, fundamental systems that help us throughout human development. And they also help us through difficulties. The basic characteristics for resilience are: Caregivers and family that are looking out for you. A human brain in good working order. A human brain that has learned through interactions and training with a lot of people who care. Parents and teachers encouraging children to pay attention, solve problems and control behavior. (Steiner, 2014)[13]

For gender-creative persons who typically suffer adverse societal, religious, and often parental deficits in care provision and encouragement, a dearth of resilience strategies can naturally follow. However, because resilience emerges from coping skills that are learned, it can be acquired and enhanced throughout the life cycle. Paradoxically, navigating through adversity leads to particularly strong resilience, so studying resilience patterns in transgender and gender-nonconforming persons illumines practices that lead to greater strength of character for persons of all genders.

Singh, along with Danica G. Hays and Laurel S. Watson, designed a phenomenological inquiry that explored resilience strategies in transgender individuals—"phenomenological" because the study sought to learn from the lived experiences of a population through its members' own descriptions of their resilience practices (Singh et al., 2011, p. 21). This is in keeping with a longstanding contention in the evolving field of transgender studies that the phenomenology of embodied experience is vital to maintaining

---

12. See also Anneliese A. Singh and Vel S. McKleroy, "'Just Getting Out of Bed is a Revolutionary Act': The Resilience of Transgender People of Color Who Have Survived Traumatic Life Events," *International Journal of Traumatology* 17, no. 2 (2011): 34–44.

13. See also Ann S. Masten, *Ordinary Magic: Resilience in Development* (Guilford Press, 2015).

and validating "the categories through which the subject makes sense of its own experience" (Rubin, 1998, p. 265). Singh and her colleagues conducted three interview rounds with transgender persons. The first round explored "general resilience strategies they had used throughout their lives and provided an everyday definition of resilience as 'overcoming difficult times and experiences'" (Singh et al., 2011, p. 22), including the context in which these experiences evolved; the second and third interviews went deeper, exploring details about the strategies shared and the meaning that the participants made of their strategies (p. 22).

Five common themes emerged across all participants, as well as two variant themes among a majority of those interviewed. I will describe briefly the themes that emerged from the study and flesh them out with first-person accounts taken from the growing literature of transgender voices.[14] I will claim that pastoral theology is a field well placed to mine these acquirable strengths for use in seminaries and congregations, and I will end by introducing the metaphor of "opening doors" to illustrate the courageous work and calling of pastoral theology.

RESILIENCE STRATEGIES FOR TRANSGENDER PERSONS

(1) The first common theme described by participants in Singh and colleagues' study as an important aspect of their resilience strategies as transgender persons was *being able to evolve "a self-generated definition of self"* (Singh et al., 2011, p. 23; emphasis added). The ways that gender-creative persons describe their placement on various gender continua can be highly varied, even within the lifetime of a particular individual. "Jamie" "identifies as genderqueer[15] and uses the singular 'they'" (Shultz, 2015, p. xx) as their pronoun:

---

14. I draw my illustrative quotations from several published collections of thematically arranged gender-creative voices: Conover (2002), Girshick (2008), and Shultz (2015). Also of note are full-length memoirs of gender-creative persons such as Jan Morris, *Conundrum: An Extraordinary Narrative of Transsexualism*, 2nd ed. (Holt, 1986); Julia Serano, *Whipping Girl: A Transsexual Woman on Sexism and the Scapegoating of Femininity*, 2nd ed. (Seal, 2016); Jamison Green, *Becoming a Visible Man* (Vanderbilt University Press, 2004); Jennifer Finney Boylan, *She's Not There: A Life in Two Genders*, 2nd ed. (Broadway, 2013); and Nick Krieger, *Nina Here nor There: My Journey Beyond Gender* (Beacon, 2011).

15. "Genderqueer" is a term falling under the transgender umbrella, "often designat[ing] a nonnormative or nonbinary gender identity or expression . . . [and] can refer to a gender identity that purposefully breaks social norms or rules regarding gender" (Shultz, 2015, p. 198).

> I enjoy labels because I can mash them all together. I like cutting up the boxes and creating pretty pictures with them, finding as many words as I can to describe different parts of me. I figured out about a year ago that there were terms for people who weren't one sex or the other, that there were a whole host of nonbinary terms. I began to think that maybe not everyone had to work as hard as I did to keep up the act of trying to fit in to their genders. It was the first time I really realized that there was something other than bisexuality happening within my life. Even a lot of mainstream transgender communities are unwelcoming to nonbinary people. They exhibit the same type of attitude you get from a lot of mainstream gay and lesbian communities: "Oh, you're bisexual? Get off the fence and decide!" They fail to understand that androgyny, just like bisexuality, is really a place. (Shultz, 2015, pp. 73–74)

Jamie's story illustrates Singh's claim that "language regarding their gender became a way for participants to actively resist the traditional binary definitions of gender" (Singh et al., 2011, p. 23). The diversity, contentious at times even *among* transgender persons, is demonstrated by Jamie's positing a *mainstream* transgender community away from which a burgeoning nonbinary population is defining itself. This nonbinary-identifying subculture is now outnumbering the more binary transgender population from which it stemmed, often entering a world of self-defining neologisms that can prove an uphill journey for the uninitiated. "Dakota" "identifies as agender and uses 'ze/hir' pronouns"[16] (Shultz, 2015, p. xx):

> It's really challenging to maintain a nonbinary identity. I have an androgynous name and appearance, but people falter with regard to pronouns . . . so I usually tell people to use whatever feels comfortable for them. I have friends who consistently switch back and forth, and others who try to avoid pronouns altogether. Our language doesn't offer a whole lot of options, and it's so heavily gendered in a lot of ways. People want to know what to do to be respectful, but there's not a lot of concrete instruction I can give them. (Shultz, 2015, p. 74)

---

16. "Agender" is "an identity that describes a feeling or state of being genderless . . . [or where] gender lies somewhere in between masculine or feminine, or beyond a masculine/feminine spectrum of gender" (Shultz, 2015, p. 195). "'Ze and hir' is the most popular form of gender-free pronoun pairing in the online genderqueer community." "The Need for a Gender-Neutral Pronoun," *Gender Neutral Pronoun Blog* (blog), January 24, 2010, https://genderneutralpronoun.wordpress.com/. "Ze" is pronounced "zee," and "hir" is pronounced "here."

In Dakota's path toward self-definition, ze is simultaneously defiant and forgiving. On the one hand, Dakota chooses pronominal designations that are particularly confounding to outsiders; on the other hand, ze lives out a generous spirit of amenability to those in hir orbit. The absence of bedrock "rules" for how to address gender-creative persons speaks to the openness to novelty through which one is invited to live in a world beyond binaries.

"Helen," who self-describes as an "androgyne-leaning femme,"[17] expresses self-determining consternation regarding the era in which she lives, one characterized by both possibilities and a lack of boundaries:

> Not only is there no "standard," generally accepted model for fitting anywhere outside the usual gender binary but there is *also* no generally accepted model for the process of questioning that binary, or for the process of formulating one's own "labels" or identity outside of that binary. . . . If none of the labels we hear "feel" right to us, how do we go about creating a new label that does? How do we know whether we've "found" the right identity/label for ourselves because it really *is* the right one, or whether we've "found" the right one mostly through default? (Girshick, 2008, p. 14)

The process of defining oneself can be an ongoing, evolving series of "trying on" monikers, terms, labels, and names that can prove dizzying but, importantly, self-constitutive and resilience-enhancing: "Although not all participants used the same language to describe their gender, all shared that being able to use their own words and terms to define their gender helped them cope with discrimination" (Singh et al., 2011, p. 23). Often, the terms settled upon are multivalent, allowing identity to be claimed intersectionally in complex ways that incorporate more than merely gender. "Rafael" "identifies as stud and aggressive and uses the pronoun yo"[18] (Shultz, 2015, p. xxii):

> These terms incorporate not only gender identity and expression but also race, which is really important to me. As an interracial individual, I try to stay away from terms like "transexual" and other identity labels that have been traditionally used in white communities. I see myself as an amalgamation within the

---

17. A person identifying as "femme" is "often a lesbian with an effeminate gender expression. However, this identity is sometimes claimed by gay or bisexual men as well" (Shultz, 2015, p. 197).

18. "Stud" and "aggressive" typically describe "masculine-presenting lesbian women" and are "used predominantly in Black or African American communities" (Shultz, 2015, p. 199).

matrices of identity: I am masculine of center, and also a person of color, and also queer. I need terminology that addresses all of these aspects because all of those things come together to shape my experience. (Shultz, 2015, p. 104)

Being able to evolve a self-generated sense of self, then, is a key step toward gender-creative persons' claiming the fullness of intersectional identities, including gender.

(2) A second common theme to emerge in the resilience strategies of transgender participants in Singh and colleagues' study is that "it was *important that they acknowledged and embraced their own self-worth as human beings*; in other words, they had the right to live their lives and exist as transgender people" (Singh et al., 2011, p. 23; emphasis added). The "imposition" that gender-creative persons can feel they are making in "demanding" recognition from an often hesitant or resistant society is subsumed under the rightness and dignity of coming to own an identity that expresses their particularity—each a reflection of the image of God. "Max," who self-describes as "transgender stone butch,"[19] raises questions about the pressures that come to bear over embodying an internal/external identity "consistency":

> Is everyone who's having SRS [sexual reassignment surgery] having it because it's consistent with their internal identity, or are some people doing it because the only images they've been shown of what a woman is are of female women with vaginas and breasts? Or tall men with penises and flat chests? I have spent much of my life desperately wishing I had a male body. But I'm starting to feel comfortable with the apparent contradictions between my female body and my male presentation. This contradiction is part of my strength and my identity, as well as part of what is hot to my lover! It's part of what makes me unique. (Girshick, 2008, p. 71)

Participants in the study shared that in a world where so many things lie outside of individual control, they feel empowered to "draw on positive beliefs about themselves to cope with stress" (Singh et al., 2011, p. 23), allowing them stand firm in their self-empowerment. The voice of "Clare" (who self-identifies as "queer") in Girshick's collection perhaps speaks for many in the study:

---

19. "Stone butch" typically refers to "a female-bodied person who is strongly masculine in character and dress, who is generally dominant in sexual relations and often does not want to be touched genitally" (Girshick, 2008, p. 206).

> To answer the homophobes becomes easy, those folks who want to dehumanize, erase, make invisible the lives of butch dykes and Nellie fags. We shrug. We laugh. We tell them: your definitions of woman and man suck. We tell them: your binary stinks. We say: here we are in all our glory—male, female, intersexed, trans, butch, Nellie, studly, femme, king, androgynous, queen, some of us carving out new ways of being women, others of us new ways of being men, and still others new ways of being something else entirely. (Girshick, 2008, p. 34)

A person's embraceable self-worth can gather strength from somewhere deep within and/or emerge bolstered by the approbation of others, whether or not those others intentionally meant to dignify a specifically transgender identity. A computer analyst wrote these words to then Vice President Al Gore upon receiving an award for developing specialized computer software:

> I am writing in advance to say thank you . . . and say that receiving your prestigious award is particularly important for me because it affirms that I, a transgendered (transsexual) woman am regarded by you as a valuable person . . . I was Richard Green when I wrote the key computer program . . . I am sending copies of the letter to The Post and other papers to advise others in advance of my preference to be regarded, treated, and referred to as the woman, Jewelia Margueritta Cameroon. (Conover, 2002, p. 107)

Embracing self-worth became for the study participants "a critical component of a positive self image. . . . They universally agreed that having a strong internal 'coach' to help them manage prejudice was instrumental in this fight" (Singh et al., 2011, p. 23).

(3) Third among common themes in the resilience strategies of study participants was *an awareness of oppression*:

> They described this awareness as being a stepwise development, in which they gradually recognized the extent of oppression they faced. Participants described their awareness of oppression as helping them to identify societal messages that were not "trans-positive." (Singh et al., 2011, p. 23)

The kinds of oppression identified by Singh and her colleagues' interlocutors ranged from the existence and experience of virulent transphobic discrimination to an awareness of the insidiousness of internalizing messages of "necessary" societal conformity. "Catherine," "an orthopedic nurse [who] transitioned male to female (MTF)" (Shultz, p. xix) and locates her community in a queer women's circle, describes the positive ripples that can come from oppression awareness:

> When I was first transitioning, I wore a lot of dresses and fingernail polish and makeup. My dyke friends were like, "Just stop. Please will you stop?" It seemed unnatural to this particular group of women that I would want to wear the sort of clothes they despised. When I asked why she was so opposed to my dress, my friend Bonnie said, "I hate wearing dresses because I was forced to." Her eyes went wide as comprehension dawned on her face. These days, Bonnie wears dresses more than she ever did, partly because now it is *her* choice and partly because it's not a political statement anymore. (Shultz, 2015, p. 79)

Often, an acute awareness of oppression emerges for transgender persons by way of contradistinction to the sometimes very different pressures and strictures faced by their "kindred" "L," "G," "B," and/or "Q" communities. Understanding the particular oppressions experienced by persons claiming the "T" allows targeted action on behalf of gender-creative persons, as does unpacking the intersectional ways that other minority group statuses can exacerbate or attenuate gender identity/expression-specific oppressions. "Mosley," who "identifies as stud, boi, and masculine of center"[20] (Shultz, 2015, p. xxi), speaks to the particularities of discrimination that fall onto both transgender and communities of color within the LGBTQ+ world she inhabits:

> When there is talk about LGBTQ issues, often issues of gay, privileged white men take center stage. The arguments become about marriage equality—and don't get me wrong I'm very supportive of marriage equality; I want my rights, dammit—but issues of homelessness, sexual violence, racial discrimination, and housing discrimination are completely ignored. These are all more pressing issues than wanting your partner to get the same benefits that you have at your really elite job. Many people in poor communities or communities of color can't even talk about benefits right now, because we're not getting work. We're not safe in our communities, and often we're not safe from the very institutions that are supposed to protect us: law enforcement, social services, and other institutions that are supposed to

---

20. "Stud" "typically describes masculine-presenting lesbian women. This term is used predominantly in Black or African American communities" (Shultz, 2015, p. 199); "boi" usually describes "a masculine woman, genderqueer individual, or young trans man" (Shultz, 2015, p. 196); and "masculine of center" is "a term for masculine women and used primarily in communities of color" (Shultz, 2015, p. 199).

help our communities [but] have often marginalized us in many ways. (Shultz, 2015, pp. 81–82)

An *awareness of the specificities of oppressions* faced by gender-creative persons both informs targeted reforms and social activism as well as helps to identify negative societal messages in order to counteract their internalization. In the process, individuals are often moved to embrace others who share their particularities and struggles, which leads to a fourth common theme in resilience strategies among the participants in the Singh et al., (2011) study: the power of belonging to a group.

(4) *Connection with supportive community.* "Olivia," a trans woman minister in the United Church of Christ denomination, stresses the importance of community in the context of her becoming aware of the differences of experienced oppressions within LGBTQ+ communities:

> Lesbian, gay, bisexual, and other people whose identities are based on *sexuality* celebrate at pride parades ... to be out in public and let everyone know that they are not ashamed of themselves. There are trans people who participate in pride, but for the most part, *trans* folk are forced to be spectacles every day so they aren't necessarily interested in throwing a parade where even more people can gawk at them. The biggest celebration in the transgender community is Trans Day of Remembrance, where we hold vigils to memorialize our dead. The rates of suicide, murder, and drug overdose in the trans community are astronomically high. People in all parts of the world gather each November with pictures of our trans loved ones. We celebrate their lives and mourn their deaths. (Shultz, 2015, p. 83; emphases added)

It is no accident that, since 2015, the Trans Day of Remembrance, which brings gender-creative persons and their allies together in communal grief, is being additionally charged through a wide-scale series of art projects as a "Trans Day of Resilience" in order to "experience a world where trans people of color don't just survive, but thrive" (Trans Day, n.d.). Shared oppression can sustain vibrant communities of joy gathered together in spite of that oppression, even in the midst of sorrow. The fact that Olivia is a Christian minister suggests that religious communities can be resources for the resilience strategies identified by Singh and her colleagues' (2011) study participants. Coming together as a community that acknowledges its common experience of oppression is itself an expression of resilience. But Singh et al. (2011) stress, based on their findings, that "although participants described having a very active role in building communities, these communities were not always transgender-only communities" (p. 24). Classrooms and congregations can become those supportive communities for building gender-creative resilience.

Optimally, support and a sense of community would be part of a person's upbringing. For some gender-creative persons (and, one hopes, for more and more of them in time), family support has been a blessing they acknowledge. "Jeff," a self-described "FtM (female-to-male)" trans man, credits his parents with allowing him the strength and resilience to embrace his trans reality:

> Probably my parents played the biggest role in my—not who I am because I don't have a choice necessarily in who I am—but in how I was emotionally ready to adapt to the world as a man. I credit my parents with being able to lay the groundwork when I was young about being who I was and about accepting yourself and about diversity, about not playing, just be yourself. (Girshick, 2008, p. 54)

The family can thereby be a prototype for the kinds of *supportive communities* gender-creative persons discover and/or create later in their journeys toward personal resilience. With parental support and communal camaraderie come more self-acceptance and the ability to look to one's future with less fear and more hope.

(5) *Cultivating hope for the future.* Participants reported using hope as a management strategy in times of felt discrimination over their gender identities and/or expression. Hope is experienced in various ways, sometimes in a wish on behalf of upcoming generations of gender-creative persons who have a wider canvas of possibilities open to them. "Catherine," the orthopedic nurse mentioned earlier, marvels at this brave new world:

> I look around at these young trans kids who pass beautifully because they got to take hormone blockers when they were still pre-pubescent and transition to hormones as teens. Many of them will never need the surgeries I had to have in order to pass. They will never face the same violence and ridicule as the people in my generation did. When I look around and see these kids transitioning, and these kids who have family support, I know that every battle we waged was worth it.[21] (Shultz, 2015, p. 194)

---

21. To "pass," which is controversial in that it suggests a necessity for, or an optimal outcome of, gender conformance (and the attendant "failures" to do so), is defined as "to be successfully recognized by others (usually strangers) as one's desired gender" (Shultz, 2015, p. 198).

Hope should be a natural outcome for gender-creative individuals seeking community in Christian churches. However, as "Olivia," the United Church of Christ minister noted earlier, understates:

> Christianity has not always been a welcoming space for LGBT people. In many churches, this is still the case. I make sure that I use my pulpit to show how welcoming the light of God can be to everyone. People cite various biblical verses to prove that homosexuality is a sin, or that being transgender is a sin. When I minister about these verses, I try to put them in a historical and cultural context so that people think about the meaning of the words in a new way. I may not be able to convince everyone that God loves and accepts homosexuals and transexuals, but I can usually help them realize that it is not their place to pass judgment on their neighbors, and that's a good place to start. (Shultz, 2015, pp. 186–187)

Cultivating hope by repositioning biblical verses that heretofore have been read and interpreted to exclude is perhaps the most powerful way pastoral theologians and ministers can begin to open the doors of Christianity to an affirmation of gender-creative promise. Hope can be cultivated in the face of oppression and discrimination, but it is inculcated best in religious community in tandem with a message of God's love and support. These reflections of "Mosley" (stud, boi, masculine of center), heard from earlier, tie together all five of the elements found in common among the study participants' resilience strategies—*self-generated definition of self, self-worth, awareness of oppressions, supportive community,* and *hope for the future*:

> Having a sense of community is vital. When you're queer, the world is actively, actively trying to get you to be anything other than who you are, so we need to provide spaces that get us to feel comfortable in our own skin. Having a sense of self [and] a sense of health and wellness is going to translate into all facets of our lives. If we feel worthy, if we feel empowered, [and] if we love ourselves, that's going to show up in our style, in the workplace, in our relationships, and [in] the way we treat others. It's going to show up in how successful we conceptualize ourselves as being. (Shultz, 2015, p. 99)

An additional two themes found in a majority of the study's participants can be seen to lead directly from a successful finding, implementation, and living out of the previous five themes held in common by all participants.

(6) A majority of Singh and her colleagues' study participants reported *the importance of engaging in social activism*; they described "both seeking

out opportunities for activism and being exposed to activism through others" (Singh et al., 2011, p. 24). The motivations for this activist work vary in the testimonies of gender-creative persons. "Kurtis," who self-describes as "transmasculine,"[22] speaks of the attendant cultural advantages that accrued to him as a result of his transitioning and his felt conviction to pay it forward:

> I woke up one day as a white man in America. I feel that it's my responsibility to do something with all that privilege, so I decided to work for a racial-justice organization. I do my best to use my powers and privileges to dismantle racism, classism, homophobia, and transphobia. I try to listen to those who are marginalized by racism and help ensure that their voices are heard. I'm not trying to sound chivalrous or gallant. The reality is I have power as a white "dude," and if I'm not actively working toward antiracism, then I'm perpetuating a system of inequality. I can't let that happen. (Shultz, 2015, p. 107)

Part of the ubiquity of activism among gender-creative persons is due to the persistence of the oppression they suffer. "Greg" refers to transgender communities as being filled with "accidental activists":

> I feel that a lot of trans folk become activists, not because they necessarily want to, but because there is a certain amount of need. You can't change the gender marker on your driver's license? You can't find a doctor willing to treat you? You can't find a safe restroom? No one else is going to take care of these issues, because their lives aren't affected by them each and every day. As you deal with prejudice on a daily basis, you start picking and choosing which battles are the most important to you and then you start educating the people around you. Even if they never intended for it to happen, I believe most trans people become accidental activists. (Shultz, 2015, p. 165)

The definitions of "activism" are wide, from advocacy in educational, social, or legislative settings to the simple activist moments of claiming aloud a marginalized identity. "Jill," who self-describes as a "male crossdresser" and "transgendered,"[23] speaks to the power of allowing more and more persons

---

22 "Transmasculine" is "the adjective form of trans man" (Shultz, 2015, p. 200).

23. There has been a historical shift from the earlier usage of "transgendered" to the current "transgender." Generally, the word "transgendered" should be avoided because "transgendered suggests that being trans is something that happens to someone, as opposed to an identity someone is born with." See German Lopez, "Why You Should Always Use 'Transgender' instead of 'Transgendered,'" *Vox*, February 18, 2015, https://

to know a gender-creative person by normalizing the experience through "coming out":

> The more transgendered people there are out, even if you're just out to your friends, even if it's just one person, I think that's activism. And that's important. It's important for the person, for both people, because the more people know that we are human beings and we're not monsters, we're not evil, that the more people can question their own ideas about gender, I think the more we will learn. (Girshick, 2008, p. 176)

"Beth," a self-described "MtF (male to female)" trans woman, would concur, evidencing her mere non-passing presence as a positive witness for the "cause":

> I do think it's important that God, the universe, whatever, decided to make me 6'3" and so masculine-looking so that I am not able to just stop and blend in and disappear into the woodwork after surgery. I'm having to be out here every day at least with people questioning. They might not know exactly, but questioning. So I think that's good. (Girshick, 2008, p. 176)

In turn, cisgender members of caring communities can engage in the "activist" endeavor of expanding the sense of their own gender and of gender in general. In finding personal placements on the various continua of gender, all persons' gender identities and expressions might be "de-normalized," creating points of gender-diverse commonality from which to create community with and for gender-creative persons. It is in the living of one's life in relationships with others that more subtle forms of activism can be deployed by persons of all genders, leading to the final theme, found among a majority of the participants in the Singh et al., (2011) study—that of educating by example.

(7) *Being a positive role model for others.* Whether it manifests in settings of work, church, family, or volunteer engagement, having a positive influence on others follows naturally from the kinds of "openly being yourself" social activism advocated by "transgendered" male crossdresser "Jill" and MtF trans woman "Beth." Becoming a positive role model for others, like "accidental activism," often starts from where one is already socially located. "Natalie" transitioned on the police force and found that she became a positive role model at her workplace by connecting with a common thread in her fellow officers:

---

www.vox.com/2015/2/18/8055691/transgender-transgendered-tnr.

> There are a lot of officers who joined the force because they wanted to make a difference and who want to uphold justice. These are the ones who truly want to protect and serve. I may not ever be able to reach the rogues, but most officers want to learn how they can help others and do their jobs better. That's why I started training squadrons on how to work with transgender suspects and inmates. It started with my own station first. My boss asked me to lead some diversity trainings that focused on LGBT issues. To my surprise, everyone was extremely attentive and asked very informed questions. From there it snowballed: I give two to four trainings at different stations each month. I occasionally feel tokenized, but I can put those feelings aside because I know that the work that I'm doing is invaluable. (Shultz, 2015, p. 181)

A lack of positive role models can cause gender-creative persons to feel isolated, to have the sense that no one could ever share their worries and struggles. The power of seeing role models in the media, on the internet, or in one's own life can often propel a transgender person to model resilience for others. Serving as a role model, in turn, better enables a person to continue gathering strength toward the vibrant living of their own life. Singh and her colleagues (2011) found that "many participants described a desire to seek out jobs and careers where they could help others and find inspiration, which helped them mitigate some of the negative effects of oppression" (p. 24). "Blake," a Native American self-described "FTM (female to male)" professor of disability studies, has found that his "teaching" extends beyond the classroom:

> Representation is incredibly important, but members of minority groups often cannot easily point to examples or positive role models or strong representatives. As an older person in the community, I feel that it is my duty to mentor youth and help guide the way for those who are taking the reins behind me. When my generation dies, the movement will fall into their hands, and we must teach them how to be strong leaders. During the summers, I go home to mentor and tutor youth on the Fort Mojave Reservation. It's good for these young kids to see that they can leave the rez and make something of themselves, and it's even better for them to see how important it is to return to the rez and give back to the community. (Shultz, 2015, p. 184)

Whether Singh and her colleagues (2011) intended it or not, each resilience strategy as enumerated can be seen to feed naturally into the next, with *evolving a self-generated definition of self* enhancing one's *ability to embrace self-worth*. Having a named identity, and self-worth attached to that identity, will steel oneself in the face of a growing *awareness of the prevalence of oppression* and enhance the attendant ability to weed out harmful tropes and influences. Awareness of oppression, in turn, puts one in touch with others who suffer in like manner, and *connecting with a supportive community* contributes to being able to *cultivate hope for the future*. Sensing a possible positive future for oneself and others leads to the kinds of *social activism* necessary to bring about the changes one seeks. Such activism can be collective action on behalf of others or simply the strength of being oneself openly and proudly, which can *furnish a positive role model for others*.

PASTORAL PRACTICE

Possible ways that a caring pastor, ministerial teacher, or pulpit preacher can contribute to, bolster, enhance—engender, even—all seven of these strengths come readily to mind: (1) inviting students and parishioners to name themselves with their own words and respecting those namings; (2) fostering positive self-images by providing affirmative messages about gender-creative persons—in casual speech, in writing, and from the pulpit; (3) critically examining societal messages to understand better the oppression the persons in one's care are experiencing; (4) providing, inculcating, and advocating for the classroom and the congregation to be the kind of supportive communities that build resilience; (5) strengthening relationships over time with those in one's care so as to connect living, unfolding life stories to hopeful outcomes; (6) attending to or sponsoring community, denominational, or academic activism by participating in rallies, religious services, and conferences that aim toward positive change in the public arena; and (7) being a positive role model on whom gender-creative persons in one's care can rely and allowing the care-receiver, in turn, to be a role model for the caregiver.

Religion and religious community, however, can be double-edged swords, sources of oppression as well as of resilience. Pastoral theology takes into serious consideration the psychological dimensions of religiosity in all their complexity and ambiguity and can help discern the aspects of religious belonging that are forces for healing from those more liable to hurt, especially those on the margins of society. Pinpointing the kinds of spiritual nourishment religious affiliation provides can guide pastoral practices for promoting gender-creative thriving and spiritual resilience. Pastoral theology has tended historically to test metaphorical ways of interpreting its own practices in constituting itself as a field and attempting to guide effective pastoral action. Dykstra (2005), in *Images of Pastoral Care*, makes a studied collection of just such vocational metaphors. His volume not only proffers rationales *for* pastoral theologians contributing to a steady stream of metaphorical images for their vocation but also allows for weighing various of those images. That process invites me, in closing, to offer a pastoral image of my own. A parable related by Jesus of Nazareth to his disciples in the Gospel of Luke (11:5–8), where the text's importuner and importuned are blurred semantically, allows me to proffer an apt metaphor for an affirmative pastoral theology beyond gender binaries.

OPENING DOORS

> And he said to them, "Among you, what man would have a friend, and *would come* to him at midnight and say to him, 'Friend, lend me three loaves of bread, Since a friend of mine has just visited me from the road and I have nothing I might set before him,' And the one inside would say in response, 'Do not present me with difficulties; the door has already been closed, and my children and I are in bed; I cannot get up and give you anything.' I tell you, even if he will not rise and give it to him because he is his friend, still on account of his persistence he will rise and give him whatever he needs."[24] (Hart, 2017, pp. 132–133; emphasis added)

This parable-text is found only in the Lukan gospel. As I began to work on a translation of the verses, I discovered two equally plausible points of view, those of the "Knocker" and of the "Sleeper."[25] While either version suffices as a translation, I suggest that *both* versions can be understood simultaneously; after all, the Knocker *was* a sleeper but for a third, usually neglected, character in the parable, that of the "Journeyer," who sets the story in motion by arriving at the house of a friend. The translation offered

---

24. Luke 11:5–8. Note: In addition to capitalizing the first word in each sentence, Hart capitalizes the first word of each new verse.

25. The Greek verb for "would come" (italicized above) in Luke 11:5 can correspond to both second and third person because the original subject combines "you" and "which." As Nolland (1993) writes, "This makes at once for an ambiguity as to who goes to whom. Does our addressee go *as* the one with an unexpected guest, or get visited *by* the one with an unexpected guest?" (p. 623; emphases added). Most English translations fall on the side of a second-person conjugation of the verb in question, such as the New Revised Standard Version, which reads as follows: "Suppose one of you has a friend, and you go to him at midnight . . ." The New English Bible translation of Luke 11:5, however, espouses the third-person alternative: "Suppose one of you has a friend who comes to him in the middle of the night . . ."

above preserves the ambiguity in the original Greek with either the Knocker version—"[the man] would come to him at midnight"—or the Sleeper version—"[the friend] would come to him at midnight"—discernible in the English wording.

The parable is set in an honor-shame cultural setting in which friendship constitutes the relationships of expected reciprocal hospitality. Each interaction between a guest in need and a resident villager involves the risk of entering into the encounter, the potential disgrace and attendant shame if the expected relationship of friendship doesn't ensue, and the opportunities for gaining honor through proffered hospitality.[26] The Journeyer has risked attendant shame by arriving unannounced in the middle of the night at the door of the future Knocker. The Journeyer, therefore, is the original knocker who sets the events in motion. The original sleeper, in order to avoid disgrace, must rise and *open the door* to provide for the Journeyer. This original sleeper, having no way of providing for the Journeyer, transitions into the Knocker of the parable who will, in turn, also have to risk shame by going to the neighbor-friend in the middle of the night to ask for food to provide for the Journeyer. So, leaving the Journeyer at home, the now-Knocker goes to the house of another friend. A second Sleeper is awakened, having put the household to bed, including children. I would imagine an initial fright, as for anyone whose door is knocked on in the middle of the night. In fact, only the importunity of the Knocker elicits any response at all from the Sleeper. A conversation ensues with the Sleeper, still in bed, who calls out, "Go away!" However, the Knocker explains the predicament, namely, that the Journeyer has risked shame and has, in turn, compelled the Knocker, too, to risk shame. The Sleeper, in turn (and in order to avoid disgrace), answers the call of the Knocker, rises, and *opens the door*. Honor is restored all around.

One can imagine Jesus's apostles gravitating toward this narrative precisely because it addressed their Knocker needs as soon-to-be itinerant ministers of the gospel. Indeed, the hospitality on which the apostles would depend is itself the content of that very gospel message: *love your neighbor-friend*. The parable illustrates God's promised benefaction through "steadfastness of hospitality." It is the bounty of God, as revealed in the sometimes-begrudging hospitality of fellow humans, on which the apostles are charged to depend. Indeed, "God" is revealed *in* this transaction of generosity.

---

26. See Halvor Moxnes, "Honor and Shame," in *The Social Sciences and New Testament Interpretation*, ed. Richard L. Rohrbaugh (Baker Academic, 1996) and Herman C. Waetjen, "The Subversion of 'World' by the Parable of the Friend at Midnight," *Journal of Biblical Literature* 120, no. 4 (Winter 2001): 703–721.

Strong claims in the passage, then, are an obligation to render care to one's fellow human despite what may be inconveniences to regular operating procedures and the reality that achieving a relationship of reciprocity can at times require persistence. By opening oneself to the plight of another in need, one has an opportunity to render care to the other by *opening the door*, and that action propels one into the godliness that exists in the knowledge of interconnectedness. The original sleeper was transformed into the Knocker as a result of the Journeyer's need. So, too, if *we* can muster the will to rise to the challenge (however burdensome it may seem) of *opening the door*, we involve ourselves in the movement of God's providence. We then are given opportunities to experience the hospitality of doors opened to *us* in the course of our duty of opening them to others. Journeyers knock, transforming sleepers into journeyers who knock, and so it goes.

Pastoral caregivers and pastoral theologians may rediscover ways to walk with God alongside their gender-creative siblings. To do so may require new metaphors, new language to describe the inherent welcome and mutuality embedded in their professions. In order to move toward an affirmative pastoral theology beyond gender binaries, caregivers can self-disclose the social locations from which they operate; learn about the existence, complexity, and diversity within the gender-creative world; gain an awareness of various gender continua and psychological models for describing the life cycles of gender-creative persons; inquire as to the resilience strategies of transgender individuals; and expand their sense of how religious affiliation and belonging are transmitted in ways benign, destructive, or transformational. If they engage in these practices while persistently wrestling with the parameters of their own gendered selves, these endeavors will contribute to a pastoral theological effort to open doors to genuine gender-diverse dialogue and care, finding the resilience and gender-creative promise that lies on the other side.

REFERENCES

Conover, P. (2002). *Transgender good news*. New Wineskins.
Crenshaw, K. (1989). Demarginalizing the intersection of race and sex: A black feminist critique of anti-discrimination doctrine, feminist theory and antiracist politics. *University of Chicago Legal Forum, 1*, Article 8.
Dykstra, R. C. (Ed.). (2005). *Images of pastoral care: Classic readings*. Chalice.
Ehrensaft, D. (2018). Foreword. In Anneliese A. Singh, *The queer and transgender resilience workbook: Skills for navigating sexual orientation and gender expression* (pp. vii–viii). New Harbinger.
Flores, A. R., Herman, J. L., Gates, G. J., & Brown, T. N. T. (2016). How many adults identify as transgender in the United States? The Williams Institute. Retrieved

January 3, 2022, from https://williamsinstitute. law.ucla.edu/publications/trans-adults-united-states/

Girshick, L. B. (2008). *Transgender voices: Beyond women and men*. University Press of New England.

GLAAD (2017). Accelerating acceptance 2017: A Harris poll survey of Americans' acceptance of LGBTQ people. https://www.glaad.org/files/aa/2017_GLAAD_Accelerating_Acceptance.pdf

Gonella, C. (2017, March 31). Survey: 20% of millennials identify as LGBTQ. *NBC News* online. Retrieved January 3, 2022, from https://www.nbcnews.com/feature/nbc-out/ survey-20-percent-millennials-identify-lgbtq-n740791

Grant, J. M., Mottet, L. A., & Tanis, J. (2011). *Injustice at every turn: A report of the National Transgender Discrimination Survey*. National Center for Transgender Equality.

Hart, D. B. (2017). *The New Testament: A translation*. Yale University Press.

Hidalgo, M. A., Ehrensaft, D., Tishelman, A. C., Clark, L. F., Garofalo, R., Rosenthal, S. M., Spack, N. P., & Olson, J. (2013). The gender affirmative model: What we know and what we aim to learn. *Human Development*, 56(5), 285–290. https://doi.org/10.1159/000355235

James, S. E., Herman, J. L., Rankin, S., Keisling, M., Mottet, L., & Anafi, M. (2015). The report of the 2015 U.S. Transgender Survey. National Center for Transgender Equality. https://www.ustranssurvey.org/ reports

Nolland, J. (1993). Luke 9:21–18:34. Word Biblical Commentary 35B. Word.

Rubin, H. S. (1998). Phenomenology as method in trans studies. *GLQ: A Journal of Lesbian and Gay Studies*, 4(2), 263–281.

Shultz, J. W. (2015). *Trans/Portraits: Voices from transgender communities*. Dartmouth College Press.

Singh, A. A. (2018). *The queer and transgender resilience workbook: Skills for navigating sexual orientation and gender expression*. New Harbinger.

Singh, A. A. & dickey, l. m. (Eds.). (2017). *Affirmative counseling and psychological practice with transgender and gender nonconforming clients*. American Psychological Association.

Singh, A. A., Hays, D. G., & Watson, L. S. (2011). Strength in the face of adversity: Resilience strategies of transgender individuals. *Journal of Counseling and Development*, 89(1), 20–27.

Steiner, A. (2014, September 17). Ann Masten: Children's natural resilience is nurtured through "ordinary magic." Retrieved January 3, 2022, from *Minn Post*. https://www.minnpost.com/mental-health-addiction/2014/09/ ann-masten-children-s-natural-resilience-nurtured-through-ordinary-m/

Steinmetz, K. (2016, May 18). How many Americans are gay? *Time* online. Retrieved January 3, 2022, from http://time.com/lgbt-stats/

Tanis, J. (2018). Transgender people in the United States. In C. Dowd, C. Beardsley, & W. J. Tanis (Eds.), *Transfaith: A transgender pastoral resource* (pp. 149–160). Darton, Longman & Todd.

Trans Day of Resilience. (n.d.). Retrieved January 3, from https://www.tdor.co

4

No Greater Love

The Light of Beauford Delaney in the Life of James Baldwin

JAY-PAUL HINDS

> No one has greater love than this, to lay down one's life for one's friends.
> —JOHN 15:13 NRSV

INTRODUCTION

You never forget your first. This often-quoted phrase is usually expressed when one thinks back, with various levels of positive or negative affect, on pivotal "first" experiences in one's life. Personally, I have too many firsts to retell here, but some are, I must admit, more cherished than others. My first trip to the Jersey Shore. My first girlfriend. My first car. My first day of high school. My first job. My first day teaching. From time to time, for some reason I have not yet completely grasped, I recall some of these firsts to give myself a sense of accomplishment or perhaps, if nothing else, to mark in my mind a pivotal point in my development. In truth, looking back on these firsts makes me feel that I have grown up a bit as I often say to myself while conjuring these memories, "Look how far I have come."

A particular first that has crept into my mind of late is my first published paper, "Traces on the Blackboard." The paper, which was written in 2010 for the New Directions in Pastoral Theology conference, was my *first* attempt to write about the lingering effects of racism on the African American psyche.

This was my *first* academic conference, and I can recall how eager I was to hear how these esteemed scholars, most of whom had already written articles and books and presented at conferences, would respond to my paper. The feedback was encouraging, so much so that I went on to submit the paper for publication in *Pastoral Psychology*, one of the most respected journals in the field of psychology and religion/spirituality. All of this—the conference, the paper, and the publication—was a wonderful first for me. But what if things had gone totally different with the conference, the paper, and the publication? How would things be different today?

For argument's sake, let us say that the respondent to my paper commented—graciously, of course—that my writing, from the grammar to the presentation of the argument, was not at the level of the other presenters'. And to make matters worse, other conference participants supported this opinion. Furthermore, what if, despite these comments, I went on submit this same paper to *Pastoral Psychology* for review, but this time, in this imagined scenario, the paper was rejected because the reviewers deemed it unfit for publication. I admit that I, as a burgeoning scholar, would have been disheartened, to say the least, by these comments and this rejection because, again, this was my first academic paper. And remember, "You never forget your first." I am grateful that things turned out differently. As it has been more than 10 years since I wrote "Traces on the Blackboard," I am now better able to see things in that article that I could not see before, such as that I was attempting, at that time, to write about the harm caused by painful firsts. These are the firsts that, unfortunately, become the traces that, in our moments of self-reflection, we see etched, indelibly, on our psyches.

In "Traces on the Blackboard," I suggested that novelist, essayist, and playwright James Baldwin was a prophetic voice who fearlessly spoke about how America's racism created an environment in which many of the firsts experienced by African Americans were contaminated by anti-Blackness. In *Notes of a Native Son*, Baldwin (1998) reveals how this environment gnaws away at the self-esteem of African Americans. An especially poignant example of this for Baldwin is that of his father, David Baldwin, of whom Baldwin says, "He claimed to be proud of his blackness but it has also been the cause of much humiliation and it had fixed bleak boundaries to his life" (p. 65). Discarded, trapped, imprisoned, enslaved—these are experiences many if not all African Americans have when they first encounter, according to Baldwin, the low value placed on their lives in America.

I spent most of "Traces on the Blackboard" attempting to understand how Baldwin sought to overcome this racially designated first experience of his Blackness through the eyes of the other. In "A Talk to Teachers," Baldwin (1998) expresses his firm conviction that this first was no accident but was rather the result of a "criminal conspiracy to destroy [African Americans]," especially their sense of self-worth (p. 685). To combat this conspiracy, Baldwin suggests that one of the African American's weapons "for refusing to make his peace with [this conspiracy] and for destroying it depends on what he decides he is worth" (p. 685). Baldwin attests that this reevaluation of worth necessitates that one reject many of the standards upheld in American society as many are "based on fantasies created by very ill people" (p. 685). New standards are needed, created by and culled from a world that is "larger, more daring, more beautiful" than the restricted world African Americans have been told they are supposed to inhabit.

In "Traces on the Blackboard," I hypothesized that this worth could be created within the pastoral counseling relationship, one in which, ideally, the counselee can be empowered to find new models and means of self-identification, leading to a revitalized sense of self-worth. I remain convinced of the value of pastoral counseling in helping African Americans overcome the traces of race and racism, but I now know that I overlooked something that is far more essential to one's recovery of self-worth, something that is evident in the life of James Baldwin, especially during a time in his development—those volatile adolescent years—when not only America but even more so his neighborhood, his family, his church, and even, one can argue based on Baldwin's own testimony, his God made him feel ugly and unlovable. James Baldwin's self-worth was restored and his life was changed through his friendship, a life-long bond, with the artist Beauford Delaney. This paper explores how, through his art, Beauford was the first for Baldwin in a significant way. Baldwin (1998) remarks, in his essay "The Price of the Ticket," that "Beauford was the first walking, living proof, for me, that a black man could be an artist" (p. 832). Through their friendship, Baldwin learned to see that art is life, art is freedom, art is redemption, and, ultimately, art is love. Delaney was the first person to give his art, which was his very life, to Baldwin so truthfully and so completely that Baldwin, through this friendship, began to see not only the world but himself anew.

THE UGLIEST BOY I'VE EVER SEEN

James Arthur Baldwin was born on August 2, 1924, in New York City's Harlem Hospital. When speaking of his childhood in *Notes of a Native Son* (1998), Baldwin shared that "the story of my childhood is the usual bleak fantasy, and we can dismiss it with the restrained observation that I certainly would not consider living it again" (p. 5). During a 1974 interview in France, Baldwin claimed, "I never had a childhood" (Campbell, 1991, p. 3). There are several factors that led Baldwin to have this negative view of his youth, but, according to biographer David Leeming, a friend of Baldwin's for over 20 years, nothing was more pivotal than his illegitimacy. "Illegitimacy and an almost obsessive preoccupation with his stepfather were constant themes in the life and works of James Baldwin," writes Leeming (1994, p. 3). *Go Tell It on the Mountain* (1952/1981), Baldwin's first and most autobiographical novel, reads like a case study of a young man experiencing the patricidal rage associated with Freud's Oedipus complex, evident in Leeming's (1994) observation that the story "recorded the killing of the father" (p. 85). John Grimes, the novel's protagonist, is in an ongoing battle, fluctuating between the physical and the spiritual, with his father, Gabriel Grimes. The significance of Baldwin's choosing to name the father Gabriel should not be overlooked. Baldwin was adept at utilizing biblical names and themes in his work, many of which were gleaned during his youth listening to sermons and songs in Mother Horn's church, the Mount Calvary Assembly of the Pentecostal Faith of All Nations, where he undoubtedly heard about the archangel Gabriel. Gabriel was God's messenger, the angel who, according to scripture, announced the birth of John the Baptist to Zechariah (Luke 1:5–25) and the birth of Jesus to the Virgin Mary (Luke 1:26–38). Gabriel Grimes, it was believed, was, like his namesake, the archangel Gabriel, set apart to be God's messenger to God's people, and no one had more faith in Gabriel's calling and power than his son John, who confesses that his father, Gabriel, "was God's minister, the ambassador of the King of Heaven" (p. 14). And if this were true, if Gabriel were in fact God's messenger, then God did not love John Grimes . . . because Gabriel did not love him.

In "The Threshing Floor," the final section of *Go Tell It on the Mountain*, Gabriel has a frightening vision about his father. In the vision, John hears his father say, "I'm going to beat sin out of [John]. I'm going to beat it out" (p. 199). By John's own admission, he committed a grave sin because he had looked upon his father's nakedness; and, similar to the sons of Noah in the book of Genesis, he would be cursed for committing this act, "a servant of servants shall he be unto his brethren" (p. 200). The curse of Ham had fallen upon John Grimes. As the vision progresses, however, we learn that this act is not the sole cause of Gabriel's hatred of his son. For Gabriel, John's greatest sin was his ugliness. And this, as his own father often told him, was also James Baldwin's greatest sin. Baldwin (1998) writes, "My father said, during all these years I lived with him, that I was the ugliest boy he had ever seen," adding, "and I had absolutely no reason to doubt him" (p. 481). Baldwin never could erase from his mind and, even more painfully, his spirit the superlative used by his real-life father, David Baldwin, to describe how he looked to him. The *ugliest* boy. But what does it mean to be ugly? And how did James Baldwin understand the term? The online *Merriam-Webster* defines ugly as "offensive to the sight" and "offensive or unpleasant to any sense." Furthermore, the ugly is "likely to cause inconvenience or discomfort" (Merriam-Webster, n.d.). Is this what his father really thought about him? Was James Baldwin, in his very ugliest-ness, the most offensive to his father's sight, just unbearable to look at? Was James Baldwin the person who caused his father the most inconvenience and the most discomfort? Whether or not David Baldwin truly believed such things doesn't matter, for the truly traumatic part of all of this is that young Jimmy put great faith in his father's hurtful words and his shaming gaze, so much so that he believed that not only his father but *everyone* saw him as the ugliest and, by extension, the most undesirable boy. Baldwin (1998) confesses in "The Price of the Ticket" that his self-identification as the "ugliest boy" caused him to push people away, to spurn the very idea that he could ever be loved, writing, "I was to hurt a great many people by being unable to imagine that anyone could possibly be in love with an ugly boy like me" (p. 833). This ugliness was the source of his intense sense of illegitimacy.

Baldwin spent most of his life searching for a cure for his illegitimacy because he had faith that only true love, expressed by someone claiming him as their beloved, could remove the curse of his ugliness. David Baldwin was the man young Jimmy called "father" during his youth, but he was not his biological father, a truth Jimmy would not learn until he was a teenager. Few biographical details are known of Baldwin's actual father except that he abandoned Jimmy before he was born, but of his stepfather he was able to piece together a narrative telling of a man who, because of tremendous hardships in his life, knew a lot about ugliness. David Baldwin was a preacher and laborer who migrated from New Orleans to Harlem in the early 1920s. The conditions that caused David Baldwin to join the Great Migration were similar to those of countless African Americans, but there were unique circumstances to his departure from the South, as Baldwin biographer James Campbell (1991) notes:

> David Baldwin had left the south partly because of an inability to communicate with people, to establish ordinary social relationships, and also because his puritan soul recoiled at the prospect of New Orleans, with its vaudeville associations, as a new-world Sodom and Gomorrah. (p. 4)

Like his stepson, David Baldwin also felt illegitimate. Unfortunately, he did not leave behind in New Orleans his inability to communicate with people and to establish ordinary social relationships. Rather, as Jimmy points out in several of his writings, David Baldwin was never able to form a healthy bond with anyone, not even his own family, due to his own sense of ugliness or what James Baldwin later referred to as his "intolerable bitterness of spirit" (Leeming, p. 7). Campbell reports that David was the son of a slave and that he himself was born before or shortly after Emancipation, possibly between 1862 and 1866. Growing up in an environment in which violence against Blacks—physical, psychological, and spiritual—was prevalent, David saw no value in his own Blackness. To be Black, for David, who had a very dark complexion, meant nothing but suffering, a life of ugliness. Preaching was David's way of overcoming the stigma of his Blackness, but his coming up north, living life in the Harlem ghetto with his wife and children expecting him to make things better, only deteriorated his faith in himself as a Black man. Ultimately, his recurring failures proved too much for him to overcome. David Baldwin eventually went mad during his final years, suffering a severe mental collapse, and in the spring of 1943 was committed to a mental hospital on Long Island, where he would remain until his death on July 28, 1943. Campbell (1991) states that when Jimmy last saw his father in a mental health facility, David was "connected to life by a tangle of tubes" (p. 26). Baldwin went home wounded by the fact that there was never anything that connected him to his father, not even their shared ugliness and illegitimacy. This yearning suggests, moreover, that both David and Jimmy needed the love of a father, an ideal father, a father who, with pride and admiration, would claim, "This is my beloved Son, whom I love; with him I am well pleased" (Matt 3:17 NIV).

Leeming (1994) asserts that "much of Baldwin's early life was concerned with a search for a father, but not for a biological father . . . rather for what an ideal father might have been for him—a source of self-esteem" (p. 3). Baldwin hoped throughout his youth that such a person not only would look past his physical ugliness but would also save him from the ugliness of his environment. The Harlem of James Baldwin's youth was becoming one of America's emerging Black ghettoes, a veritable slum. Historian Gilbert Osofsky (1966) contends,

> The most profound change that Harlem experienced in the 1920s was its emergence as a slum. Largely within the space of a single decade Harlem was transformed from a potentially ideal community to a neighborhood with manifold social and economic problems called "deplorable," "unspeakable," "incredible." "The State would not allow cows to live in some of these apartments used by colored people . . . in Harlem," the chairman of a city housing reform committee said in 1927. The Harlem slum of today was created in the 1920s. (p. 135)

Overcrowding was a major problem in Harlem as people lived so packed together. For instance, when former one-family apartments were cut up into one-room flats, living conditions became inhumane. In "The Harlem Ghetto," Baldwin (1998) reports on what he saw every day in the Harlem of his youth, stating, "All of Harlem is pervaded by a sense of congestion, rather like the insistent, maddening, claustrophobic pounding in the skull that comes from trying to breathe in a very small room with all the windows shut" (p. 42). Baldwin is not guilty of embellishment when he describes how the Harlem of the 1920s was suffocating its residents. The Harlem air was, in fact, harming its residents, especially its children. Osofsky (1966) reports that a city official called Harlem's houses "diseased properties" (p. 142). Diseases were not found only in homes, however; the neighborhood itself was diseased, evident when an Atlanta University professor discovered that "Harlem's death rate, for all causes, was 42 percent in excess of that of the entire city . . . almost twice as many Harlem children 'passed' as did infants in the rest of New York" (p. 141). The rates of all sorts of maladies were higher in Harlem. Tuberculosis was higher in Harlem. Pneumonia was higher in Harlem. Heart disease was higher in Harlem. Cancer was higher in Harlem. Stillbirths were higher in Harlem. Malnutrition was higher in Harlem. "Whatever the causes of Harlem's health problems . . . a good deal can be laid at the door of the slum environment," writes Osofsky (p. 143).

In addition to the deleterious health environment, Harlem residents were also subject to the trauma of fractured relationships. As sociologist Lee Rainwater (1970) argues in *Behind Ghetto Walls*, his study of Black families living in a St. Louis housing project, "Closely entwined with this generalized judgment about respectability is a *basic trust* [emphasis added] of other persons, no matter how close they may be by blood or affection" (p. 55). Rainwater observes that there are two sources of this distrust: (1) ghetto residents' vulnerability to exploitation by other persons in the environment, even family members and friends; and (2) ghetto residents' lack of dependable others to assist them in times of great difficulty (p. 55). During his youth, Jimmy Baldwin, like so many young African Americans, was conditioned to believe that no one in Harlem—not a friend, not a family member—would help him.

Jimmy was an ugly young man who, by no fault of his own, was forced to live in an ugly environment. As he matured, however, particularly during his later teenage years, he began to consider that all of his suffering was being caused by what Clarence E. Hardy (2003), scholar of African American religion, terms "a malevolent God" (p. 39). Baldwin often said that he was born in the church, and he remained there until the age of 17. During that time, however, he had moved from the pew to the pulpit, garnering attention for his dynamic preaching style, a skill that earned him the nickname "Little Minister" (Leeming, 1994, p. 30). Though he proclaimed the goodness of the Lord from the pulpit, Jimmy's heart was filled with doubt, always questioning the reality of a God whom he felt was ignoring his plight. "Baldwin struggles with great difficulty," Hardy (2003) claims, "to see how a caring god could exist in a world weighed down with the ever-present reality of suffering" (p. 39). Hardy explains,

> When Baldwin writes how God "would not hear me," he suggests that God might have been able to answer his petition but for whatever reason refused. It is an active, divine disregard and not God's impotence and apparent irrelevance that finally pushed Baldwin to leave the faith. In some of his early fiction, published in his high school magazine before he left the ministry and the church, Baldwin dramatizes the loss of faith he himself experiences.... In the end, Baldwin's hopes for eternal glory are shattered before the seemingly permanent reality of black suffering. Any promise he initially found in the faith of his youth was undermined by the betrayal of a god who was not only silent but also hostile to the life chances of black people and their own sense of worth. (pp. 39, 41)

The God that young Jimmy, the "Little Minister," had learned about in Mother Horn's church had left Black people to suffer. But Jimmy's lack of trust in and anger towards God was far more personal than that. God had made Jimmy live a life filled with ugliness. When Jimmy crossed the doors of the church for the last time as a believer in the spring of 1941, he looked around him knowing there was more to see, somewhere, out in the world. He had caught glimpses of this renewed vision a year prior when he, "in poverty and uncertainty," knocked on the "unusual door" of the Black artist Beauford Delaney (Baldwin, 1998, p. 720). It was Delaney who, through his art, would make Baldwin believe that even the ugliest boy from the ugliest part of the city could be loved. "In Beauford Delaney . . . Baldwin found what he was looking for" (Leeming, 1994, p. 33).

LET THERE BE LIGHT

On the advice of his friend Emile Capouya, Jimmy went to Greenwich Village, the haunt of artists and bohemians, to visit Beauford Delaney for the first time. Jimmy was at a terribly vulnerable point in his life. His faith in the church was waning. His performance in school was becoming erratic. The most troubling occurrence, however, was that he had recently learned, through overhearing an argument between his parents, that he was illegitimate. At the age of 16, he finally discovered why he was not, and would never be, David Baldwin's beloved son. Troubled in mind and spirit, Jimmy took what little hope he had and made the journey, as though it were a spiritual pilgrimage, to Beauford's home. Baldwin, in "The Price of the Ticket" (1998), tells of their first meeting.

> I was terrified, once I had climbed those stairs and knocked on that door. A short, round brown man came to the door and looked at me. He had the most extraordinary eyes I'd ever seen. When he had completed his instant X-ray of my brain, lungs, liver, heart, bowels, and spinal column (while I had said, usefully, "Emile sent me") he smiled and said, "Come in," and opened the door.
> He opened the door all right.
> Lord, I was to hear Beauford sing, later, and for many years, open the unusual door. (Baldwin, 1998, p. 830)

Unusual is the appropriate adjective to describe not only Beauford's door but even more so the artist himself. Beauford Delaney, who was in his 30s when he and Baldwin met, shared a lot of similarities with young Jimmy. He, too, was the son of a minister. He, too, was gay. He, too, was born in poverty. Baldwin, though, was most drawn to Beauford because Beauford, too, knew what it meant be ugly. "He comes from darkness—as I do," comments Baldwin (1998, p. 720). Beauford's greatest gift, however, was that he used his art to turn the darkness around him into light. He was able to do so without escaping into the fantasies of reaching a sweet by and by, the hereafter wherein the sufferers in this world would finally receive their reward. Rather, Beauford wrestled with the here and now as his art "leads the inner and outer eye, directly and inexorably, to a new confrontation with reality" (p. 721). And it is for this reason above others that, even in his later years, Baldwin remained awestruck by Beauford's "example of courage and integrity" (p. 832). These laudable attributes were requisite for Beauford, especially as he, a queer Black artist, had to confront the darkness of poverty, racism, homophobia, and physical and mental illness to see light in the world. Seeing light was his way of staying alive. This is not a quality Beauford was born with, however. It was created and strengthened in living a life filled with darkness.

Delaney was born in Knoxville, Tennessee, in 1901. He was the son of parents who knew well the horrors of slavery. His mother, Delia Johnson, was born into slavery in Richmond, Virginia, in 1865. His father, John Samuel Delaney, was born in Bristol, Tennessee, in 1859. The name

Delaney came from a former slave master who, according to the historical record, freed Samuel Delaney's mother from slavery. John Samuel, who later became a Methodist preacher, met Delia Johnson at a church event, and the two quickly fell in love, getting married on April 9, 1885. David Leeming (1998) reports that Delia was a natural artist. "Not only was she a fine singer and storyteller," says Leeming, "she was a fine seamstress and quilt-maker" (Leeming, chap. 1, "Knoxville"). Oftentimes, the children would watch Delia create a quilt, taking a mental note of every step from start to finish, which included creating a pattern on paper, "then used the tracing as the pattern for cutouts made from odd bits of colorful material" (Leeming, 1998, chapter. 1, "Knoxville"). She undoubtedly passed on this artistic talent to her son Beauford. Samuel Delaney was a faith-filled man, committed to his religion and the ministry. Leeming (1998) remarks that "he was called Brother Delaney by all who knew him and he spent much of his adult life as a circuit-riding preacher, finding black communities that lacked a Methodist Episcopal Church, helping them construct church buildings, then moving on" (Leeming, chap. 1, "Knoxville"). He earned very little as a minister and part-time barber. His was a life devoted to serving those in need, even when he didn't have enough to take care of himself and his family. He undoubtedly passed on this commitment to serving others to his son Beauford.

The Delaney family soon moved to Jefferson City, where they lived in a poor, rural community and socialized almost exclusively with the parishioners of Boyd Chapel Methodist church, a small congregation led by Samuel Delaney. Things improved somewhat when the family moved back to Knoxville in 1915 after Samuel answered a call to lead another Methodist congregation. Tragedy struck the Delaney household shortly before this last move, though, as Ogust Mae, Beauford's older sister, died of a severe respiratory disease. She was 19 years old. The haunting circumstances surrounding her death are recaptured in a 1961 journal entry written more than four decades after her death by Beauford.

> We became alarmed because [from] the first time the doctor came it was always something the matter with Sister. Mama would quit her job and come home, the house became very quiet and we were awake late at night [talking] in hushed voices in fear for Sister's recovery. She was strong willed and survived most difficulties and would seem to be well and we would rejoice. So much of the sickness . . . came from improper places—long distances to walk to schools improperly heated . . . natural conditions common to the poor that take the bright flowers like terrible cold in nature. (Leeming, 1998, chap. 1, "Knoxville")

Beauford never stopped grieving the loss of his sister, even as life in Knoxville began to offer some small comforts to ease his emotional pain. He started drawing and soon began to take personal painting lessons with a local artist named Lloyd Branson, Knoxville's first full-time professional artist. Branson was a White man who was born and bred in the South and therefore found it hard to put aside "the prejudices inherent in his politics and point of view" to teach Beauford (Leeming, 1998, chap. 1, "Knoxville"). But he did. He was Beauford's first art teacher. It was Branson who taught Beauford that "all painting . . . should be studies in light" (Leeming, 1998, chap. 1, "Knoxville").

Branson recognized that there was little opportunity for a young Black artist to pursue an art career in the segregated South, and so, seeing so much potential in his young protégé, he helped send Delaney up north to pursue further professional training at the Massachusetts Normal School. Delaney was 21 years old when he left home in September 1923. While in Boston improving his drawing skills, Delaney earned a living doing several menial jobs. He soon started to take night classes at the South Boston School of Art, supplementing his formal art education with countless impromptu trips to the Boston Museum of Fine Arts, where he first encountered works created by master artists such as Claude Monet and John Singer Sargent. Delaney's next major move was to Harlem in 1929. He expanded his artistic talents as he began to make portrait paintings, some of which were of prominent African American figures such as W. E. B. Du Bois, Marian Anderson, and W. C. Handy. African American artist Romare Bearden and art historian Harry Henderson (1993) observe that, although Delaney did create portraits, "Much of his work was completely abstract—bright, thick impasto swirls of color" (p. 282). Though surrounded by the beauty of the Harlem Renaissance, led by such noted figures as Zora Neale Hurston, Langston Hughes, and Claude McKay, Delaney had to face the ugliness of everyday life in Harlem. Art historian and curator Eloise Johnson (2005) reports that "on Delaney's first day in New York, he was robbed and forced to roam aimlessly around the city without resources or a place to stay" (p. 47). Soon after, Delaney states that he found himself in the company "of a multitude of people of all races—spending every night of their lives in parks and cafes and seeming very much in a good mood" (Leeming, 1998, chap. 2, "Boston and Harlem"). This was his best attempt to put a positive spin on the fact that he was homeless in Harlem, spending most nights sleeping on a Union Square Park bench. Leeming (1998) notes that Delaney was intrigued by the community of homeless people he encountered; "these people and their outdoor city life would become the subject of some of Delaney's greatest New York period paintings" (chap. 3, "Boston and Harlem"). The most famous of these works is Delaney's 1946 *Can Fire in the Park*. Even with the great difficulties he faced—the extreme poverty, the homelessness—Delaney remained committed to his life as an artist.

A small amount of recognition for his artistic talent would come in the following years, most notably when he shared his portfolio at the Whitney Museum (a 1930 exhibit that garnered him a great deal of recognition), the Schomburg Center, and, later, the Vendome Art Gallery. During this time, though sometimes making portraits of elites, Delaney continued to draw and paint pictures of the ordinary people and the ordinary scenes of New York. During the 1930s, despite the ups and downs of his artistic success, Delaney's personal problems began to mount. He was coming to grips with his homosexuality. He was overwhelmed by the guilt he felt due to his art and his life being supported, almost exclusively, by White patronage. Most troubling of all, however, were the early signs of severe mental illness—he was hearing voices "that argued with each other and taunted their host—gently at first, more harshly later" (Leeming, 1998, chap. 3, "New York: The Early Years"). The haunting voices, all in his head, served to remind him that he was suffering from the ugliest of mental illnesses: schizophrenia.

David Leeming reports that other problems began to arise for the struggling artist during his time in New York. Delaney had moved from Harlem to Greenwich Village, and one particularly cold day in the winter of 1935, he "noticed that he had difficulty walking, that his feet felt numb" (Leeming, 1998, chap. 3, "New York: The Early Years"). The bizarre reason for his physical ailment was that the pipes under the floor of his apartment were leaking severely, and, in effect, a quasi-frozen lake had formed under his apartment floor. After this calamity, along with other mishaps that were caused by the apartment's poor condition, he moved to 181 Greene Street, whose unusual door young Jimmy Baldwin would walk through. The apartment itself was nothing special, at least not aesthetically. It was only a single-room apartment, without much space, and the walls were cracked, signs of deterioration that Delaney attempted to cover with pieces of drawing paper. Like the apartment on Downing Street, however, the Greene Street abode was terribly cold in the winter. "In the winter the studio was so cold that Beauford wore a wool ski cap, several layers of clothing, and an overcoat," says Leeming (1998, chap. 4, "New York: Pre-War Greene Street").

Cold, poor, lonely, battling mental illness, and marginalized in the art community—none of these challenges stopped Delaney from remaining committed to refining his skills as an artist because his art was his life, and it was how he expressed love. "To Delaney," comments art curator Stephen Wicks (2020), "art was an act of love and faith capable of revealing inner truths and of offering entry into a world of illumination" (p. 2). With his illuminated vision, Delaney used his brush, some paint, and his imagination to speak to the darkness all around him and declare, "Let there be light." Wicks observes that "Delaney in his portraits, for example, employed vibrant color and expressive brushwork in a way that increasingly sacrificed superficial physical qualities in order to project what he considered the more important and essential spiritual identity of the sitter" (p. 4). Delaney worked on perfecting this technique by shedding light on the everyday life he saw in Greenwich Village, particularly those things—ignored people and blighted places—that many deemed too insignificant, even too dark and ugly, to be beautiful. This light, according to Leeming, expressed the true "reality of the subject" (Leeming, 1998, chap. 4, "New York: Pre-War Greene Street"). Delaney would finally get a chance to display these light-filled works during a one-man exhibition at the Vendome Art Gallery, which lasted from January 18 to February 2, 1941. Large oil landscape paintings, such as *Greene Street* (1940), caught the attention of viewers, but nothing represents the power of Delaney's light more than *Dark Rapture* (1941). This was the first known image Delaney created of his new young friend James Baldwin.

Dark Rapture was symbolic of the love between Jimmy and Beauford. From their first encounter in 1940, the two had developed a friendship that was filled with music, laughter, and, most of all, light. Beauford was the first person to see light in Jimmy. The loving bond between the two had re-established a basic trust in Baldwin, so much so that he posed nude for *Dark Rapture*, believing that he could be totally vulnerable in Delaney's presence. He trusted that Delaney would look beyond his frog eyes, his dark skin, and his crooked body caused by scoliosis and find the light in him. Wicks (2020) points out that the unique color scheme used by Delaney in *Dark Rapture* "presents Baldwin's visage as if illuminated" (p. 11). Delaney continued to portray Baldwin's light in such works as *Portrait of James Baldwin* (1944), and in each subsequent portrait one can see increasing light in Baldwin, the most radiant of which is *James Baldwin* (1957), created after Baldwin moved to Paris in 1953. Baldwin proclaimed that Delaney would become the person who, above all others, looked beyond his flawed physical features and beheld an enduring inner beauty. Thus, Delaney's paintings caused Baldwin to see himself differently, to recognize that light still exists even in the darkness, to recognize that beauty can be seen in the ugliest of things. The power of Delaney's light in Baldwin's life cannot be overstated. As Baldwin remarks, "This light began to stretch back for me over all the time we had known each other, and over much more time than that, and this light held the power to illuminate, even to redeem and reconcile and heal" (1998, p. 721).

NO GREATER LOVE

LOOKING MATTERS

Baldwin's meditation "On the Painter Beauford Delaney" (1998) serves as a love letter telling of how his beloved friend caused him to see. During the early years of their friendship, young Jimmy developed the habit of following Delaney around Greenwich Village and other parts of Manhattan, paying close attention to the master's gaze "so that he could see what Beauford saw" (Leeming, 1994, p. 34). On a rainy day in the winter of 1940, just a few months after their first encounter, Baldwin became fascinated by Delaney's gaze, which was focused on something amidst all the hustle and bustle on Broadway. Baldwin (1998) writes,

> What I saw, first of all, was a brown leaf on black asphalt, oil moving like mercury in the black water of the gutter, grass pushing itself up through a crevice on the sidewalk. And because I was seeing it with Beauford, because Beauford caused me to see, the very colors underwent a most disturbing and salutary change. The brown leaf on the black asphalt, for example—what colors were these, really? To stare at the leaf long enough, to try to apprehend the leaf, was to discover many colors in it; and though black had been described to me as the absence of light, it became very clear to me that if this were true, we would never have been able to see the color, black: the light is trapped in it and struggles upward, rather like that grass pushing upward through the cement. It was humbling to be forced to realise that the light fell down from heaven, on everything, on everybody, and that the light was always changing. (1998, p. 720)

Leeming (1994) provides more details about this lesson about looking, underscoring the fact that it took some time before Jimmy could follow Delaney's gaze. According to Leeming, Delaney stood on a street corner, waiting for the light to change, when, as though in a trance, he began to stare at a stream of water flowing down the curb. Then, suddenly, Delaney, filled with awe, shouted, "Look." Baldwin tried to see what Beauford saw, but, with his limited vision, young Jimmy could see only filthy water and tattered leaves flowing into an urban gutter. Beauford's gaze persisted, until, once again, he shouted, "Look again" (p. 34). Look . . . look again. Look . . . look again. Look . . . look again. That is the lesson. Baldwin (1998) remarked that Delaney was "*seeing* [emphasis in original] all the time" (p. 720). Delaney's gaze—his seeing—allowed him to see things—even things regarded as insignificant and unappealing, such as a tattered leaf—anew every day. It was not long before Jimmy understood that when he first met Delaney and knocked on that unusual door, the "X-ray of my brain, lungs, liver, heart, bowels, and spinal column" (1998, p. 830) that Delaney performed on Jimmy was, in fact, the artist searching for, discovering, and being in awe of Jimmy's light. He saw so much beauty in James Baldwin.

Look... look again.

In "Dialogues with Paintings: Notes on How to Look and See," philosopher Amélie Rorty (2014) mentions that "there is no such thing as art" (p. 1). Rorty's point is that art is not about the object—paintings, sculptures, drawings, etc.—created by the artist as much as it is about the act of looking. "We can look at *anything*—clouds, a tree, a face, a road, a herd of cows in a field—as if they were works of art, finding a composition of patterns and resonances of color, texture, and form," says Rorty (p. 1.). One must avoid the traps, Rorty advises, of ready-made 'isms' when encountering an artwork, that is, eagerly searching for various modes of classification that, oftentimes, restrict a painting's meaning. Time is important when looking at a painting, particularly as "it takes concentrated time to see" (p. 1). Similar to the lesson Delaney taught Jimmy on that Broadway corner, Rorty instructs that things are always changing when we take the time to look: "Your eyes change; the painting changes as you look: light, coloration, distance, perspective" (p. 1). Rorty maintains that the time one invests looking and seeing enables one to engage in a dialogue with the painting, a conversation that is guided by several questions. First, one questions the painting as a physical object: "How do the size, shape, height, and location of the painting structure your perception?" (p. 2). Second, one questions the painting's parentage and place: "How does the painting's location [e.g., a church, a museum, or a public building] affect what you see and how you react to it?" (p. 3) Third, one questions the painter's elements: "How does the painter direct the sequence of visual attention? ... What are the sources of light?" (p. 4). Fourth, one questions the painting's representation: "What—if anything—does the painting represent? ... Who are the people represented? How are they identified and characterized?" (p. 7). Last, one finishes with questions focused on theory, and then one conducts an evaluation of the painting: "What makes a painting good or successful?" (p. 8). Ideally, these questions also help the observer better understand the various biases they bring to their dialogue with a painting as, undoubtedly, these questions make one aware of how much of the painting remains unseen. Rorty ends her meditation on looking and seeing with the following advice.

> Having addressed some of these questions, stop questioning and just sit and *look* [emphasis in original] *at the painting again* [emphasis added]. How does it affect you, what have you learned, what does it make you realize or question? What does it enable

you to see? Then, after a time, consider whether how you see it—its effect on you—has been changed by your "dialogue" with it. (p. 9)

Look . . . look again.

In his influential text *Black Skin, White Masks* (1952/1967), activist, writer, and psychologist Franz Fanon discusses the entrapment of Blackness. "Look, a Negro!" He goes on to discuss the fragmenting experience that Black people have when they are attacked, and rendered inferior, by the "glances of the [White] other" (p. 109). "Look, a Negro!" A young White child looked at Fanon and cried out, "Mama, see the Negro! I'm frightened! Frightened! Frightened!" Fanon attempted to console himself by the fact that he, as an educated man, an educated man of the West, no less, could not be classified, on account of a child's jejune glance, as a Negro. What, after all, is a Negro? Why is the child so afraid of the Negro? What does the child see? "The Negro is an animal, the Negro is bad, the Negro is mean, *the Negro is ugly* [emphasis added]" (p. 113). This is the only way, Fanon argues, that the Other world, the White world, looks at Black life. There's no beauty to be seen there, no matter how many times the White world looks; it's all ugly.

This was also the case when it came to looking at Black art, unfortunately. Cultural historian Clyde R. Taylor (1998) contends that, during the Enlightenment, "the idea of black humanity as beautiful was unthinkable, threatening the universal order with chaos . . . destroying the foundations of universal standards, and even harboring the possibility that Whiteness is not universally good and beautiful" (p. 30). Taylor's text provides a trenchant analysis of the violence Western aesthetics has done to non-Western peoples. He is particularly concerned with the cultural trauma that occurs when the Western art world, including curators and art critics, designate an object from a non-Western context as art. "The works become art only through violence done to their original meanings," writes Taylor. For example, he tells of the paintings created by Australian Aboriginal people that served as "chartings of ancestral spiritual journeys" (p. 296). So much of the original meaning is lost in such works when observers are looking for only Westernized notions of "beauty or satisfaction of the aesthetic gaze [i.e., the look] that the curator and her public are interested in" (p. 297). No wonder, then, that Beauford Delaney, like so many African American artists of his time, failed to amass a long list of museum credentials, prizes, and awards. In his art, he communicated "his attack on the conventional" (Bearden & Henderson, p. 282). More to the point, Delaney, with his brush and imagination, fought against the "lack of meaning, dehumanization, and mechanical banality of much of American life" (p. 283).

Look... look again.

Look at James Baldwin... look again. What do you see? Following Rorty's advice, one can begin by looking at his physical characteristics. The frog eyes. The dark skin. The small frame. What of Baldwin's parentage and place? He was born and raised in the Harlem ghetto. Let us move to the most important question of all: what does this represent or re-present? His physical attributes, his class and status, his racial heritage—all this re-presents someone who evokes fear and, by extension, must be avoided. Look at James Baldwin... look again. Can you see what Delaney dared to see? And if not, ask yourself why not? Rorty (2014) suggests that we cannot be concerned with only the natural representation of a painting but rather should ask, "How does the painting interpret/represent divinity of supernatural forces/beings/powers?" (p. 7). Delaney kept looking until he saw more than the physical James Baldwin, the person that had been abused by his father, shamed by his church, and rejected by America. As already noted, Wicks (2020) commented that "Delaney in his portraits... increasingly sacrificed superficial physical qualities in order to project what he considered the more important and essential spiritual identity of the sitter" (p. 4). Look at James Baldwin... look again. Do you see the light? Do you see the love? Do you see what Beauford Delaney's spiritual vision allowed him to see? Baldwin followed Delaney's vision until he saw the light within himself. This was the love that Baldwin, "in poverty and uncertainty," was looking for. Therefore, in tribute to his beloved friend, who sacrificed his life for his art, the art that turned darkness into light, Baldwin writes,

> For Beauford's work leads the inner and outer eye, directly and inexorably, to a new confrontation with reality. At this moment one begins to apprehend the nature of his triumph, and the proof that it is a real one, is that he makes it ours. Perhaps, I should not say, flatly, what I believe—that he is a great painter, among the very greatest; but I do know that great art can only be created out of love, and that no greater lover has ever held a brush. (p. 721)

REFERENCES

Baldwin, J. (1981). *Go tell it on the mountain*. Bantam Dell. (Original work published 1953).

Baldwin, J. (1998). *Baldwin: Collected essays*. Literary Classics of the United States.

Bearden, R., & Henderson, H. (1993). *A history of African-American artists: From 1792 to the present*. Pantheon.

Campbell, J. (1991). *Talking at the gates: A life of James Baldwin*. University of California Press.

Fanon, F. (1967). *Black skin, white masks* (C. L. Markmann, Trans.). Grove. (Original work published 1952).

Hardy, C. (2003). *James Baldwin's God: Sex, hope, and crisis in Black holiness culture*. University of Tennessee Press.

Hinds, J.-P. (2010). Traces on the blackboard: The vestiges of racism on the African American psyche. *Pastoral Psychology, 59*, 783–798.

Johnson, E. (2005). Out of the ashes: Cultural identity and marginalization in the art of Beauford Delaney. *Source: Notes in the History of Art, 24*, 46–55.

Leeming, D. (1994). *James Baldwin: A biography*. Knopf.

Leeming, D. (1998). *Amazing grace: A life of Beauford Delaney*. Oxford University Press. https://www.amazon.com/Amazing-Grace-Life-Beauford-Delaney-ebook/dp/B001F0RIX6.

Merriam-Webster. (n.d.). Ugly. In *Merriam-Webster.com* dictionary. Retrieved May 2, 2023, from https://www.merriam-webster.com/dictionary/ugly.

Osofsky, G. (1966). *Harlem: The making of a ghetto*. Elephant Paperbacks.

Rainwater, L. (1970). *Behind ghetto walls: Black families in a federal slum*. Aldine.

Rorty, A. (2014). Dialogues with paintings: Notes on how to look and see. *Journal of Aesthetic Education, 48*, 1–9.

Taylor, C. R. (1998). *The mask of art: Breaking the aesthetic contract—Film and literature*. Indiana University Press.

Wicks, S. (Ed.). (2020). *Beauford Delaney and James Baldwin: Through the unusual door*. Knoxville Museum of Art.

5

When Empathy Is Not Enough
A Reflection on the Self-Experience of Black Boys in Public Spaces

DANJUMA G. GIBSON

> They approach me in a half-hesitant sort of way, eye me curiously or compassionately, and then, instead of saying directly, *How does it feel to be a problem?* they say, I know an excellent colored man in my town; or, I fought at Mechanicsville; or, Do not these Southern outrages make your blood boil? At these I smile, or am interested, or reduce the boiling to a simmer, as the occasion may require. *To the real question, How does it feel to be a problem? I answer seldom a word.*
>
> (DU BOIS 1903, EMPHASIS ADDED)

BACKGROUND AND CONTEXT

In the above passage, W. E. B. Du Bois outlines for us a familiar interaction. It is the kind of red-herring, small-talk conversation that witnesses to contexts where the very presence of Black bodies (especially Black male bodies) precipitates anxiety, uncertainty, or gazing. When Du Bois postulates what he believes to be the real question (i.e., how it feels to be a problem), he is capturing in literary form the deadly psychosocial practice that has infested the Western psyche for centuries: the unconscious and implicit practice of demonizing, criminalizing, and objectifying the Black male body.

This chapter offers a psychodynamic framework for explicating the unconscious propensity to objectify and criminalize the Black male body—particularly Black boys—in public spaces along with the deleterious emotional effects this objectification has on the lives of these boys. Instead of examining the lives of Black boys through caricatured images and stereotypes that inundate television and social media (and only exacerbate the problem of objectification), I highlight their *self-experiences* through the power of their own voices. Using salient themes derived from qualitative interviews of Black boys on the south side of Chicago, I draw attention to the *self-experience* of the boys as they strive to exist in public spaces that are generally antagonistic to their presence, bodies, and personhood. The field of practical and pastoral theology has long viewed empathy as a critical component of redemptive praxis. *But what happens when empathy—the capacity to imaginatively place oneself in the context of another—is simply not enough to bring about healing to the wounded and flourishing to the marginalized?*

The idea for this project, in large part, is in response to the negative portrayal of Black males—particularly boys—in the national spotlight. Especially in Chicago, images of life on the south side of the city commonly associate negative story lines and imagery with Black male youth. Across the country, narratives of Black people being vilified in public spaces are becoming common. The latent elements of an intergenerational, deep-seated racial animus (and hatred) is rising to the surface of the collective American psychic space. It is becoming commonplace for Black people to have the police called on them—by White people—for the most mundane acts in public spaces (sitting in Starbucks without buying coffee, barbequing in a public park, sleeping in a student lounge in an Ivy League school, etc.). Deadly encounters with law enforcement (and other self-appointed enforcers of the law) have reached epidemic proportions: Eric Garner, Walter Scott, Michael Brown, Laquan McDonald, Tamir Rice, Freddie Gray, Sandra Bland, Alton Sterling, Philando Castile, and Trayvon Martin are but a few of the victims. As it relates to lost life, the ultimate tragedy is not only these deaths but also the potential for life that has been foreclosed. Even as I initially penned this short manuscript, my community of Grand Rapids, Michigan, internalized images of police officers holding five Black boys at gunpoint because an anonymous caller to 911 indicated one of the boys *might* be armed. None of the boys were armed. Hearing some of the boys cry out "I don't want to die" is the stuff of nightmares.

It is important that I specify my social location in proximity to this project. I am a Black male scholar, born and raised on the south side of Chicago. It pains my entire being to see the media portrayal of Black boys in Chicago—as if the only existence these youths know is one of violence, guns, and death. My observations and lament are in no way meant to minimize the epidemic of violence in the city. Indeed, the proliferation of gun violence in Chicago is not beyond my scholarly purview. In the very contentious sociopolitical environment where we find ourselves, some might find it conceivable that I would focus more on the intracultural violence that transpires between Black males rather than reflecting on the violence between law enforcement and Black people (particularly Black males) or the tenuous self-experiences of Black boys in public spaces. In part, my point is to argue that the Black male imagery commonly highlighted in the media is a far cry from the *actual lives* of Black boys and teenagers in Chicago.

On a more personal note, after I was pulled over in the Hyde Park area of Chicago for talking on the cell phone, a White female police officer approached my vehicle and asked for my license, registration, and insurance. While keeping both of my hands on the steering wheel, I explained to the officer everything I was about to do *before I did it* (e.g., reach for my wallet in my back pocket or reach for my glove compartment for registration and insurance). The officer smiled in response to my actions, but for me it was no laughing matter. It was only when I reached to open the glove compartment that I noticed in the passenger-side mirror another police officer flanked to my right with his hand clearly in the vicinity of his holster. Ostensibly, the responding officer had requested backup for a stop related to my talking on the cell phone. Since that incident, I have often pondered how quickly something could have gone wrong if the officer flanked to the rear of the car had *thought* I was reaching for something else in my glove compartment. As I have occasionally shared this story with others, the responses I get ranged from empathic reactions of disdain and frustration to more paternalistic diatribes explaining that the officers were within their rights and acted according to their training or that they hadn't broken the law. But whether we are considering this personal encounter or any of the preceding incidents mentioned at the beginning of this paper, the point of this project is not to determine the legality of any action per se.

My decision to take up this topic does not mean that I am oblivious to intracultural violence among Black males any more than a White scholar taking up an issue that affects the lives of White people suggests that she is somehow oblivious to intracultural violence among White people. The *myth of Black-on-Black violence* as a unique ontological category has for far too long represented an uncontested stereotype. This is not to deny the reality of intracultural violence but only to recognize that White people commit violence against other White people, Latino and Latina people commit violence against other Latinos and Latinas, human beings kill other human beings—you get my point. The point of this project is to *examine the psychodynamics behind why some people or groups in the psychosocial space of our society disproportionately and implicitly experience anxiety or fear in the presence of Black male bodies and experience a sense of civic or moral justification when exacting any form of violence (emotional or physical) against Black male bodies—especially Black boys.*

A BRIEF HISTORICAL ANALYSIS

The objectification of Black male bodies in the Western imaginary is not a recent phenomenon. It has a long-standing tradition in modernity. Fanon (1952) understands it as a fundamental *Weltanschauung* of the colonial project. It operates with ruthless efficiency in the unconsciousness of the colonial subject (both victims and benefactors). For Fanon, the violence inherent in Western expansionism effectively forecloses psychic countermeasures within the subaltern against the imposing imagination of Eurocentric fantasy. That is to say, "Not only must the black man be black; he must be black in relation to the white man" (pp. 82–83). This objectification of Black male bodies can come across in the most seemingly innocent manner—even from children: "Look, a Negro. Mama, see the Negro! I'm frightened" (p. 84). Fanon recognized that his very existence was manifested not only in the time and space he occupied at any moment but by the weight of his ancestry and history and the legacy of colonial fantasy: "I was battered down by tom-toms, cannibalism, intellectual deficiency, fetishism, racial defects, slave-ships, and above all else . . . 'Sho' good eatin'" (pp. 84–85).

Even in America, the deadly effects of this racialized imaginary are self-evident in the terror of lynching inflicted on Black lives—namely, Black males—in the early twentieth century. The ubiquitous and unconscious nature of this racialized imagery comes to light especially well in an exchange between Jane Addams (an acclaimed pioneer in the field of social work) and Ida B. Wells-Barnett (a well-respected female Black journalist and activist best known for her work related to the anti-lynching campaign). What makes this case most intriguing is that Jane Addams is (deservingly) recognized and celebrated for her work in women's suffrage, feminism, and the establishment of Chicago's Hull House—a settlement house for European immigrants. Nevertheless, Addams's (1901) notable regard for human experience falls short in her examination of lynching in the Jim Crow South and her explanation of why so many Black men were being victimized. According to Addams, the epidemic of lynching was in reaction to an *assumed rise in crime* committed by Black males. She further argued that Southerners had a right to self-govern, to determine how to deal with this *alleged rise* in crime, that *criminals* should not be hanged without a trial by jury, and that the *primary mistake* of Southerners was the false assumption that "criminality can be suppressed and terrorized by exhibitions of brutal punishment; that crime can be prevented by cruelty" (p. 18). Her entire analysis stems from the implicit and unconscious criminalization of Black males. To support her position, Addams grants robust hermeneutical privilege to the supporters of lynching (participants, observers, and bystanders) when she posits:

> *Let us then assume* that the Southern citizens who take part in and abet the lynching of negroes *honestly believe* that that is the only successful method of dealing with a certain class of crimes; that they have become convinced that the Southern negro in his present undeveloped state must be frightened and subdued by terror; that, acting upon this theory, they give each lynching full publicity and often gather together numerous spectators . . . let us *give the Southern citizens the full benefit of this position*, and *assume* that they have set aside trial by jury and all processes of law because they have become convinced that this brutal method of theirs is the most efficient method of dealing with a particular class of crime committed by one race against another. (Addams 1901, p. 18, emphasis added)

In her analysis, why must we assume that Southern citizens honestly believe lynching is the only successful method? Who cares if they believe this? Why must we give them the full benefit of this position? The position that somehow the lynch mob should be excused for their actions if they honestly believe they are in danger is precarious at best and sociopathic at worst when it comes at the expense of Black lives. Even today, we hear a similar train of thought used to justify violence committed against Black boys in public spaces (i.e., did the actor honestly believe there was imminent danger) whereas *other lighter-skinned bodies* move about relatively invisible in the public sphere and tend to get the sociopolitical benefit of the doubt. Addams's entire analysis was based on an unconscious racialized imagination that *seemed and felt right* to her. For Addams and many others in the Western psychic space, the presumed danger and guilt of Black male bodies are akin to psychic muscle memory; Black culpability is an unconscious, foregone conclusion. Unfortunately, the application of the colonial logic has real and deadly implications. That is to say, implicit and unconscious racial bias and animus often yield explicit and material reactionary violence.

How might we account for the contradiction and irony of Addams's assessment of lynching? How does a tireless advocate of human rights concede the barbarity of lynching and at the same time—through the uninterrogated, presumptive, and unconscious criminalization of Black males—craft an empathic argument that favors the architects and supporters of such demonic brutality? Wells-Barnett (1901) cogently debunks these implicit biases and assumptions of Black criminality in her response to Addams:

> It is unspeakably infamous to put thousands of people to death without a trial by jury; *it adds to that infamy to charge that these victims were moral monsters*, when, in fact, four-fifths of them were not so accused even by the fiends who murdered them . . . [I]*t is this assumption, this absolutely unwarrantable assumption, that vitiates every suggestion which it inspires Miss Addams to make.* It is the same *baseless assumption which influences ninety-nine out of every one hundred persons who discuss this question.* Among many thousand editorial clippings I have received in the past five years, ninety-nine per cent discuss the question upon the *presumption* that lynchings are the desperate effort of the Southern people to protect their women from *black monsters*, and while the large majority condemn lynching, the condemnation is *tempered with a plea for the lyncher*—that human nature gives way under such awful provocation and that the mob, insane for the moment, must be pitied as well as condemned. (pp. 1133–1134, emphasis added)

The same observations that Wells-Barnett made over a century ago still hold true today in terms of the unconscious demonization and criminalization of Black males in public spaces. Yet the question remains: How can a person or society extol democratic values while simultaneously condoning, justifying, or ignoring violence commonly exacted on Black male bodies?

GROUP-LEVEL RACIAL DELUSION

One possible response to this question relates to individual or group splitting.[1] One side of the split (for an individual or group) reflects a reactionary

---

1. Kohut's (1979) conception of a vertical split is persuasive for the purposes of this paper. In the vertical split, an individual (or group) experiences self in two distinctly separate ways—ways that are antagonistic toward each other or that could represent such wide contrasts that the vertical split becomes a source of cognitive or emotional dissonance within a person or group. In the case of racial oppression, one side of the split of the oppressor reflects grandiose-exhibitionistic self-experiences related to Western superiority or potential death-dealing "acting out" by the individual (or group).

violence toward Black male bodies in the public sphere or a self-experience of anxiety, fear, or even rage at the sight of Black boys or teenagers in public spaces. The other side of the split reflects the unconscious self-experience of innocence, virtue, exceptionalism, or any other experience of the self that is *necessary to prop up the ideology of Whiteness and Western superiority*. That is to say, one side of the split adheres to the values and principles of democracy and American idealism while the other side of the split justifies and normalizes brutality and violence on the bodies of the subaltern—in this case, Black male bodies. The psychic structure of the split allows for widely competing ideas. The concept of splitting accounts for the requisite mental, emotional, and spiritual resources that enable an individual, group, or empire to simultaneously inflict heinous violence against subaltern bodies—to be oblivious to the interior hatred, biases, and bigotry that underwrite such violence—and at the same time to be fully convinced (religiously, socially, and politically) that its actions are morally justifiable. When this psychic structure—and the resulting affective state of the individual or group—undermines all other psychological or spiritual faculties at the expense of objectifying, violating, or indiscriminately killing Black people in public spaces (especially Black males), I refer to it as *group-level racial delusion*. To this end, I suggest that what Wells-Barnett witnessed in the early part of the twentieth century in the terror of lynching, and what Addams (and many of her White contemporaries) fell victim to, was *group-level racial delusion*.

Given the long history of the objectification and criminalization of Black male bodies, this project reflects on how young Black males on the south side of Chicago experience themselves in public spaces. How can Black boys experience themselves in a life-giving way that is accretive to human flourishing when colonial fantasy, *group-level racial delusion*, and death-dealing stereotypes have all but stamped out any substantive or life-giving symbols in the occidental public sphere? The insatiable media appetite for negative Black male imagery reflects a long history of colonial images that

---

These grandiose self-experiences and acting out are primarily driven by archaic nuclear ambitions and ideas related to Western exceptionalism. The question of whether or not these nuclear ambitions and ideas are life-giving, especially in Western society, is open for debate and was beyond the work of Kohut. The other side of the split represents American and religious idealism that is necessary to prop up Whiteness or the *images and facades of Western innocence and exceptionalism*. The split itself reflects disavowal—a maladaptive but formidable ego strength that enables the person or group to possess the capacity to know and not know at the same time. Underneath this entire psychic structure is a horizontal repression barrier that represses the realities (for both the individual or group) of a violent Western history, a history that turns the very ideas of American innocence and virtue on its head. It also represses experiences of guilt, shame, anxiety, or condemnation stemming from the violence or injustice that is necessary to underwrite Whiteness and the political ideology of Americanism.

play out in the psyche and emotional field of Western civilization, effectively reducing the bodies of Black men and boys to objects of fear, suspicion, and abjection. Morris (1999) sums the problem up succinctly, noting that "the popular imagination, the media, and social science literature have focused on the Black male as criminal, violent, family deserter, lazy and shiftless predator, and extremely self-centered . . . thought to be a creature of emotion and impulse rather than intellect . . . dangerous, menacing, and a drain on the resources of the larger society" (p. xii).

A BRIEF HISTORY OF THE OBJECTIFICATION OF BLACK BODIES

Although it is problematic to assume a linear trajectory between contemporary racial oppression and precolonial or Victorian-era images of sub-Saharan Africans or Black and Brown peoples of the earth, the psychosocial and anthropological antecedents of contemporary racial pathology are deeply entrenched in the Western collective psyche. Scholars such as Braude (1997), Blackburn (1997), Morgan (1997), and others have cogently demonstrated that the complexities of racial formation and identity originated east of the Atlantic during the medieval and enlightenment eras and cannot be reduced to how race is conceived in the modern-day West. Still, the primary hegemonic tool that seems to remain characteristic of the oppression and enslavement of human beings throughout the history of Western expansionism is the *animalization of the subaltern*: associating individuals and groups—through idealization or objectification—with beast-like features (Davis 1997).

The subjugated caricatures of Black life and Black bodies in classical media, literature, and entertainment only served to further ingrain abject imagery in the psychic space of the West. Victorian depictions of the Black and Brown peoples from the African continent tended to highlight difference and thereby underwrote the requisite ideologies of inferiority and subcategories of humanness (Vaughan & Vaughan 1997). The effect on the English imagination was (and remains) clear and self-evident: "A black African provoked curiosity at the very least and often marvel; rarely, if ever, did the sight inspire admiration. Judging from the writings of George Best and all of his contemporaries whose ruminations survive, *contempt was the prevailing response*" (p. 27, emphasis added). Given the ubiquitous distribution of contemptuous literature and caricatures of abject Black bodies juxtaposed against the Elizabethan imagination, it is preposterous to think that the effect of such imagery was delimited to Shakespearian theater or other forms of classical entertainment. For Vaughan and Vaughan, the implications for a nation are clear:

> These negative representations of alien black Moors were perhaps symptomatic of what Richard Helgerson calls "nation formation," in which *accounts of exotic peoples helped England define itself.* As a nation being formed, insecurely groping toward common ground in religion and politics and searching for national symbols in literature and art, England was *as concerned with what it was not as with what it was.* And the English public acquired its images of alien Others to an appreciable extent in the theater. (p. 38, emphasis added)

If there is to ever be a redemptive path forward beyond racial oppression, the utilitarian purposes of Black objectification—especially that of males—must be understood as far more than morally objectionable; the criminalized Black body in public spaces *helps America define itself . . . as Western exceptionalism is continuously concerned with what it is not and with what it is.* Interrogating American identity politics, then, especially in the post-Obama sociopolitical environment, is inseparable from truly comprehending the self-experience of Black boys in public spaces.

RACIAL DELUSION AND RELIGION

Negative imagery related to Black bodies has long infected the religious realm as well. In addition to discrediting alternative epistemologies (i.e., ways and means of knowing) from marginalized groups that had been *otherized* in the colonial project, the colonization of Christianity not only anthropologically redefined what it meant to be human but also engaged religious categories such as demonic, heretical, or unorthodox to describe the practices and experiences of the Amerindian and African *other* (Wynter 2003). For example, as I periodically reflect on my own experiences in various religious denominations or in the halls of theological education, I am amused at how poverty-stricken communities, individuals at the margin, or groups of Black boys that leisurely congregate in public spaces all become targets of *alleged evangelism or missionary work.* The subaltern, the marginalized, and the poor are commonly experienced by the church as needing spiritual aid and assistance. Of course, the implicit assumption made by these religious organizations is that marginalization reflects a person's meager spiritual condition or divine punishment or wrath (or that the privilege of those who exist at the center is reflective of a healthier spiritual condition or divine affirmation). It never occurs (it seems) to such actors that people can *be forced to exist at the margin and simultaneously possess a life-giving faith*, often a faith that looks radically different from religion of the powerful and privileged. That is to say, *marginal social location and raced bodies* (especially the bodies of Black boys in public spaces) tend to become implicit, unconscious markers of irreligiosity in the colonial project.

This presumptuous tendency in religion, especially in Western Christianity, is rightfully located in colonial history. Building on the work of anthropologist Jacob Pandian, Wynter (2003) highlights a critical feature of Western expansionism—"the West's transformation of the indigenous peoples of the Americas/the Caribbean . . . together with the population group of the enslaved peoples of Africa, transported across the Atlantic into the physical referents of its reinvented True Christian Self, as that of the Human other to its new 'descriptive statement' of the ostensibly only normal human, Man" (p. 265). That is to say, instead of Christian God-talk being used to live more faithfully and to foster a radical love of neighbor, in the colonial project theology effectively becomes a tool that legitimates who is human and who is less than human, which bodies are important, and which human experiences will be recognized or discarded. Given this historical propensity to associate the subaltern with non-Christian themes, Ray (2003) cogently observes that those with the least amount of power (socially, economically, and politically) tend to be the object of Christian sin-talk. The material danger of such demonizing sin-talk cannot be overemphasized. Ray observes two presuppositions typically held in most Cristian circles: "sin destroys, and God punishes sin . . . [S]in-talk is therefore serious business because once the source of social sin is named, the impulse to stigmatize it is strong and the desire to destroy it even stronger" (p. 1). This, in part, might go toward the inexplicable silence the Church tends to maintain when it comes to the topic of violence perpetrated toward Black men—especially Black boys—by law enforcement: *Black boys have long been negatively stereotyped and associated with sin and the need for salvation.*

RACIAL DELUSION IN PUBLIC SPACES

This public portrayal of negative Black male imagery works in tandem with social, cultural, and historical fantasies in the American collective psyche, a psyche underwritten by a racialized imagination. The insatiable appetite of the media (including social media) for negative Black male imagery reflects a perverse group-level functioning that entails elements of splitting, projective identification, valence and container functions, and psychotic anxiety (Cytrynbaum 1993). Psychotic anxiety relates to anxiety that is irrational in its prima facie functioning and experienced as persecutory. Such anxiety stems from fears of personal, cultural, or social annihilation. In-group/out-group dynamics, or intergroup bigotry, derives its energy from psychotic anxiety. Group-level functioning suggests that groups take on a mind and life of their own that are far more complex than individual psychic functioning. For our purposes here, projective identification reflects undesired elements that individuals or groups have projected (or scapegoated) onto the Black male body. Ultimately, this contributes to the constant negative media imagery and resulting fear and anxiety related to Black male bodies in public spaces. The identification counterpart (of projective identification) reflects the possible internalization (by Black boys) of racialized projections materializing in a variety of ways, including cultural trauma, depleted self-worth, or even the commercialization of negative imagery (in the music entertainment industry or Hollywood) that plays off of racialized stereotypes.

The volume of negative imagery related to Black males in the media suggests a valence and container function (on the part of the media industry) wherein the media acts as a container that holds the racialized fantasies, resentments, and anxieties of society. These media moguls exhibit a valence (or archaic disposition) to focus on (or exacerbate) false or negative story lines of marginalized individuals or groups. This form of cultural trauma flattens the histories and life stories of Black boys, effectively preventing their voice and agency from articulating their own life stories and human experiences. In their psychosocial analysis of group dynamics through the lenses of race and culture, McRae and Short (2010) offer up a cogent analysis of projective identification at the social level, suggesting that when it occurs it "is often a microcosm of what occurs in society ... subgroups that may have greater access to power and privilege may seek to maintain status by disowning undesirable and ambivalently held aspects of themselves by projecting negative attributes onto other subgroups ... recipients of stereotyped, racist, discriminatory projections" (pp. 62–63).

Of all the group-dynamic themes mentioned, splitting provides the requisite emotional repertoire for an individual or group to unconsciously enact racial ideology, embody injurious behaviors and attitudes, and exact violence while at the same time extolling values of human decency and liberty, democracy, and good will. Although not comprehensive in its explanatory power, the concept of splitting—applied to group-level functioning—provides compelling historical insight into how some of the most heinous atrocities committed against humanity (the trans-Atlantic slave trade, American slavery, the Holocaust, Native American genocide, etc.) were carried out by groups and nations that espoused moral virtue and democracy. More specific to this project, splitting provides significant insight into how the bodies of young Black males can be objectified and brutalized in public spaces with little to no public outrage. In this paradigm, I suggest that the Black male body becomes a theological and religious scapegoat—the societal fetish necessary to underwrite the group-level split. Without a scapegoat, the group disavowal that sustains the split would collapse. Borrowing from Freud's work on fetishism and disavowal, Hook (2005) sums up the emotional impasse that is the result of this inner working[2]:

> Racism functioning at this level is very difficult to eradicate. Why so? Well, *because the racist has more often than not already assimilated the lesson of anti-racism.* Disavowal works . . . by being a less than fully adaptive attempt at adapting to a threatening state of affairs, by saying . . . I believe x, I just choose, every once in a while, to believe not x anyway . . . As pessimistic as such an implication is, it is important to confront, otherwise we are left with less than effective ways of countering racism. What is particularly important about this understanding of fetishistic disavowal is that it reminds us again of the limitations of the myth of racism as mere ignorance: *one can repeatedly challenge racists with the proof of racial equality in all the ways that matter, without making the slightest dent in their racist perceptions, because after all, they have already acknowledged that race makes no difference*—they just opt to act as if it did, anyway. (pp. 715–716, emphasis added)

A notable historical example of racial delusion in public spaces is evidenced in Dr. Martin Luther King Jr.'s (1986) letter from a Birmingham, Alabama, jail cell in April of 1963. Far more than simply composing poetic prose, he succinctly captures the phenomenon of group-level racial delusion (along with its splitting and disavowal functions) when he writes with utter frustration:

> I have traveled the length and breadth of Alabama, Mississippi, and all the other southern states. On sweltering summer days and crisp autumn mornings I have looked at her beautiful churches with their lofty spires pointing heavenward. I have beheld the impressive outlay of her massive religious education buildings. Over and over again I have found myself asking:

---

2. Challenging disavowal is important, but some groups lack sufficient ego strength to even critically engage in redemptive conversation that could expose and challenge splitting or group-level racial delusion. Such groups tend to psychically decompensate to such an extreme (via passive aggressiveness or claims of unfair treatment) that any form of empathic interpretation (about racial delusion) is nearly impossible—especially if the individual or group is part of the power structure.

> "*What kind of people worship here? Who is their God?* Where were their voices when the lips of Governor Barnett dripped with words of interposition and nullification? Where were they when Governor Wallace gave the clarion call for defiance and hatred? Where were their voices of support when tired, bruised and weary Negro men and women decided to rise from the dark dungeons of complacency to the bright hills of creative protest?" (p. 299, emphasis added)

When he questions the kind of people who worship there and the nature of their God, King wrestles with how people can simultaneously hold Christian principles and racial ideology without any *apparent* anxiety or discomfort—a perfect example of *group-level racial delusion* and splitting. On the night before he was assassinated, in his final sermon, King responds to this long-standing practice of *American splitting and disavowal* by preaching "All we say to America is, 'Be true to what you said on paper . . . If I lived in . . . any totalitarian country, maybe I could understand some of these illegal injunctions. Maybe I could understand the denial of certain basic First Amendment privileges . . . But somewhere I read of the freedom of assembly . . . the freedom of speech . . . [and] the freedom of press."[3]

DEMONIC TRANSFERENCE

In addition to splitting, the concept of transference offers compelling explanatory power for both the propensity to objectify Black boys in public spaces and also the mechanism by which it becomes easier to inflict psychical violence. Expanding how we understand the concept of transference and how we examine the content of this transference is beneficial to this work. The classic definition of transference delimits our understanding of the possibilities of human connectedness to the therapeutic encounter. As traditionally understood in a Freudian paradigm, transference describes the unconscious displacement of past affect related to significant others onto the person of the therapist, commonly due to emotional deficits related to unresolved conflict(s).

Schaeffer (2007) suggests a basic possibility behind transference in the human situation, suggesting that "though the conscious mind knows

---

3. This is an excerpt from the last sermon of Dr. Martin Luther King Jr., preached on April 3, 1968, at the Masonic Temple—the world headquarters of the Church of God in Christ—in Memphis, Tennessee. See source at https://kinginstitute.stanford.edu/king-papers/documents/ive-been-mountaintop-address-delivered-bishop-charles-mason-temple

that past conflicts need to be resolved, the unconscious mind uses transference as a means of avoiding conflict resolution" (p. 4). According to Schaeffer, our understanding of transference (since Freud's conception of the phenomenon) has expanded to include fantasizing (i.e., the transferor does not subject the transference to reality testing), positive and negative components or emotions, the conflictual nature of transference (i.e., interior anxiety related to frustrated desire), transference understood as a re-enactment of past negative intersubjective experiences, and the dynamic nature of transference (i.e., even though it reflects a past encounter, the emotional outcome upon the transferor is subject to the response of the present therapist). Summed up then by Schaeffer in what she refers to as a totalistic definition, "Transference is the client's unconscious displacement of attitudes, feelings, sensations, and thoughts from another person in the client's life, past or present, to the therapist in an attempt to re-enact and resolve conflict; it presumes the therapist's unconscious participation in these efforts" (p. 9).

The totalistic definition incorporates a more comprehensive understanding of transference, but more recent definitions of transference have sought to include the impacts of culture, ethnicity, and race in the therapeutic encounter. The term 'ethnic unconscious' has been employed to account for the unconscious workings of sociocultural themes and symbols within transference and the therapeutic space (Hersch 1980; Javier and Rendon 1995). Altman (2010) employs what he has termed a three-person model (juxtaposed against the traditional one- and two-person models) "so a larger social perspective can enrich our understanding at the level of both individual and dyad" (p. 61) and to focus "our attention not only to the analytic dyad, but also to the patient's and the analyst's relationship to the social context within which the analytic dyad functions" (p. 86). Further highlighting the potency of thirdness, Aggarwal (2011) goes as far to suggest that the sociocultural subjectivity generated by the patient and the therapist has the capacity to "take on a life of its own in the culturally inflected, interpersonal field" (p. 212). Lastly, a growing number of theorists and practitioners are recognizing that the larger sociohistorical context does indeed manifest itself in the therapeutic encounter via transference and countertransference (Altman 2004; Bonovitz 2005; Gump 2010).

What seems then to be absent from reflections on transference in the literature is its usage beyond the therapy room in a way that sheds light on interpersonal and psychosocial interactions. Specific to this project, I am concerned with transference and how it affects tenuous interactions with Black boys in public spaces, whether it be with law enforcement, the media, or any other societal stakeholder that has an interaction with Black boys.

An expanded conception of transference (in terms of both its content and its usage beyond the therapeutic paradigm) seems to hold tremendous interpretive power. For example, it could go a long way toward explaining the growing amount of quantitative data that substantiates the material reality of adverse interactions between law enforcement, the criminal justice system, and Black males (Goff et al. 2016; Ross 2015; Spencer and Charbonneau 2016).

Similar to when it occurs in the therapy room, *it is not beyond the pale to suggest that transference can be precipitated when there is any interpersonal or group interaction that triggers strong emotional or affective states, especially an encounter that entails a power dynamic whereby one person or group is subordinate to another person or group.* For example, it is very conceivable that transference is involved when ethnic minorities are mistreated at the hands of law enforcement or when unarmed Black men and boys are callously gunned down because they are *experienced or perceived as dangerous*. Quantitative data in implicit bias research continues to suggest a greater statistical likelihood of negative encounters between police and people of color than between police and Whites that cannot be explained by crime rates. Transference holds significant explanatory power. Further on in her expository on transference, Schaeffer (2007) highlights several triggers (or what she refers to as archetypes) that precipitate and influence transference in the therapeutic encounter. This includes experiencing the therapist (or, for my purposes, the one perceived as having more power or authority) as a mother, as a father, as a god or goddess, as a sibling, or as the source of completion a person seeks from the opposite gender. She does not give much attention to it, but Schaeffer does suggest that other cultural phenomena could precipitate transference as well.

One such cultural phenomenon that I suggest precipitates and shapes transference is the fantastic hegemonic imagination as elucidated by Townes (2006). Building on Michel Foucault's conception of fantasia and Antonio Gramsci's understanding of hegemony, Townes argues that the fantastic hegemonic imagination perverts and distorts history and memory in a way that hijacks personal and social imagination in order to erect and sustain structures of evil. In the Townesian paradigm, the "fantastic" renders evil banal and latent, such that anyone is susceptible to its influence. Likewise, the essence of the hegemonic in this paradigm rests in its ability to seduce the subjugated into acquiescing (across numerous disciplines and institutions) to the rules and ideologies of domination (both consciously and unconsciously), thereby creating what Townes refers to as a "false conscious." I believe it is this "false conscious" that, psychodynamically speaking, makes hegemony *feel right to those it oppresses*. In her project, Townes locates the etiology of the death-dealing stereotypes imposed on Black women within the fantastic hegemonic imagination. I would further add that it is the fantastic hegemonic imagination that has produced and maintained colonial fantasy, racial delusion, rabid stereotypes, and the criminalization of Black boys in public spaces. At this point, considering Schaeffer's observation that other cultural phenomena can prompt transferences and my suggestion that Townes's conception of the fantastic hegemonic imagination represents one of those cultural phenomena, I introduce *demonic transference*. *In this proposed conception of demonic transference, I am arguing that the fantastic hegemonic imagination, when left unchecked over the long run (individually, socially, or culturally), creates an antagonistic or hostile interpersonal or group transference that potentially leads to brutal or death-dealing encounters with Black male bodies in public spaces.*

Tillich's (1936) conception of the demonic is useful here as well. According to Tillich, the demonic is not about a spirit (as object) per se but is nonetheless still spiritual (i.e., part of the human situation that is concerned with the divine or the ultimate concern). The demonic finds its realization in the spirit. For Tillich, the demonic is primarily manifested in the personality of the individual or group. The essence of demonry reflects the cleavage of that personality. That is to say, for Tillich possession reflects the division of consciousness. Similar to how Kohut conceives of the vertical split, Tillich suggests that in the individual or group personality, "Its power over itself is founded in its unity, in the synthetic character of consciousness . . . [but] the possessed state is the attack on the unity and freedom, on the center of the personality . . . cleavage of consciousness has always been held a sign of the possessed state" (p. 87). Because demonry, for Tillich, represents a cleavage of the personality (as opposed to an overtaking of consciousness), mind and being remain in place such that the possessed "recognize Christ as Christ" (p. 87).

Consequently, a Tillichean lens reveals the demonic (both individual and socially) as a *cleavage* in group or individual personality such that *individuals and groups can be both spiritual and spirit-deforming at the same time*, capable of revealing the divine but only "as a reality which it fears, which it cannot love, with which it cannot unite" (p. 88). Religious groups and institutions thus can create good, but they can also exact a perversion of creativity that generates destruction. The ultimate paradox of the Tillichean lens of demonry is that an individual or institution—even an established religious institution—can simultaneously do great good and great evil (in its pursuit of what it thinks is good). *That is to say, religious people and institutions can exact some of the greatest crimes against humanity while in the pursuit of goodness or the holy.*

Consequently, in both Townes's explication of the fantastic hegemonic imagination and Tillich's understanding of the demonic, anyone is subject to its influences. The fantastic hegemonic imagination has the potential to captivate anyone—Black or White—in a way that objectifies and vilifies Black boys in public spaces. The Tillichean lens on the demonic turns the rhetorical question of Christian racial culpability on its head—that is to say, Western Christianity and racial oppression are not mutually exclusive. Both narratives are independent. Western Christianity is implicated in North American racial oppression. The concept of *demonic transference* is helpful in explaining violent events such as those that occurred in Charlottesville, Virginia, on August 12, 2017. Individuals and groups can profess religious values and—at the same time—march and demonstrate for neo-Nazi and White-supremacist values.

A BRIEF CONVERSATION WITH BLACK BOYS

The ongoing negative portrayal of Black boys in Chicago has the potential (if it has not already happened) to create a permanent psychic caste system because these boys are constantly experienced as threatening (at best) or abject (at worst) by the larger society. This death-dealing psychosocial cast system provides little to no spiritual, emotional, or psychological resources that are accretive to the emotional and spiritual well-being of Black boys. Life-giving identity formation is foreclosed. Therefore, this project asks questions of these boys about their *self-experience* in an intersubjective global world that (implicitly and explicitly) relegates the bodies of Black men and boys to the lowest rungs of an interpsychic caste system.

In this project, I interviewed two groups of Black boys: one group of high school juniors and seniors and another group (at a different location) that ranged in age from 13 to 21 years old. I asked questions informed by a Kohutian framework. This was not because of any predisposed affinity for Kohut's work but because of the context (Nazi Germany atrocities against Jews) in which, as one who fled from the Nazis, he likely conceived and fashioned his theory of the human project. According to Aron (2007), for Kohut the ultimate horror one could experience in life was to exist in an environment where one was not deemed to be human. This seems to be the context of Black boys in America.

Below, I briefly reflect on five salient themes/questions I posed to both groups: (1) What is your experience of self in various public spaces throughout Chicago or when you see Black males depicted in the media? (2) If you had a worldwide audience, what would you want them to know about you as a Black male? (3) Describe an instance or situation in your life that was a high point, a time when you thought you could conquer the world? (4) Who do you admire most, such that being around them (or in that place) gives you a sense of being *uplifted* or encouraged, and, (5) If you could have anything or any type of life after graduation, what would it be?

Regarding the first question on self-experience in public spaces (and the media), the responses included experiences of being stressed, being depressed, being enraged (because of negative stereotypes), and being hurt (because of implicit biases relative to Black boys). Both groups seemed to share the belief that the negative media depictions or negative social responses served to motivate them to personally succeed and defy low expectations or beat the odds. Salient comments included (1) "It's hard to be a black male in Chicago"; (2) "It's motivating, you see this bad stuff and want to do better, but it is scary, it is a life-and-death situation"; (3) "The media does not try to tell the whole story. They will always show killings. They will not show graduations or other good things about Chicago. Focusing on the killings makes their jobs easier"; (4) "No one is talking about the kids in my high school that won first place in drama. No one is talking about the girl that got pregnant and still got accepted to college and plans to attend"; and (5) "The negative portrayals are especially hurtful when they come from other Black people." There was a general sense of existential fatigue associated with the negative media depictions or the negative stereotypes they faced in the public spaces of Chicago. One student summed it up by saying, "It is stressful and depressing but beneficial because when you have been through so much, you don't feel it anymore. I learned to bottle it up and not to show emotion. But now I am finding myself around people that help me express myself and not be a shell. Teachers and friends in school help take stress away."

For the question related to what they would want the world to know about them as Black males, the prevalent theme seemed to focus on their being no different than any other human being. A sample of responses includes the following: (1) "Never judge a book by its cover. You never know what a person goes through. Nobody's opportunities should be taken from them because of the way they look. Know what people stand for!" (2) "Other races do the same [presumably negative] things as Black people, but Black people are the face of all things bad . . . *they make us the face of the world's problems*"; and (3) "We are something greater than what you see on television. We are in school trying to do great things."

Responding to the question about a high point in life when they felt as if they could conquer the world (i.e., affirming self-object needs), the responses coalesced around school, sports, and the arts. In several cases, the most important element for the boys seemed to be what they accomplished with their fellow classmates. A sampling of responses included the following: (1) "I feel most alive when I am doing what I do best: playing a sport like football—doing what I do best and showcasing it"; (2) "When we put that helmet on, *winning together is what counts because we are from the south side* [of Chicago], *and people automatically think we don't amount to anything*"; (3) "Graduating from elementary school was the highlight of my life"; (4) "A high point for me was when I transcribed a piece of music that my instructor didn't believe I could transcribe . . . he was surprised"; and (5) "Band camp was a high point for me."

Regarding the question of who they admired or liked being around because they *uplifted* them (i.e., idealizing self-object needs), in both groups the boys' identified one of their fellow classmates or friends, a teacher, an administrator, someone at their church, or one of the boys in the room where we were having the group interviews. Interestingly enough, when I prodded them about admiring a famous athlete or entertainer, the overwhelming response was that because they didn't have access to such individuals, they felt no strong admiration for them.

Finally, in response the question about what they wanted if they could have anything (or live in any way) after graduation, every response—in both groups—centered on giving back to their community or somehow making *their world* a better place. One might think that because there were other adults present observing the group interview or because the boys were aware of the topic being discussed (i.e., Black males in public spaces), they were possibly embellishing their responses to look better. But as the empathic investigator in the room, I did not sense that this was the case. My impression was that the responses were genuine. A sample of responses included the following: (1) "I would like to have peaceful communities, no crime, and be successful so I can take care of everyone in my family"; (2) "I want to be an entrepreneur to make things better for the community and provide jobs for youth, not just Black youth but all youth"; (3) "I want to be able to give back to the community, have different resources to give to poor communities, not just Black communities but everybody in the city of Chicago"; (4) "I want to work for a world where we can be all together. I desire for Black people to be free from White people or anybody who stigmatizes different races. Black people are stigmatized the most, like dirt. Everybody else is respected for who they are. If everyone works together, we will be surprised at what we can accomplish"; (5) "I just want peace of mind"; and (6) "I want peace of mind that stems from people coming together, loving each other, and understanding what's going on in [the] press. Instead of just showing violence, show the people who are trying to do something about it. With understanding comes resolution of issues."

FINAL THOUGHTS AND FUTURE WORK

The reactions of the adults who observed the boys being interviewed was visceral, emotional, and tearful but also included frustration. Instead of idealizing the responses of the boys, the general communication from several administrators was that the boys should not have to be in a situation or context to respond in such a serious manner. In their general assessment, Black boys do not have the opportunity to be children. Based on their years of experience as educators, clergy, and law officers, several of the adult observers even suggested that White children can be just that—children—and would have responded differently to the questions.

In reflecting on the interviews and the overall project, I cannot overstate how important it was that the teachers and other adult observers did not idealize the boys' responses and refer to them as *young men*. Instead, they lamented the inability for Black males to live lives in which they are first Black *boys*. Vaughans and Harris (2016) pick up on the deleterious psychological effect that Black boys suffer when they are not allowed the developmental period whereby they can be boys and experience insecurity, vulnerability, and ambiguity. The authors assert "in the national media, Black boys are in legal trouble because they are not described as such . . . we hear phrases such as 'young man' or a statement of their age . . . unlike their White counterparts there is no questioning in the media about their psychological state of mind" (p. 174). Furthermore, Black boys can be objectified in public spaces and also within their own care communities. The temptation to idealize their responses to interview questions (and experience them as young men) possibly reflects internalized stereotypes that strip the boys of their agency and voices and flattens their life stories.

When asked about what it took to do their jobs, one of the teachers lamented, "We can equip younger teachers and staff with certain skills that will allow them to be relatively successful, but we cannot teach younger teachers *how to give a shit. You have to give a shit.*" Another senior faculty member added, "*You have to love them and be willing to do things outside of your official job description.*"

The comments from these caregivers caused me to ponder this question for future research: As pastoral psychotherapists—or practical, pastoral, or public theologians—what if our *ideological golden calf called empathy* is not enough? This is not to suggest that empathy is not fundamentally important.

But does empathy solve all? In the colonial logic and the Western racial imagination that is fundamentally designed and structured to subordinate the Black male body, how far will empathy go in relation to dismantling structures of evil and providing life-giving spaces for Black boys? I wonder, then, what is the theoretical and theological correlate to giving a shit? That is to say, what does a pastoral theological and psychological praxis of giving a shit entail? I suspect that more than having empathy for Black boys, there is a larger (more substantive) question to investigate. What does it look like (and mean) to believe in Black boys, and what is the redemptive effect on the lives of Black boys when their caregivers and community believe in them?

REFERENCES

Addams, J. (1901). Respect for law. *The Independent, 53*(2718), 18–20.

Aggarwal, N. K. (2011). Intersubjectivity, transference, and the cultural third. *Contemporary Psychoanalysis, 47*, 204–223.

Altman, N. (2004). History repeats itself in transference: Countertransference. *Psychoanalytic Dialogues, 14*, 807–815.

Altman, N. (2010). *The analyst in the inner city: Race, class, and culture through a psychoanalytic lens* (2nd ed.). Routledge Taylor & Francis.

Aron, L. (2007). Reflection on Heinz Kohut's religious identity and anti-Semitism: Discussion of Charles B. Strozier's "Heinz Kohut and the meanings of identity." *Contemporary Psychoanalysis, 43*(3), 411–420.

Blackburn, R. (1997). The Old-World background to European colonial slavery. *William and Mary Quarterly, 54*(1), 65–102.

Bonovitz, C. (2005). Locating culture in the psychic field: Transference and countertransference as cultural products. *Contemporary Psychoanalysis, 41*, 55–76.

Braude, B. (1997). The sons of Noah and the construction of ethnic and geographical identities in the medieval and early modern periods. *William and Mary Quarterly, 1*, 103–142.

Cytrynbaum, S. (1993). *Implications of the Tavistock model for group psychotherapy.* American Group Psychotherapy Association Annual Meeting.

Davis, D. B. (1997). Constructing race: A reflection. *William and Mary Quarterly*, Third Series, *54*(1), 7–18.

Du Bois, W. E. B. (1903). *The souls of black folk.* McClurg.

Fanon, F. (1952). *Black skin, White masks.* (C. L. Markmann, Trans.). Pluto.

Goff, P. A., Lloyd, T., Geller, A., Raphael, S., & Glaser, J. (2016). *The science of justice: Race, arrests, and police use of force.* University of California, Los Angeles, Center for Policing Equity.

Gump, J. P. (2010). Reality matters: The shadow of trauma on African American subjectivity. *Psychoanalytic Psychology, 27*(1), 42–54.

Hersch, J. (1980). The ethnic unconscious. *Journal of Analytical Psychology, 25*, 181–191.

Hook, D. (2005). The racial stereotype, colonial discourse, fetishism, and racism. *Psychoanalytic Review, 92*, 701–734.

Javier, R. A., & Rendon, M. (1995). The ethnic unconscious and its role in transference, resistance, and countertransference: An introduction. *Psychoanalytic Psychology, 12*, 513–520.

King, M. L. (1986). Letter from Birmingham city jail. In J. M. Washington (Ed.), *A testament of hope: The essential writings and speeches of Martin Luther King Jr.* (pp. 289–302). HarperCollins.

Kohut, H. (1979). The two analyses of Mr. Z. *International Journal of Psycho-Analysis, 60*, 3–27.

McRae, M. B., & Short, E. L. (2010). *Racial and cultural dynamics in group and organizational life: Crossing boundaries*. Sage.

Morgan, J. (1997). "Some could suckle over their shoulder": Male travelers, female bodies, and the gendering of racial ideology, 1500–1770. *William and Mary Quarterly, 54*(1), 167–192.

Morris, A. D. (1999). Forward. In D. C. Hine & E. Jenkins (Eds.), *A question of manhood: A reader in U.S. Black men's history and masculinity* (p. xii). Indiana University Press.

Ray, S. G. (2003). *Do no harm: Social sin and Christian responsibility*. Fortress.

Ross, C. T. (2015). A multi-level Bayesian analysis of racial bias in police shootings at the county-level in the United States, 2011–2014. *PLoS One, 1*–34.

Schaeffer, J. A. (2007). *Transference and countertransference in non-analytic therapy: Double-edged swords*. University Press of America.

Spencer, K. B., & Charbonneau, A. K. (2016). Implicit bias and policing. *Social and Personality Psychology Compass, 10*(1), 50–63.

Tillich, P. (1936). *The interpretation of history*. Scribner.

Townes, E. M. (2006). *Womanist ethics and the cultural production of evil*. Palgrave Macmillan.

Vaughan, A. T., & Vaughan, V. M. (1997, January). Before Othello: Elizabethan representations of sub-Saharan Africans. *William and Mary Quarterly, 54*(1), 19–44.

Vaughans, K. C., & Harris, L. (2016). The police, black and Hispanic boys: A dangerous inability to mentalize. *Journal of Infant, Child, and Adolescent Psychotherapy, 15*(3), 171–178.

Wells-Barnett, I. B. (1901). Lynching and the excuse for it. *The Independent, 53*, 1133–1136.

Wynter, S. (2003). Unsettling the coloniality of being/power/truth/freedom: Towards the human, after man, its overrepresentation—An argument. *New Centennial Review, 3*(3), 257–337.

6

The Organ of Tactility
Fantasy, Image, and Male Masturbation

JACO J. HAMMAN

Masturbation is widely practiced, though rarely discussed. It has eclipsed what has been called the coital imperative, as an estimated 98% of men (and 87% of women) masturbate (Kahr 2007). With masturbation—which *The Kinsey Report* defines as "the deliberate self-stimulation which effects sexual arousal"—almost always culminating in orgasm, it is a practice that delivers what it promises (Kinsey et al. 1948, p. 133). Still, Western culture remains ambivalent about masturbation. The Swiss physician Samuel-August Tissot (1728–1797) exploited this ambivalence, arguably more than anyone else. Long before Tissot, however, Catholic monks tried to starve, freeze, or castrate their sexual desire to death, thereby giving us an ironic understanding of masturbation as self-abuse. Etymologically, the word has from *manus* ('hand') and *stuprum* ("debauch") and *perpetrare* ("to perpetrate"). Slang terms describing the intimate act are legion. The practice has also moved out of the private sphere, as many online sites, one being www.beautifulagony.com, give ordinary people ways to upload their non-pornographic pleasure for others to witness.

Tissot's *The Diseases Caused by Masturbation*, published in 1760 in French, recounts numerous patient narratives, all leading to dire consequences (Tissot 2015). Tissot, as did many physicians in his day, believed that the body contains the right amount of fluids, and if the balance is disturbed, illnesses set in. "There is another seminal fluid," he writes, "which has so much influence on the strength of the body and on the perfection of digestion which restores it, that physicians of every age have unanimously admitted, that the loss of one ounce of it, enfeebles more than forty ounces of blood" (2015, p. i-ii). Ejaculation is dangerous. Tissot depicts the frightening results of losing one's precious seminal fluid (humor). He quotes Aretaeus of Cappadocia, the first-century Greek physician, who paints an equally dire picture: "Young persons assume the air and the diseases of the aged; they become pale, stupid, effeminate, idle, weak, and even void of understanding; their bodies bend forward, their legs are weak, they have a disgust for every thing, become fit for nothing, and many are affected by paralysis" (as quoted in Tissot 2015, p. 3). Echoing Celsus, the second-century Greek philosopher, Tissot states that only the weak masturbate.

Tissot, placing himself among distinguished physicians and philosophers who warned against masturbation—Galen, Pliny, Aetius, Sanctorius, Lomnius, Tulpius, Blancard, and Muys, to name but a few—paints a grim picture for all who masturbate. Masturbators suffer from deranged stomachs, sunken eyes, loss of appetite, impaired memory, digestive problems, insensible perspiration, sleep disturbances, and physical deformation, as well as "apoplexies [strokes], lethargies, epilepsies, loss of sight, trembling, paralysis, and all kinds of painful affections" (2015, p. 4). Some may even develop "spontaneous gangrene" and die if coitus follows masturbation (p. 5). Feeling the need to repeat himself, Tissot quotes the Dutch (Christian) physician, Herman Boerhaave (1668–1738): "Too great a loss of semen produces weakness, debility, immobility, convulsions, emaciation, dryness, pains in the membranes of the brain, impairs the senses, particularly that of sight, gives rise to dorsal consumption, indolence, and the several diseases connected to them.... We are ignorant what sympathy the testicles have with the body, but particularly with the eyes" (as quoted in 2015, p. 7). It is no surprise that he discourages fantasy, since imagination that leads to sexual arousal also overheats the brain, equally ominous. Today, Tissot is read with amusement. Not all voices from previous centuries, however, followed Tissot.

Samuel Langhorne Clemens (1835–1910)—better known as Mark Twain—delivered a speech during his 1879 tour of Europe at a Parisian men's club entitled "Some Thoughts on the Science of Onanism." The talk was later published as *On Masturbation* (Twain 2017). Despite the puritanical thought thriving during Twain's life, he exposes the Victorian culture's rich ambivalence towards masturbation. He opens his speech by admitting (or confessing) the obvious—men masturbate:

> My gifted predecessor has warned you against the "social evil"—adultery. In his able paper, he exhausted that subject; he left absolutely nothing more to be said about it. But I will continue his

good work in the cause of morality by cautioning you against that species of recreation called self-abuse—to which I perceive that you too are much addicted. (Twain 2017, p. 7)

The fact that persons from a wide range of disciplines, especially medicine, philosophy, and religion, write on masturbation, Twain concludes, speaks to masturbation as a "stately subject; this shows its dignity and importance" (2017, p. 8). Although Twain states he wants to caution men "against that species of recreation called self-abuse" (p. 15), his speech is essentially a celebration of this intimate practice. Referencing scientific, literary, political, and cultural "masters," Twain shifts the power held by Tissot's treatise. Twain quotes Homer (7th to 8th century BCE), who said: "Give me masturbation or give me death" (p. 10). That Homer was a blind poet and bard—and Tissot warns against going blind when one masturbates—does not go unnoticed. Twain builds his argument by referencing Julius Caesar (130–85 BCE), who highlighted the egalitarian nature of masturbation: "To the lonely it is company; to the forsaken a friend; to the aged and the impotent it is a benefactor; they that be penniless are yet rich, in that they still have this majestic diversion" (p. 10). He reminds his audience of Daniel Defoe's Robinson Crusoe, who said "I cannot describe what I owe to this gentle art" (p. 11) and of President Benjamin Franklin, who described masturbation as "the mother of invention" (p. 14). One senses that Twain appreciates "the Old Master" Michelangelo who told Pope Julius II, "Self-negation is noble, self-culture is beneficent, self-possession is manly, but to the truly great and inspiring soul they are poor and tame compared to self-abuse" (p. 14). Twain ends his speech by describing masturbation as "a science" (p. 15).

Just as one thinks Twain fully affirms masturbation, however, he addresses the consequences of "excessive indulgence in this destructive pastime . . . : A disposition to eat, drink, smoke, to laugh, to joke, and tell indelicate stories—and mainly, a yearning to paint pictures" (2017, p. 24). Twain, of course, was poking fun at the members of the men's club. Still, he channels Tissot:

> The results of this habit are loss of memory, loss of virility, loss of cheerfulness, loss of hopefulness, loss of character, and loss of progeny. Of all the kinds of sexual intercourse, this has the least to recommend it. As an amusement it is too fleeting; as an occupation it is too wearing; as a public exhibition there is no money in it. (Twain 2017, p. 25–26)

Twain notes that masturbation is mostly banned as a conversation topic unless it appears in some male conversation. With the admonition not to "play a Lone Hand too much" (p. 28), Twain concludes his speech. We have, of course, come a long way since Twain's speech. We've moved from fantasy and printed materials to living increasingly digital lives.

The developmental importance, psychodynamic impact, and motivation for masturbating to pornography are well researched (Carvalheira et al. 2015; Diorio 2016; Goren 2003; Garlick 2012; Kaestle and Allen 2011; Kwee and Hoover 2008; Lillie 2002; Staehler and Kozin 2017; Strager 2003; Uebel 1999; Wood 2011; Yule et al. 2017). These studies, recognizing the ambivalence and changing nature of sexual expression and increased masturbatory practices, rarely discuss the intimate relationship between sexual fantasy and image and how image may be replacing fantasy. Before I proceed, two terms central to this chapter need definition. *Pornography* is understood as any sexually explicit image or depiction other than the naked body of one's partner. *Sexual fantasy* may be defined as "an image, a thought or a fully elaborated drama, which passes through our mind principally during sexual activity, either coital or masturbatory, often resulting in orgasm" (Kahr 2007, p. 547).

Dismissing Tissot's warnings about the dangers of masturbation comes naturally to a culture that has had numerous sexual revolutions since the 1960s. Twain's satirical wit can only take us that far. This chapter addresses the interplay of sexual fantasy and pornographic images in male masturbation. It does not seek to address the meaning of sexuality, or the ethical, moral, and religious issues tied to pornography, such as the exploitation of women and minors; stereotyping of race; the commodification of lives; nonconformity; sexual aggression, power, and control; or legal matters. Rather, the focus is on sexual fantasies and men masturbating to online images. As pornography scholar Stephen Strager (2003) states, "The masturbating man is pornography's audience" (p. 51). Having the masturbating man in mind, this chapter asks, Are images, masquerading as fantasies, possibly replacing the erotic imagination in the Internet age? And do images merely serve the deeper unconscious fantasies a person holds?

Writing about masturbation and pornography in a way that invites deeper personal, pastoral, theological, and psychodynamic reflection is challenging, for words are easily assigned sexual innuendo. The title of this chapter with its inclusion of the word "organ," Tissot often repeating the diseases caused by masturbation, and Twain speaking to the "members" of a men's club all demonstrate this difficulty. Our minds do sexualize what we experience, as well as what we read. Care has been taken in this regard in writing this chapter, and only three brief sexual fantasies are mentioned.

Brett Kahr, in turn, provides verbatim fantasies of more than a thousand persons; some are titillating whereas others might be seen as gross (Kahr 2007, 2008).

First, this chapter reflects on the case of Jude, given to us by British psychotherapist John Woods (2015). Jude, who was referred to counseling after periods of school absenteeism, used Internet pornography excessively and masturbated compulsively. The sheer number of images Jude consumed became a burden he was unable to bear. Jude's case introduces the question for this essay of whether modern masturbation is driven by fantasy or by image (upon image). The chapter next explores the role of fantasy in the rich and storied history of masturbation, followed by a discussion of Brett Kahr's (2007, 2008) epic study on sexual fantasy. Identifying a shift from fantasy to image, the chapter then appropriates Australian philosopher Michael Taussig's (1993) concept of the eye as "the organ of tactility" as he reflects on mimetic desire. The chapter concludes by offering a framework for discerning whether masturbating to images might be disordered and life-depriving. Counselors and therapists, when they facilitate the exploration of sexual fantasies and masturbatory practices, can assist others to hold the tension around "the masturbatory paradox"—that sexual fantasies and practices that provide pleasure can also instill guilt and confusion and even become addictive. They can also encourage nonvisual sexual arousal (the use of fantasy) and mindfulness to achieve relief from the tyranny of the eye.

A YOUNG MAN'S MASTURBATORY PRACTICES

London-based therapist John Woods explores the psychodynamics of masturbation and pornography in the Internet age in his essay "Seeing and Being Seen: The Psychodynamics of Pornography Through the Lens of Winnicott's Thought" (2015). Woods warns against the danger of pornography: "A compulsive form of voyeurism means that the young person cannot bear to be seen and becomes painfully alone with his violent masturbation fantasies" (p. 163). He introduces the central concern that drives this essay: *Contemporary masturbatory practices are now driven by the eye and pornographic images, even if they serve a deeper, unconscious fantasy.* Woods sees contemporary masturbatory practices, now part of the sexualized self, as remaining insatiable despite consuming images online. He quotes a British study that found that one quarter of boys between 14 and 18 years of age are concerned about the amount of pornography they personally consume. The same study found a relationship between the frequency of using pornography and problems related to employment, relationships, and sexual intimacy.

Woods references researcher Jill Manning's (2006) landmark meta-analysis on the use of pornography in the United States, "The Impact of Internet Pornography on Marriage and the Family: A Review of the Research." A brief detour from Woods's article to look at Manning's research is informative. Manning writes that "Internet pornography is distinct from other forms of pornography because of the 'Triple-A Engine' effect of Accessibility, Affordability, and Anonymity—a combination of traits unique to the virtual square" (p. 133). Her research found that pornography (a) leads to sexual deviance, especially in the form of ritualistic masturbation; (b) increases the possibility for sexual perpetration (rape), (c) changes intimate relationships (due to viewing persons as sexual objects or part objects, such as a breast, a vagina, a penis or a butt), (d) instills the acceptance of the rape myth (believing women cause rape), and (e) causes behavioral and sexual aggression. Tested on these variables, users of pornography generally tested 20–31% higher than the general population. Amongst the many studies Manning quotes, a study by Zillman and Bryant indicated 68% of their respondents, all active users of pornography, experienced decreased sexual intimacy with their partner, and 52% lost interest in relational sex, preferring solitary masturbation.

Manning's analysis of the impact of pornography on children and adolescents showed that users:

> (a) can be easily coerced into viewing pornography or manipulated into the production of it, (b) have limited ability to emotionally, cognitively, and physiologically process obscene material they encounter voluntarily or involuntarily, (c) can be the victims of another's pornography consumption in ways adults are often more resilient to, (d) can have their sexual and social development negatively impacted through exposure to fraudulent and/or traumatic messages regarding sexuality and relationships, and (e) can develop unrealistic expectations about their future sexual relationships through repeated exposure to fantasy-based templates. (p. 146)

Manning's research is echoed by Heather Wood (2011), who found that the use of Internet pornography fuels manic defenses (feelings of power and omnipotence), offers an escape from real relationships, invites part-object relating, is a vehicle to express sadism (or sadism by proxy), allows scenes where desire and arousal can meet, and avoids or subverts the superego. Similarly, a study of nearly 600 heterosexual married men by

Ana Carvalheira and her colleagues (2015) showed that 70% of the men masturbated at least once a week to pornography. The frequency of their masturbation was related to sexual boredom, frequent use of pornography, and low relationship intimacy. As John Woods's work with Jude indicates, the combination of a visual image, a sexual fantasy, a hand, and a penis can have serious psychodynamic and relational implications.

Woods (2015) introduces his readers to Jude, a 17-year-old who withdrew from the world after being bullied and was referred to counseling for school absenteeism. As with most boys, "The first sexual experience [for Jude did] not begin with a nervous request to meet or get to know someone; it [was] watching a parade of grotesquely degrading images of women, often mixed with violent abuse" (p. 165). Jude did not masturbate to conscious fantasies, but he did masturbate to images. The images were "fused with a state of sexual arousal and masturbation" (p. 165). The school social worker who referred Jude, not knowing the extent of his involvement with pornography, also expressed concerns about his excessive use of the Internet. One attempt by the social worker to get Jude out of his home and bedroom failed when, at a day center, he made an advance to a girl who did not reciprocate his move. As identified by Manning (2006), pornographic use can limit a man's ability in face-to-face intimate relationships. Jude felt rejected, wanted to stab the girl, and said he wanted to kill himself due to his failure to relate to girls. To Woods, Jude described how he felt ugly and angry and wanted to break things; he admitted watching Internet pornography for many hours and enjoyed seeing women being abused. One scenario was that of a man grabbing a woman's throat and punching her in the face. After masturbating, he would "crash," feeling low and guilty. But he maintained he would never give up pornography because he might become more dangerous on the street (Woods 2015).

Jude was emotionally and physically distant from his father, and he had much contempt for his mother as she tried to hold things together after a divorce. He was proud of his vast collection of digital pornographic images, ready at hand, which he carefully labeled and catalogued. He relied on the images to fuel his masturbatory practices, for fantasy alone was too weak to arouse him (a sign of erectile dysfunction). Woods suggested that Jude turned the absence of his father into victory by accumulating the images and wondered out loud whether the images were "real." Woods sought ways to make conscious to Jude the fantasy that fueled his masturbatory practices. Jude initially remained dismissive of the counseling journey, fearing that Woods would ask him to give up his images. In a session where he admitted to illicit online activity and stalking behavior in real life, Jude stated: "I feel dehumanized.... It is being seen by you. I don't want you to see everything, but you have to see it all" (Woods 2015, p. 169). Jude confessed to Woods that he watched films of women urinating and defecating, sometimes covering themselves in excrement. Other films were filled with violence. Woods observed that Jude was projecting his self-disgust onto his mother and other women.

Although Woods does not address the neuroscience behind Jude's practices and behavior, Gary Wilson's (2014) *Your Brain on Porn: Internet Pornography and the Emerging Science of Addiction* offers a deeper understanding of what Jude was experiencing. The neuroplasticity of the brain—the fact that the brain or biology can shape itself after an environment such as online pornography—demands that we remain mindful of the impact of our use of technology. The brain is responsive and malleable. For Wilson, there is a strong correlation between the addictive brain and the brain of someone compulsively engaging in pornography. "Most users regard internet porn as a solution—to boredom, sexual frustration, loneliness or stress," Wilson writes (p. 9). When a person "faps," the slang for masturbating to porn, the person has an experience stronger than masturbating to "static" porn (print media). Free and abundant online galleries of short movies (including GIFs) not only flood the pleasure centers of the brain but also can wear those centers out. For many using pornography, as was true for Jude, pleasure can only be found by engaging increasingly graphic material. The shortness of the clips demand clicking and searching for additional material to maintain interest and stimulation.

Wilson (2014) describes how pornography stimulates the reward circuitry of the brain—the amygdala, the prefrontal cortex, the nucleus accumbens, the ventral tegmentum area (midbrain), and the hypothalamus's suprachiasmatic nucleus. These areas also govern emotions, drives, and unconscious decision-making and release dopamine, which not only is the feelgood (pleasure) opioid of the body but also places the brain in a state of seeking and searching. Dopamine prompts nerves to synchronize the ways they transfer signals ("firing" together), a state needed for orgasm and active in addiction. Dopamine also facilitates the creation of new neural connections (a "wiring" together called Hebb's Law). The dopamine and its neural effects increase as anticipation grows and novelty surprises. "Internet porn is especially enticing to the reward circuitry because novelty is always just one click away. It could be a novel 'mate,' unusual scene, strange sexual act, or . . ." (p. 60).

Your Brain on Porn (Wilson 2014) identifies pornography's "supernormal stimulation," a state of arousal that leads not only to *desensitization*, a numbed response to stimulus, but also *sensitization*, having a powerful memory of the kinds of images that bring pleasure. Furthermore, the brain experiences *hypofrontality*, "reduced brain activity in the prefrontal regions, which weakens willpower in the face of subconscious cravings" (p. 81). *Dysfunctional stress circuits* mean that minor stress causes cravings and relapses. A period of noFapping—also called "rebooting," restores neural functioning to men (p. 18). NoFapping (See: www.nofap.com), which is a cultural movement built on a simplistic morality, has been questioned as a sustainable path honoring the complexity of human desire and sexuality and the ambivalence of being embodied (Staehler and Kozin 2017). Jude's adolescent brain, vulnerable to overstimulation, was strained by the cost of fapping.

As Jude's journey with Woods deepened, he felt attracted to a new girl. When the relationship did not work out, Jude was appropriately sad. Woods found Jude less angry and showing signs of developing what D. W. Winnicott (1994) called "the capacity to be alone" (in the presence of others). This capacity calls on a person to contain emotion in one's body and to have appropriate relationships with other bodies. Slowly, Jude began to find pornography boring. His regression to a pornographic universe, where there are no rules but a sense of omnipotence and control, stopped. Jude's accompanying splitting and projection, especially towards his mother and women, diminished. His bedroom became a place of rest and relaxation as he was in touch with his personal exhaustion, with no felt need for pornography and compulsive masturbation.

In reflecting on Jude's case, Woods (2015) states that Internet pornography and compulsive masturbation is first a defense against loneliness and isolation and then becomes a catalyst for those very experiences. From a neurological perspective, *Your Brain on Porn* (Wilson 2014) affirms Woods's observation. Pornography causes a break between the subject and the object viewed. This break, for Jude, was repaired as he entered into a significant relationship with Woods, the only father figure that modeled maturity to him. It was Woods and Jude seeing each other, and more specifically Jude being seen by Woods, that removed Jude's desire to watch image after image. "Mother and baby usually look into each other's eyes, the baby sees itself, and the mother's liveliness reflects the baby's" (p. 171), Woods (2015) reminds his readers. Emotional belonging and security are instilled as eyes meet. The irony of Jude's journey is this: As he was seen by Woods, Jude no longer felt the need to look at pornographic images, and a normal fantasy life—including the fantasy of being with another person—returned. I am reminded of Numbers 6:24–26, where God states, "The Lord bless you and protect you. The Lord make his face shine on you and be gracious to you. The Lord lift up his face to you and grant you peace" (CEB). We live a facial existence, which pornography and masturbation try to mimic but fail to do.

Jude shows that for many boys and men, masturbation comes fused with images and personal as well as interpersonal burdens. The images serve unconscious fantasies and desires. Jude's practices also show that masturbation today is very different compared to the masturbatory practices of pre-Internet eras.

A VERY BRIEF HISTORY OF MASTURBATION

Pastoral theological evaluations of masturbation have been done by James Nelson, Donald Capps, Judith and Jack Balswick, and earlier by William Phipps, to name but a few pastoral theologians (Balswick and Balswick 1999; Capps 2003; Nelson 1978; Phipps 1977). Phipps (1977), who taught religion and philosophy at Davis and Elkins College, writes positively about "fantastic images . . . the picture on the screen of the mind" (p. 193) that accompanies healthy masturbation. Even 5000 years ago, masturbation has intrigued people enough to have drawn on ancient Egyptian papyri the god Atum masturbating with his own mouth. The intrigue continues as sex historians remind us that our sexual practices may not have changed much over the last few thousand years: "Sexual manuals written thousands of years ago in ancient China covered almost all the same techniques one would find in a sex manual today, with only one major exception" (Baumeister and Bushman 2017, p. 49). The exception is sadomasochism.

In the next paragraphs, I consult three histories of masturbation, keeping the intimate relationship between fantasy, image, and masturbation in mind. The histories are Stengers and Van Neck's (2001) *Masturbation: The History of a Great Terror*, Thomas Laqueur's (2003) *Solitary Sex: A Cultural History of Masturbation*, and Mels van Driel's (2012) *With the Hand: A Cultural History of Masturbation*. Each book approaches the topic in a unique manner. Stengers and Van Neck offer a defined historical and feminist take on masturbation. Laqueur, whose book is twice the length of the other two, addresses masturbation (although he prefers the term "solitary sex" to describe the habit) as a problem. Van Driel, in turn, offers an unabashedly positive, although not without concern, review of the solitary practice.

Belgian feminist historians Stengers and Van Neck (2001) look at Western attitudes toward masturbation in the late 1800s and the 1900s and the social forces that informed and also followed this era. They show how Tissot's thoughts—a chapter is dedicated to him—are reflected in the typical European attitudes toward this practice during that era. According to that view, no bodily system remained untouched by masturbation: the nervous system, the sense organs and phonation, the skeletal system, the muscular system and how the body stores fat, the respiratory system, the cardiovascular system, the digestive system, the genitourinary system, and ultimately the process of dying (Stengers and Van Neck 2001). Masturbation leads to total physical and moral failure and agony, as many a physician and theologian argued. Antidotes during this time were thought to be gymnastics, swimming, a clean diet (Sylvester Graham and his crackers, John Harvey Kellogg and his cereal), and the memorization of poetry. The purpose was a dead-tired boy or man who would fall asleep before the temptation of masturbation set in. Mechanical "instruments" were developed, such as a penis ring with sharp teeth, to be worn to prevent "the bad habit" (Stengers and Van Neck 2001). Some men resorted to infibulation, piercing the foreskin in two places and inserting a metal ring, disallowing the foreskin to retract and thus stopping erections. When everything else failed, the Church recommended marriage. Stengers and Van Neck note that *all the social anxiety against masturbation came from the bourgeoisie*. The authors explore how different economic and social classes engaged in masturbation. They argue that the campaign against masturbation starting in the seventeenth century was a deliberate attempt by the upper class to control the minds of the lower classes. It is the bourgeoisie who turned the moral attitudes toward masturbation into a medical concern and an outrage against society.

Masturbation (Stengers and Van Neck 2001) does have a few telling references to sexual fantasy. The Franciscans and Benedictines of the late sixteenth century warned against the pollution that "is provoked through diabolical illusion," which is the work of the devil himself. Here, fantasy is judged harshly by moral theology. Likewise, the seventeenth-century French physician and sexologist Nicolas Venette (1633–1698), following the Benedictine tradition, warned against "venereal illusions which trouble the imagination" (as quoted in Stengers and Van Neck 2001, p. 32). Venette, who held strong patriarchal and chauvinistic attitudes, believed that women struggle with these illusions more than males do. Stengers and Van Neck also give much weight to *Onania, or, The Heinous Sin of Self-Pollution*, a 1712 book by British surgeon John Marten that went through numerous printings. Marten was one of the first creators of printed soft-core porn. *Onania* indicates the moral turn against masturbation similar to that of Tissot. The book, inspired by the biblical narrative of Onan, informed Tissot's writing. Marten emphasized the belief that masturbation is a physical threat to one's health and society and also saw masturbation as morally wrong. Marten's authority as a physician gave his writings credence few could challenge. He was a good salesman and placed advertisements in his book for vaginal oils and various cures of self-abuse.

By the eighteenth century, Stengers and Van Neck (2001) note, the focus had turned to the masturbatory practices of children. They refer to Jean-Jacques Rousseau (1712-1778), who, in his *Emile* (published in 1763), warns the young boy not to succumb to the "instinct," which is a "deadly habit." Later, Rousseau wrote about his personal introduction and experience of "this deplorable advantage" in his *Confessions* (published in 1778), a vice "particularly attractive to active imaginations" (as quoted in Stengers and Van Neck, ibid.). This imagination, Rousseau states, avail a woman to a man "without needing to obtain her consent." The authors remind their readers that Rousseau masturbated for much of his life.

Stengers and Van Neck (2001) next turn to *The Diseases Caused by Masturbation* by Tissot (1728-1797), who identifies the pleasures "solicited by the imagination" as disrupting the seminal fluids of the body. When semen is spilled because of the imagination, more so than when it happens naturally, a man is at grave risk for the illnesses mentioned in the introduction to this chapter. Tissot saw the imagination as being so powerful that it can control the senses, even attack the brain, as can be seen in the chronic fatigue manifested in masturbators. Like many Germans, Immanuel Kant (1724-1804) followed Tissot and warned parents and educators in his *On Pedagogy* (1803) to protect children from "the evil thoughts from one's mind," recommending spending as little time as possible in a bed (Stengers and Van Neck 2001, p. 90). Kant too saw masturbation as having disastrous implications for one's wellbeing.

Stengers and Van Neck notice a slight change in attitude toward masturbation with Sir James Paget (1814-1899), Queen Victoria's physician, who first challenged the popular masturbatory beliefs of his day, especially the ones arguing that mental and physical illness is the result of masturbation. Still, he strictly forbids "fornication." Jules Christian, a French physician, also noted in 1881 that masturbation is so widespread that "very few people can boast having escaped it completely" (as quoted in Stengers and Van Neck 2001, p. 90). Tissot, Christian felt, was wrong, for the number of persons affected by masturbation was too low. Still, the focus remained on morality and compromised physical health. *Masturbation* also discusses Sigmund Freud (1856-1939). Stengers and Van Neck highlight Freud's warning about "a preponderance for a fantasy life over reality, a situation that forms a pattern for a number of other functions" (as quoted on p. 140). The three pages addressing Freud identify his ambivalence toward the practice but do not exhaust Freud's contribution.

One of the few references to looking at images surfaces in Stengers and Van Neck's (2001) discussion of *Scouting for Boys*, the 1914 manual by Robert Baden-Powell (1857-1941), who warned that "trashy books and looking at lewd pictures are very apt to lead a thoughtless boy into the temptation to self-abuse. This is the most dangerous thing for him, for should it become a habit, it quickly destroys both health and spirits" (as quoted on p. 146). *Scouting for Boys* was translated into many languages as the Boy Scouts moved from the United States across the globe. The attitudes of Baden-Powell, according to Stengers and Van Neck, remained in place until World War II, when cultural shifts regarding sexuality were documented in *The Kinsey Report* of 1948 (to be discussed in a following section). By 1972, research showed that the majority of persons no longer saw masturbation as physically detrimental or a personal sin, although religious doctrine persisted in seeing it as a moral failure, even as it was judged less harshly. *Masturbation* is a rich book tracing a large number of philosophers, educators, physicians, and theologians who created a culture that awakened terror around the practice of masturbation. With its emphasis on morality and physical health, the book rarely reflects on sexual fantasy and the use of images. The next book on the history of the practice, by Berkeley historian Thomas Laqueur, does pay significant attention to the role of the imagination.

Laqueur's (2003) *Solitary Sex: A Cultural History of Masturbation* is a tome of more than 500 pages. It primarily covers the period from the seventeenth century to the dawn of cyberspace, more or less the same period Stengers and Van Neck covered, but with more depth and detail. Laqueur shows that masturbation was not a primary issue in the ancient world but really came into focus in the 16th through 18th centuries. Laqueur too argues that the strong taboo against masturbation was driven by wealthy, progressive Enlightenment thinkers, not the religious powers of the day. For Laqueur, the date of a cultural shift around masturbation is "in or around 1712," when *Onania*—which he identifies as "masturbation's primal text" (p. 25)—was published. Coincidentally, 1712 is also the year Joseph Addison (1672–1719) published his essay "The Pleasures of the Imagination or Fancy." Addison, a poet and politician, declared: "Our imagination loves to be filled with an object... The mind of man naturally hates every thing that looks like restraint upon it and is apt to fancy itself under a confinement when the sight is pent up in a narrow compass.... Everything that is new or uncommon raises a pleasure in the imagination" (as quoted in Laqueur 2003, p. 318). Addison's quote, which seems timeless and drafted without knowledge of Marten's *Onania*, describes the trend that placed the imagination, seen as the negotiator between the senses and the mind, under suspicion, even though Addison attempted to elevate its importance.

Laqueur (2003) finds it ironic that, just as a profoundly individualistic culture came into being through the notion of morality as self-government and self-sufficiency—the self being "autarkic"—masturbation came into its own as a grave physical threat and moral failure. He identifies the imagination and sexual fantasy as one reason why masturbation became such an offense, as the act, always done secretly and excessively, was not rooted in reality. It is "the disconnected, imaginative, individualist, resolutely ahistorical qualities of masturbation" (p. 22) that continue to inform its taboo nature. The eternal challenge for masturbation, Laqueur identifies, remains how to have a relationship with oneself without losing a relationship with others.

Solitary Sex (Laqueur 2003) covers *religion* (Judaism and Christianity), *medicine* (Marten and Tissot as the main figures), *moral philosophy* (Rousseau), *pedagogy* (Kant), *psychogenesis* (Freud), *research* (Kinsey), and *gender studies* (Marie Bonaparte, Jill Johnson, and Betty Dobson). The book also addresses the pre-1712 era, looking at Greek mythology, early Judaism and Christianity, and Roman culture when masturbation was recognized but never seemed to be placed in anxious focus. For Laqueur, sexual fantasies or the role of the imagination never strays too far from any discussion of masturbation, for the passion that emanates from the imagination also must be managed by society. He references Kant on the imagination as representative of the general attitude toward masturbation and fantasy or the imagination:

> [It is unnatural] if a man is aroused . . . not by its real object, but by his imagination of this object, and so stray in a way contrary to the purpose of the desire, since he himself creates its object. For in this way the imagination brings forth an appetite contrary to nature's purpose . . . [or to the contract of mutual pleasure that is marriage]. (quoted in Laqueur 2003, p. 60)

Imagination—as "the theater of the mind"—serving the solitary vice is guilty of moral failure. The charge came easy due to the excesses of the imagination. Kant's thoughts are not much different from the Talmudic interpretation that views "imaginations [as] more injurious to health than the sin itself" (Laqueur 2003, p. 122). The danger and misuse of the imagination when it comes to masturbation remain tied, though after the *Kinsey Report* (1948) the attitudes of danger and misappropriation began to change.

In a chapter titled "The Problem with Masturbation," Laqueur (2003) discusses the intimate relationship between fantasy and masturbation. Especially during the Enlightenment, he suggests, masturbation and the social outcry against the act were "motivated not by a real object of desire but by a phantasm; masturbation threatened to overwhelm the most protean and potentially creative of the mind's faculties—the imagination—and to drive it over the cliff" (p. 210). By focusing on and even eradicating the act, the imagination could be saved. By calling on Freud to name the problem with masturbation, Laqueur also indicates that attitudes toward the imagination had not changed much between the 17th and the mid-19th centuries: "Masturbation contributes to the substitution of fantasy objects for reality" (p. 210). A belief during this enlightenment period was that the practice "heats" the imagination, which turns it into a dangerous idolatrous instrument. The problem, however, is difficult to solve, for the imagination, which is "voluptuous, fiery," is not easily constrained (p. 213). Since using the imagination during masturbation is a conscious act, the moral judgment on a person using his imagination in this way was severe. "Fictions and phantasms—the made-up, imagined, self-fashioned products of the mind—always at the ready, were the real villains of the piece," Laqueur concludes (p. 214).

One Enlightenment opponent of fantasy, the German physician Christoph Hufeland (1762–1836), felt that youth turned to self-pleasuring too early, causing them to postpone marriage. "The expansion of flaming of fantasy with all sorts of indecent and unworthy pictures," Hufeland stated, leads to "fantasy [being] armed and [it] takes over the whole being" (as quoted in Laqueur 2003, p. 215). Other opponents referred to the imagination as "the fatal rage of masturbation," able to excite all the organs, including emotion, and thereby claiming power over a person's life. Nocturnal emissions were less morally fraught than emissions that were weakened by the imagination. "That which sullied, that which transgressed, was no longer semen in all its sticky specificity, but rather the imagination reveling in desires of its own, unnatural creation" (Laqueur 2003, p. 216).

In the absence of a proper object for sexual intercourse, the imagination provided where reality failed. "The mind's eye," the English physician Alexander P. Buchan (1716–1824) declared, interferes with the normal "indulgence of sexual appetite [and causes the] evil consequences of this vicious habit" (as quoted in Laqueur 2003, p. 216). With few exceptions, European progressive intellectuals saw the imagination as a vice. Laqueur faults the Enlightenment for coming to a place of seeing the imagination in a completely different light compared to classical medicine, where someone such as Diogenes the Cynic (412–323 BCE) saw masturbating to one's imagination as the most efficient, dignified, and satisfying of practices, an act of much higher standing and causing less self-depletion than visiting with a prostitute. Not surprisingly, masturbation had its Enlightenment proponents too, in the person of John Hunter (1728–1793). Hunter, a British physician, stated that the only affliction persons had was reading the misinformation regarding "solitary friction." Hunter—in the tradition of Diogenes the Cynic—was adamant that "masturbation does less harm than the natural [act]" (as quoted in Laqueur 2003, p. 217). In the second and third editions of his book *A Treatise of the Venereal Diseases* (first published in 1786), however, Hunter's support of masturbation was edited out, and he merely questioned whether masturbation caused medical illness as popular belief dictated.

Laqueur (2003) also identifies Rousseau as the Enlightenment person who viewed masturbation's use of the imagination as "deceitful and counterfeit," a description he gives in his *Emile*. Furthermore, Rousseau argued that the imagination, an admirable faculty that should have fueled democratic values or economic products, was tainted by the solitary practice. "The onanist mobilized the imagination not to produce art and poetry or compassion; in fact he or she produced nothing at all or, worse, nothing but bottomless self-absorption at the expense of any possible social good" (Laqueur 2003, p. 221). As the nineteenth century approached, masturbation remained a problem because it was "*the* solitary vice," "*the* secret vice," and "antisocial." Laqueur (2003) refers to the secrecy of the act and its excesses as a threat to heterosexuality because the act establishes communities not under the control of any authorities.

In concluding his chapter "The Problem with Masturbation," Laqueur (2003) identifies two primary reasons for the negative evaluation of masturbation that spanned much of the 17th–19th centuries: First, "Anxiety about masturbation was an expression of anxiety about the new political economic order writ large on the body" (p. 280). The solitary vice undermined authoritarian systems. Second, print media became a prominent market player, and pornographic or antisocial material could not be controlled. Europe's social values were under threat. Erotic literature, sometimes referred to as "pillow books" or "books to be read with one hand," were popular. Paintings of nude virgins, sometimes masturbating while reading (*Midday Heat* by Emmanuel de Ghendt, *Solitary Pleasure* by Pierre-Antoine Baudouin, *The Dangerous Novel* by Isidore Stanislas Helman, and *Lonesome Pleasures* by Thomas Rowlandson would be examples), made it into print and into personal collections (Laqueur 2003). Society depended on the very media it feared. Laqueur summarizes the West's dilemma as follows: "Print culture, the essential communication network of civil society and the teacher of its most basic ways of being and feeling, depended on and encouraged precisely the qualities that made masturbation so threatening" (p. 303).

By the beginning of the twentieth century, illnesses were no longer ascribed to masturbation. Although medical understanding increased significantly, religious and moral values mostly resisted change. Rather, the attention shifted away from illness to guilt, neurosis, and personal failure. Viewing masturbation through the lens of "fantasy, excess, and secrecy on the one hand and incompleteness, falseness, and lack of sociability on the other" maintained culture's ambivalent relationship with the practice (Laqueur 2003, p. 365). Laqueur has a rich discussion of Freud on masturbation, which is outside the scope of this essay. Suffice it to say that Freud, in 1895, "argued that there was a specific *somatic*, depleting quality to masturbation that resulted in neurasthenia—nervous debility—and that this neurosis could be distinguished from *Angstneurose*, anxiety neurosis" (Laqueur 2003, p. 367). Freud, however, rejected a generalized view on masturbation, saying it had to be evaluated case by case. *Solitary Sex* also references Sándor Ferenczi (1873-1933), Freud's Hungarian colleague, who saw the imagination doing all the heavy lifting during masturbation as the other senses are "silent" during the practice, and this "work" causes the fatigue and debility the masturbator experiences. When one has sex with a partner, Ferenczi believed, the imagination could rest and the man would be "invigorated in the act" (Laqueur 2003, p. 219). Laqueur faults Freud and Ferenczi for not escaping the legacy of *Onania* and the Enlightenment's turn against masturbation. The views of Freud, Ferenczi, and other nineteenth-century psychoanalysts, however, did not have nearly the impact *Onania* and Tissot had on the general cultural attitudes towards masturbation. Rather, Laqueur (2003) argues that it was feminist scholars, including psychoanalysts such as Melanie Klein and Helen Deutsch and feminists such as Anne Koedt, Joan Garrity, and even Betty Dobson (who wrote *Sex for One: The Joy of Self-Loving*, published in 1995) who, in changing views of women's masturbation, changed masturbatory perceptions for men, too.

Laqueur does not discuss the late twentieth century in depth, a time in which computer technology forever changed the practice of masturbation. However, modern influences such as a new political order, printed media, globalization, the Internet, and the growth of social media is changing cultural values toward masturbation. Furthermore, religion and medicine have been stripped of their role as authorities in the postmodern world. This change is noticeable in the next history to be discussed, that of the Dutch urologist and sexologist Mels van Driel, who describes the pornification of masturbation.

Van Driel (2012), in his *With the Hand: A Cultural History of Masturbation*, explores his topic thematically. In this engaging book, he weaves together mythological, historical, biblical, religious, philosophical, and contemporary beliefs about masturbation. He discusses the attitudes toward the act within Christianity, Judaism, the Islamic tradition, and Taoism and addresses the demographics around masturbation, education, sex aids, doctors, scientists, writers, poets, artists, entertainment, and even animal masturbation.

Van Driel (2012) approaches his readers with humor and Dutch open-mindedness:

> In itself it stands to reason that the habit of masturbation can lead to passivity. But what's wrong with that? For many people an active, mutually satisfying sex life is bound up with self-esteem and hence far from idyllic. All in all, however, it is not a good idea for men to masturbate five times in quick succession. The seminal vesicles empty and finally all that comes out is a little liquid, or in the worst case, blood. Apart from that, after fourteen days of complete abstinence—no masturbation or coitus—the sperm will find their own way out via the urine. (p. 13–14).

Van Driel (2012) is the reverse incarnation of Tissot because he seeks to undo the taboo of masturbation. He takes physicians such as Tissot to task for the ways they influenced the Western mindset toward masturbation. Following Stenger, Van Neck, and Laqueur, Van Driel argues that much of masturbation's taboo serves "the creation of a perfect society" (p. 184). The concern during the 17th to 19th centuries was, in part, that if the wealthy masturbate, the poor, who fornicate, will outnumber the ruling class by larger numbers they already do. He addresses the relationship between fantasy, images, and masturbation when he writes, "Perhaps many persons masturbate with their loved one's image in front of them. So, isn't that love? A lesser kind of love? What is love?" (p. 14). Van Driel raises questions of what is real and whether masturbation helps or hinders the building of intimate relationships. The topic of whether or not masturbating is actually self-love still needs to be researched, Van Driel states, though he has doubts. Still, Van Driel appreciates fantasy and quotes research in which 42% of respondents masturbated to their own fantasies without using images. He identifies fantasy as central to masturbation and laments that "unfortunately, the role of fantasies is not given sufficient prominence in [educational] publications" (p. 27). As long as the emphasis remains on the genital and physical, Van Driel states, fantasies will be neglected. Fantasies, of course, do not always assist a person in reaching orgasm through masturbation. When they are traumatic fantasies or exclude the self, Van Driel sees a severing of the relationship between fantasies, well-being, and pleasure.

In his chapter "Artists," Van Driel (2012) discusses depictions, drawings, paintings, and etchings from the sixth century BCE to the twentieth century CE that depict persons masturbating. He does not discuss the images per se—which are reproduced in the book—but highlights the fact that masturbation has been a topic of interest to painters such as Rembrandt and Dali, and the artist Jordan McKenzie (who paints with sperm), and the photographer Serrano.

As Van Driel concludes his book, he turns to the use of pornography in the service of masturbation. He judges "the pornification of our society" harshly. The availability of pornography causes "masturbation addicts. Marriages break up because men creep out of bed at night, penis in hand, and sit in front of the computer," Van Driel attests (p. 236). Especially for young people, "Porn removes sex from the realm of human relationships and locates it purely in the genitalia and in mechanical movements" (p. 237). When masturbating to images replaces relationships, it fuels narcissism, leads to objectification, and cuts off the ties that bind people together. Education, Van Driel suggests, is the only approach to combat the use of pornography and to change the taboo of masturbation into the celebration of solitary sex.

As I conclude this brief look at three histories of masturbation, Western culture's deep ambivalence towards this universal practice remains intact. As sociologist Steve Garlick (2012) writes, the histories of masturbation and anti-masturbation are complex and can focus on procreation, heteronormativity, social order, religion, morality, philosophy, notions of the body, scientific knowledge, capitalism, film, ethics, and medicine, to name but a few approaches. Yet, the common theme is one of moral judgment and a call to revisit our relationship with an intimate practice. The research of Brett Kahr on the sexual fantasies of contemporary Brits, arguably more than anybody else, addresses not only the proliferation of masturbatory practices but also the role of fantasy. His work is discussed next.

BRETT KAHR AND MEN'S SEXUAL FANTASIES

"The central masturbatory fantasy ... provides the most important insights into the core of the human mind," writes research therapist and London-based analyst Brett Kahr (2007, p. 76). Our sexual fantasies indicate who we are. Kahr surveyed more than 19,000 men and women as part of the British Sexual Fantasy Research Project. His research was first published in *Sex and the Psyche: Revealing the True Nature of Our Secret Fantasies from the Largest Ever Survey of Its Kind* (Kahr 2007) and reprinted in revised form as *Who's Been Sleeping in Your Head? The Secret World of Sexual Fantasies* (Kahr 2008). I will draw on *Sex and the Psyche* unless otherwise indicated. Most of the fantasies in the book were given by the respondents in the survey, but some are also from Kahr's case material. The fantasies were reported online, some written down and sent to him and others recorded as an audio file.

Kahr himself interviewed hundreds of persons. He warns his readers that the fantasies—from ordinary Brits of all standings and religions who lived "a reasonably healthy life"—shock, disgust, titillate, and arouse even to the point of climax. Here, the focus will not be on the fantasies per se—revealing as they are—but rather on what Kahr learnt about *the nature, role, and function, even the importance of sexual fantasies*. Kahr, identifying with Theodor Reik, states he listens to fantasies with his "third ear . . . concentrating not only on what the patient says, but also on what the patient does not say, attempting at all times to decipher the secret meanings of the patient's dilemmas, meanings which remain obscure even to the patient" (2007, p. xix).

"Sexual fantasies," Kahr (2007) writes, "can serve not only as a source of deep pleasure, but also as a cause for great shame. Often our fantasies will stimulate both excitement and revulsion simultaneously, and this produces a great deal of psychological turmoil" (p. xxiii). Living between orgasms and despair and between pleasure and pain or even disgust—often fueled by a singular fantasy—Kahr's patients reveal that sexual fantasies are deeply rooted in their lives. Reflecting on fantasizing about someone else other than one's partner, he writes that "we do not yet have a sufficiently clear idea about whether our fantasies may be good for us; they may, in fact, induce the most potent of orgasms . . . [but might fantasies about someone else] indicate that our relationship at home might be in trouble?" (2007, p. xxvii).

Sex and the Psyche opens by telling of Jasper, who ritually masturbates to videos of women boxing "Mohammed Ali-style." Like many, Jasper's inner life is "dominated by . . . a perplexing sexual fantasy," now mirrored back to him from a screen, which awakens "shame and suffering about his internal world" (Kahr 2007, p. 9). When Jasper does have sex with his model girlfriend, he does so with the lights off and fantasizing about boxing women. Having introduced Jasper, Kahr (2007) raises significant questions about sexual fantasies:

> What is a sexual fantasy? What constitutes a "normal" fantasy? Why do we have sexual fantasies in the first place? What purpose or purposes do our sexual fantasies serve? . . . If we fantasize about someone other than our partners during sex or masturbation, does that mean that our relationship might be in trouble? . . . Is there a difference between the fantasies that we have during sex with a partner and the fantasies that we indulge in during private masturbation? Do we control our fantasies, or do our fantasies control us? (p. 9–10)

"I have come to the conclusion," Kahr (2007) writes, "that a significant majority of adults maintains a most uncomfortable relationship with their private sexual fantasies, in spite of the fact that most fantasies culminate in orgasm" (p. 11) a dynamic he calls "the masturbatory paradox." This paradox might be the *first* truth to be accepted in reflecting on sexual fantasies and is fueled, in part, by the fact that one may not know the person "who *has been sleeping in your head*," the person being masturbated to or who becomes the fantasy partner during sex (p. 12).

In laying the foundation for his book, Kahr (2007) normalizes sexual fantasies: "I regard our sexual fantasies as completely normative experiences, which develop from our earliest infantile fantasy capacities and become increasingly sexualized as we progress through the life cycle" (p. 25). By its very nature, a fantasy is always transformed and invested with personal desires and pleasures. He also provides a brief synopsis of "the sexperts," primarily analysts who have reflected on sexual fantasies. He identifies Heinrich van Kaan, a German physician, who in 1844 published *Psychopathia Sexualis*, a book on the mental pathologies of human sexuality. Like Tissot, Van Kaan held grave concerns about masturbation, which he saw as a sexual perversion, especially since it was often tied to fantasy. Kahr also names the Austrian psychiatrist and professor Richard von Krafft-Ebing, whose *Eine klinisch-forensische Studie* (*A Clinical Forensic Study;* published in 1886) was more liberal than van Kaan's. Von Krafft-Ebing writes about a man with masochistic fantasies he had entertained since childhood but found very dissatisfying when he enacted them with a prostitute. Since sexual fantasies follow masturbation and vice versa, he referred to fantasies as "psychical onanism" and launched the discipline of sexual fantasy studies. "Psychical onanism," Von Krafft-Ebing believed, is more prevalent in those with masochistic traits.

Freud, who met Von Krafft-Ebing at conferences, is the next person Kahr (2007) discusses. Freud qualified in medicine at the University of Vienna in 1886, just as von Krafft-Ebing's work was published. Freud's argument for a connection between early childhood experiences and neurotic illness was not well received by Von Krafft-Ebing, who called it "a scientific fairy tale" (Kahr 2007, p. 28). Freud, of course, continued with his research and argued that all people have erotic and violent fantasies and urges. Kahr reminds us that in his *Three Essays on the History of Sexuality* (published in 1905), Freud identified a relationship between "perverse" sexuality (sucking, biting, and licking) and infantile experiences of the breast, thereby legitimizing foreplay. Not surprisingly, Kahr sees Freud as the first to explore the origins of sexual fantasies and how they relate to a person's early life, especially the life around mother and father. Still, Freud "regarded much of human sexual functioning as degenerate" (Kahr 2007, p. 29). Freud's contribution, according to Kahr, was showing that sexual fantasies "serve as the fulfillment of primitive, unbearable wishes, and that sexual fantasies also protect the mind from often even more uncomfortable thoughts" (p. 29). Later, Freud linked sexual fantasies to mental turmoil, writing in his essay "Creative Writers and Day-Dreaming" that "we may lay it down that a happy person never phantasies, only an unsatisfied one. The motive forces of phantasies are unsatisfied wishes, and every single phantasy is the fulfillment of a wish, a correction of unsatisfying reality" (as quoted in Kahr 2007, p. 33).

Kahr (2007) interprets Freud's famous statement, "I am accustoming myself to the idea of regarding every sexual act as a process in which four persons are involved," as meaning that Freud had the male and female elements of a person in mind or that every lover fantasizes about someone else during sex. The latter scenario Kahr identifies as "the intra-marital affair," which is a separate chapter in *Whose Been Sleeping in Your Head?* (Kahr 2008). Before Freud's death in 1939, Freud wrote of a man whose only path to sexual arousal was fantasizing about his mother *and* father (Kahr 2007). Still, sexual fantasy, Kahr concludes, was never a primary focus for Freud. For Kahr, who appreciates Freud more than Laqueur does, Freud's work initiated a more humanist understanding of sexuality and sexual fantasy.

The final "sexpert" Kahr addresses is Alfred Charles Kinsey, the Indiana University sexologist who published *Sexual Behavior in the Human Male* in 1948. Kinsey had recently returned from World War II when he exposed the subterranean sexuality of the American male after interviewing 12,000 males. He also opened interest in the sexuality of women after he published *Sexual Behavior of the Human Female* in 1953. Kinsey's work initiated the academic study of sexuality in the United States.

In a chapter called "The Science of Psychological Fingerprints," Kahr (2007) explores different aspects of sexual fantasies beyond the masturbatory paradox. He argues for the normalcy of sexual fantasies: "I would regard the capacity to fantasize as completely normal. . . . In fact, I would be extremely concerned if I met a patient who could not fantasize, as this might indicate an impoverishment of mental functioning" (p. 15). His research also indicates that "technological distractions do not prevent fantasy; in many cases [digital images or videos] will inflame fantasy" (p. 16). Jude's case, discussed earlier, would be an example of this statement. For many of Kahr's subjects, sexual fantasies, which can be conscious or unconscious, promise "escape from the confining strictures of ordinary reality" (p. 15). Serving as a specific kind of daydream, fantasies are also vulnerable to one's specific contexts and relationships. Most often, however, desires and needs that resist awareness drive our fantasies. If the unconscious fantasy is one of self-destruction, as was the case for a number of Kahr's patients, self-sabotage permeates their lives, but they remain unaware how this dynamic determines much of their lives.

Furthermore, sexual fantasy can be simple and brief or elaborate, with an intricate or complicated narrative, and it can be entertained with or without the aid of mind-altering substances such as alcohol, marijuana, or other drugs or sex toys (Kahr 2007). There might be a single person in one's fantasy or there might be a great many, the latter more likely causing one to feel "perverted," Kahr writes. Kahr's subjects entertained sexual fantasies at all hours of the day, outside or during sexual intercourse and exploration and when alone or with others. Some of the fantasies were very personal—and thus rarely appealing to someone else and best not shared—or imbedded in cultural and historical behavior. Some reflected mild "vanilla sex" whereas others were extreme forms of sadomasochism, violence, and perversion. Kahr distinguishes "pub fantasies," those fantasies we'll readily share with friends, from fantasies that remain private. One might share how one would like to make love to the person across the bar but not reveal one's homosexual fantasies. The more disturbing the fantasies are, the less likely we are to share them with others. Some persons return to the same fantasy or structure (dominance or fetish)—such as the "central masturbation fantasy," as Jude showed—whereas "others utilize a broader variety of different fantasies" that may include persons, animals, objects, and places (Kahr 2007, p. 22). In addition, Kahr illustrates how people's fantasy lives can be fixed, rigid, predictable, and even logical or more fluid, plastic, open to new experiences, or even illogical, with those traits being the poles of a very large spectrum. Some men only fantasize about their partner, some never about their partner; some men will have sexual relations with women only but fantasize exclusively about males.

Psychodynamically, these fantasies serve many purposes, which are evident in the numerous case discussions Kahr (2007) provides. Some people fantasize to repair narcissistic wounds; to hide concerns of genital or bodily inadequacy; to allow for the exploration of latent homosexual wishes; to recreate pleasurable or painful childhood or sexual experiences (which are then incorporated, disguised, and transformed); to reflect the nature of the caregiving received in infancy and childhood; or to voyeuristically reflect on the parents' bedroom—the Oedipal crisis. Giving his readers a summary of the functions of sexual fantasies, Kahr identifies fourteen meanings of sexual fantasies in a chapter with the same title. The meanings are wish-fulfillment, self-comfort and self-medication, trial action and experimentation (of personal and sexual identities), elaboration of childhood play, establishment of object relationships, transitional objects and transitional phenomena (symbolic mothering), communication of inner unconscious or unanalyzed conflict, indulgence in masochistic punishment, defenses against intimacy and merger, discharge of aggression, avoidance of painful reality (by using aspirational wishes), evacuation of sadistic strivings, mastering trauma (as well as shame and loss), and establishing equilibration of the self (as part of the capacity for creativity). Kahr (2007) warns that "we cannot ever attain absolute certainly in our psychological detective work [about the meanings of sexual fantasies], instead, we present *hypotheses* to our patients, so that we can use the observations as a starting point for a psychotherapeutic conversation" (p. 380). We are best reminded that fantasies originate in '*biography*' and not in a person's '*bloodstream*,' genetic make-up, or hormone levels" (p. 435).

After discussing some of the key figures on sexual fantasy and the key findings of his research project, Kahr (2007) turns to a discussion of specific sexual practices, including masturbation. Even though the medical profession deems the practice "a perfectly reasonable, pleasurable and normal form of sexual self-expression and self-pleasuring," he writes, "psychotherapists and psychoanalysts have long known that masturbation may also serve some more defensive and complicated functions for the human being" (p. 79). The practice, first discovered by the infant, is practiced by 97% of males and 87% of females, and it is practiced equally across race, religion and class. As a "positive" practice,

> masturbation can provide bodily pleasure, reduce depression, stress or anxiety, facilitate sleep, be used as an erotically arousing adjunct during lovemaking with one's partner, help to prevent the spread of sexually transmitted diseases, provide a vehicle in which loving fantasy can be utilized and so much more . . . Furthermore, masturbation may serve as a source for sexual release for the widowed, the handicapped, the celibate, or anyone else who does not have access to a regular sexual partner. It may even be a means of indulging in fantasies which one could not, would not or perhaps should not enact with one's regular partner or partners. (Kahr 2007, p. 80)

Kahr, as if reflecting on a reason a man can give for masturbating, says the idea that the emission of semen prevents prostate cancer is yet to be fully proven.

Highlighting the role and function of masturbation in ordinary lives, Kahr, as Wilson does, points out masturbation's addictive potential, which can minimize the potential of finding a real partner. Furthermore, it may lead to "the reinforcement of dangerous or sexually perverse fantasies," as is true for many pedophiles masturbating to the images of minors (Kahr 2007, p. 80). Sadistic and perverse fantasies can also induce guilt and shame, and being deemed a "wanker" is almost always an insult, not a compliment. Wondering why men tend to masturbate more often than women, Kahr suggests that men have a less complicated relationship with their external genitalia compared to women. Whereas a man touches his penis to urinate from a young age and many times a day, women can urinate without touching their "internal genitals." Psychodynamically, some men masturbate to unconsciously see if their genitals—forever vulnerable—are still there (p. 81). The act resists castration fear.

Not surprisingly, Kahr's research also indicates a strong relationship between pornography and masturbation. Eighty-seven percent of males and 56% of females in Kahr's study have used pornography to stimulate sexual arousal and increase sexual experience. Virtual content is fueling masturbatory practices. One reason Kahr identifies is that "the vast proportion of males would claim not to have had a fully satisfying sexual experience without achieving orgasm; and many, though certainly not all, women would agree" (Kahr 2007, p. 93). Pornography and masturbating to orgasm provide satisfaction and release.

Kahr's work is important because it offers a deeper understanding of the paradox and complex nature of sexual fantasies. The chapters after "The Science of Psychological Fingerprints"—discussed in the preceding paragraphs—focus on the varied ways the British practice their sexuality. Some fantasies are depictions of straight sex, others focus on gay sex; some fantasies are with known persons, but the majority of fantasies include strangers; some are fantasies of solitary activities, others include groups or crowds. Fifty-eight percent of the men in Kahr's study fantasized having sex with more than one person (p. 167). Some fantasies include persons, other fantasies include things or objects or demand a certain context; some fantasies seem normal, others are dirty; some fantasies speak of love and romance, others of domination, penetration, humiliation, power, and control. Persons perceived to be predominantly ordinary have fantasies across this wide spectrum. "We notice," Kahr (2007) writes, "not only the wide range of content, revealing the breadth of secret sexual thoughts, but also an extraordinary diversity in terms of style" (p. 117).

Kahr writes that, in his experience, therapists and counselors typically view sexual fantasies in one of six ways: (1) fantasies are the products of deeply disturbed minds and traumatized persons; (2) fantasies are not serious compared to those who violate others sexually, as in rape, for example; (3) fantasies are symptoms of unresolved aggressive conflicts that will impact everyday living; (4) fantasies are symptoms of unresolved aggressive impulses that remain tied to inner worlds; (5) fantasies are potentially creative ways to deal with life and powerful emotions such as aggression; and (6) some therapists are caught between their desire to address pathology and their open-mindedness and compassion related to matters of sexual and personal experience (p. 388).

Kahr's (2007) work beckons us to understand ourselves more deeply, a task that is unlikely to happen if we do not explore the unconscious fantasies and their wish fulfillments that fuel our masturbatory practices. When we ritually and compulsively seek image upon image with increased intensity, as Jude did, one can even argue that the eye has replaced fantasy as a source of stimulation. It is not surprising that Kahr, towards the end of his book, briefly discusses the impact of online pornography on the fantasy lives of persons (p. 515). He describes the use of pornographic images as "an area of growing concern" and "a troubling and preoccupying issue" (p. 515). The case Kahr discusses of a couple in their 30s who were rarely intimate shows the destruction that unfolded when the husband first denied masturbating but then got caught red-handed, asleep in front of graphic, sadistic pornography. Much courageous work led the couple back to sexual relations that were life-giving to both in the partnership. Whereas Kahr's work highlights the prevalence and passion of ordinary persons' fantasy lives, this chapter asks what happens to a male who primarily masturbates to images, even if those images serve an unconscious fantasy. What happens when the "mental infidelity" and the "intra-marital affair," as Kahr identifies cheating on one's partner in one's imagination or with pornography, are reinforced by *visual infidelity*, the inevitable result of pornography (p. 138–139)? The eye and the ritual of looking at a screen mandate revisiting the role of the eye in human nature (and sexuality). I will do so by following the thought of Michael Taussig, who explores the eye within mimetic desire.

THE EYE AS THE ORGAN OF TACTILITY

The eye has eclipsed fantasy. Furthermore, sexual fantasies now rely on the eye for their own stimulation. Whereas the eye seeks constant stimulation, the fantasies in Kahr's study show that they are especially sustained by and tied to early—and often traumatic—life experiences. The mind typically does not rapid-fire through fantasies to build arousal. Rather, it usually returns to a familiar (or even the same) mental picture, which is slowly built. In addition, it seems as if the eye has bound the hand. The hand, now serving the eye, swipes a screen for minutes or even hours on end as the perfect image is sought to briefly touch a penis to orgasm. In the language of philosopher Michael Taussig (1993, p. 20), the eye is "the organ of tactility."

In his *Mimesis and Alterity* (1993), Taussig argues that culture is built on two opposing but intimately connected dynamics: imitation and difference. Human beings seek to take nature and build a second nature that is alike yet dissimilar. We copy, especially through our tools and machines, but do so imperfectly. Creating social constructions through our mimetic capacities, we seek to invigorate life with what Taussig calls "the true real" (p. xvii). We know, however, that there is a difference between "the real and the really made-up," yet we continue to live as if what is real and what we create are the same. The only way to proceed, Taussig states, is to "retreat to the unmentionable world of active forgetting" as we "marvel at [mimesis'] wonder or fume at its duplicity" (p. xvii). We'd rather forget the original experiences that now seek mimetic replication. An in-depth discussion of Taussig's fascinating work, in which he draws extensively on the work of Walter Benjamin but includes numerous anthropological studies, lies outside the scope of this essay. His construct of "the eye as the organ of tactility," however, is instructive for this project.

The Cuna Indians of Panama's San Blas Islands created shamanistic curing icons and protective spirits—*nuchus*—in the shape of their Spanish colonizers. This fact has intrigued anthropologists, as the colonizers brought nothing but disease and destruction. After reflecting on the Cuna Indians, Taussig (1993) turns to the eye. In a chapter entitled "Physiognomic Aspects of Visual Worlds," Taussig begins with a 1933 quote from Walter Benjamin: "[Man's] gift for seeing is nothing other than a rudiment of the powerful compulsion in former times to become and behave like something else. Perhaps there is none of his higher functions in which his mimetic faculty does not play a decisive role" (as quoted in Taussig 1993, p. 19). The eye, Taussig suggests as he follows Benjamin, is the organ by which we not only "other" an object or a person—we also use the eye to become someone else. We mimic to return to a primitive state, to a time and place where we lived a simpler, ritualized life that made more sense.

"Every day the urge grows stronger to get hold of an object at very close range by way of its likeness, its reproduction," Taussig (1993) quoting Benjamin (p. 20). Mimesis not only *copies* but creates *contact*, a "palpable, sensuous connection between the very body of the perceiver and the perceived" (p. 21. The eye, more so than the other organs, is used to build contact. The advertising world knows this best and readily exploits the eye's power. Through the eye, the intricate relationship between producer, laborer, and product that Karl Marx highlighted is severed. Taussig does not address masturbation or pornography, but drawing on his thought, one can say that the eye creates the contact between a man, his digital screen, and a pornographic image that serves deeper desires. We use our eyes to touch and be touched. Fantasy, which can play a similar function, becomes work when one can swipe one image after the next.

"The organ of tactility" is an optical analogy used not only to describe how mimesis functions but also to serve what Benjamin refers to as "the optical unconscious," that world we mimetically long for (Taussig 1993, p. 24). Film, Taussig shows, often portrays the optical unconscious, a new subject-object relation that serves mimetic desire. Men, for example, who will never cry in real life may shed tears while watching a movie. Specifically, the construct implies a world in which personal experience is diminished and dominated by the images that are being perceived. Returning to his discussion of Marx and the eye breaking the production cycle, Taussig (1993) broadens his picture of the optical unconscious world, a world in which production has "the increasingly modest role of the hand" and in which "the constellation of the eye, hand and soul, is torn apart by the division of labor" (p. 36). Taussig reflects that as machines manufacture, the product dominates both the creator and the laborer alike.

We minimize the stronghold of the eye as the organ of tactility by insisting "on breaking away from the tyranny of the visual notion of image" (Taussig 1993, p. 57). Identifying the West as disembodied, Taussig references Amazonian healers whose healing is always embodied and filled with sensual (and non-visual) stimuli, whether it is singing, dancing, smelling, inducing nausea (which Taussig characterizes as "untheorized territory"), or leaving the body as spirit. It is by focusing on the body, on the senses that can awaken "interior images," and on the non-visual that a person can break the power of the eye, Taussig suggests (p. 58). Of course, this break is not easily navigated because the image sensorizes or stimulates the body too much, as masturbating to pornography teaches us.

The eye as the organ of tactility, considering our discussion thus far, informs this project in at least six ways. *First*, Taussig persuasively argues that the eye is the organ of tactility. We touch ourselves not by the hand but with our eyes. When the touching eye is placed in the context of masturbating to pornography, the insatiable nature of desire meets an infinite source. The self can consume image upon image and rarely tires, even if the life holding the eye is filled with despair and is depleted.

Second, the eye serves the desire to be or to become someone else. As it serves imitation, the eye forgets the difference inherent to mimetic desire. Specifically, the eye creates the illusion of relationship, desirability, control, sexual omnipotence, and potency. Although the desire to be someone else is natural, the eye rarely delivers on this promise of alterity. The powerful, mimetic relationship one experiences with the image is not the same as a relationship such as the one Woods (2015) had with Jude, where each person was recognized in deep mutuality. Rather, mimetic relationships with online images lead to isolation and alienation.

Third, just as photos and film awaken an optical unconsciousness, pornography too awakens a world where relationship is promised, where pleasure is always available, where boredom never exists and stimulation is a mere click or swipe away. As Kahr (2007) showed, masturbating to sexual images can serve unconscious memories and desires. The mimetic magic of optical unconsciousness can be understood in a variety of ways, whether religious, economic, or psychodynamic. The fourteen meanings of sexual fantasies Kahr identifies, whether self-comfort and self-medication or trial action and experimentation, and the establishment of object relationships or communication of inner conflict, describe the optical unconsciousness of masturbating to pornography.

A *fourth* way Taussig's work informs this project is the acknowledgment that there is a difference between mental images internally created and images (or imitations) internalized from outside sources. A man masturbating to personal fantasies deeply linked to his repressed unconscious, for example, rarely becomes bored of those images, whereas the images found online easily lose their titillation and the eye will seek images more explicit, vile, or violent, as the above discussion on the neuroplasticity of the brain also indicates.

Fifth, the organ of tactility facilitates and engages in touch. Mimesis not only copies but also creates contact. The physical touch of a screen or a mouse as images are being consumed, the "foreplay" that precedes masturbation to pornography, gives new meaning to touching oneself. This touch can be so profound that the question can be raised on the difference between "the true real" and "the real and the really made-up" (Taussig 1993, p. xvii). The eye as the organ of tactility entices but never remains focused on an object too long. Doing just that, focusing on an object—even a pornographic one—may break the power of the eye as the urge to seek a new image is resisted. Also, being mindful—to encourage emotional regulation and minimize disembodied masturbation—may change one's masturbatory practices (Reid et al. 2014; Reid et al. 2011).

And *sixth*, Taussig shows how mimesis leads to forgetting, as demonstrated by the Cuna Indians' puzzling creation of healing icons in the image of the very colonizers who had destroyed their way of living and who had introduced catastrophic illnesses. As the relationship between the eye, the hand, and the penis deepens, so too may the repression of the original experiences that gave content to one's sexual fantasies strengthen. One can also expect a repressed person to be more defensive when challenged on the role and function of masturbating to pornographic images in the service of certain fantasies.

Taussig's work, when combined with Kahr's, broadens our understanding of masturbating to pornographic images, even if those images serve deeply personal fantasies. "The wonder of mimesis," Taussig (1993) writes, "lies in the copy drawing on the character and power of the original, to the point whereby the representation may even assume that character and power" (p. vxii). As Woods already indicated in his discussion of Jude, "the original" can be understood in terms of D. W. Winnicott's capacity to be alone. In the remainder of this chapter, I return to Kahr's (2007) work as I ask, When does masturbating to pornography become an addictive and thus life-depriving practice?

WHEN THE EYE DOMINATES OVER FANTASIES

The history of masturbation shows that images, whether mental or in print, are inherent to its practice. In today's Internet culture, the eye reigns supreme. Brett Kahr's research shows that sexual fantasies are a normal part of almost all persons' sexual (including masturbatory) practices. He names, with great concern, the prevalence of pornography and notes that images can ruin lives and relationships. In a chapter called "Normality and Perversion in the Bedroom and the Boardroom," Kahr (2007) asks, "Is your fantasy perverse?" In light of the severe moral judgment masturbation has received in history, however, it is important for us not to hear the question as a moral judgment on a normal behavior. Using the term "disordered"—rather than "perversion"—to describe masturbation that depletes personal well-being can help us move beyond the moral connotations of being "perverse." Still, talking about the dangers of masturbating to pornography does awaken images of Tissot and his message of doom, even as clinicians and researchers are unanimous in recognizing life-depriving elements in some masturbatory practices.

Reflections on how the *Diagnostic and Statistical Manual for Mental Disorders* (5th ed.; *DSM-5*; American Psychiatric Association 2013) identify addiction and recent discussions on hypersexuality as a disorder are informative. The *DSM-V* frames addiction as "impaired control, social impairment, risky use, and pharmacological criteria," the latter speaking to increased tolerance (APA 2013, p. 516). This framework may inform our discussion better than the criteria for paraphilic disorders, which address voyeurism, exhibitionism, frotteurism, masochism, sadism, pedophilia, fetishism, and transvestic disorder, even as these disorders also cause distress or impairment.

A proposal to include "hypersexual disorder" in the *DSM-V* was unsuccessful despite clinicians' arguments in favor of its inclusion (Kafka 2010, 2014; Reid 2015). Rory Reid, a psychologist and sex researcher from the University of California Los Angeles, played a significant role in proposing the inclusion of hypersexual disorder in the *DSM-V*. He admits that the topic of hypersexual behavior is in its infancy. He defines the disorder as "a repetitive and intense preoccupation with sexual fantasies, urges, and behaviors, leading to adverse consequences and clinically significant distress or impairment in social, occupational, or other important areas of functioning" (Reid 2015, p. 221). Reid's definition supports my argument that masturbating to images can be disordered. A defining feature of hypersexual disorder is "multiple unsuccessful attempts to control or diminish the amount of time an individual engages in sexual fantasies, urges, and behavior in response to dysphoric mood states or stressful life events" (ibid.). However, looking at symptoms only and counting those to assess severity, Reid warns, is not an effective way to measure disorder because it assumes that a single criterion is equal to other criteria. Time spent serving the disorder, Reid argues, is also not an effective measure of severity. Masturbating "once a week for 15 minutes might not be considered excessive or problematic whereas sex with an extra-dyadic partner outside a monogamous committed relationship once a week for 15 minutes is likely both problematic and excessive," Reid writes (ibid.).

Martin Kafka, a psychiatrist and fellow sex researcher, joined Reid in arguing for the inclusion of hypersexuality disorder in the *DSM-V* (Kafka 2010, 2014). Kafka, however, mentions "persisting general criticisms that the proposed revision potentially would add many new diagnoses that pathologize normal behaviors, including sexual behavior" and provide "a medicalized excuse for immoral conduct" as additional reasons why hypersexuality disorder was excluded from the *DSM-V* (Kafka 2014, p. 1259. Questions were also raised as to whether hypersexuality is a behavioral and non-substance-related addiction (such as gambling) or a sexual disorder (Kor et al. 2013). The lack of consensus on symptoms, frequency, and risk and the insufficient empirical and epidemiological research led to hypersexuality disorder not being included in the *DSM-V* as a distinct clinical syndrome.

Still, the proposed criteria (excluded from the current *DSM-V*) for hypersexuality disorder are helpful because the criteria can also be used to assess disordered masturbation:

A. Over a period of at least six months, recurrent and intense sexual fantasies, sexual urges, and sexual behavior in association with four or more of the following five criteria:

   1. Excessive time is consumed by sexual fantasies and urges, and by planning for and engaging in sexual behavior.
   2. Repetitively engaging in these sexual fantasies, urges, and behavior in response to dysphoric mood states (e.g., anxiety, depression, boredom, irritability).
   3. Repetitively engaging in sexual fantasies, urges, and behavior in response to stressful life events.
   4. Repetitive but unsuccessful efforts to control or significantly reduce these sexual fantasies, urges, and behavior.
   5. Repetitively engaging in sexual behavior while disregarding the risk for physical or emotional harm to self or others.

B. There is clinically significant personal distress or impairment in social, occupational or other important areas of functioning associated with the frequency and intensity of these sexual fantasies, urges, and behavior.

C. These sexual fantasies, urges, and behavior are not due to direct physiological effects of exogenous substances (e.g., drugs of abuse or medications), a co-occurring general medical condition, or to manic episodes.

D. The person is at least 18 years of age.
   Specify if: Masturbation, Pornography, Sexual Behavior With Consenting Adults, Cybersex, Telephone Sex, Strip Clubs. (Reid 2015, p. 222)

Kahr (2007) can inform this discussion, too, as he draws on the work of British psychiatrist Estela Welldon, a specialist in forensic psychotherapy. Although Welldon writes about "perversion" and I prefer to use "disordered," masturbating to pornography does lead to addictive behavior and personal and relational alienation (Kahr 2007, pp. 534–535). Welldon's work, in addition to the *DSM-V* criteria for addictions, provides an additional framework that can inform a conversation between a therapist and a client to discern whether masturbation has become disordered or not. We can deduce the following criteria for disordered masturbation:

Impaired Control

- The person masturbates to pornography.
- He masturbates without mindfulness.
- He masturbates compulsively and repetitively.
- He experiences an urge or intense desire to masturbate.
- He sees his own actions as bizarre or inexplicable.
- He spends much time accumulating and curating images.
- He has unsuccessfully tried to stop the practice.
- He carries significant guilt feelings or has no feelings about the practice.

Social Impairment

- Shows little regard for his own emotional and relational well-being.
- He treats others as objects, rather than as people.
- Masturbatory practices keep the person from seeking or initiating intimacy with a partner.
- He is increasingly lonely and isolated, without any close friends.
- He shows little concern for the women in the images.
- Masturbating to pornography is done in secrecy and leads to a life of deceit.
- He uses masturbation as the only way to release pent-up social and sexual anxieties.

Risky Use

- He is generally unable to mourn early losses or to address trauma, which may have contributed to the seeking of pornographic images.
- He uses masturbating to pornography to self-medicate an underlying depressive state.
- He masturbates in public spaces or settings where others can expose the act.
- The practice is complemented by stalking behavior or interpersonal violence.

- The practices interfere with other areas of life, such as being a professional or being economically responsible.

Increased tolerance (the need for more extreme images)

- Disturbing images of increased humiliation, violence, or dysfunction are needed to achieve or sustain arousal (sadism and masochism).

The challenge masturbators, clinicians, and researchers alike face is knowing whether masturbating to pornography is disordered or not. It is very likely that the next iteration of the *DSM* will include a category of hypersexuality or a similar disorder. Until then, conversation between a clinician and a client needs to suffice. The patient Jude, in working with Woods (2015), came to understand that his behavior was outside the parameters of normalcy. Still, cause and effect are not easily determined here. It does seem, however, that masturbating to pornography easily escalates to the point where it becomes a concern.

Kahr (2007) provides a case of disordered masturbation similar to Jude's case. Julius is a man in his late 70s who has been masturbating twice daily since his mid-teens. Julius has had the same fantasy his entire life: He ties up the teenage girl who rejected him in real life and sadistically rapes her in fantasy while masturbating to great orgasmic pleasure. Julius has dated intermittently for more than 50 years but has been unable to sustain a relationship with any woman. "Many men have aggressive fantasies about women," Kahr writes, "but the vast majority manage also to make love to their female partners in tender and sensitive ways, thereby offering evidence of a more adaptable, creative erotic love. But in Julius' case, the fantasies became so compelling that they may well have prevented him from becoming more intimate" (2007, p. 536).

With the dawn of Internet pornography, sexual fantasy and masturbation—inherent parts of human sexuality—have gained the potential to destroy lives and relationships. Pastoral psychotherapists, in particular, can help persons with their understanding of behavior that is natural.

CONCLUSION

"And if your right eye causes you to fall into sin, tear it out and throw it away. It's better that you lose a part of your body than that your whole body be thrown into hell" (Matt 5:29 CEB) is an intriguing verse. Over the past

2000 years, men have defied this text. Men do not cut off their penises or pursue lobotomies (if one accepts that we truly have sex in our brains). One would think that "psychical onanism" (Von Krafft-Ebing's term) would lead persons of faith to entertain castration, blindness, or even traumatic brain injuries. Yet, men who self-abuse do not self-mutilate. Despite parents who might threaten their son by saying "I will cut off your Willy if you touch it again . . .," men show another logic in their relationship with their penises.

Pastoral theologians and psychologists need to remain curious about this intimate practice. Masturbation might be the most common form of relaxation for persons who are stressed by their private, relational, and professional lives (Rosewarne 2014). This arguably includes the majority of teenagers and adults. Relaxation and escape from the stresses of life not only *sustain* a person but also *prevent* destructive coping mechanisms. Lester, played by Kevin Spacey in Jinks et al. (1999) *American Beauty*, validates this argument as he speaks to a co-worker: "My job consists of masking my contempt for the assholes in charge, and at least once a day retiring to the men's room so I can jerk off while I fantasize about a life that doesn't so closely resemble hell" (Quoted in Weeks 2015, p. 50). Lester describes the ambiguity of being enslaved by a specific economy and free at the same time. The enslavement that comes from watching pornography, however, is qualitatively different from what Lester experienced. This demands that we continually explore the intimate relationship between the eye and fantasy and their respective roles in masturbation. When Lester had to defend himself for masturbating when his wife Carolyn (played by Annette Benning) caught him in the act, he was fantasizing about Angela (the teenage daughter of a friend played by Mena Suvari). Internet pornography was not his practice.

When masturbation is dissociated from sexual desire and fantasy, the role and function of the act changes. Woods (2015) showed in his work with Jude that a significant relationship, one in which a form of reparenting can occur and meaning can be explored, can empower a person to deepen his relationship with self and other. Fantasy returned to Jude as images began to disappear. Kahr's (2007) research similarly indicates the thin line where fantasy and pleasure crosses over into compulsion and disorder. Masturbation plays a central role in the formation of a boy's or man's identity. Doing so with a rich fantasy life continues a tradition that spans millennia.

In this chapter, masturbation is described as a *practice*. Pastoral and especially practical theologians have identified the importance of religious practices in recent years (Bass and Copeland 2010; Conner 2011; Doehring 2015; Dykstra 2005; Miller-McLemore 2012; Swinton 2007). A practice, one can argue, *is behavior a person or persons do over time and in specific contexts that has meaning and purpose.* Whereas practical theologians look at religious practices, pastoral theologians are also called to look at practices that may not easily fit into a narrow Christian worldview. Practices such as masturbation, pimple picking, checking (on one's phone), collecting, forgetting (even if part of an illness), and avoiding can teach us much about human nature and how we relate to God. When it comes to masturbation, no man should be left to his own devices.

REFERENCES

American Psychiatric Association. (2013). *Diagnostic and statistical manual of mental disorders* (5th ed.). American Psychiatric Association.

Balswick, J. K., & Balswick, J. O. (1999). *Authentic human sexuality: An integrated Christian approach.* InterVarsity.

Bass, D. C., & Copeland, M. S. (2010). *Practicing our faith: A way of life for a searching people* (2nd ed.). The Practices of Faith Series. Jossey-Bass.

Baumeister, R. F., & Bushman, B. J. (2017). *Social psychology and human nature* (4th ed.). Cengage Learning.

Capps, D. (2003). From masturbation to homosexuality: A case of displaced moral disapproval. *Pastoral Psychology, 51*(4), 249–272.

Carlin, N., & Capps, D. (2015). *Gift of sublimation: A psychoanalytic study of multiple masculinities.* Cascade.

Carvalheira, A., Bente, T., & Stulhofer, A. (2015). Masturbation and pornography use among coupled heterosexual men with decreased sexual desire: How many roles of masturbation? *Journal of Sex and Marital Therapy, 41*(6), 626–635.

Conner, B. T. (2011). *Practicing witness: A missional vision of Christian practices.* Eerdmans.

Diorio, J. A. (2016). Changing discourse, learning sex, and non-coital heterosexuality. *Sexuality and Culture, 20,* 841–861.

Doehring, C. (2015). *The practice of pastoral care: A postmodern approach* (rev. & expanded ed.). Westminster John Knox.

Dykstra, C. R. (2005). *Growing in the life of faith: Education and Christian practices* (2nd ed.). Westminster John Knox.

Garlick, S. (2012). Masculinity, pornography, and the history of masturbation. *Sexuality and Culture, 16,* 306–320.

Goren, E. (2003). America's love affair with technology: The transformation of sexuality and the self over the 20th century. *Psychoanalytic Psychology, 20*(3), 487–508.

Jinks, D., & Cohen, B. (Producers), & Mendes, S. (Director). (1999). *American beauty* [motion picture]. DreamWorks Pictures.

Kaestle, C. E., & Allen, K. R. (2011). The role of masturbation in healthy sexual development: Preceptions of young adults. *Archives of Sexual Behavior, 40,* 983–994.

Kafka, M. P. (2010). Hypersexual disorder: A proposed diagnosis for DSM-V. *Archives of Sexual Behavior, 39*(2), 377–400.

Kafka, M. P. (2014). What happened to hypersexual disorder? *Archives of Sexual Behavior, 43*(7), 1259–1261.

Kahr, B. (2007). *Sex and the psyche: Revealing the true nature of our secret fantasies from the largest ever survey of its kind.* Allen Lane.

Kahr, B. (2008). *Who's been sleeping in your head? The secret world of sexual fantasies.* Basic.

Kinsey, A. C., Pomeroy, W. B., & Martin, C. E. (1948). *Sexual behavior in the human male.* Saunders.

Kor, A., Fogel, Y., Reid, R. C., & Potenza, M. N. (2013). Should hypersexual disorder be classified as an addiction? *Sex Addict Compulsivity, 20,* 27–47.

Kwee, A. W., & Hoover, D. C. (2008). Theologically-informed education about masturbation: A male sexual health perspective. *Journal of Psychology and Theology, 36*(4), 258–269.

Laqueur, T. W. (2003). *Solitary sex: A cultural history of masturbation.* Zone.

Lillie, J. J. M. (2002). Sexuality and cyberporn: Towards a new agenda for research. *Sexuality and Culture, 6*(2), 25–48.

Manning, J. C. (2006). The impact of internet pornography on marriage and the family: A review of the research. *Sexual Addiction & Compulsivity, 13,* 131–165.

Miller-McLemore, B. J. (2012). *Christian theology in practice: Discovering a discipline.* Eerdmans.

Nelson, J. B. (1978). *Embodiment: An approach to sexuality and Christian theology.* Augsburg.

Phipps, W. E. (1977). Masturbation: Vice or virtue? *Journal of Religion and Health, 16*(3), 183–195.

Reid, R. C. (2015). How should severity be determined for the DSM-5 proposed classification of hypersexual disorder? *Journal of Behavioral Addictions, 4*(4), 221–225.

Reid, R. C., Garos, S., Carpenter, B. N., & Coleman, E. (2011). A surprising finding related to executive control in a patient sample of hypersexual men. *Journal of Sexual Medicine, 8*(8), 2227–2236.

Reid, R. C., Bramen, J. E., Anderson, A., & Cohen, M. S. (2014). Mindfulness, emotional dysregulation, impulsivity, and stress proneness among hypersexual patients. *Journal of Clinical Psychology, 70*(4), 313–332.

Rosewarne, L. (2014). *Masturbation in pop culture: Screen, society, self.* Lexington.

Staehler, T., & Kozin, A. (2017). Between platonic love and internet pornography. *Sexuality & Culture.* Advance online publication.

Stengers, J., & Van Neck, A. (2001). *Masturbation: The history of a great terror.* Palgrave.

Strager, S. (2003). What men watch when they watch pornography. *Sexuality and Culture, 7,* 111–123.

Swinton, J. (2007). *Raging with compassion: Pastoral responses to the problem of evil.* Eerdmans.

Taussig, M. T. (1993). *Mimesis and alterity: A particular history of the senses.* Routledge.

Tissot, S.-A. (2015). *Diseases caused by masturbation, or onanism.* Gottfried & Fritz.

Twain, M. (2017). *On masturbation.* CreateSpace Independent Publishing.

Uebel, M. (1999). Toward a symptomatology of cyberporn. *Theory and Event, 3*(4), Project MUSE, muse.jhu.edu/article/32565.

Van Driel, M. (2012). *With the hand: A cultural history of masturbation.* Reaktion.

Weeks, M. (2015). American Beauty: The art of work in the age of therapeutic masturbation. *European Journal of American Culture, 34*(1), 49–66.

Wilson, G. (2014). *Your brain on porn: Internet pornography and the emerging science of addiction*. Commonwealth.

Winnicott, D. W. (1994). The capacity to be alone. In D. W. Winnicott (Ed.), *The maturational processes and the facilitating environment: Studies in the theory of emotional development* (pp. 29–36). International Universities Press.

Wood, H. (2011). The internet and its role in the escalation of sexually compulsive behaviour. *Psychoanalytic Psychotherapy, 25*(2), 127–142.

Woods, J. (2015). Seeing and being seen: The psychodynamics of pornography through the lens of Winnicott's thought. In M. B. Spelman & F. Thomson-Salo (Eds.), *The Winnicott tradition: Lines of development (evolution of theory and practice over the decades)* (pp. 163–174). Karnac.

Yule, M. A., Brotto, L. A., & Gorzalka, B. (2017). Sexual fantasy and masturbation among asexual individuals: An in-depth exploration. *Archives of Sexual Behavior, 46*(17), 311–328.

7

You Are My Friends

Pastoral Care with Young Mexican Men

RUBÉN ARJONA

"*Aquí no eres un cliente más, eres un amigo*" ("Here you are not only a client, you are a friend") are the words printed at the bottom of the receipt one is given upon ordering a *torta* (Mexican sandwich) at Las Tortas, a sandwich shop in Denver, Colorado. These words are a reflection of the cultural significance of friendship for Mexican identity. My purpose in this chapter is to discuss the significance of friendship in caring for and counseling with young Mexican men. My main claim is that despite the power differential and imperfect mutuality between the minister and the care seeker, ministers can effectively counsel young Mexican men who are both their parishioners and their friends.

FRIENDSHIP IN COUNSELING

"Can the pastor counsel with parishioners who are also his [or her] friends?" In the fourth issue of the first volume of *Pastoral Psychology*, Seward Hiltner (1950) posed this question. Although this is an old question, I believe it continues to be a relevant one. To answer this question, Hiltner made a distinction between friendship and friendliness. He explained that whereas friendliness "plainly refers to the approach of warmth, genuine interest, and real concern for people," friendship implies "not merely a relationship to which the pastor gives something, but also one from which he [or she] gets something" (p. 28). From this point of view, Hiltner posited that although friendliness ought to be a component of every counseling and pastoral relationship, personal friendships and counseling cannot be "in operation at the same time" (p. 28). He conceded, however, that it might be possible to temporarily redefine a relationship with a friend in order to counsel him or her as long as "both persons understand and accept the limitation which the counseling places temporarily on the relationship" (p. 28). For Hiltner, insofar as friendship implies a sense of mutuality and "counseling is a relationship in which two people concentrate on the needs of one" (the care seeker), friendship "has no place in counseling" (p. 34).

Although I find Hiltner's distinction between friendliness and friendship useful, I don't think friendship and counseling are incompatible. I agree that in counseling friends, ministers ought to focus on the needs of their friends, but I don't think counseling requires a redefinition of friendship, especially if this redefinition requires suspending the sense of trust and intimacy that friendship implies. Reflecting on the significance of friendship for Mexican identity, Mexican psychologist Díaz-Guerrero (1975) posits that "the environment of friendship is sufficiently fertile to bring to the surface the lost vocations, the obscured potentials, and the deep and creative aspects of the Mexican's personality" (p. 42). If Díaz-Guerrero is right—and I believe he is—in counseling with young Mexican men, rather than redefining friendship the minister ought to embrace friendship and its potential to facilitate pastoral conversations and deepen trust. Because I focus in this chapter on the care of young Mexican men, in what follows I offer an overview of the significance of friendship in Mexican culture and identity.

FRIENDSHIP FROM A MEXICAN PERSPECTIVE

Friendship is at the core of Mexican identity. In his book *El amor y la amistad en el mexicano* [Love and friendship in the Mexican], Mexican writer Reyes Nevarez (1952) explains that "friendship is one of the forms of community that we better and more constantly cultivate in Mexico" (p. 73). He adds that Mexicans uphold "with passion and absolute sharpness, enthusiastically and exclusively, a primordial type of community: family; and a second type, of peculiar characteristics, the community of friendship" (p. 74).

Like Reyes Nevarez, Mexican psychologist Rogelio Díaz-Guerrero emphasizes the centrality of friendship for Mexican identity. Drawing on Mexican philosopher Samuel Ramos's understanding of the inferiority complex of the Mexican, Díaz-Guerrero (1975) posits that Mexicans have a profound hunger for developing their self-esteem (p. 39). Friendship, he points out, can be "the easiest and most felicitous means of maintaining self-esteem"

(p. 40). In the "smiling and accepting faces" of one's friends, the Mexican finds "a garden in the midst of a desert of low self-esteem" (p. 41). Given this sense of radical acceptance, Díaz-Guerrero posits that "with friends one can brag without the criticism that demands evidence" (p. 40). With their friends, Mexican men brag, for example, about their sexual prowess, their physical strength, or their ability to maneuver a car. To be sure, the braggart is sometimes so obvious or ridiculous that he provokes the laughter of his audience. For Díaz-Guerrero, bragging can be transformed "into a suitable form to develop self-esteem, through a healthy, profound, active, and original sense of humor" (p. 41). But bragging among friends can also lead to a constructive moment (p. 41). In fact, Díaz-Guerrero posits that "the greatest creative efforts of our [Mexican] culture are produced in contact with friends" (p. 41). To illustrate his point, Díaz-Guerrero quotes journalist Ángel de Campo. De Campo (1991) recounts that a North American tourist once complained that Mexican writers do not write books that deserve the title of "novels" but instead write books that replicate foreign literature (p. 123). De Campo replied that each Mexican carries a novel in his or her head, "but inspiration escapes through our mouths, and one should not look for the works of our genius in pamphlets, in bookstores or in libraries, but in bars, cafés, corridors, newspaper premises, offices, intimate visits, and after-dinner conversations" (p. 123). In other words, where friendship is, there creativity will be.

The fruits of friendship, however, may not always be as evident as those of other human relationships. Pastoral theologian Culbertson (1996) maintains that friendship, especially male intimate friendship, oftentimes is deemed useless because it is *unproductive* (p. 172). He explains, for example, that male friendships do not produce tangible results such as an attractive home, a successful career, or a multigenerational family (p. 172).

Culbertson's observation may be accurate in some contexts, but in Mexican culture and society friendships are productive in many ways. After all, Mexican society *functions* under the premise of friendship. Mexican philosopher Zea (1952) describes Mexican society as "a citizen-less society, a society of friends and relatives" (p. 103). Indeed, for a wide array of projects and tasks, Mexicans tend to initiate action through the mediation of a friend. If one's child is sick, for example, one would tend to look for a pediatrician who is a friend, or at least one who is a friend's friend. If one is planning to buy a car, it wouldn't be uncommon to seek out a friend who works at a dealership or a friend who is an expert on cars.

To be sure, this tendency has a negative side. On the one hand, Mexicans can become overdependent on friendships, and this sometimes leads to a sense of stagnation, particularly if one is unable to find a friend who will support a particular need or project. On the other hand, an exaggerated dependence on friendship can generate maladaptive social behaviors such as *amiguismo* (from the word *amigo*), a form of nepotism quite common in Mexico. Zea describes the pervasiveness of *amiguismo* when he points out that the Mexican's aspiration to be friends with the president of the country, or friends with the president's friends or at least friends of the friends of the president's friends, can become an endless chain (pp. 103–104). To be sure, in conferring positions, politicians and entrepreneurs, for example, tend to favor their friends, often without taking into account whether a candidate's talents and experience match the job profile. Obviously, such *amiguismo* can lead to corruption and inefficiency.

Despite such risks, Díaz-Guerrero is right in reclaiming the capacity of an environment of friendship "to bring to the surface the lost vocations, the obscured potentials, and the deep and creative aspects of the Mexican's personality." I believe this kind of environment is precisely what Mexican men need in order to voice their most intimate concerns. A Mexican man will often find an *amigo* in the taxi driver, the convenience store attendant, or the barber.[1] These friendships often offer healthy avenues of expression, of good humor, and of nonjudgmental support.

Late in his life, my father developed the habit of visiting a small convenience store around the corner from our home. My mother sometimes got angry at him because she thought he spent too much time in that store "drinking with his friends." One day, a few weeks after my father died, I visited that store. The owner, Don Modesto, notably touched by my visit, recounted that in those conversations with friends and neighbors Don Rubén (my father) often talked about how proud he was of his children.

I have no doubt that my father and his friends found some form of care in those informal meetings. Don Modesto, perhaps unknowingly, was the minister of that "parish." I believe, however, that men like my father could also benefit from an intimate relationship, akin to friendship, with a minister. By virtue of their vocation, ministers can offer their perspectives on the horizontal axis of life, but along with these, with informed knowledge and insight, they can "adequately express the vertical dimension" (Tillich 1984, p. 199). Expressing their interpretations of how God may be at work

---

1. In *Love Undetectable: Notes on Friendship, Sex, and Survival*, Sullivan (1998) points out that for the Greeks "friendship was a somewhat promiscuous thing." He explains, for example, that in Aristotle's Books Eight and Nine of the *Nicomachean Ethics*, the word *philia* "covers a multitude of connections." According to Sullivan, "In Aristotle's hermetically sane universe, the instinct of human connection is so common and so self-evidently good that there is little compunction to rule certain relationships out of the arc of human friendliness" (pp. 186–187).

in actual human situations is part of what ministers do, for example through counseling and preaching. Although this task is inherently complex, I believe it can be especially challenging to express the vertical dimension in the midst of caregiving situations that entail matters of human intimacy, including, of course, sexual intimacy. In these cases, an environment of friendship can facilitate pastoral conversations and deepen the sense of trust between caregiver and care seeker.

SEX AND THE SEMINARY: TWO SEMINARIANS AND TWO FRIENDLY MINISTERS

In what follows, I offer two stories of ministers who aptly expressed the vertical dimension in caregiving and counseling situations that involved a young man's sexuality.

For a number of reasons, some young adults may have a difficult time expressing sexual concerns. This difficulty is often related to religious scruples that foster a split between body and spirit and that label an individual's sexuality as inherently sinful. If parishioners encounter only rigid "interpretative structures" within their communities of faith, they will be forced to "dissociate large parts of their experience or emotions from their Christian faith" (Waters 2015, p. 781).

A common feature of the two theological students in the following stories is that both of them encountered ministers who took care of the young men's desires by offering fresh perspectives on their inner conflicts. Each of these ministers was empowered by his theology to see the young man under his care in his wholeness. Based on the belief that God takes pride in both a person's spirit and body, these ministers welcomed the young men's desires along with their faith. But along with a pertinent theological framework, these ministers embody a friendly disposition, or, as Hiltner (1950) put it, the minister's friendliness, that is, "the approach of warmth, genuine interest, and real concern for people" (p. 28).

JEREMÍAS

In reference to the sixth stage of human development (young adulthood), Erik Erikson points out that young adults tend to "experiment in many ways with intimacies" before they can develop "true intimacy" (Evans and Erikson 1967, p. 50). This does not imply that it is the minister's task to encourage a young man to experiment sexually. In some cases, however, by suggesting a new perspective on a conflictual situation, a young man may experience the freedom to modify his sexual behavior. This was the case, for example, for Jeremías, a man now in his mid-30s, whom I met more than a decade ago when I was an instructor and he was a student at a Presbyterian seminary in Mexico City.[2]

From the moment we met, Jeremías and I began to develop a close relationship. Jeremías, who was born in a rural community in the State of Chiapas, Mexico, had never been to the capital city. Early on I perceived Jeremías's eagerness to learn but also noticed that he needed additional support to navigate life in the city. Jeremías became my protégé. Since then, we have shared many meals and spent numerous hours in conversation, first in person and lately through social media. I have directed much time and effort to encourage him to embrace his whole self, that is, to reconcile his desires with his Christian faith.

After a few years of accompanying him, Jeremías began to share with me some of his inner conflicts, especially those that arose from the tension between his faith and his sexual longings. Like many other young Christian men, Jeremías was convinced that masturbation is a sin. Some churches in Mexico continue to use the story of Onan (Genesis 38) to sustain the idea of the so-called sinfulness of masturbation. I recall discussing with him the theme of masturbation on several occasions. I explained that masturbation was a normal component of an individual's sexual development and that I saw no biblical basis for calling it a sin. In doing so, based on my understanding of the vertical dimension, I simply offered a fresh perspective that I hoped could help assuage Jeremías's inner conflicts. In a recent conversation with him, several years removed from those discussions, I asked if he recalled any of our conversations. He recalled discussing with me "delicate topics" about his sexuality. When I asked if he could specify any of these topics, Jeremías referred to our conversations about masturbation. Then he told me, "Your accompaniment has helped me to know myself better." I believe Jeremías is right in describing my caregiving with him as "accompaniment." For more than a decade, I have sought to walk with him, to listen to him, and, sometimes, to offer my perspective. To be sure, Mexican ministers, like ministers in general, have significant constraints on the amount of time and resources that they can invest in accompanying, in this case, young men. I believe, however, that every now and then, through God's providential intervention, ministers are led to care seekers who, like Jeremías, require extraordinary attention.

2. Jeremías has granted me permission to tell this portion of his life story and to use his actual given name.

In caring for men like Jeremías, ministers will benefit from cultivating a friendly disposition that will encourage the care seeker to voice his most intimate concerns. As I reflect on more than a decade of ministry with Jeremías, however, I realize that in addition to much warmth, genuine listening, and understanding, Jeremías needed, quite desperately, a new interpretation of the vertical dimension. It is no exaggeration to say that Jeremías's conscience was tortured by a religious framework that persecuted him for his sexual longings and diminished the importance of his body's overall well-being. Jeremías's life-limiting theology was so deeply ingrained that it took him years to start moving toward an alternative paradigm. In this process, changes in his theology played a crucial role. Jeremías was particularly impressed by liberation theology, especially by what Mexican theologian Cervantes-Ortiz (2003) describes as Rubem Alves's "liberating-poetic-ludic theology."[3]

Little by little, through much listening, understanding, and logistical support, Jeremías began to move toward a theological framework that affirmed the goodness of his whole being. This life-giving theology has led Jeremías not only to reclaim his sexuality but also to commit to the care of his body through, for example, physical exercise and healthier eating. In line with Alves's theology, he has also cultivated a profound love for painting.

Because Mexican men in general have difficulty voicing their sexual concerns, and because some of these men—like Jeremías—belong to faith traditions that tend to exacerbate shame and guilt, in caring for and counseling with young Mexican men, a minister's theology matters. Sometimes, as in the case of Jeremías, ministers have to engage their protégés in explicit theological discussions. In other cases, however, theology may be implicit although nevertheless present. To reflect on a case in which the minister communicated his theology more subtly, I turn to the case of another young seminary student.

PRAYERS IN A LIBRARY

In "Finding Language for What Matters Most: Hosting Conversations about Sexuality in Pastoral Counseling," Dykstra (2015) posits that *"a given*

---

3. Rubem Alves, who was born in a conservative Presbyterian family in Brazil, completed his doctorate in theology at Princeton Theological Seminary in 1968 under the advisement of Richard Shaull. In the acknowledgments of his dissertation, Alves (1968) refers to Shaull as "a close friend for more than fifteen years." Cervantes-Ortiz (2016) explains that with his dissertation Alves established himself as one of the founders of liberation theology, and, in some respects, he anticipated the future works of Gustavo Gutiérrez and Hugo Assmann (p. 9).

society's conventions concerning its range of acceptable interests and practices inexorably take their toll among its more vulnerable citizens" (p. 667, emphasis in original). Then he explains that "when our parishioners, students, or counselees summon up courage to confide in us as counselors about the idiosyncratic ways these societal tolls manifest as symptoms in their personal lives, they should feel less rather than more lonely for having done so" (p. 667, emphasis in original).

As an illustration of how a minister may help a young man feel less lonely, Dykstra (2015) refers to a case in which he counseled "a young seminary student tormented over his sexual longings for other men" (p. 678). Dykstra recounts the story of an incident that had occurred during this student's senior year at a conservative Christian college:

> Entering the college library one day for what he considered routine study and without an overt sense of distress, he sat down at a table and took out a piece of paper. For some unknown reason, however, all at once he found himself overcome by what he knew even at the time was an accumulation of internalized frustration over his inability to free himself of homoerotic desire. Finding himself suddenly in tears there in the library, this upright man vigorously started writing *Fuck you, Fuck you,* over and over again on the page, until a point where his rage turned inward, such that with equal fervor he began writing *Fuck me, Fuck me,* again and again instead. Finally, still angry but now exhausted, the paper filled with obscenities, he pulled a random book from the stacks, put the paper inside, and replaced the book on the shelf. The next day, having had second thoughts about someone happening upon that piece of paper in the book, he returned to the library to retrieve it, found the book, but discovered that the paper was already gone. (pp. 678–679)

Dykstra adds that after the student told him about this incident, "his head and eyes were downcast with tears of shame" (p. 679). Sensing the student's weary spirit, Dykstra responded, "It sounds like you were praying" (p. 679). Perceiving the student's disbelief about what he had just heard, Dykstra added, "That may have been your first real prayer. What if you were finally asking God for what you really want? You may have been asking for that much intimacy with God" (p. 679). After a moment of silence, the student's tears of shame became tears of release (p. 679). Dykstra concludes, "At this point in our conversation, it seems pretty safe to suggest, we were both feeling much less lonely" (p. 679).

The story of Dykstra counseling this young seminary student is a remarkable illustration of a minister's ability to curate—to take care of—a young man's desires. Rather than attempting to educate this young man on the nature of his desires or on theological disputes with his conservative college, Dykstra listens to the student attentively and empathically. Instead of lecturing the student on how he should claim his sexual identity, Dykstra enters the student's world respectfully and gently offers an alternative interpretation of his actions that affirms the student's faith and personal experience. Solution-focused therapists Berg and Dolan (2001) refer to this kind of response as the counselor's ability to "lead from behind" (p. 3). Berg and Dolan explain: "From this position, the therapist gently 'taps the client on the shoulder' and asks whether she noticed the beautiful sunset in the sky . . . These 'taps on the shoulder' are the questions the therapist asks in order to stimulate a fresh look at the same old picture" (p. 3). In the young seminarian's case, Dykstra offers a fresh look at the student's writing of obscenities on a piece of paper. Rather than shaming the student for writing obscenities, the counselor suggests that those words may have been a prayer. He says the right thing at the right time in the right way. Dykstra could have jeopardized this moment of empathic connection if he had begun educating the student, for example, on the nature and applicability of prayers of lament. The counselor's response is certainly constructed upon a set of theological convictions, but in service to the counseling process he chooses not to disclose his rationale. But a certain theological framework—a certain interpretation of the vertical dimension—is nevertheless present. Ultimately, this case evokes the pastoral theologian's ability to bring into the counseling moment both sound theological wisdom and pertinent psychological insights.

The previous two stories illustrate the usefulness of the minister's counseling skills, the value of friendliness in caregiving relationships, and the significance of the minister's theology. First, these stories emphasize attentive listening, empathic attunement, and, particularly in the second case, the ability to lead from behind. Generally speaking, congregants and pastors in Mexican churches expect that the pastor will *guide* them to the truth. In other words, after listening briefly to the congregant's problem or dilemma, the minister tends to do all the talking. This approach may have the disadvantage of undermining the care seeker's agency and overemphasizing the minister's authority. In this context, ministers and pastors in Mexican churches would benefit from a caregiving approach that incorporates the skills of attentive listening, empathic attunement, and the ability to lead from behind. Although these skills underscore the care seeker's sense of agency, they leave space for the minister's creative involvement. By listening attentively and empathically to the care seeker's story, the minister upholds the value of the story and the care seeker's sense of agency as teller and interpreter of his or her story. At the same time, by suggesting fresh perspectives and new interpretations, the minister can influence and motivate the care seeker.

Second, these stories illustrate the role of a friendly disposition in caregiving and counseling. I believe the quality of the relationship between caregiver and care seeker affects the way stories are told. If Díaz-Guerrero is right in pointing out that "with friends one can brag without the criticism that demands evidence"—and I believe he is—then conversations among friends must have a different quality than, for example, conversations between bosses and their subordinates. Although the minister as counselor is in a position of power in relation to his or her parishioner, when parishioners perceive their relationship with their minister as friendship they are more likely to voice their intimate concerns more freely, without fear of criticism or judgment. Ultimately, the accepting environment of friendship empowers young men to reclaim their lost vocations and actualize their potentialities.

Third, these stories point to the crucial role of the minister's theology in caregiving and counseling. The men in these stories, like other men who have difficulty voicing their intimate concerns, would benefit from consultation with professional therapists. For example, although I have continued to accompany Jeremías, he has also benefited from therapy with a psychiatrist and, more recently, from an exploration of Mayan spirituality. But given the nature of his conflicts—the tendency to dissociate parts of himself from his faith—Jeremías, like the seminarian in Dykstra's case, benefited from the care of a *minister*. Of course, the minister's theology matters. The minister's interpretation of the theological dimension can further oppress a young man or can contribute to his liberation. The ministers in these stories communicated, either explicitly or implicitly, their theologies. In one way or another, these ministers conveyed the message that God delights in a young man's physical body and sexual interests (Dykstra 2007, p. 64).

Although at the time of their encounters with the young seminarians the ministers in the previous two cases were *friendly*, neither of them was, strictly speaking, friends with his care seeker. Nevertheless, the ministers' friendliness was crucial in empowering the young men to voice their intimate concerns. In other cases, caregiving and *friendship* are intertwined in intricate ways. Can a minister counsel a parishioner who is also a friend? In order to answer this question, I present and discuss the case of Alonso and Pastor Garza.

COUNSELING WITH YOUNG MEXICAN MEN: THE CASE OF ALONSO AND PASTOR GARZA

Scholars Sperry and Pies (2010) discuss three ways of ethically employing case material in therapeutic writing: seeking the client's permission; disguising the case material; and developing composite case material (pp. 88–102). Although Sperry and Pies write for clinicians, the guidelines they recommend are applicable to ministers and pastoral theologians who write about counseling relationships within the parish context. In this case, even though I obtained Alonso's and Pastor Garza's permission to tell their story, I agreed with them that I would disguise the material to protect their rights to privacy and confidentiality.[4]

Background

Pastor Garza, a Mexican male minister in his late 30s, and Alonso, a young Mexican man in his late 20s, had met each other many years earlier when Garza was appointed as the pastor of the congregation where Alonso was a new member. Although Garza was in charge of pastoral care for the whole congregation, as a young pastor he initially spent most of his time in youth ministry. Little by little, Pastor Garza and Alonso began to develop a relationship of trust. Alonso often visited Garza at his office to discuss personal issues and matters of faith, and he sometimes volunteered to help Garza by running errands.

In an interview with Alonso, he explained to me that he regards Pastor Garza not only as his pastor but as his *friend*. In fact, Alonso believes that his friendship with Pastor Garza preceded the pastoral relationship: "I have to say he was first my friend and then my pastor." I believe Alonso is able to voice his intimate and sexual concerns to Garza precisely because he perceives this relationship as akin to friendship.

Before I present and discuss the verbatim of a pastoral conversation between Garza and Alonso, a word about my relationship with these men is necessary. I met Pastor Garza when we were both students at a seminary in Mexico City. During our time at the seminary, we became friends, and although we have lived in different cities since then, we have kept in touch

---

4. The names in this story (Alonso, Pastor Garza, Erika, Vanessa) are pseudonyms. I have also disguised the case by altering a few demographic descriptors, by adding "extraneous material," and by excluding certain information, such as Alonso's profession. For a discussion of these three disguise strategies, see Sperry and Pies (2010, pp. 93–95).

via phone and social media. Given my interest and formation in pastoral care and theology, he has sometimes consulted with me about some difficult pastoral care cases, including some of his personal concerns. I should note, however, that I do not know any of his congregants except for Garza's family and Alonso, whom I have met through social media. On several occasions in recent years, I have had the opportunity to share and discuss pastoral care matters with Garza.

Several months ago I shared with Pastor Garza the focus of my research, and he suggested somewhat in jest that he could become my case study. A few weeks later, we talked more, and I expressed my interest in including the case of Garza's pastoral relationship with Alonso in an academic paper. With Alonso's permission, Pastor Garza shared with me a verbatim account of several of their conversations. These conversations took place in Spanish, and I have translated them into English. I have sought to maintain, as much as possible, the zest of the original.

The Conversation

Some months ago, Alonso asked whether he could come talk to Pastor Garza about a difficult situation he was facing. Pastor Garza (PG) arranged a meeting with Alonso (A) in the church's office. Afterward, Pastor Garza constructed the following verbatim of their pastoral conversation.

> A1: I need your help, friend. This is a case for you. There's a woman in my life. There is nothing yet; we aren't lovers. She has a boyfriend. We've been working in the same office for about a year. When we first met, she really liked me. She keeps saying I'm a very smart guy, a very special *caballero* [gentleman]. She is not married, but she has been with her boyfriend for about ten years. She knows that I'm married and that I have kids, but we keep saying nice things about each other. She really wants to be respectful of my situation, but at the same time she seems to enjoy talking to me. She seems so righteous, and that is precisely what makes her so beautiful to me.
>
> PG1: I notice a lot of emotion in your words. You really seem to enjoy the mutual flattery . . .
>
> A2: Yes. When I try to change my attitude, she gets angry, unconsciously, I think. But when I suggest that destiny has brought us together, she seems happy. You see, we know that this might not be our destiny, but maybe friendship. . . . I don't think that can happen either.

PG2: Are you saying you can't be just friends?

A3: Look, I believe my wife [Vanessa] is the love of my life and that I have two wonderful kids. I like my family, but I don't see Erika as just any friend. My relationship with her is *so* personal, as if a pearl was waiting for me.

PG3: And so the question is what to do with this pearl . . .

A4: If I let it go, it will get lost; if I take it, I'll enjoy it. If she gives herself to me, I don't know what might happen. You see, she has said nicer things to me than my wife, even though we have never kissed or had sex.

PG4: That seems to be hitting you hard . . .

A5: Yes, of course.

PG5: This must be a very difficult situation, considering that you interact with her frequently at work.

A6: We usually have lunch together. We do work together, and then we start writing things on paper, like chatting on paper. We find any number of excuses to run into each other. Today, however, we only greeted each other twice, at the beginning and at the end of the day. I asked what was going on, and she replied that she wanted to respect both me and her boyfriend. The problem is that she may say one thing but suggest something else with her attitudes. I told her that her refusal to open up is not going to help us. I told her it would be important to know the limits of our situation and that I have limits as to how long I can hold my desire.

PG6: What do you desire, Alonso?

A7: She makes me feel important. My wife does that too but in a different way, perhaps more holistically. Erika does it like the girl I never had as a girlfriend; young and mature at the same time; with a sense of purpose Listen, I like her; she likes me, but we don't go beyond a certain point. But in the way we talk, you could say we make love.

PG7: Your idea of making love by talking and spending time together but without actually having sex seems interesting to me . . .

A8: You get why the situation is driving me crazy?

PG8: Yes, of course.

A9: And if I did it . . . I don't even want to tell you . . .

PG9: If you told me that you'd like to make love to her?

A10: Well, why not? After all, we're both opening up to each other.

PG10: Is there anything that worries you about having sex with Erika?

A11: Yes. I'm concerned about her. I, after all, have my wife and kids.

PG11: Not being able to offer her a more permanent relationship worries you?

A12: If I hadn't met my wife, Erika would have been an excellent candidate. Yes, for sure [brief silence]. This situation makes me feel so nostalgic. You know, nowadays I listen to a lot of jazz and country music.

PG12: It sounds like that kind of music helps you take care of your feelings.

A13: Yes, it helps me *feel*. I actually introduced jazz to Erika, and she couldn't believe it. She thought that this kind of music was only for old and rich people. She tells me that I am different from other men, and she seems so delighted about it.

PG13: And that makes you feel good.

A14: Yes, it makes me feel unique. Although my wife makes me feel that too . . . [Brief silence.] You know, unlike other times, I haven't exploited this. I don't demand love. Rather, I try to understand . . . and that is painful.

PG14: Well, it seems to me that you're taking care of your feelings and thoughts rather than ignoring those feelings or acting impulsively.

A15: Yes, but to tell you the truth, sometimes I want it all.

PG15: Yes, I can see that.

A16: When I think things through carefully, I come to the conclusion that I really want to enjoy life, despite the possible consequences.

PG16: In that case, I'm wondering if it would be helpful to anticipate possible scenarios.

A17: Yes, of course.

PG17: Rather than leaving things to chance, it might be good to think what you are and what you are not willing to do and, of course, what might be the possible consequences in each case.

A18: Yes. I want to enjoy life. We only get to live one life. Sometimes I wonder, why now? Will I be able to contribute something to her life? I really don't know, but I know that I like her.

PG18: Well, I'm glad you're being honest with yourself.

A19: Yes. I don't want to deceive myself.

PG19: This isn't an easy situation, Alonso, but I trust you'll know how to respond.

A20: What should I do? You are my very best confidant. Tell me; only you have the right words for me.

PG20: At the end of the day, only you can decide what to do. I would suggest considering your options and deciding which is best. My job is not to impose this or that path on you.

A21: [Brief silence.]

PG21: But I can certainly accompany you in this dilemma. Having an extramarital affair can put great pressure on your life, but, of course, this is not the only factor that you ought to consider.

A22: Yes.

PG22: You know, there are different paths that you can take, but which of these paths is best for you?

A23: My family. And if I get to know another part of love, then let it be.

PG23: Are you aware of or can you imagine the consequences that an extramarital relationship might entail?

A24: Well, I might never have one.

PG24: Maybe, but it would be really helpful to know what those relationships can imply. I know that you wouldn't ever buy a car without knowing what kind of car you're buying, what kind of engine it has, what advantages or disadvantages it might have compared to other cars.

A25: Yes, you're right. You've really made me think [brief silence]. I ought to enjoy life responsibly [brief silence]. Thanks, friend; I love you a *fuckload*.

PG25: Same here. You know you can count on me if you get stuck.

A26: I know, that's why I came. And you know you can count on me too.

PG26: Thank you.

A27: God was good to me giving me you as a friend. God gave me an angel.

PG27: [Smiling] Take care, Alonso. Call me if you'd like to talk again.

About a week later, Alonso came back to the church office to see Pastor Garza. Alonso informed Pastor Garza that he had talked to Erika and had decided to be friends only. He said that he would stay with his family and that his heart would remain happy. Alonso acknowledged that talking to Pastor Garza had helped him a lot.

As the conversation continued, Alonso explained that his relationship with his wife was facing a difficult period. What follows is an excerpt from a later part of this second conversation between Alonso and Pastor Garza:

A28: I'm really scared about falling in love with another woman and betraying my awesome wife. And I say this without sarcasm, okay?

PG28: Which came first, the chicken or the egg? In other words, because things were not good with Vanessa you fell in love with Erika, or because you fell in love with Erika things got bad with Vanessa?

A29: Both.

PG29: Are you suggesting that these processes reinforced each other?

A30: Maybe the lack of tenderness, affection, flattery . . . and then along comes Erika. As simple as that.

PG30: I see. You distanced yourself from Vanessa for a number of reasons. This is when Erika came into your life.

A31: Yes, lack of sex, touching, kisses, and nice words. This is when Erika came into my life, and she started offering tender words without me even asking for them.

PG31: *Bueno, eso sí que debió sacudir el tapete* [That really must have shaken your world].

A32: Yes, it really did.

PG32: Now that you mention sex, what happened? I'm guessing it wasn't like that at the beginning of your relationship with Vanessa.

A33: Yes, you're right. [Brief silence.] She caught me watching porn several times. Even so, I don't think this should prevent her from being with me. After the birth of my second child, I don't know, perhaps hormones did their thing.

PG33: Have you talked about it?

A34: Yes, but she demonizes me. Then I tell her that she must be rejecting me because I don't satisfy her. This goes on and on.

PG34: What do you mean when you say she demonizes you?

A35: Well, she thinks I'm a *depravado* [depraved person]. She says I'd rather watch [porn] than be with her.

PG35: Is that true?

A36: No, not at all. These are two different things. She is real; porn is fantasy. With her, I go crazy. It's just that I got used to masturbating when I was a teenager. And then, if you have stimuli, it is really great. That's how I endured [not being intimate with my wife] all this time.

PG36: What do you mean by "endured"?

A37: You know, almost a year, pregnancy and then the baby. Until today.

PG37: Today?

A38: Yes, we went back to it today.

PG38: I'm guessing you may be feeling better.

A39: Yes. And I learned two things today. My wife and kids are the best part of my life. Second, although I may have other relationships, I will not let myself be swallowed by them.

PG39: Well, there is one thing that you certainly cannot change: you now have two kids. Life will never be the same, including your sexual life. What do you think you might have to do to foster a satisfactory sexual life at this new stage of your life?

A40: Be authentic.

PG40: And how would you be sexually authentic?

A41: Being true to my desire. Never by force.

PG42: And this would apply to both of you, right?

A43: Yes.

PG43: Let me go back to the issue of porn. Is there anything that concerns you about your use of porn?

A44: Not really. This is a very personal thing. It is a habit that I can eradicate.

PG44: Do you think watching porn is a depraved behavior?

A45: No. It is just a personal fantasy. It may [do] damage if one uses it excessively.

PG45: Do you think watching porn affects your sexual relationship with your wife in any way?

A46: No. It is definitely something personal. A utopia.

PG46: Does this mean you get to experience "things" that are beyond your reality, things that your wife may not be willing to explore?

A47: Yes, things that I may never do with anyone [brief silence]. My wife is open to exploring, but it isn't the same. Porn lasts; real life doesn't. Maybe this is why one enjoys porn.

PG47: I see. What do you mean by "lasts"?

A48: You know, when you're masturbating, you decide when to end. With one's partner, things are already decided because of the intensity of passion. You see what I mean?

PG48: I think so. Are you saying that porn allows you to be in control of the situation and extend enjoyment? [Brief silence.] Might there be ways to extend sexual enjoyment with your wife?

A49: [Brief silence.] Well, yes. I guess so.

PG49: I tell you what. Why don't you think about this possibility, and if you'd like, we can talk some more in the coming weeks. In the meantime, I will find a book for you that may give you two some ideas to foster deeper and more joyful sexual encounters with your spouse.

A50: Thank you, brother. I look forward to reading that book [laughing]. Thank you, again. You really are my guru.

DISCUSSION

The preceding conversations illustrate a caregiver's deep respect for the uniqueness of a care seeker. Pastor Garza conveys radical respect for Alonso's alterity by mirroring Alonso's thoughts and feelings and by asking multiple questions and following Alonso's responses.[5] Simple affirmations of Alonso's thoughts and feelings (e.g., Garza's responses 1, 3, and 5) give Alonso permission to talk and experiment with his ideas. Although Garza allows Alonso to talk and experiment, at times Garza offers a bit of guidance and a few suggestions. In the first conversation, Alonso seems to resist the

---

5. Carrie Doehring defines alterity as "an evocative term describing each person's otherness: those aspects of an individual's religious or spiritual world hidden by what seems similar or familiar to us." She explains that "radical respect for alterity describes the quality of relationship that awaits the emergence of mystery" (Doehring 2015, pp. 2–3).

need to reflect on the possible consequences that an extramarital relationship would entail. At this point, Pastor Garza offers an allegory that seems to connect well with Alonso (24). Without explicitly saying so, Garza seems to imply that entering an extramarital relationship without considering its possible consequences would be as unwise as blindly buying a car. In the second conversation, Garza, as if tapping on Alonso's shoulder, suggests a new possibility (48). If one of the reasons Alonso watches pornography is to extend the duration of his sexual pleasure, Garza suggests that there might be ways of doing so *within Alonso's relationship with Vanessa*. In other words, Garza wants to redeem the obscured potential of their relationship. What seems to be at stake here, as psychoanalyst Phillips (2016) puts it, is "finding the unforbidden in the forbidden; or acknowledging that forbidden pleasures can be distortions or perversions of unforbidden pleasures" (p. 156).

At different points in their conversations, Pastor Garza resisted the option of scolding Alonso or educating him on a number of issues. The first conversation could have prompted a lecture on adultery in the Bible. In their second conversation, Garza could have asked whether pornography might evoke the biblical concept of *porneia*. This is not to say that Alonso might not benefit at some future point from biblical instruction on these or any other themes. But if Pastor Garza had taken the occasion to instruct Alonso, Alonso wouldn't have had as much space to talk and experiment with his ideas. Moreover, it is likely that if Garza had used scripture to "correct" Alonso's behavior, Alonso would have shut down or perhaps challenged Garza's biblical interpretations.

The case of Alonso and Pastor Garza supports my argument that young Mexican men are more likely to voice their sexual concerns and other intimate conflicts more openly when their relationship with their ministers is perceived as a personal relationship akin to friendship. In an interview with Alonso (via Facebook video calling) about his relationship with Pastor Garza, I asked him to comment on his ability to talk about sex with Garza. He responded, "Friendship has built the necessary trust to talk about sex. Through friendship we removed social barriers and built a bridge of intimate trust to the point that I can say anything without fearing what he may think of me. I also trust him because his responses are sustained by the testimony of Christ."

In a separate video call, I asked Pastor Garza to reflect on his relationship with Alonso. Garza said: "I am aware that I am Alonso's and his family's pastor, but we've spent so much time together over a period of so many years that I guess you can say we're friends. He really likes to talk, to tell me about his conflicts, dilemmas, and joys, and he is aware that I listen to him." I asked Pastor Garza if his relationship with Alonso might be risky or perceived as too intimate. Garza responded,

> That's an excellent question. I've thought about that myself. Several years ago I had to visit a family in a *ranchería* [a small rural settlement], and Alonso volunteered to come with me. We had to stay overnight, and the family we were visiting gave us a double bed to share. That was an awkward moment for us; after all, you are not supposed to sleep with other men, much less with your minister. But we survived the night without a problem. Of course, I wouldn't take a minor or a female parishioner with me on this kind of visit, but I have found that young men like Alonso really open up if I spend a little extra time with them.

In a second video call with Alonso, I asked him if he remembered his trip to the *ranchería* with Pastor Garza. He certainly did, and I asked him what he thought about having had to share a bed with him. Alonso said, "His presence didn't bother me, but I should acknowledge that I felt something strange ... At the end of the day, I was glad I went with him. It made me feel important."

AWKWARD FEELINGS

Following these conversations, I began to wonder whether I could perhaps further explore with both Garza and Alonso why it had felt "awkward" to share a bed on that night. I decided to ask Pastor Garza whether it was viable for him to explore that feeling of awkwardness in a future conversation with Alonso. He replied that it was probably too risky, but he offered to think about it. To my surprise, a couple of weeks later Garza called me and told me that he had a "gift" for me. He then sent me an email with a verbatim portion of a recent conversation with Alonso, one in which he had ventured to talk with Alonso about the night they shared a bed. What follows is an excerpt from the latter part of that conversation:

> PG51: Alonso, Rubén called me a few weeks ago, and he asked me if I was willing to explore a few more things about our relationship.
>
> A51: Hey, that guy really wants to know everything, doesn't he [laughing]?
>
> PG52: I guess so ...
>
> A52: Not a problem. *Tú sabes que soy materia dispuesta* [You know I'm up for it].

PG53: In relation to the night that we spent in that *ranchería* [rural settlement], Rubén noticed that both of us described the experience of sharing a bed as "awkward." He was wondering if we could say a bit more about that.

A53: Oh, I see [brief silence]. Well, for me it was strange because it was unusual. Sometimes I've shared a bed with my brother, but I had never shared a bed with a man outside of my family.

PG54: I see [prolonged silence]. I have to confess that for me it was strange in another way [brief silence]. I kind of wanted to be even closer to you . . .

A54: You mean . . .

PG55: Yes, like I felt the desire to touch you [brief silence].

A55: Look at you, man; you're blushing as red as a tomato!

PG56: Well, this isn't an easy thing to say.

A56: Don't worry, friend. You didn't do anything wrong.

PG57: I know. Even though I felt that desire, I also knew that I was your pastor and that I had to take care of you.

A57: And you've done it. You've always taken care of me [brief silence].

PG58: Can I ask . . . what would have happened if I had touched you?

A58: Very likely, I would have stopped you right away.

PG59: How would this have affected our relationship?

A59: I would have forgiven you, that's for sure, but I don't think we'd have the same level of trust that we have today.

PG60: So maybe the fact that I didn't act on my desire has strengthened our relationship.

A60: Yes, for sure [brief silence]. You didn't do anything wrong. You know how I know this?

PG61: I guess simply because I didn't act on my desires.

A61: Yes, but more than that. I know it because no one, not in the church, not in our families, ever suggested that there was anything inappropriate about our relationship. People knew, my mother knew, that you really cared about me. That's why she didn't mind me hanging out with you. On the contrary . . .

PG62: [Crying.] Thank you for saying all this.

A62: Let me put it this way. You've been for me what Barcelona has been for Messi.⁶ When he played in Argentina he was a good player, but when he went to Barcelona he became the best [football] player in the world. Thanks to you, I have conquered my fears and have learned to be authentic. Thanks to you, I can stand up and speak in public. I can say what I think. I can fight for what I want. Your model of care to me has been the model of the Teacher [Jesus], of the Spirit.

PG63: How do you know it was the Spirit working in me and not a demon?

A63: Because you taught me freedom with responsibility. Even when we drank beer, it was always one or two. No more than that. Freedom with responsibility. That's how I know you really cared for me.

In the email in which Pastor Garza shared with me this conversation, he wrote: "Brother, thanks for encouraging me to explore this point with Alonso. This was a conversation that I needed to have. I think we closed a circle that needed to be closed, and I have no doubt that Alonso trusts me more than ever before."

DISCUSSION

The preceding conversation illustrates what Greenspan (1996), a feminist psychotherapist practicing in Boston, calls "the healing paradoxes of the therapeutic relationship": cultivating equality in a hierarchical relationship, mutuality in an inherently non-mutual relationship, and empowerment in a power-imbalanced relationship" (p. 134). When Garza confesses his homoerotic desire, the conversation shifts powerfully. The roles reverse and Alonso, in the way of a friend more than a parishioner, becomes Garza's caregiver. With the allusion to a tomato, Alonso seeks to assuage the intensity of Garza's feelings and normalize the conversation (55). Alonso then embarks on a mini-monologue to express his gratitude for Garza's ministry (61–62). He uses a football simile to convey the impact of Garza's ministry in his life (62) and concludes by assuring Garza that his model of care comes from the Spirit of Christ (62). In these ways, Alonso became the curator of Garza's desires.

But there is also a sense in which Pastor Garza continued to take care of Alonso's desires. By reflecting together on his erotic feelings toward Alonso,

---

6. Lionel Andrés "Leo" Messi is an Argentine professional football player who plays as a forward for the Spanish club FC Barcelona.

Pastor Garza is showing, perhaps inadvertently, that it is possible to have erotic feelings but not to act on them for the sake of a greater good (D.V.D. Hunsinger, personal communication, March 8, 2017). In other words, Pastor Garza is implicitly suggesting that Alonso may continue to be friends with Erika while honoring his marriage vows (D.V.D. Hunsinger, personal communication, March 8, 2017). By the end of the conversation, it is safe to say, Alonso and Pastor Garza knew each other better, and they were both feeling much less lonely.

In the case of Alonso and Pastor Garza, as in the stories of Jeremías and the seminarian who sought Dykstra's counsel, the minister's counseling skills mattered. Pastor Garza listened to Alonso attentively and empathically. He also introduced a few motifs to offer fresh perspectives. Like Dykstra, Pastor Garza communicated his theology in subtle ways. His theology, nevertheless, mattered. Garza's most explicit theological statement came right after he had revealed his erotic feelings toward Alonso. At Garza's most vulnerable moment comes the statement: "Even though I felt that desire, I also knew that I was your pastor and that I had to take care of you" (57). Garza's is a theology of desire, but it is also a theology of pastoral responsibility. Notice that Alonso appears to have perceived Garza's theological tone because Alonso responded with two religious references. First, he underscored the positive testimony of his relationship with Garza (61). Then, at Garza's most vulnerable moment, Alonso assured his minister that his model of care with him was "the model of the Teacher, the Spirit" (63). The conversation concludes with another theological statement by Alonso. He maintains that Garza's model came from the Spirit because his minister taught him "freedom with responsibility" (63).

The last conversation between Alonso and Pastor Garza raises the theme of homoerotic desire among men in caregiving relationships. Commenting on classical and patristic writers' understanding of love among men, Culbertson (1996) posits that "homosocial love must not only precede heterosexual love, but must continue alongside it, in order for heterosexual love to survive" (p. 170). But whether homosocial love is possible without homoeroticism is another question. Freud thought that all expressions of love have their roots in some form of sexual energy. Freud (2011) distinguished between "those love instincts which ... pursue directly sexual aims" and those "love instincts which have been diverted from their original aims" (p. 32). Interestingly, Freud posited that "it is precisely those sexual tendencies *that are inhibited in their aims* which achieve such lasting ties between men" (p. 43, emphasis added). Pastor Garza's insight that by deciding not to act on his desire he strengthened his relationship with Alonso (60) seems congruent with Freud's views. But what might be the implications of these insights for ministers like Garza and parishioners like Alonso?

More often than not, I believe intimate pastoral relationships like Garza's and Alonso's entail not only homosocial love but some form of conscious or unconscious erotic attraction, even if men self-identify as heterosexual. Although Alonso did not acknowledge any homoerotic feelings toward Garza, he is clearly *attracted* to Garza's personality, beliefs, and values. The probable existence of homoerotic feelings between them does not mean, of course, that male ministers and male young adults should act on their desires. This would constitute a boundary violation and harm both minister and parishioner. Rather than acting on his desires, a minister ought to "constructively process erotic countertransference" (Gabbard 1994, p. 1083). Although countertransference enactments entail risk, Gabbard posits that "only by tiptoeing on the edge of that abyss [of unethical transgressions] can we fully appreciate the internal world of the patient and its impact on us" (p. 1103).

I want to underscore that although countertransference feelings like those of Garza for Alonso are not unusual in therapeutic relationships, in the typical (U.S.) literature on boundaries in counseling the therapist would be instructed to explore these feelings with a supervisor or another therapist, not to share them with the counselee.[7] As a general rule of thumb, in almost any imaginable pastoral counseling scenario ministers ought to analyze countertransference feelings with the help of a counselor rather than share them with their parishioners. *In this particular case*, Garza's sharing of his desires (the night they shared a bed) was, however risky, somehow appropriate. The fact that Alonso could so beautifully take care of Garza's feelings of vulnerability after Garza shared about his desire when they were in the bed together that night is perhaps the strongest proof that their relationship has, indeed, acquired a level of trust that surpasses that of usual pastoral relationships. As Garza put it in his email to me, "I feel like we [Garza and Alonso] closed a circle that needed to be closed, and I have no doubt that Alonso trusts me more than ever before."

In any case, in caregiving and counseling with young men, ministers ought to keep in mind that young men may experience, both consciously

---

7. See, for example, Glen O. Gabbard's discussion of the case of Dr. A and Mr. B. Aware of her countertransference feelings for Mr. B., Dr. A. began a process of self-analysis that entailed consultation with a colleague. In this way, Dr. A was able to contain and process constructively her erotic countertransference. Gabbard (1994) explains, "Erotic countertransference becomes less mysterious and compelling when exposed to the light of the day and discussed as a matter of rational discourse between analyst and consultant" (p. 1100).

and unconsciously, homoerotic desire. I believe Dykstra (2012b) is right in pointing out that ministers as "curators of funny emotions"[8] and, I would add, as curators of desire, ought to "simply honor the need for . . . young men to keep silent about the uncomfortable truths of their lives—maybe not forever silent but at least for a time, possibly a long time" (p. 69). After a long time, it is possible that some men, like Garza and Alonso, will trust the strength of their friendship to a degree that they can, indeed, break the silence. More often than not, however, a minister's task will simply be to curate, to take care of a young man's desires, by offering an empathic and compassionate environment where the young man can explore his desires and feel less lonely. Dykstra (2012a) notes that "effective caregiving does not mean having to say everything one notices, thinks, or feels in the relationship, especially with older adolescent boys and young men" (p. 74). Rather, "curators *notice, nurture, and uphold*" desires and funny emotions in men's lives (p. 74). The minister as curator of desire accompanies the young man's journey and willingly embraces the uncertainties that an unknown road entails, assured that the Spirit of Christ is leading him and his parishioner to a place of healing and liberation.

Would I encourage a male minister to share a bed with a male parishioner, even if he is an adult? Would I allow my own adolescent son to accompany a male minister to visit a family in a faraway town? These are hard questions to answer. Even if both the minister and the parishioner are male adults, boundary violations, including sexual boundary violations, can occur. Ministers ought to monitor their countertransference enactments judiciously, including their thoughts, feelings, bodily sensations, and dreams, and avoid situations that are likely to lead to boundary violations.

While the framework of pastoral accompaniment upholds the minister's fiduciary responsibility, it also rejects rigid boundaries. To paraphrase Ingram (1991), at the end of the day, the intimacy of a caregiving or counseling situation proceeds at a pace that is highly specific to the caregiving relationship of a particular caregiver with a care seeker (p. 410). This therapeutic insight affirms the commitment of pastoral care and counseling to a radical respect for the uniqueness of each care seeker. On the other hand, this caveat adds a level of complexity to a model of intimate care insofar as it refuses to establish one prescription for every caregiving situation. From a theological perspective, however, this is precisely what is needed. By

---

8. Dykstra borrows the term "funny emotions" from literary critic Abelove (2003). According to Abelove, "emotions are funny when, on the one hand, they are associated with fun or pleasure, and when, on the other, they are likely to be made fun of—mocked, derided, trivialized, even stigmatized" (xii).

embracing those spaces of uncertainty and risk, the minister affirms his or her belief in the life-giving intervention of the Spirit of Christ.

As I reflect on my caregiving with young Mexican men, I have no doubt that the Spirit of Christ has often intervened in my favor. After many years in ministry, the words of Jesus in Luke 12:12 remain true to me: "the Holy Spirit will teach you at the very hour what you ought to say" (NRSV). Interestingly, the purpose of these words in the context of Luke 12 is to assuage the "anxious" feelings of a disciple who has "to conduct a defense at law" before a court (Evans 1990, p. 519). Because issues of boundaries in caregiving relationships may foster anxiety, the words of Luke 12:12 are quite relevant for ministers who care for and counsel with young people. This does not mean, of course, that a minister should not be intentional about maintaining healthy boundaries.[9] But ministers ought to remember that in moments of uncertainty and risk the Spirit will teach them what to say "at that very hour" and will empower them to maintain "appropriate witness."[10]

Ministers who work with young Mexican men ought to remain open to the possibilities that new roads entail. Colombian psychiatrist Restrepo (1997) argues for this sense of openness: "In order to access the gratuity of existence, it is indispensable, it is imperative to be completely open to chance, light, ready to weave at the compass of life, allowing ourselves to be trapped by the rhythm that life proposes" (p. 105).[11] For those of us in ministry, Restrepo's words may ring truer if we say that to access the graciousness of life, ministers have to allow themselves to dance to the rhythm that the Spirit of God plays. Ministers in many places and times have followed the Spirit's rhythm and, in doing so, have effectively cared for young men and women. As this article attests, some of these stories continue to be told and inspire others to keep on caring.

---

9. Evans explains that the Greek verb *merimnān* may mean "to be unduly concerned," "to be anxious," but its basic meaning is "to care" or "to be concerned about" (as in Philemon 2:20). As Evans (1990) puts it, "The question then at issue is when a proper concern has become an improper anxiety" (p. 526).

10. Kuecker (2011) explains that Luke 12:12 refers to the disciple's "testimony before antagonistic judges," but it can also be understood, more generally, as "the role of the Spirit in the cultivation of appropriate witness" (p. 212).

11. The phrase *tejer al compás de la vida* (weave at the compass of life) is difficult to translate. Women (and perhaps a few men) in Mexico and other Latin American countries used to gather to knit or weave while listening to a phonograph. In a sense, the rhythm of the music determined the rhythm of the weaving. The idea of knitting or weaving at the compass of life may be a reference to this practice.

CONCLUSION

When it comes to the care of men, for many years I have been impressed by the friendship motif in the Gospel of John. Given its interweaving of friendship and food, one of my favorite biblical narratives is the story of Jesus' encounter with his disciples by the Sea of Tiberias (John 21). According to the narrative, when the disciples—to whom he had previously referred as *friends*—came to the shore, "they saw a charcoal fire there, with fish on it, and bread" (v. 9). Later on, "Jesus said to them, 'Come and have breakfast'" (v. 12a). In full color and flavor, this story evokes accompaniment, and, as Goizueta (1995) notes, accompaniment (*ad-cum-panis*) implies breaking bread with (p. 205).

Given the interplay between friendship and food, the story of the breakfast by the Sea of Tiberias offers a fitting metaphor for the pastoral accompaniment of young men. Many of my pastoral conversations with young Mexican men have happened in *taquerías* (taco shops). Insofar as they are usually crowded and noisy, *taquerías* may not be ideal spaces to talk. They are, however, excellent spaces to cultivate friendship.[12] And when a minister cultivates with a young man a personal relationship akin to friendship, the young man is more likely to express his intimate concerns.

Pastoral relationships akin to friendship do not entail the elimination of the power differential between minister and parishioner. Such pretension would only reinforce the power differential (Capps 2001, p. 220). Rather, I believe that caregiving relationships between male ministers and young adult men over time enable a new kind of friendship. In this kind of ministerial friendship, the pastor intentionally and judiciously endures the tension between the power differential and the search for mutuality. In other words, while acknowledging the asymmetry of the pastoral relationship and honoring his professional commitments, the minister facilitates an intimate environment of care and understanding.

In the farewell discourse of the Gospel of John, Jesus adopts the language of friendship to describe his relationship with his disciples: "I do not

---

12. Although Sullivan (1998) does not suggest that only gay men can be friends, he explains that "the trajectory of a homosexual life often places, in a way unique to itself, a focus on friendship that many heterosexuals, to their great loss, never quite attain" (p. 230). I suggest that, by virtue of their vocation, ministers may be in a unique position to foster friendships with and among their male parishioners. By doing so, ministers can enrich the spiritual and emotional life of men, especially those heterosexual men who may be secretly longing for significant male friendships. As Sullivan points out, "The fear of male intimacy, which is intrinsically connected to the fear of homosexuality, has too often denied straight men the bonds they need to sustain themselves through life's difficulties" (p. 234).

call you servants any longer, because the servant does not know what the master is doing; but I have called you friends, because I have made known to you everything that I have heard from my Father" (15:15 NRSV). Biblical scholars have different opinions about the meaning of friendship in this verse and throughout the Gospel of John. Crook (2011), for example, posits that John 15:12–17 is an example of "fictive-friendship." Crook explains that fictive-friendship refers to the practice in the Greco-Roman world of adopting the language of friendship "to mask a relationship of dependence and to diminish the attendant stigma" (p. 5). In the Gospel of John, Jesus is "essentially equal to God," Jesus is superior to his disciples and cannot be a real friend to them (p. 6). In other words, Crook claims that the relationship between Jesus and his disciples is "one of fictive-friendship, not actual friendship" (p. 6).

Interestingly, Crook (2011) notes that the fictiveness of a friendship does not preclude its effectiveness, nor does he "cast aspersions on [such] a relationship" (p. 7). Using Crook's model, one could posit that the ministerial friendship I'm advocating in this chapter is fictive-friendship. Is the relationship between Alonso and Pastor Garza a fictive-friendship? Insofar as Mexican culture tends to be hierarchical, one could argue that the idea of ministerial friendship among Mexicans is just a way of masking power inequality. Ultimately, however, even if Alonso and Garza are fictive friends, one would have to concede that their relationship is nevertheless intimate and effective. I conclude, however, by considering an alternative interpretation.

In *Echoes of Friendship in the Gospel of John*, Culy (2010) argues that in the Gospel of John, Jesus invites his followers "to enjoy a level of intimacy with him that can actually (and perhaps only) be compared to the level of intimacy that he enjoys with the Father" (pp. 178–179). Jesus and his followers are not equal, but this does not imply that their friendship is fictive. For Culy, the Gospel of John makes the startling claim that "ideal friendship *can* exist where ontological equality is absent" (p. 177, emphasis in original). Ultimately, the Johannine motif of an ideal friendship is "theologically revolutionary" precisely because it makes the radical claim that friendship between God and human beings is possible (pp. 187–188).[13]

The idea of genuine friendships within caregiving relationships does not imply that the power differential between ministers and parishioners

---

13. According to Sullivan (1998), Aristotle believed that two unequal partners could be friends as long as each of them recognized "the unequal nature of their relative positions" (p. 245). Aristotle (1980) pointed out, however, that when there is a great distance between parties, friendship is no longer viable: "when one party is removed to a great distance, as God is, the possibility of friendship ceases" (p. 204).

can be eliminated or that absolute mutuality within these relationships is possible or even desirable. Rather, it asserts that Christianity and friendship are intimately connected. After all, "One becomes a Christian to aspire to friendship, to become a better friend" (Dykstra 2012a, p. 80). And if one becomes a better friend, one is more likely to care effectively for others.

Jeremías, the young man to whom I referred earlier in this chapter, used to address me as *hermano* (brother). Although this is the conventional salutation among Christians in Mexico, Jeremías is right in pointing out that the word *hermano* communicates respect but also conveys "a sense of distance." Recently, Jeremías began to call me *amigo* (friend). When I asked him to explain this shift, he responded: "One cannot open one's heart to everyone. I call you friend because I have opened my heart to you." In all my years of ministry, I have known no greater honor than the invitation to enter an open heart. Upon entering, the minister discovers that taking care of a young man's desires and hopes demands much time and effort. But with great demand comes the promise of an inner reservoir of creative energy that defies responsibly the rigidity of human boundaries. If in caring for and counseling with young Mexican men ministers embrace the promises of Jesus—the one who calls them friends—it is likely that these young men will not only develop enough trust to voice their most intimate concerns but also that they will gather the courage to actualize their creative energy, uncover their obscured potentials, and reclaim their sense of vocation.

REFERENCES

Abelove, H. (2003). *Deep gossip*. University of Minnesota Press.
Alves, R. A. (1968). Towards a theology of liberation: An exploration of the encounter between the languages of humanistic messianism and messianic humanism. (Unpublished doctoral dissertation, Princeton Theological Seminary).
Aristotle. (1980). *Nicomachean ethics* (D. Ross, Trans.). Oxford University Press.
Berg, I. K., & Dolan, Y. M. (2001). *Tales of solutions: A collection of hope-inspiring stories*. Norton.
Capps, D. (2001). *Giving counsel: A minister's guidebook*. Chalice.
Cervantes-Ortiz, L. (2003). *Series de sueños: La teología ludo-erótico-poética de Rubem Alves*. Departamento de Comunicaciones Consejo Latinoamericano de Iglesias.
Cervantes-Ortiz, L. (2016). A theology of human joy: The liberating-poetic-ludic theology of Rubem Alves. *Perspectivas, 13*, 6–26.
Crook, Z. A. (2011). Fictive-friendship and the fourth gospel. *HTS Teologiese Studies/Theological Studies, 67*, 1–7. https://doi.org/10.4102/hts.v67i3.997/.
Culberston, P. (1996). Men and Christian friendship. In B. Krondorfer (Ed.), *Men's bodies, men's gods: Male identities in a (post-) Christian culture* (pp. 149–180). New York University Press.
Culy, M. M. (2010). *Echoes of friendship in the Gospel of John*. Sheffield Phoenix.

De Campo, A. (1991). *Pueblo y canto* (3rd ed.). UNAM, Coordinación de Humanidades.
Díaz-Guerrero, R. (1975). *Psychology of the Mexican: Culture and personality*. University of Texas Press.
Doehring, C. (2015). *The practice of pastoral care: A postmodern approach* (2nd ed.). Westminster John Knox.
Dykstra, R. C. (2007). The spiritual quest of the loser. In R. C. Dykstra, A. H. Cole Jr., & D. Capps (Eds.) *Losers, loners, and rebels: The spiritual struggles of boys* (pp. 45–76). Westminster John Knox.
Dykstra, R. C. (2012a). Friendly fire. In R. C. Dykstra, A. H. Cole Jr., & D. Capps (Eds.) *The faith and friendships of teenage boys* (pp. 71–84). Westminster John Knox.
Dykstra, R. C. (2012b). Subversive friendships. In R. C. Dykstra, A. H. Cole Jr., & D. Capps (Eds.) *The faith and friendships of teenage boys* (pp. 43–69). Louisville: Westminster John Knox.
Dykstra, R. C. (2015). Finding language for what matters most: Hosting conversations about sexuality in pastoral counseling. *Pastoral Psychology, 64*, 663–680. https://doi.org/10.1007/s11089-015-0656-2.
Evans, C. F. (1990). *Saint Luke*. SCM.
Evans, R. I., & Erikson, E. H. (1967). *Dialogue with Erik Erikson*. Harper & Row.
Freud, S. (2011). *Group psychology and the analysis of the ego*. Empire.
Gabbard, G. O. (1994). Sexual excitement and countertransference love in the analyst. *Journal of the American Psychoanalytic Association, 42*, 1083–1106.
Goizueta, R. S. (1995). *Caminemos con Jesús: Toward a Hispanic/Latino theology of accompaniment*. Orbis.
Greenspan, M. (1996). Out of bounds. In K. H. Ragsdale (Ed.), *Boundary wars: Intimacy and distance in healing relationships* (pp. 129–136). Pilgrim.
Hiltner, S. (1950). Friendship in counseling. *Pastoral Psychology, 1*, 28–34.
Ingram, D. H. (1991). Intimacy in the psychoanalytic relationship: A preliminary sketch. *American Journal of Psychoanalysis, 51*, 403–410.
Kuecker, A. (2011). *The Spirit and the "other": Social identity, ethnicity and intergroup reconciliation in Luke-Acts*. T. & T. Clark.
Phillips, A. (2016). *Unforbidden pleasures*. Farrar, Straus & Giroux.
Restrepo, L. C. (1997). *El derecho a la ternura*. LOM.
Reyes Nevarez, S. (1952). *El amor y la amistad en el mexicano*. Porrúa y Obregón.
Sperry, L., & Pies, R. (2010). Writing about clients: Ethical considerations and options. *Counseling and Values, 54*, 88–102.
Sullivan, A. (1998). *Love undetectable: Notes on friendship, sex, and survival*. Vintage.
Tillich, P. (1984). *The meaning of health: Essays in existentialism, psychoanalysis, and religion*. (P. D. LeFevre, Ed.). Exploration.
Waters, S. (2015). Identity in the empathic community: Alcoholics Anonymous as a model community for storytelling and change. *Pastoral Psychology, 64*, 769–782. https://doi.org/10.1007/s11089-015-0649-1.
Zea, L. (1952). *Conciencia y posibilidad del mexicano*. Porrúa y Obregón.

8

Men, Warriorism, and Mourning
The Development of Unconventional Warriors

RYAN LAMOTHE

> Let's put the imagery in a nutshell: an Airborne Ranger executes daring missions to rescue humanity at the cost of his own life. That's exactly what Jesus does for us.
>
> (MCDOUGALL 2015, P. 6)

> Its [Warrior Culture's] martial ethic connects American warriors today with those whose previous sacrifices allowed our nation to persevere. You, the individual Soldier, are the foundation for the Warrior Culture.
>
> (U.S. ARMY 2008, P. 1-3)

> Human beings love their weapons, crafting them with the skills of Hephaistos and the beauty of Aphrodite for the purpose of Ares.
>
> (HILLMAN 2003, P. 125)

> America has always had a warrior culture.
>
> (GIBSON 1994, P. 17)

MEN, WARRIORISM, AND MOURNING

Since its founding, the United States has relied on its military to expand its territory, subdue and remove native populations (Welch 2004), secure trade routes, topple governments (Kinzer 2006), train indigenous paramilitary groups (Zinn 2005), and threaten noncompliant states and their peoples. The government's use of the military has required establishing and maintaining a warrior ethos that enshrines obedience to the Constitution, the people, the government, and the nation. For centuries, then, young men have been motivated to join the military for various reasons.[1] The allure of the military and its warrior ethos is, for many, almost religious, providing men with a sense of identity, a close-knit synchronic and diachronic community, a way of life, and a transcendent mission. For those who elect to remain in the military, only a few become unconventional warriors, questioning and critiquing their political masters.

In this chapter, I consider the interrelation between the warrior ethos, warriorism, and mourning. More specifically, the question I seek to answer is how a young man moves from warriorism—an uncritical idealization of warrior values and beliefs—to being an unconventional warrior who, although remaining attached to the warrior ethos, is critical toward a government that uses its military to further the aims of political and economic elites. To understand this process, I rely on psychology of religion perspectives to understand warriorism, because it has many parallels to religion. In addition, I find Nathan Carlin's (2014) discussion of religious mourning helpful in framing this process of change or conversion, though I amend his view of mourning as reversal and restoration of religion. Finally, to illustrate my claims, I use the life of Marine Major General Smedley Butler—a two-time recipient of the Medal of Honor, the nation's highest award for valor. I begin with a discussion of the attributes of the warrior ethos and its

---

1. The use of the term "young men" is fluid, since there is no clear social-cultural marker in U.S. history that indicates the transition from boyhood to manhood, though legally 18-year-old males are considered men. In U.S. history, males under the age of 18, like Smedley Butler, joined the military as teenagers and were considered men. Pressfield (2011) notes that the military and its attending warrior ethos provides many young men, including boys who are under the age of 18, with the rituals and ordeals to secure their identity as men in the warrior ethos. One other point concerns this chapter's focus on men, warrior ethos, and warriorism. Ehrenreich (1997) writes that war and the warrior ethos have been, throughout history, the province of men. Indeed, she argues that "war is . . . one of the most rigidly 'gendered' activities known to humankind" (p. 125). Nevertheless, women warriors, as Ehrenreich notes, have taken part in wars and revolutions (pp. 128–129, 154–156). The gendering of war remains largely true, but the recent graduation of women from the U.S. Army's elite Ranger School and the U.S. Defense Department's change in policies regarding women in combat suggests a less rigid gendering. In this chapter, however, I restrict my focus to male warriors, though it would be interesting to explore the differences between female and male warriors.

psychological allure for young men. This lays the foundation for indicating how the adoption of the warrior ethos can lead to warriorism, which fosters conventional, obedient, and unquestioning warriors. In this section, I describe the psychosocial features of warriorism and identify how it parallels religious fundamentalism. The final section depicts the process of Butler's mourning, moving from being a conventional warrior to an unconventional warrior.

Before taking up my argument, I offer a few clarifying remarks. The reader may wonder why I am choosing to address this subject regarding the vicissitudes of male identity in relation to warrior ethos, warriorism, and mourning. I offer several responses. First, from its beginnings the United States has been, in many ways, a martial culture (Gibson 1994). This is evident in its violent territorial expansion and in its economic expansionism throughout the continent and other parts of the globe. Indeed, the notion of "citizen soldier" reflects the intersection of a putative democratic society and the warrior culture, which the state made use of vis-à-vis its imperial aims. Also, this martial ethic was and is frequently supported and justified by Christian individuals and groups.[2] If we turn from history books to the media, the martial culture appears in the news media, movies (Gibson 1994), and, more recently, the plethora of violent military electronic games (Capozzi 2013; Happ and Melzer 2014). In brief, the warrior ethos is part of our cultural DNA, which suggests that the phenomenon of warriorism is prevalent and, therefore, a necessary focus for analysis. Second, and relatedly, the expansion of violent military electronic gaming raises new questions and problems. Before electronic games, the media and entertainment industry, more often than not, promoted the warrior ethos, which often drew men to the ranks of the military. Gibson notes that the portrayals of the military and combat were mostly fantasies and heightened the fantasies of boys and men who were attracted to a military ethos. When young men joined the military, these illusions confronted very real physical and mental ordeals, as well as violence and the horrors of military life and combat, making it possible for men to be disillusioned. The proliferation of military gaming expands identification of the warrior ethos among boys and men without any connection to reality—unless, of course, men join the military. This reality of the proliferation of war gaming, along with the media spectacle of U.S. military operations in other countries, means that the warrior

---

2. In U.S. history, we see the intersection of Christianity and the martial ethic in Harriet Beecher Stowe's (Kaplan 2002, pp. 29, 32) and Senator Beveridge's (Johnson 2004, p. 43) evangelical desire to bring civilization to the "uncivilized." The military, in these instances, becomes the "civilizing" element. A more recent illustration of this is Rev. MacDougall's (2015) book on the warrior Christ.

ethos is increasingly divorced from the consequences of becoming a real, not virtual, warrior. The result of this is that mourning or disillusionment is less likely, which, in turn, means a decline in the presence of unconventional warriors. In short, a virtual warrior society, cut off from the realities of war and military life, is caught up in the pleasures of virtual aggression without having to experience the sweat, fear, pain, chaos, guilt, and horror of real combat. It is a spectacle-driven society of conventional, virtual warriors—a society more dangerous for its lack of questioning and critique.

My final remark is a confession. Wittingly or unwittingly, scholars in the human sciences, at times, take up questions to understand themselves. When this topic emerged, I was initially unaware that it involved me personally. At the age of 18, I entered West Point (United States Military Academy), an educational institution that prepares warrior leaders. During my four years at West Point and six years in the Army I went to Ranger School (the Army's "elite" warrior training), Airborne School, and SERE (Survival, Escape, Resistance, and Evasion). I drank deeply from the well of the warrior ethos and only became "unconventional" years later, after leaving the total environment of the military and marrying a left-wing activist. Perhaps this is why I was attracted to Smedley Butler and his journey.

WARRIOR ETHOS AND WARRIORISM DESCRIBED

Geertz (1973) writes that a "people's ethos is the tone, character, and quality of their life, its moral and aesthetic style and mood; it is the underlying attitude toward themselves and their world that life reflects" (p. 127). The group's tone, character, and quality of life are shaped by narratives, rituals, and daily practices that comprise the shared beliefs, expectations, mores, values, customs, and aims that provide individuals and the group with a shared identity, ways of being in the world, and vision. Although Geertz is thinking of a people from a particular culture, this perspective easily fits with military individuals who adopt the group's warrior ethos. Of course, it is more accurate to say that the group that adopts the warrior ethos is also part of the ethos of the larger society. So, along with the similarities, we would expect to see some differences between the warrior ethos of one society and the warrior ethos of another.

The United States' warrior ethos is spelled out in the U.S. Army's Field Manual (2008), *The Warrior Ethos and Soldier Combat Skills*. In the first section (Warrior Ethos), the Soldier's Creed is presented:

> I am an American soldier. I am a warrior and a member of a team. I serve the people of the United States and live the Army

values. I will always place the mission first. I will never accept defeat. I will never quit. I will never leave a fallen comrade. I am disciplined, physically and mentally tough, trained and proficient in my Warrior tasks and drills. I always maintain my arms, my equipment, and myself . . . I stand ready to deploy, engage and destroy the enemies of the United States of America in close combat. I am a guardian of freedom and the American way of life. (U.S. Army 2008, p. 1–1).

The values that an American warrior is to live by are loyalty, duty, respect, selfless service, honor, integrity, and personal courage (p. 1–2). These values undergird the combat skills depicted in the remaining chapters of this training manual.

There are a number of important features about this creed of the warrior. The individual is the obvious speaker, but it is clear that he is a loyal member of a group of warriors and of a larger group—the people of the United States. In being part of the group, one is expected to be loyal as well as to be willing to serve others, even to the point of the ultimate self-sacrifice.[3] As a warrior, one is also expected to be proficient in using and maintaining military equipment, skilled in the martial arts, and disciplined in mind and body. With these skills, the warrior stands ready to engage and destroy "enemies" that threaten the United States. The vision—in this case, an extremely vague one—that guides the warrior is not combat per se but the protection of freedom and the American way of life.[4] Moreover, a cursory view of the larger U.S. culture shows that this warrior ethos is supported by U.S. patriotism and exceptionalism.[5] The *conventional* U.S. warrior, in short, abides by the warrior creed as well as uncritically proclaims his patriotism, believing wholeheartedly in U.S. exceptionalism.[6]

3. Pressfield (2011) emphasizes selflessness as a common value in various warrior creeds, dating back to the Spartans (pp. 42–45). Selflessness and trust are crucial if a group is to be successful in combat.

4. Bacevich (2002, 2005) notes that the warrior ethos, such as self-sacrifice and commitment to the good of the group, is at odds with many of the mores of contemporary culture, which emphasizes individualism and acquisitiveness. It is ironic that U.S. warriors are asked to protect an American way of life that touts individualism, materialism, and a profligate way of living.

5. Numerous authors address the pervasiveness of U.S. exceptionalism in the wider culture. See Chomsky (2003, 2005), Fullbright (1966), and Johnson (2010).

6. The warrior ethos can also be intertwined with and supported by religious beliefs. As Barbara Ehrenreich (1997) notes, many warrior cultures have religious underpinnings. Two contemporary examples of this are Weber's book *Tender Warriors* and McDougall's book *Jesus Was an Airborne Ranger*. In my view, these books heighten or, more accurately, ontologize the transcendent feature of the warrior ethos and warriorism, making it even more difficult to develop a critical stance. In other words,

A young man who joins the military is introduced to the warrior creed in boot camp, and it is re-emphasized in field exercises, combat training, parades/awards, promotions, and other forms of training (French 2005). The aim is not to say the creed, as if one is citing the Nicene Creed in church, but to live and embody the creed, which diverse military practices and rituals inculcate and strengthen. And since I mentioned church, let me add that the United States military is a near total environment that serves as a disciplinary regime that forms, maintains, and reinforces the warrior ethos and community. By total environment, I mean the reality of military bases where soldiers are housed, shop (at the PX or Post Exchange), obtain medical care (from military doctors), and seek entertainment (at Officers' and NCOs' clubs). As James Hillman (2003) notes, "The military have their own jurisdiction, their own courts, their own prisons; they obey their own codes, observe their own remembrances, march to their own music, care for their own graveyards" (pp. 88–89). In this total environment, soldiers adopt language that is familiar to them and not to civilians, reinforcing group solidarity and their identity as warriors (Beder 2012). It is difficult to convey, but once a recruit enters this total environment, it is nearly all-encompassing. From a psychological perspective, this warrior environment functions, in part, to excise the civilian self and form a warrior self. The new soldier, in other words, begins to internalize the warrior ethos, eventually making it a significant part of his identity. He no longer identifies himself as a citizen but as a soldier-warrior. That said, the warrior ethos of the U.S. military is deeply attached to a wider, socially held idea of U.S. exceptionalism and civilian expressions of patriotism, as mentioned above. The total environment is, therefore, not separated from the larger culture's patriotic fervor and U.S. exceptionalism. Indeed, the warrior ethos and the total environment of the military are supported by the patriotic fervor of citizens.

Considering the traits of a warrior ethos naturally leads one to wonder about what draws boys and men to enlist, submitting to physical-mental ordeals and placing themselves, at times, in peril. First, I note that the rigors of military life seem more fitting for the physical strengths and endurance of young men. Typically, the age group that joins this total environment is 17- to 20-year-olds,[7] though the Air Force has raised the age limit in recent years.[8] This is not simply because young men, guided by the illusions of

---

Christianizing the warrior ethos further secures the inevitability of the development of conventional warriors.

7. Are you eligible to join the military?, Military.com, http://www.military.com/join-armed-forces/join-the-military-basic-eligibility.html.

8. Chris Carroll, Air Force raises enlistee age limit from 27 to 39, *Stars and Stripes*, http://www.stripes.com/news/air-force/air-force-raises-enlistee-age-limit-from-27-to-

omnipotence or phallic narcissism, are needed to engage in the rigors of combat. There are other attractions. In Western cultures, because of the lack of social rituals that function to facilitate the transition from boyhood to manhood, many boys and young men are predisposed to find military life captivating. Two psychoanalytic perspectives are helpful in understanding the allure of the warrior ethos for boys and young men. Erik Erikson (1963) believed that there were eight stages in human lifespan development. The stage that corresponds to most new recruits is "when childhood comes to an end [and] the individual moves into the fifth stage, which is termed identity versus role confusion" (p. 261). In this period, adolescents are "now primarily concerned with what they appear to be in the eyes of others as compared with what they feel they are . . . and they are ever ready to install lasting idols and ideals as guardians of a final identity" (p. 261). Put another way, an adolescent individual is differentiating from earlier familial identifications while forming new extra-familial identifications and loyalties (Erikson 1982, pp. 56–57). This suggests, then, that establishing an identity and integrating earlier identifications with new ones means that the adolescent is motivated to join a particular group and adopt its ideals. Indeed, Erikson notes that adolescent "'falling in love,' which is by no means entirely, or even primarily, a sexual matter . . . is an attempt to arrive at a definition of one's identity" (1963, p. 262)—an identity that is linked to both meaning and purpose. The underlying anxiety, or what Erikson calls danger, is role confusion, and this anxiety motivates adolescents to seek out clear ideals to establish a secure identity within the confines of a group of like-minded people. Erikson suggests further that adolescents are particularly vulnerable to over-identifying with a particular group (p. 262), which means that they will be unlikely to possess a critical self-reflective stance toward the group.

In an earlier section of *Childhood and Society*, Erikson (1963) depicts the Sioux people and an adolescent boy's transition to manhood by way of the group's rituals—rituals that help solidify the identity of and concomitant ideals associated with being a hunter and warrior (pp. 145–153). As a hunter and warrior, the young Sioux man obtains a clear sense of meaning and purpose vis-à-vis the group and the collective vision of the group. Similarly, Ehrenreich (1997), in her historical and cross-cultural research, notes the varied rituals involved in boys becoming warriors, which by definition means men (pp. 117–131). These rituals, she notes, provide individuals with meanings and purposes associated with the protection and flourishing of the group. Likewise, Pressfield (2011) depicts the importance of warrior rituals in facilitating the process of boys establishing their identities as men (pp.

27–29). The allure, then, of the warrior ethos for adolescent boys and young men is understood in terms of psychosocial developmental needs wherein young males seek a secure identity that is joined to higher or transcendent meanings and purposes.

One may wonder why adolescent boys do not join chess or book clubs instead of joining the military with all of its rigors and dangers. Are not there other groups that would provide the allure of a secure identity? The simple answer is yes, but in a warrior society the collective ego ideal is the warrior. The allure, then, is not only a secure identity but a secure identity that is highly prized by the larger culture. Even if a chess club provided rituals, ordeals, and clear markers of identity, it could not compete with the idealization associated with being a warrior in a warrior society.

An illustration of the allure of the military or warrior ethos for young men is seen in Smedley Butler's decision at age 16 to join the U.S. Marine Corps. Schmidt (1987) writes that Butler was "swept up in the enthusiasm for the Cuban War" (p. 6), which was widely popular in the United States at the time. Young Butler's enthusiasm was no doubt linked to the media that fanned the flames of war, but it was also part of his family upbringing, even though they were Quakers. Schmidt notes that Smedley's father was celebrated as the fighting Quaker and was "well known for staunch sponsorship of the navy and marines during a tenure lasting three decades on the House Naval Affairs Committee" (pp. 6–7). Thus, it was not a stretch for Smedley Butler to enlist in the Marines, which at the time was a small cadre of warriors. Schmidt notes that Butler "quit school in favor of a military initiation into manhood" wherein he "picked up the warrior cult of physical masculinity and a corresponding anti-intellectualism" (pp. 9–10). With this group and this war, young Butler could attain manhood and, like his father, be known as the fighting Quaker.

In Smedley Butler's training to become a warrior, Schmidt writes, there was "heavy emphasis on blind obedience and rote learning" (p. 7), which one might say is the initial price the young Butler paid to be assured of a warrior identity and inclusion in the group. Along with blind obedience and rote learning, the military values of courage and honor were repeatedly preached, which Butler clearly internalized—the evidence of which is his being awarded two Congressional Medals of Honor. Given his teenage psychosocial developmental needs and attributes, his attraction to military life in the Marine Corps would mean that Butler was seeking an identity as well as a secure sense of meaning and purpose. And, like many boys and young men, Butler's enthusiasm almost certainly led to an over-identification with the group and its warrior ethos of obedience, loyalty, and sacrifice. This initiation into military life, in other words, meant Butler was well on his way to becoming a conventional warrior, obedient to and acritical of military and civilian authorities.

Erikson's comment about adolescent love not being entirely or primarily a sexual matter hints at another related allure of the warrior ethos for both adolescents and adult men. To understand this, I rely on Carlin and Capps's (2015) work on sublimation vis-à-vis masculinities. They argue that men often sublimate their erotic desires in their engagement and cooperation with other men, which, for instance, they contend is illustrated in the mutual affection and shared work of Sigmund Freud and James Jackson Putnam (pp. 18–29). If we transpose the notion of sublimation to the realm of the military and its warrior ethos, it is possible to see that part of the allure of the warrior ethos for both boys and men is male cooperation and bonding—what is commonly referred to as comradeship, which many authors describe as a key element and result of joining a group of warriors (Gray 1970). James Hillman (2003), for instance, using different language, recognizes the presence of love and the erotic in military life. He writes:

> There is tenderness. One man diverts another from self-centered preoccupation. A man helps another man to die . . . Men in small units care for each other, cover for each other.
> *Kamradschaft* is the German word for this kind of intimacy. (p. 147).

Distinguishing between comradeship and friendship, Gray (1970) writes, "Suffering and danger cannot create friendship, but they make all the difference in comradeship" (p. 89). Friendship, Gray notes, can fade, but the feelings of comradeship remain long after men leave the military. Similarly, Butler, in his autobiography, recalls "an easy and friendly relationship [that] prevailed between officers and enlisted men on the march. We were sharing the same hardships . . . I've always had a deep affection for the veterans who brought me up" (as quoted in Schmidt 1987, p. 26). Thus, the warrior ethos and attending military life are inextricably linked to camaraderie and a kinship with previous service members throughout history (Ehrenreich 1997). The allure, then, is not simply identity or even a shared identity but the sublimation of the erotic in the form of comradeship.

There are two important clarifications to make. First, comradeship and loyalty are not necessarily dependent on engaging in combat. Long before men go to war, if they go to war, they are engaged in demanding shared physical ordeals and rituals that stress the necessity of group cooperation and the subordination of the individual to group goals. Combat training is rigorous, focusing on teamwork, self-sacrifice, and the achievement of the mission. As noted in the warrior ethos above, individuals are to place their ego or self in the service of the group's aim. This collective self-surrender, which can be understood in terms of the notion of sublimation, fosters comradeship, even if warriors never experience the indelible stench of cordite, blood, sweat, and feces. A second point of clarification concerns the transition from boyhood to manhood. Above, I suggested that one of the allures of a warrior ethos is its clear rituals for establishing one's identity as a man. This is alluring for boys and young men, yet, once this is attained and secure, how do we account for the continued allure of military life? To be sure, there are other possible motivations for remaining in the military (e.g., job security, lust for war, prestige, etc.), but I argue the experience of comradeship is an important motivator. Hillman (2003) notes the power of comradeship, remarking that soldiers "who had been lightly wounded or briefly relieved sometimes sneaked back to their units, called by solidarity with their buddies" (p. 147). Schmidt's (1987) biography of Smedley Butler's life in the military reveals this as well. Butler, when wounded, did not want to be away from his men. In his biography, there is a constant thread of his love for his men and his comradeship with fellow officers. So, long after Butler attained a warrior identity, the warrior rituals and practices continued to provide the bonds of shared cooperation with other men—younger and older.[9]

The warrior ethos informs us about the values and virtues held by men who seek to become warriors. We can even ascertain the allure of this ethos. However, an ethos does not reveal the kind and strength of group attachments and identifications. When we peer more closely at the total aspects of military life, we note that it is, in many ways, akin to religion, which can help us to understand the particular binding features of the warrior ethos. To understand this kinship, I first delve into the contested notion of religion. Durkheim, a sociologist, argued that religion is "a set of beliefs and practices relative to sacred things ... which unite one single moral community" (as quoted in Morris 1987, p. 115). Avoiding the notion of the sacred, Geertz (1973), a cultural anthropologist, proposed that religion is: (1) a system of symbols which acts to (2) establish powerful, pervasive, and long-lasting moods and motivations in men by (3) formulating conceptions of a general order of existence and (4) clothing these conceptions with such an aura of factuality that (5) moods and motivations seem uniquely realistic" (p. 90). Instead of five features, Allport identified six features of religion, five of which fit the military: (1) it encompasses and orders a complex array of objects, interests, and issues; (2) it offers a system of high ethical standards; (3) it is

---

9. I mention this here because several men served as father figures for Smedley Butler, and later he served as a father figure to officers and enlisted men (Schmidt 1987, pp. 170–172).

comprehensive, "seeking to encompass the totality of human existence... in a unified framework"; (4) it attempts to "form elements into a harmonious whole"; (5) it "infuses life with energy and conserves fundamental values" (as quoted in Wulff 1996, p. 60). When it comes to identifying the connections between these definitions of religion and the military, one might wish to eschew the term "sacred" in describing the religious aspects of military life. This is acceptable, though it is important to recognize that there are clearly transcendent elements in the warrior ethos, such as sacrificing for the greater good, for the nation, etc. Moreover, at times these secular transcendent elements are intertwined with theological beliefs, which can reinforce individuals' motivations to identify with the military's transcendent object and aims (e.g., McDougall 2015). These shared transcendent objects are joined to a complex system of symbols and attending beliefs, values, expectations, and meanings that are collectively used to (1) bind people into a community, (2) provide group members with high ethical standards connected to an overarching moral vision, (3) proffer explanations of the world and the warrior's actions, and (4) establish powerful, pervasive, and long-lasting moods and motivations that are accompanied by an aura of factuality such that moods and motivations seem uniquely realistic. This said, I am not, of course, implying that the military is a religion, rather, that it has similar features associated with religions, especially in its ability to motivate people and deeply bind individuals in shared worldviews and experiences. It is this close kinship with religion that makes it possible to see warriorism as a species of fundamentalism and that allows me to use a psychology of religion approach to understand warriorism and conventional warriors.

Warriorism, which breeds and attracts conventional warriors, is akin to religious fundamentalism, which points to, in part, an unwavering attachment to a set of irreducible beliefs (Nagata 2001). This unwavering attachment accompanies literalism vis-à-vis interpreting scripture or other "sacred" texts. Literal affirmation is one of the four attitudes in religion and the one associated most closely with fundamentalism (Wulff 1997, pp. 635–636). This attitude eschews complexity, ambiguity, and critical reflection. Binary or black-and-white thinking is dominant. The fundamentalist's mind "ceases to be complex, achieving a simplicity held together initially by bindings around the signs of the ideology" (Bollas 1992, p. 201). Ideological or religious certainty reflects the process of simplification, which can be understood in terms of the lack of critical thinking. I would add that a fundamentalist attitude denotes a failure of introspection, which is integral to homogenized minds or groupthink. Fundamentalism, then, results in conventional subjects—individuals who (1) frame questions in ways that confirm their already existing worldview; (2) seek to conserve traditional views without change; (3) only question authority if authority critiques or questions received traditions; and (4) expect group members to hold identical beliefs.

Much of Smedley Butler's early life in the Marine Corps can be understood in terms of warriorism. As Schmidt (1987) points out, Butler was indoctrinated in a system that placed a "heavy emphasis on blind obedience and rote learning" (p. 7). This included a kind of anti-intellectualism associated with lower class military mores (p. 10) and led to a homogenization of military thinking. Early on, Butler unquestioningly accepts orders to fight in Cuba, Philippines, and China. Indeed, he petitions his mother to have "Papa go to the President . . . and request that I be ordered for duty with one of the army regiments up at the front" (p. 11). As a young captain, his considerable mental energies vis-à-vis planning, tactical thinking, and strategizing; his capacities for reflection and introspection; and his critical acumen were all focused on being a warrior leader (p. 19). Put another way, Smedley Butler became a conventional warrior, unquestioning, obedient, and unambiguously certain of the warrior ethos, his duty to his men and nation, and the mission of the Marine Corps.

The attributes of religious fundamentalism detailed above can only take us so far in understanding warriorism. Lacking is how both fundamentalism and warriorism reflect a type of strong emotional attachment and identification of an individual vis-à-vis religion or the military and warrior ethos. To understand this strong attachment and to later depict the change from conventional to unconventional warriors, I turn to two psychoanalytic concepts, namely, adhesive identification and idealization. These concepts set the stage for understanding the process whereby one moves from the conventional warrior of warriorism to being an unconventional warrior. Bick (1968) and Meltzer (1975) initially used the concept of *adhesive identification* to refer to early self-states characterized by the construction of experience around bodily surfaces. Anzieu (1990), Ogden (1989), Tustin (1980, 1984), and others have built on Bick's idea of the earliest stage of development, positing, for instance, auto-sensual forms of relating or autistic forms of organizing experience. The term "adhesion" signifies the baby's intense clinging to the object-surface that provides him or her with a sense of security and continuity. In this early stage of development, the object-surface is the nascent self. Ogden (1989) argued that this early, pre-symbolic mode of organizing experience continues to be present throughout development, though it is altered by and interacts with new cognitive capacities used to construct experience and communicate with others. Ogden's notion of the intersection of modes of organizing experience in adult life is important and helpful in arguing that the presence of an adhesive mode of organizing experience in adult interactions is *not* necessarily regressive, pathological, or primitive. Indeed, Ogden is arguing that strong identifications in adolescence and adult life, although they have connections to earlier forms of organizing experience, are common.

Before moving to the notion of adhesive idealization, I return to Smedley Butler's story as a young warrior in the Marine Corps. We would expect, following Erikson (1963), that any teenage boy seeking to "arrive at a definition of [his] identity" would be vulnerable to over-identifying with the group and its ethos (p. 262). By vulnerable, I mean that Butler, at age 16, was, like other adolescents, in search of an identity distinct from but related to his family. This normal insecurity, I suggest, would have motivated him to identify strongly with the warrior ethos. Of course, the warrior ethos and identity are closely allied with group identification, which the Marine Corps appears to be particularly adept at fostering.[10] Young Butler's enthusiasm for training, for going to war in Cuba, and for petitioning his parents to aid him so that he could join a fighting unit in the Philippines are evidence of his strong or adhesive identification with the Marines and its warrior ethos.

The adult Smedley Butler also strongly identified with the Marine Corps and its warrior ethos. Indeed, despite the changes he made in terms of his political views and attitudes toward military and political leaders, Butler remained attached to the warrior ethos as a major feature of his identity. At the same time, he never lost affection for the soldiers, even when, toward the end of his life, he was considered a pariah. This said, I do not equate the adolescent Butler's strong identification with the kind of identification the older Butler displayed. As an adolescent and young man, Butler did not question military or political leadership. His main focus was being a Marine and leading soldiers in combat. I consider all of this as illustrative of adhesive identification. It was only later in life that Butler became more critical of civilian and military leadership, though he retained a strong identification with the warrior ethos. To understand this metanoia, I turn to the notion of adhesive idealization.

The concept of adhesive identification is close to idealization, but there is an important distinction. Not all adhesive identifications, especially those of early infancy, manifest the capacity for idealization. Idealization (McWilliams 1994; Schafer 1959) is a type of identification that develops later in childhood and has been considered to be important for the development of a child's secure sense of self. In general, idealization involves assigning special, positive value to the object or person, which provides a child or

---

10. The strong bonds forged and identification with the Marine Corps are illustrated in the adage that no Marine obtains a mental discharge from the Corps—once a Marine, always a Marine.

adult with self-esteem and a secure sense of attachment to the object or person. Anxiety-driven idealization, however, is reflected in defensive positive valuations of an object or person, which, in turn, screens pervasive anxiety associated with an insecure self and the threat of loss of one's attachment to the prized object (McWilliams 1994, p. 106). Adhesive idealization, then, refers to a self-state and corresponding organization of experience that reflects a person's strong positive idealized identification with an object, often a shared object, as well as an underlying anxiety. Ogden is helpful in furthering the distinction. From Ogden's viewpoint, the psychological organization related to adhesive identification in early childhood is transformed by the later capacity of idealization. Adhesive idealization, then, is a form of identification characterized by a passionate or intense, rigid, positive valuation of an object (e.g., idea(s), story, individual, group). Put differently, adhesive idealization involves an unyielding identification with the cherished object such that the individual derives an *unquestionable* sense of self-esteem, security, continuity, belongingness, and shared meaning. The metaphorical use of the term adhesive, then, signifies this type of rigid attachment wherein an individual seeks to secure esteem, meaning, belongingness, security, and continuity.

Another important point regarding adhesive idealization has to do with aggression and grandiosity. Some analysts (e.g., Kernberg 1991; Stolorow and Atwood 1978) suggest that grandiosity is a form of adhesive idealization that guards against aggression and disappointment vis-à-vis the idealized object. Moreover, there are secondary gains in bolstering the grandiose self that is associated with the idealized object—security, pleasure, and continuity—though, in the end, these gains are illusory. In adhesive idealization, aggression is deflected toward the devalued Other, which preserves the grandiose sense of self and its positive identification with the beloved object. In other words, aggression toward the devalued Other functions to protect the cherished object and secure a sense of continuity and esteem. When adhesive idealization is shared, aggression is collectively aimed at real or imagined enemies who are believed to threaten the cherished object, and this casts a shadow of grandiosity on its adherents.

I wish to stress here that adhesive idealization in adulthood is not necessarily pathological or primitive or regressive, signifying some early form of attachment. That is, to identify the presence of earlier modes of organizing experience in an adult's adhesive idealization (and devaluation) does not necessarily imply the presence of pathology, immaturity, early deprivation, or developmentally archaic patterns of relating. The adult self-state associated with adhesive idealization signifies modes of organizing experience characterized by intense, positive valuation of the object and, correspondingly, a devaluation of the Other. Patriotic fervor, in other words, is not, in and of itself, pathological or regressive, and, therefore, adhesive idealization simply signifies shared forms of constructing experience whereby participants defensively and rigidly (unquestioningly) assign positive value to an object. This provides members with the shared illusion of a secure, grandiose self as well as a sense of belongingness and continuity, while at the same time screening anxiety.

The early period of Butler's time in the Marine Corps reflects this adhesive idealization of the warrior ethos and the Marine Corps. Shortly after leading his men in a combat with Philippine insurrectionists, Butler went to a local tattoo shop. Schmidt (1987) writes, "In a blatant act of consecration to the marine cult and to manhood attained, Smedley had himself tattooed from the throat to the waist with a Marine Corps globe-and-anchor insignia" (p. 12). Here we have a wonderful example of adhesive identification and idealization wherein the idealized warrior values are etched onto his body. In psychoanalytic parlance, this "adhesion" signifies that the pre-symbolic (skin-object) and symbolic (Marine insignia) organization of experience are joined, providing Butler with a sense of physical and psychological security and continuity. Note, as well, that this is not a small tattoo on his arm but one that covers his entire chest, suggesting grandiosity. Shortly after this, Butler's exuberance and grandiosity are seen in a letter to his mother. "Needless to say," Butler writes as his company is sailing to China, "I am the happiest man alive and that the last few days my feet have not touched the ground at all." The grandiosity of adhesive idealization is further seen in his motivation "not to be outdone in heedless bravery," which "he proved in these weeks of death defying heroism" (p. 15). Schmidt notes that this was connected to hero worship, which "was another enveloping persuasion in the marines . . . that impelled Smedley forward as a teenage daredevil" (p. 16). Finally, the tendency to secure positive idealization by way of aggression vis-à-vis foes is noted when Butler boasted that 1000 Marines could beat 10,000 soldiers—inter-service rivalry.

It is not uncommon that the ordeals of military life and training, as well as the travails of combat, temper one's idealization and identification with the warrior ethos. This seems not to be the case in Butler's long career. Even when he entered civilian life to become police chief of Philadelphia, Butler maintained and lived out the values of the warrior ethos. This said, the almost religious zeal (warriorism) displayed in Butler's early years as a Marine shifted later in his life. The warriorism of his early years—as an obedient, unquestioning, conventional officer—and the attending adhesive identification and idealization changed later in his life. Toward the end of his career and after his retirement, Butler converted to an anti-war, anti-imperialist stance, though he retained his identification with the warrior ethos.

WARRIORISM AND MOURNING

In 1929, while still on active duty, Butler made an after-dinner speech in front of 700 guests. He told the guests "how marines had cynically rigged elections in Nicaragua in 1912, and how they controlled the client president and manipulated politics in Haiti" (Schmidt 1987, p. 204). After that, he became more outspoken and, as a result, was encouraged to retire in 1931. Schmidt notes that Butler's "political views shifted ever more outspokenly toward a radical critique of contemporary events" (p. 217). In an article published in *Common Sense*, Butler wrote:

> I helped make Mexico and especially Tampico safe for American oil interests in 1914. I helped make Haiti and Cuba a decent place for the National City Bank boys to collect revenues in. I helped the raping of a dozen Central American republics for the benefit of Wall Street. The record of racketeering is long. I helped purify Nicaragua for the international banking house of Brown Brothers in 1909–12. I brought light to the Dominican Republic for American sugar interests in 1916. I helped make Honduras "right" for American fruit companies in 1903. In China in 1927 I helped see to it that Standard Oil went its way unmolested . . . Looking back on it, I feel I might have given Al Capone a few hints. The best he could do was to operate his racket in three city districts. We Marines operated in three continents. (Schmidt 1987, p. 231).

During that same year, Butler published a book, *War is a Racket*, that was derived from articles he had written earlier. In this book, he rails against the rich and corporations that profit from war. "At least 21,000 new millionaires and billionaires," he wrote, "were made in the United States during the World War . . . How many of these war millionaires shouldered a rifle?" (1935, p. 23). These business and political leaders "used propaganda to make the boys accept conscription. They were made to feel ashamed if they didn't join the army. So vicious was this war propaganda that even God was brought into it" (p. 36). And who bears the brunt of the economic, physical, and psychological costs of these hugely profitable wars? Regular citizens. Butler acknowledges that "the soldier pays the greater part of the bill, but his family pays too. They pay it in the same heart-break that he does. As he suffers, they suffer . . . And even now the families of the wounded men and of the mentally broken and those who never were able to readjust themselves are still suffering and still paying" (pp. 36–37). Citizens also pay by purchasing war bonds, while war profiteers reap the benefits.

In the last few years of his life, Butler could hear the rattling of sabers as the next world war loomed. Today he would have been called an isolationist, but he could see "the coming interventionist sanctification of war, and spent the last years trying to demystify it" (Schmidt 1987, p. 241). He knew that "Japan happens to be the enemy this year. Next year it may be somebody else" (p. 242). In my view, he was fighting the warriorism prevalent in society and the military.

It is important to point out that Butler was not simply concerned with war and its effects on soldiers and families (and the citizens of other countries who were on the receiving end of U.S. aggression). His critique of big business's use of the military to secure profits was also connected to his recognition that big business colonized citizens. As he remarked, "One class believes that the country was made for them. The other class would like to come in somehow. A few people on one side, and the masses on the other" (Schmidt 1987, p. 218). Still adhering to the warrior ethos, Butler fought for the rights and needs of the lower classes.

These critiques, laments, and confessions are not those of a conventional warrior. There is no hint of warriorism and its adhesive identification/idealization. Butler is no longer the obedient soldier, stifling questions and critiques, though he clearly continued to identify with soldiers and the warrior ethos. The Butler in these excerpts is unconventional, fighting against the principalities of Wall Street, the White House, and other political leaders that send the military to faraway places so that corporate coffers can be filled and careers advanced. How did Butler move from the adhesive identification of warriorism to an unconventional warrior?

In his book, *Religious Mourning*, Nathan Carlin (2014) notes that some "students of religion become disappointed and disillusioned with religion, and they subsequently mourn religion in various ways, often by means of their scholarship" (p. 12). These scholars, he argues, "are still religious but in unconventional ways" (p. 13). Instead of fasting and prayer, they research and write, and maybe go to conferences (p. 13). What Carlin is arguing is that these scholars mourn religion and, in the process, find other ways to be religious and to appreciate religion. In other words, mourning involves a reversal and restoration of religion. Carlin's psychology of religion approach to mourning religion is helpful here as well, though with modifications. For Smedley Butler, the process of "mourning" involved changing from being a conventional warrior to an unconventional one. He replaced planning battles and fighting with fighting for peace, fighting against Wall Street and its politicians, and fighting for soldiers and families that suffered—including the suffering of the lower classes. Butler's change or mourning was a reversal to the extent that the unconventional warrior no longer blindly accepted the government's reasons for the use of the military. However, it was not restoration because, as an unconventional warrior, he never discarded the warrior ethos and his allegiance to his fellow warriors. It is the process of this change that I briefly explain, relying on the notion of adhesive identification and idealization.

For Butler, the seeds of change away from the adhesive identification and idealization of warriorism lay not in the ordeals of military life or in the perils and fears of combat. Recall that Butler thrived in military life and combat. Rather, the seeds lay in his painful disillusionment vis-à-vis military and government bureaucracies. Butler and his men were sent to Honduras in 1903 because of a suspected revolution and concern about American financial interests. Having arrived, Butler regarded the military intervention as pointless (Schmidt 1987, p. 31). Seven years later, Colonel Waller, one of Butler's friends and mentors, was up for commandant of the Marine Corps. Waller failed because of the "fickleness of Washington politics" (p. 37). Although Butler was not above asking his politically connected father (and mother) to help him, he experienced a dawning recognition and disillusionment about political leaders and the decisions they made in relation to the Marine Corps and the consequences of those decisions for the soldiers he led.

After Colonel Waller failed to obtain the promotion, Butler was involved in a number of U.S.-led interventions in Central America and the Caribbean. While tasked to protect American property in Grenada, Butler wrote that he hated the job, "but orders are orders and of course I had to do it" (Schmidt 1987, p. 51). Here we see the ethos of obedience, but it is no longer a blind obedience. During this same campaign, Butler met with the rebel general and told him that if he surrendered, General Mena would be taken to Panama [to safety]. "For Butler," Schmidt writes, "there was one more trauma." He was ordered "to arrest and hand over to the client government all captured rebels" (p. 52). Butler knew what would happen to Mena, and he felt helpless to aid this man that he respected. These are important moments to focus on. His "hate" represents not simply disagreement with his leaders but disillusionment. And yet, he falls back on the warrior value of obeying orders regardless of their soundness. In my view, he was still caught in the net of warriorism and its adhesive idealization, but the net was fraying because of his questions and criticisms.

Another seed of disillusionment was the commonplace resentment among fellow officers of the "crass economic motives behind military interventions" (p. 54). This recognition and critique would emerge more forcefully later in his life. In the meantime, Schmidt points out that Butler's "skepticism regarding American motives and resentment at being shamed in deceitful subterfuges were offset by personal and professional achievements" (p. 54). Although these achievements were gratifying, Butler's distaste for bureaucrats and politics returned to the foreground when he was dismissed from command at Grenada.

There would be other campaigns (e.g., Veracruz, Haiti) and Butler would distinguish himself, leading to more promotions, awards, and public recognitions. We have seen so far that, early in his career, Butler was beginning to be more aware of the flaws and machinations of political and business leaders vis-à-vis their use of the Marine Corps, but he still identified closely with the Marine Corps and its warrior ethos. This was still, in my view, an adhesive identification, though the glue was rapidly dissolving in the face of the harsh realities of military life and bureaucratic entanglements. Butler, in other words, was no longer the young officer who had blindly accepted orders and carried them out. To be sure, he did his duty, but he was more questioning and critical, which suggests he was a step or two away from the adhesive identification and idealization of the conventional warrior.

Before moving to other events in his career that would lead him to greater differentiation from the glories of warriorism, I will mention two other factors that I believe had some influence in his mourning and moving toward becoming an unconventional warrior. Butler acknowledges his affection for enlisted men. As a commander, he became concerned about their welfare, but he also was determined to share in their sacrifices. As Schmidt points out, Butler became more egalitarian in his stance toward his soldiers (p. 109), which likely had roots in his Quaker upbringing. One notes in this connection to his soldiers a close identification with and affection for them, which would necessarily mean that Butler understood their suffering and the sources for their suffering.

Butler's egalitarianism was also part of another trait, namely, his concern with people whose suffering resulted from exploitation by the wealthy and political classes. Although Butler came from a privileged class, his stint in the Marine Corps and overseas deployments led to a greater identification with soldiers and other less privileged folk. Butler observed the incredible poverty of Central American and Caribbean nations, recognizing, in time, poverty's close connection to capitalist expropriation of resources and money. As a commander in Haiti, he gained affinity for "the black peasant masses" (p. 88). As he stated to a U.S. Senate committee in 1921: "One class wears shoes and the other does not" (p. 88). The ones without shoes were exploited by "scheming politicians who were being artificially kept in office under the American protection" (p. 88). Lest one think he was critical only of foreign countries, Butler, Schmidt notes, "was prescient in seeing that the old cavalry-to-the-rescue theme was one aspect of racist-colonial lore that would survive into the postcolonial era" (p. 175). In his return to China in 1927, Butler showed "sympathy for Chinese suffering" and the Chinese people's desire for self-determination (p. 179). Recognizing that soldiers on foreign soil tended to be arrogant," Butler warned his men that "this country belongs to the Chinese, and I tolerate no clashes between my men and the Chinese people. If a man so much as slaps a rickshaw coolie or lays a hand upon a servant, he gets a general court-martial" (p. 189).

Recall that warriorism tends toward an idealization of one's group and denigration of outsiders. This is not uncommon among conventional soldiers, who may display disdain for civilians, enemies, and foreign peoples. It is likely that, when Butler was a young officer, he identified with the officer class and that he would have tolerated, if not participated in, racist or jingoist speech. As Butler remarked, it was only later that he drew closer to his men by sharing in their suffering. Butler's egalitarian streak and his empathy toward the needs of people in other countries shaped him as a leader, making him a more complex and unconventional leader. In brief, his close identification with his men and the poor peoples of other nations accompanied his growing disillusionment with political and business leaders who used the military for imperial gains.

Toward the end of his successful career, Butler confided in his old friend General Lejeune that the highest position in the Marine Corps was of no interest to him. "I can do no good in the Marine Corps after you have gone," he wrote to Lejeune, who was retiring from being commandant of the Marine Corps. With clarity, he continued, "I would never be any good as Commandant myself, as I simply could not get along with politicians. Their insincerity and duplicity would eat my vitals out" (p. 200). A short time later, he confided to his father that he hoped to obtain one more star (become major general) so that he could retire with a bit more financial security. Without reading too much into these letters, it is safe to say that Butler was torn between his affection for the soldiers (and the Marine Corps) and his having to obey or follow orders from political leaders. A conventional warrior might have similar disdain for politicians but compartmentalize this and continue to serve the masters obsequiously. I think what Butler was recognizing is that he was getting to the point where he could no longer keep his questions and critiques stowed safely in his Marine duffle bag. He was a warrior, and his desire for one more star was pragmatic—it was not a desire for prestige and glory that had been part of his motivations as a young officer and a signifier of warriorism. He continued to have great affection for his men. But his earlier zeal and unquestioning devotion to duty had confronted too many machinations of politicians and military leaders.[11] His mourning, his disillusionment (de-idealization), did not lead to cynicism or disidentification with the warrior ethos but to a shift in how his warrior ethos would be directed.

Butler, as an unconventional warrior, came out of the closet a few months before he retired from the Marine Corps. This occurred at the after-dinner speech mentioned above at which he derided imperialists. Perhaps knowing he was close to retiring and would be offered no more promotions freed him to be more public in his criticisms of people who delighted in the glories and riches of war. Not surprisingly, Butler received a great deal of criticism from the press as well as from conventional military and political leaders. He was "called on the carpet" by the secretary of the Navy, and Butler walked back some of his criticisms (p. 205). He continued to do damage control, but the unconventional side of him could no longer be fully contained by his beliefs in obedience and duty. Indeed, the speech, in my view, represents his re-evaluation of duty and obedience. A conventional warrior obeys his military commanders and political leaders. An unconventional warrior is more critical, possessing a sense of duty toward the people and not merely the state.

Once Butler retired, he was more free to turn his passion toward the public-political sphere. He ran for office and was roundly defeated (p. 216), but this did not slow him down from throwing himself into public life. In the summer of 1932, Butler stood up for the veterans who had camped out in Washington demanding compensation. Disgusted with the brutality of the Hoover Administration toward the veterans and the poor, Butler campaigned vigorously for Franklin Roosevelt—a significant change from his conservative Republican roots. At the same time, Butler railed against the "elitist managerial trends in the military" (p. 220). In 1935, Butler published a short book, *War Is a Racket*, detailing how business and political leaders sheltered themselves from the sufferings of war while adding to their coffers. At the same time, Butler acknowledged he was a mercenary for Wall Street (p. 211). In the months and years leading up to World War II, Butler continued to argue against war.[12] As noted above, according to Schmidt, Butler "could clearly foresee the coming interventionist sanctification of war and spent his last years trying to demystify it" (p. 241). Butler was engaged

---

11. Butler also acknowledged his own participation in subterfuges in some of the campaigns in Central America and the Caribbean.

12. Butler was not a pacifist by any means. He argued against imperial wars, but not wars that were waged in defense of the country. By this, he meant that the United States territorial boundaries would have to be attacked for war to be just.

in a vigorous public speaking tour just weeks before his death in 1940. His public life reveals the absence of idealized identification with the military, yet his public life also reveals the continued presence of his identification with the warrior ethos. Years of confronting the realities of military life in an imperium led to a process of disillusionment, of mourning, in which he gradually let go of the adhesive idealization of and identification with warriorism but retained the values of the warrior ethos. Butler started his military career as a conventional warrior—obedient and duty-conscious toward his superiors—and he retired an unconventional warrior—critical of military and political leaders who used the military and lower classes to obtain and retain power, privilege, and prestige.

CONCLUSION

The U.S. empire cannot exist without a warrior culture, which attracts many boys and young men who end up strongly identifying with its values and aims. A danger of submitting to a warrior culture is succumbing to the acritical adhesive idealization of and identification with warriorism, which I argue is akin to religious fundamentalism. Warriorism breeds conventional warriors, though it is possible for a warrior, after encountering the harsh realities of military life, the horrors and chaos of combat, and the machinations of political leaders, to enter a process of disillusionment and mourning. In so doing, a warrior's adhesive idealization and identification changes, lessens, and in time fades. To be sure, the pain of disillusionment can lead to cynicism and rejection of the warrior ethos, but it can also result in a change wherein one retains one's identification with the warrior ethos and affection for his comrades but becomes more critical of the larger system. In addition, an imperium dominated by virtual wars (games, movies, etc.) is more likely to breed a type of warriorism that is immune to mourning, precisely because war spectators and gamers have no opportunities to experience the realities of military life or war. Warrior fantasies, when divorced from reality, are seemingly impervious to disillusionment, resulting in acritical followers who are slavishly patriotic. Unconventional warriors like Smedley Butler are rare in a warrior culture and, likely, even rarer in a warrior culture in the thralls of virtual war.

REFERENCES

Anzieu, D. (1990). Formal signifiers and the ego-skin. In D. Anzieu (Ed.), *Psychic envelopes* (pp. 1–25). Karnac.

Bacevich, A. (2002). *American empire.* Harvard University Press.
Bacevich, A. (2005). *The new American militarism.* Oxford University Press.
Beder, J. (Ed.). (2012). *Advances in social work practice with the military.* Routledge.
Bick, E. (1968). The experience of the skin in early object relations. *International Journal of Psychoanalysis, 49,* 484–486.
Bollas, C. (1992). *Being a character.* Hill & Wang.
Butler, S. (1935). *War is a racket.* Feral House.
Capozzi, P. (2013). Spectacular war: Media, militainment, and the new imperialism. In K. McLoughlin & M. Forte (Eds.), *Emergency as security: Liberal empire at home and abroad* (pp. 111–120). Alert Press.
Carlin, N. (2014). *Religious mourning: Reversals and restorations in psychological portraits of religious leaders.* Wipf & Stock.
Carlin, N., & Capps, D. (2015). *The gift of sublimation: A psychoanalytic study of multiple masculinities.* Cascade.
Chomsky, N. (2003). *Hegemony or survival: America's quest for global dominance.* Metropolitan Books.
Chomsky, N. (2005). *Imperial ambitions.* Metropolitan.
Ehrenreich, B. (1997). *Blood rites: The origins and history of the passion of war.* Owl.
Erikson, E. (1963). *Childhood and society.* Norton.
Erikson, E. (1982). *The life-cycle completed.* Norton.
French, S. E. (2005). *The code of the warrior: Exploring warrior values past and present.* Rowman & Littlefield.
Fullbright, J. W. (1966). *The arrogance of power.* Random House.
Geertz, C. (1973). *The interpretation of cultures.* Basic.
Gibson, J. (1994). *Warrior dreams: Violence and manhood in post-Vietnam America.* Hill & Wang.
Gray, J. G. (1970). *The warriors: Reflections on men in battle.* University of Nebraska Press.
Happ, C., & Melzer, A. (2014). *Empathy and violent video games.* Palgrave Macmillan.
Hillman, J. (2003). *A terrible love of war.* Penguin.
Johnson, C. (2004). *Sorrows of empire.* Owl.
Johnson, C. (2010). *Dismantling the empire.* Metropolitan.
Kaplan, A. (2002). *The anarchy of empire in the making of U.S. culture.* Harvard University Press.
Kernberg, O. (1991). Aggression and love in the relationship couple. *Journal of the American Psychoanalytic Association, 39,* 45–70.
Kinzer, S. (2006). *Overthrow: America's century of regime change from Hawaii to Iraq.* Times Books.
McDougall, J. (2015). *Jesus was an airborne ranger: Find your purpose following the warrior Christ.* Multnomah.
McWilliams, N. (1994). *Psychoanalytic diagnosis.* Guilford.
Meltzer, D. (1975). Adhesive identification. *Contemporary Psychoanalysis, 11,* 289–311.
Morris, B. (1987). *Anthropological studies of religion.* Cambridge University Press.
Nagata, J. (2001). Beyond theology: Toward an anthropology of "fundamentalism". *American Anthropologist, 103*(2), 481–498.
Ogden, T. (1989). *The primitive edge of experience.* Aronson.
Pressfield, S. (2011). *The warrior ethos.* Black Irish Entertainment.
Schafer, R. (1959). *Aspects of internalization.* International Universities Press.

Schmidt, H. (1987). *Maverick marine: General Smedley D. Butler and the contradictions of American military history*. University of Kentucky Books.

Stolorow, R., & Atwood, G. (1978). A defensive-restitutive function of Freud's theory of psychosexual development. *Psychoanalytic Review, 65*, 217–238.

Tustin, F. (1980). Autistic objects. *International Review of Psychoanalysis, 7*, 27–39.

Tustin, F. (1984). Autistic shapes. *International Review of Psychoanalysis, 11*, 279–290.

U.S. Army. (2008). *The warrior ethos and soldier combat skills. Field Army manual 3-21.75*. Department of the Army.

Welch, S. (2004). *After empire: The art and ethos of enduring peace*. Fortress.

Wulff, D. (1996). The psychology of religion: An overview. In E. Shafranske (Ed.), *Religion and the clinical practice of psychology* (pp. 43–70). American Psychological Association.

Wulff, D. (1997). *Psychology of religion: Classic and contemporary*. Wiley.

Zinn, H. (2005). *A people's history of the United States*. HarperPerennial.

9

Moral Injury

Care and Politics

ADAM TIETJE AND JOSHUA MORRIS

Several pastoral theologians have recently begun examining the spiritual struggles of soldiers and veterans[1] through the lens of moral injury (Graham, 2017; Moon, 2019; Ramsay & Doehring, 2019). This interest is timely—coming toward the end of America's Global War on Terrorism and wars in Iraq and Afghanistan—and represents an important shift away from the notable silence of the field during and after the Vietnam War. Perhaps there were some, even many, who spoke out against the war. However, we have been unable to find any who attended to the care of the Vietnam veterans themselves. There are many potential reasons for this silence, which we explore below. Our contention, however, is that the recent pastoral theological scholarship on moral injury has not yet fully metabolized the liberative trajectory of the field of pastoral theology. In contrast with this trajectory, the care of those who come home from war remains largely depoliticized. The wounds of war are personal *and* political, and care requires attending to the political dimension (Kinghorn, 2012; Wiinikka-Lydon, 2017).

In this chapter, then, we attempt that much needed metabolization. In the first section, we examine the current pastoral theology conversation around moral injury and set it within the historical context of the field around the care of veterans and the depoliticized nature of the clinical literature. In the next section, we argue that the trajectory of the field provides not only

---

1. We use the term soldiers throughout this paper to refer to current U.S. service members of any branch, including those in the National Guard and Reserves. We use the term veteran to refer to service members who have separated from service in any branch or component and under any condition of discharge.

MORAL INJURY

a basis for a robustly political response but also sets of relevant conceptual categories and care resources. Finally, we conclude with a programmatic outline for bringing the wisdom of the wider field to bear within the context of the care of soldiers and veterans as well as naming key external resources and considerations to which pastoral theologians need also attend.

PASTORAL THEOLOGY AND THE DEPOLITICIZATION OF MILITARY MORAL INJURY

Moral injury first emerged in the clinical world as a conceptual and therapeutic response to the ways in which the moral dimensions of the trauma of war veterans exceeded the bounds of the conceptualization of post-traumatic stress disorder (PTSD) in the *Diagnostic and Statistical Manual of Mental Disorders* (*DSM-III*; American Psychiatric Association, 1980) (even granting that the *DSM-III* included guilt). Jonathan Shay (1994), a United States Department of Veterans Affairs (VA) psychiatrist, first used the term moral injury to capture that excess in light of the experiences of betrayal the Vietnam veterans he worked with named. Shay's conception focuses on the way that war corrupts character and how that corruption is linked to failures of leadership. Shay (2014) defines moral injury as "a betrayal of what's right, by a person who holds legitimate authority (e.g., in the military—a leader) in a high-stakes situation" (p. 183). That betrayal could come at the hands of one's immediate leadership or be tied all the way back to the actions or inaction of those holding political power. Shay's account of moral injury built on the clear connections that Vietnam veterans made between their personal suffering and the politics and prosecution of the war itself.

More than a decade later, and many years into the wars in Iraq and Afghanistan, Brett Litz et al. (2009)[2] took up the concept of moral injury as a way to name and respond to the moral pain of veterans that is connected to their own agency or perceived failures and also results in some form of psychosocial impairment or maladaptive or destructive behaviors. Moral injury, as Litz frames it, involves a perceived moral violation that leads to painful moral emotions and cognitions with a resulting inability to navigate that pain toward meaning and connection. These violations include violations in which the self is perpetrator, with attendant moral emotions of guilt and shame, and/or violations as victim, with attendant moral emotions of anger and disgust (Currier et al., 2021).[3] Litz shifts the focus of moral injury

---

2. The authors are all VA providers/researchers, with the exception of William Nash, who at the time was a psychiatrist in the United States Marine Corps.

3. There are, however, no established criteria for what constitutes a potentially

away from the wider institutional (or even national) context with which Shay is concerned and zooms in on the individual agency of soldiers and veterans.

Pastoral Theology and Depoliticized Care

Larry Graham's (2017) book *Moral Injury: Restoring Wounded Souls* is the first full-length treatment of moral injury by a pastoral theologian. At first glance, it might seem that Graham's work actually sets the field up for a robustly political account of military moral injury. This would be in keeping with the overall oeuvre of Graham's career that focuses on relational justice, signaling a shift away from the diagnosis-dependent aspects of the clinical pastoral paradigm. This shift moved the parameters of pastoral theology from just an individual to an individual's community (and the social and political implications of communities). People come *from* communities, and return *to* communities; therefore, an analysis of communities and systems is paramount for pastoral theology. Graham conceptualizes moral injury as not just personal but as experienced on interpersonal and collective levels.

Moreover, Graham argues for a normalization of moral injury and strives to take it out of a pathologizing clinical context (even within the clinical context there is a strong bias against pathologizing moral injury). In Graham's "normalized" account, moral injury flows out of moral dissonance and moral dilemmas. He doesn't put it in these terms, but his work suggests something like a moral injury equivalent to the trauma-stress continuum (Dulmus & Hilarski, 2003). He even directly states that "there is no way to disconnect the personal and the public in understanding moral injury and fashioning healing responses to it" (Graham, 2017, p. 40). Unfortunately, Graham has mostly removed moral injury from its initial context among soldiers and veterans.[4] Thus, while he can imagine the integration of care and politics (or, at least, the public) with respect to thinking about moral injury and racism (the context of the previous quote), nowhere in Graham's account does he trace a similar line of thinking with respect to thinking about war and moral injury.

---

morally injurious event. Neither is there any consensus on the symptoms that would signify being morally injured (Currier et al., 2021; Jinkerson, 2016).

4. This avoidance of context is surprising as Graham (2015) states, while summing up his career, "[A]s pastoral theologians, we are already well aware of the physically embodied and socially embedded nature of our lives. To a greater or lesser degree, all of our pastoral theological paradigms are sensitive to the embodied and embedded character of human life in the world" (p. 177).

Zachary Moon, another pastoral theologian and a former military chaplain writing about moral injury (and Graham's student) ends up in a similar place but for different reasons. In *Warriors Between Worlds: Moral Injury and Identities in Crisis*, Moon (2019) argues that the problem of moral injury is a matter of moral dissonance between the moral orienting systems of military and civilian worlds. The solutions Moon offers, then, are focused on reintegration and how "warriors" (veterans) reintegrate into the civilian world. Moon seeks to do this culturally, intersectionally, and communally (elsewhere, he names this the "social-relation dimension" [2020]) and recognizes a kind of political responsibility of communities to care for those whom they have sent to war. Moon's response, too, does not address military moral injury as a political problem. Moon seems averse to considering war to be the moral problem that moral injury is naming, and he categorically excludes it from the outset of his study as a kind of poison pill that risks alienating the very veterans he has in view. In Moon's view, "[T]his tension is instructive for further work and may reveal how antiwar positions can limit access to communities who don't share those values and beliefs" (2019, p. 16).[5]

Nancy Ramsay (as director of the Soul Repair Center at Brite Divinity School), Carrie Doehring, and others have offered up helpful care resources, most recently in an edited volume *Military Moral Injury and Spiritual Care: A Resource for Religious Leaders and Professional Caregivers* (Ramsay & Doehring, 2019). While many of these resources open up avenues for liturgical and communal modes of care, none of them offers a robustly political conception of either moral injury or its care. Given that this cuts against the grain of the general trajectory of the field (which we will get to in a moment), it seems appropriate to pause and ask, why? While there is no straightforward or obvious answer, we suggest this gap persists for two reasons. First, the field of pastoral theology developed largely under the influence of mainline Protestants in the wake of mainline Protestant opposition to Vietnam. The churches' opposition to the Vietnam War, which generally came late, was largely accompanied by silence concerning soldiers and veterans, if not open blame and hostility, including toward military chaplains (Loveland, 2014, p. 22–25). Second, the field has historically been tied to clinical and psychological models and methods that prioritize the care of the individual. Even as Graham and others push back against the clinical conceptualization and treatment of moral injury, Litz's highly individualistic account is generally their starting point.

---

5. Of course, the equal and opposite point can be forcefully made. Not taking a stand against a particular war can also be costly. We suspect this would be the rejoinder of the likes of Rita Brock and Gabriella Lettini (2012).

The story of the development of diagnosis of PTSD highlights both the ways some clinicians ignored, shamed, and mistreated returning Vietnam veterans *and* how others showed up as powerful allies in the protest against the war and advocacy for the recognition and care of veterans (Scott, 1990). Even in the context of that story, it is not the case that mainline Protestant churches completely ignored or abandoned veterans. The National Council of Churches proved to be an early ally for the Vietnam Veterans Against the War as they began to form. The council even financially supported the organizational work that led to the codification and inclusion of post-traumatic stress disorder in the *DSM-III* in 1980 (Scott, 1990, p. 302). It would certainly be inaccurate to make sweeping statements about local church pastors and their treatment of Vietnam veterans.

What we can say is what did not happen at the level of academic discourse. In the wake of Vietnam, there was little to no attention paid to the care of veterans from within the field of pastoral theology. To be fair, pastoral theologians did not constitute themselves a "guild" until the creation of the Society for Pastoral Theology in 1985. As Nancy Ramsay relayed to us in an email: "If we had gathered a decade earlier in 1975, the War in Vietnam may well have been more present in our conversations. If the notion of military moral injury had been articulated or if a similar conflict had arisen, I think we would have made that a focus. Sadly, concepts such as moral injury were not with us" (personal communication, March 18, 2022). We are grateful for Ramsay's recollections on the guild in its early days both here and elsewhere (Hunter & Ramsay, 2017). While the guild may have not formally emerged until 1985, many of the people who were its antecedents had been in the academy for decades prior. And while Vietnam may have left the collective radar of those first members of the Society for Pastoral Theology, it was very much in the wider American consciousness.[6] There

---

6. It is almost impossible to overstate the social, cultural, and political impact of the Vietnam war, even well into the 1980s. While there was never a true political reckoning over Vietnam, there was certainly an ongoing and evolving cultural reckoning, which was well underway in the 1980s. The blockbuster war films of the era are illustrative. The most famous line from *First Blood* (Kotcheff, 1982) was Rambo's question: "Sir, do we get to win this time?" In *Uncommon Valor* (Kotcheff, 1983), one of the characters says to a team of fellow veterans on their way to rescue some MIAs: "No one can dispute the rightness of what you're doing." *Platoon* was released in 1986 (Stone) and *Full Metal Jacket* in 1987 (Kubrick). These films provided a forum for both re-narrating a win (*First Blood, Uncommon Valor*) and recognizing the profound immorality and suffering of the war (*Platoon, Full Metal Jacket*). Throughout the 1980s, the "Vietnam vet" also emerged in film and other media as a trope, someone deeply wounded psychologically and often physically unkempt and unfit for society. Further cultural markers of the salience of the war and its ongoing impact on veterans can be seen in the inclusion of PTSD in the *DSM-III* (1980) and the completion of "the Wall," the Vietnam Veterans

was widespread talk of post-Vietnam syndrome, and then PTSD, and then both as deeply personal and political wounds (Lifton, 1973/2005; Shatan, 1972, 1973). Perhaps it was simply an anti-war bias (no doubt the norm for mainline church clergy and seminary professors of the day) that accounts for pastoral theologians neglecting the deep wounds of Vietnam veterans and the ways those wounds were explicitly political.

We welcome the newfound interest in and scholarly attention upon the needs and concerns of veterans. The consequences of this interest and attention emerging quite late—after more than a decade into the wars in Iraq and Afghanistan—are notable. The pastoral theological consideration of the situation of veterans has not occurred organically over the last 50 years, alongside the many developments in the field when it comes to feminist, Black, and womanist pastoral theology, for instance. Given that is the case, there is much in the pastoral theological conversation left unaccounted for in terms of both the development of the study of war trauma *and* in the application of the discipline's own best insights within the context of the military and veteran communities. The interest in moral injury surged only after the publication of Litz's work. Litz's clinical conception of moral injury is ready-made for pastoral theological use within the clinical pastoral paradigm.[7] Clinical forms of knowledge still hold significant esteem within the guild, and it is no surprise that it is fundamentally Litz's conception of moral injury as personal transgression that predominates in the work of Graham, Moon, and others. Even as they seek to move beyond it (as articulated above), they are beholden to it as their starting point.[8] So it is that moral injury has largely remained a highly individual and personal wound for veterans within the context of pastoral theology.

Politics and the Care of Moral Injury

It is in this context of a largely depoliticized account of moral injury that we suggest a much needed repoliticization of care. On the surface, it would seem rather pedestrian to say the experiences and suffering of veterans

---

Memorial, in 1982. Again, with all this as backdrop, the lack of engagement by pastoral theologians at the time is surprising.

7. And yet, Litz himself describes his adaptive disclosure method as "ill advised" for chaplains, who are not psychotherapeutically trained, to utilize as it is an "intensive, totally secular, step by step manualized psychotherapy" (personal communication, February 2016).

8. Elsewhere, Graham (2015) notes that the clinical pastoral paradigm "is still the default paradigm organizing pastoral theology and care" (p. 174). We agree—especially as it relates to moral injury—and this is problematic.

is political. Working as they do to defend the polis, of course their work is political. In reality, though, America's national narratives about its war making serve to depoliticize and then to privatize the trauma of veterans. The narratives grant meaning to the experiences and suffering of soldiers to the extent that they conform to a certain civil religious orthodoxy. They mask the reality of the moral suffering of soldiers behind the veil of personal sacrifice. America's stories about war can affirm that war is horrible and that soldiers suffer because they do so *pro nobis*.

Recent pastoral theological work on moral injury inadvertently recapitulates this dynamic. Privatizing the trauma of veterans ensures both that America's stories about war remain uninterrogated by the actual experiences of veterans and that veterans themselves often remain subject to these stories in the context of care. The moral and political landscape of American wars provides the context in which soldiers imagine and narrate what they do on the battlefield, even if the stories they tell stand in opposition to the story of American exceptionalism. If current pastoral theologians and caregivers proceed as if the larger context of war is irrelevant, then they, too, are liable to a similar judgment wrought in the wake of the critiques of liberation theologies. The care they provide may simply help veterans accommodate to the oppressive patriarchal dynamics of military service rather than bear witness to the liberating hope of the gospel.[9]

While troubling these distinctions is precisely our point, historically, care has been conceptualized as "private," of and proper to the *oikos*. The church is *both* oikos and polis. As pastoral theology developed as a discipline, it emerged as the study of an activity of the private sphere, the care work of pastors in the context of the church as oikos. The work of Black, feminist, and womanist pastoral theologians challenges this depoliticized orientation. We affirm this political trajectory of pastoral theology. Following Luke Bretherton, we see three dimensions to politics as a moral good. The first dimension refers to the good of the common life as such,

9. We suggest that the challenge for military chaplains is exacerbated by the fact that they function within the very system that both valorizes its warriors while both medicalizing and individualizing their maladies (as precisely *their* maladies). There are legal, political, and biopolitical regimes that all but guarantee military chaplains provide pastoral care that brackets out any wider moral and political questions about war. Thus, it must be acknowledged up front that the care of soldiers and veterans (properly inflected by the wider moral and political context of America's wars) remains a tall order. The institutions where pastoral caregivers most directly attend to the soul care of America's soldiers and veterans—the United States Department of Veterans Affairs and the United States Department of Defense—are the very institutions in which such care will be least welcomed. We believe that churches and other religious bodies bear much of the blame for having de facto ceded responsibility and authority over their clergy to the state.

the nature of the polis. The second dimension refers to the structures that give shape to the polis, statecraft (constitutions, laws, bureaucracy, etc.). Finally, politics includes the relational practices and prudential judgments that enact the good of association (Bretherton, 2019, pp. 32–34). To argue for the re-politicization of care, as we do, is to recognize the ways in which war, soldiering, and the aftermath of war for soldiers is bound up with all three dimensions of politics (or, in the case of the third dimension, the lack of political agency).

A political account of moral injury is attentive to war as an activity aimed (ostensibly) at preserving the polis as such (the first dimension), armies (and soldiers) as located within the bureaucracies of statecraft (the second dimension) *and* structurally subordinated to them and excluded from the relational domain of politics (the third dimension), relegated to live within the precarity of the permanent state of exception (Agamben, 1995/1998, 2003/2005). Soldiers are included within the polis through their exclusion and subordination. This political dynamic and the way it is narrated and oriented toward sacrifice (and justified theologically) parallels the ways that women were traditionally included within the polis through their exclusion from the oikos (state of nature) as wives and mothers (Tietje, 2021). Moral injury is best understood as located within this wider political context. We argue that a politically oriented conceptualization of moral injury and care stands in deep continuity with the overall trajectory of pastoral theology as increasingly attentive to contextualizing care within the larger political dynamics of exclusion and subordination, care not as accommodation to oppression but as a means of survival and even liberation.

Pastoral theology is not averse to the consideration of the personal *and* the political. The various 20th -century theologies "from below"[10] have

---

10. This phrasing comes from the theological fragments of Dietrich Bonhoeffer during the early days of his imprisonment, possibly in late 1942. In an unfinished paragraph, Bonhoeffer (1997) writes: "We have for once learnt to see the great events of world history from below, from the perspective of the outcast, the suspects, the maltreated, the powerless, the oppressed, the reviled—in short, from the perspective of those who suffer" (p. 17). This quote represents a rather significant turn in 20th-century theology. We do not mean to read Bonhoeffer or this quote as the sole fulcrum that turned theology in a new direction. But, this quote does capture a shift that was already well underway. Bonhoeffer is indeed influential among early Latin American liberation theologians in this regard (Gutiérrez, 1983/2004; Weidersheim, 2021). *Below* and *above* are prepositions. They orient something (or someone) in relation to something else (or someone else). In this quote, below is an orientation in relation to history, privilege, and power. Those below are those crushed rather than propelled by the forward march of history: "outcasts, suspects, the maltreated, the powerless, the oppressed, the reviled." Theology "from below" is theology "from the perspective of those who suffer." The important work of liberation theologies has been to show that in Jesus God turns history

forcefully asserted that "the personal is political." Feminist theology (it is a feminist slogan, after all), Black liberation theology, womanist theology, Latin American liberation theology, queer theology, and other theologies "from below" have made significant contributions to the development of the field of pastoral theology. They have found deep resonances between the basic methodological stance of pastoral theology and theology "from below." Pastoral theologians, from the outset, have seen their work as tending to persons in all their particularity (Anton Boisen's living human document) and developing theologies that grow from the interplay of person(s) and theology.[11]

Early pastoral theologians embraced ego psychology as offering liberating possibilities, even liberation from oppressive moral frameworks. However, psychology is not amoral, and over time it became clear that the psychological theories to which pastoral theologians were turning came with their own moral assumptions and problems. The overarching problem for these psychologies and the pastoral theologies that employed them was the extent to which they simply reflected the White, middle-class, and male perspective of the thinkers who had crafted them. That, at least, was the pushback pastoral theology faced beginning in the 1960s. Feminist and Black pastoral theologians began to question whether the frameworks they were employing, rather than provide a path for liberation, simply helped women and Black people accommodate to White male power in the midst of oppression. The time has come for a similar reappraisal of the soul care of soldiers and veterans.

A LIBERATIVE TRAJECTORY

Feminist, Black liberation, and womanist pastoral theological conversations provide significant resources for the care of veterans. Moreover, the present state of the pastoral theological conversation is replete with untapped pastoral theological resources for thinking about war "from below,"[12] espe-

---

on its head. The crucified God is at the heart of history. Salvation, then, is not an escape from history but God's solidarity within history with the "crucified peoples of history" (Ellacuría & Sobrino, 1993; Sobrino, 1994). Theologies "from below" begin from the perspective of those who are oppressed and suffering.

11. The terminology "from below" is technically anachronistic as applied to early pastoral theologians, Boisen in particular.

12. We recognize that "from below" has largely been jettisoned in favor of "from the margins" or "from the periphery" because it is hierarchical imagery. With respect to the situation of soldiers, we think below is actually the most apt preposition precisely because soldiers are subject to patriarchal dynamics of subordination within the military

cially the turn to post-colonial (Lartey, 2013; McGarrah Sharp, 2019) and political pastoral theology (LaMothe, 2017a; Rogers-Vaughn, 2014, 2015). We intend to make explicit the latent resources within pastoral theology for thinking about war and the care of soldiers and veterans "from below," from the perspective of their subordinated positionality. Much pastoral theological work has already been done to connect the personal (soul care) and the political (political and moral theology). Our modest hope is to bring the care of veterans into these wider conversations. In turn, we examine key Black, feminist, and womanist pastoral theological resources.

Before we do so, however, we want to pause and offer a caveat. We are speaking of soldiers (and veterans) who are (or were) situated within the U.S. military. We are aware of this institution's death-dealing. We have very much been a part of it.[13] In other places we have imagined ways in which pastoral theology could think counterhegemonically in providing care to soldiers and veterans (Morris, 2020, 2021). Therefore, as we learn from Black, feminist, and womanist colleagues, we are keenly aware of the potential misuse and appropriation of caregiving competencies that are born from oppression and marginalization. Our goal, however, is to honor those communities by noting similar dynamics of exclusion and subordination for soldiers and veterans. These dynamics doubly impact soldiers who are also members of marginalized communities, Black women in particular (Fox, 2019; Melin, 2016). With that, we now explore, trace, and synthesize these liberative themes through the work of Edward Wimberly, Archie Smith, Bonnie Miller-McLemore, and Carroll Watkins Ali.

Black Liberation Pastoral Theology: Edward Wimberly and Archie Smith

Edward Wimberly wrote the first pastoral theology text from the perspective of Black experience. In *Pastoral Care in the Black Church*, Wimberly employs the four functions framework outlined by Clebsch and Jaekle (Hiltner's healing, sustaining, and guiding with their addition of reconciliation) but focuses on sustaining and guiding as the two functions that have been most prevalent in the Black church. Wimberly (1979) writes:

> The racial climate in America, from slavery to the present, has made sustaining and guiding more prominent than healing and

---

hierarchy.

13. Of course, so have all American citizens, whether they know or acknowledge it or not.

> reconciling. Racism and oppression have produced wounds in the black community that can be healed only to the extent that healing takes place in the structure of the total society. Therefore, the black church has had to find means to sustain and guide black persons in the midst of oppression. (p. 21)

For Wimberly, healing and reconciliation entail structural economic and political changes that have yet to be realized. The ongoing oppression of Black people makes "wounds almost irreparable" (p. 38). For White churches, by way of contrast, Wimberly writes:

> Healing has been the dominant function in these white denominations largely because of the absence of economic, political, and social oppression. The healing model of modern pastoral care goes back to the early 1920s, and it was predominantly influenced by the one-to-one Freudian psychoanalytic orientation to psychiatry. To learn the methods and skills of the one-to-one healing model required economic resources and extensive clinical and educational opportunities to which many black pastors did not have access until very recently. (p. 22)

Black pastors, instead, drew on the resources they did have. The care of souls in the Black church has thus been more "corporate and communal." Worship is at the heart of Black life, the Black church, and Black soul care. Wimberly offers a good outline of the history of the sustaining and guiding ministry of the Black church from slavery through the 1960s.

While Wimberly's (1979) work precedes later womanist writers, his focus on the sustaining and guiding functions comports well with a key aspect of womanist ethics and care: survival.[14] Pastoral care in the Black church sustains and guides Black souls in the midst of ongoing oppression. Black pastors serve as "symbol(s) reflecting the hopes and aspirations of Black people for liberation from oppression in this life" (p. 20). Black pastoral care is *not* simply accommodation to oppression. It is the creation of conditions for survival in the midst of oppression.

While Wimberly treats the pastoral functions as conceptually distinct from the prophetic and political work of the Black church, from the outset it is clear that in reality no such distinction is possible. Wimberly himself acknowledges that healing is impossible because there is no path to personal

---

14. Of course, womanism is focused not only on survival but also on well-being and thriving. Melanie Harris (2010, pp. 114–123) highlights seven virtues that promote survival, well-being, and thriving that women of African descent embody: generosity, graciousness, compassion, spiritual wisdom, audacious courage, justice, and good community/good accountability.

healing for Black Americans apart from political healing. The care of souls in the Black church is intimately related to the Black church as an alternative space of political agency and the ongoing work of the Black church for civil rights. Current clinical and pastoral moral injury interventions, unintentionally, largely help soldiers and veterans adjust to political conditions that are unjust. With Wimberly, we affirm the need for pastoral care that empowers soldiers for survival, even and especially when political healing is not readily forthcoming. We turn next to Archie Smith Jr., who makes these connections much more explicit.

In *The Relational Self: Ethics and Therapy from a Black Church Perspective*, Smith (1982) builds on the work of Wimberly and others by explicitly putting Black liberation ethics into conversation with the therapeutic modalities in which he is trained. If healing for Black Christians demands political and social work, then ethics and therapy need to be brought to bear together in the work of the Black church for care and liberation. The two are, in reality, inseparable. Unfortunately, as Smith points out, sociological and psychological theoretical frameworks have been developed in support of social and political projects that may be fundamentally at odds with Black theology. Smith (1982) explains:

> Sociologies or psychologies based upon and supportive of modern bourgeois individualism and materialism, or that fail to analyze the system and history of exploitative capitalism serve to delude both victims and social scientists while claiming to be value neutral. Social science and psychoanalysis premised on a different, but historically self-critical and liberating paradigm, will require the support of a different human subject and social order to be effective. (p. 25)

Because these sociologies and psychologies have been supportive of individualism and materialism, they have largely served "to adjust the individual *within the* established norms and structures of society, thereby strengthening the status quo" (Smith, 1982, p. 26). Psychology holds the potential for social criticism and change. Indeed, the task of psychology is to "free the inner life of the human subject from ... internalized oppression" (p. 26). Yet, "it has often served to dull ... the potentially critical and emancipatory" (p. 26). The Black church, too, has often been viewed as "an opiate to militant action" (p. 26). What is needed, according to Smith, is a therapeutic *and* prophetic orientation. In this way, the Black church can support both "outer and inner transformation" (p. 27). Thus, Smith concludes that

> [e]thics and therapy can find common cause in liberation struggles among oppressed groups that seek to build a sense of

solidarity and respect for life where issues of self-contempt and demoralizing relational patterns are common. Both Christian social ethics and therapy are complementary when set within the context of liberation, reconciliation, and the relational self—expressed in the age old African proverb: "One is only human because of others, with others, and for others." (p. 27)

With a communal focus in mind, Smith argues for a relational paradigm that sets persons within a web of relations that links "private troubles . . . with broad public issues" (p. 27). There is ever-present interconnection and dialectical exchange between inner and outer worlds. Indeed, "[M]orality is constituted through this web of dynamic relations" and is constitutive of our common moral life together.[15]

Smith powerfully unites the personal and the political and argues for a dialectal relationship between ethics and therapy that puts both in the service of liberation. Smith's work places pastoral psychology and therapy into conversation with Black liberation theology and points us toward the radical possibilities of doing pastoral theology "from below." Pastoral theology can and does have a role to play in the liberation of the oppressed. Smith also provides us with the necessary critical tools for reorienting our work when the relationship between ethics and care has gone awry. He writes:

> Therapy [or, spiritual care] may serve to adjust the individual within the limited horizon of the dominant ideology. Therapy in this case, may be seen as a delusional system, perpetuating the split between the person and the system. Therapy is then itself in need of emancipation. In order for therapy to serve its own implicit emancipatory interest, it needs to function in a different context and under social conditions that are more supportive of this interest. In this light, it may be argued that the interest of liberation ethics in social transformation takes priority over an interest that takes for granted the assumptive world of individuals. (p. 153)

We suggest this is precisely the danger inherent with present clinical and pastoral theological conceptualizations and interventions around military moral injury. In cases where "therapy is then itself in need of emancipation," Smith suggests it needs critical and dialectical engagement with liberation ethics. This is precisely what we have set out to do with respect to current pastoral conceptualizations of moral injury. With this in mind, we turn

---

15. Smith's work is thus a clear antecedent of Bonnie Miller-McLemore's later "living human web."

our attention to another movement to do pastoral theology "from below," feminist pastoral theology.

Feminist Pastoral Theology: Bonnie Miller-McLemore

We have just narrated the initial efforts toward a Black liberation pastoral theology. Feminist pastoral theology was a parallel development as feminism and feminist theology made its way into the pastoral theology conversation. The challenge, of course, as with the development of Black liberation pastoral theology, was that the overwhelming majority of pastoral theologians remained White men well into the 1990s.[16] This was certainly the case in the 1960s and 1970s when both feminist and Black liberation theology were developing.

Bonnie Miller-McLemore stands out as one of the most significant pastoral theologians of the "second wave" of feminist pastoral theologians, not only as a feminist but as a leader in the discipline(s) on many fronts.[17] We want to articulate here two conceptual contributions she makes that unpack her synthesis within our trajectory. In turn, we examine her widely taken up expansion of Boisen's living human document to the "living human web" and her addition of four core functions of pastoral care: resisting, empowering, nurturing, and liberating. The latter examination is central to our own constructive proposal.

Miller-McLemore's "The Human Web: Reflections on the State of Pastoral Theology" (1993) points to both the centrality of care as the focus of pastoral theology and also the ways in which that care is now informed by "the study of sociology, ethics, culture, and public policy" (p. 367). Pastoral theology's embrace of resources beyond the field of psychology represents a central aspect of the shift from Boisen's "document" to Miller-McLemore's (and Smith's) "web." Miller-McLemore directly ties this to the feminist slogan we have already embraced here: "the personal is the political." The living human document implies the gaze of an external observer, one no doubt deeply embedded in the dominant societal power structures. The

---

16. We recognize though, that many women were *already* at work shaping pastoral theology and practice. The literature in pastoral theology, as in any field, recognizes those who have the positions, power, and influence to publish. There are always others doing important work "from below."

17. Further, building on our previous note, a potential frustration with any trajectory are those critical voices that are omitted. We are beginning with Miller-McLemore as she pulls our liberative threads in complementary ways, especially with respect to Smith. However, the groundbreaking work of Peggy Way should be acknowledged. We recognize her influence on the entire field and especially on Miller-McLemore.

living human web is an image that highlights connectedness and its interdependence. If documents can be examined in isolation, a web implies an inextricable connection and embeddedness. Persons are always already enmeshed in social and political realities, notably systems of racist, capitalistic, and patriarchal oppression.

Crucially, if documents can be read, those embedded within the web must be empowered to speak for themselves. Miller-McLemore (2018) notes three significant trends in pastoral theology that lie behind this shift from the personal to the political: an increased interest in congregational studies, a new public theology, and the rise of liberation movements (p. 313). Boisen's (1936/1971) turn to the living human document represents an important movement in theology away from abstraction. In its own right, it was a step toward doing theology "from below," from the perspective of those who are suffering. The shift to thinking about the living human web further frames the work of the pastoral theologian in relation to the care of persons embedded within unjust social and political realities. Here, we have named this move as Miller-McLemore's. She readily acknowledges her use of the web was already in the discipline's ether; as we have seen, it was clearly already present in Smith's work more than a decade earlier.

The turn to persons as embedded within the web thus evokes a new set of pastoral functions. Miller McLemore consolidates the additional pastoral functions suggested by feminist pastoral theology around the headings of resisting, empowering, nurturing, and liberating. Her summary of these functions bears quoting at length:

> *Compassionate resistance* requires confrontation with evil, contesting violent, abusive behaviors that perpetuate underserved suffering and false stereotypes that distort the realities of people's lives. *Resistance* includes a focused healing of wounds of abuse that have festered for generations. *Empowerment* involves advocacy and tenderness on behalf of the vulnerable, giving resources and means to those previously stripped of authority, voice, and power. *Nurturance* is not sympathetic kindness or quiescent support but fierce, dedicated proclamation of love that makes a space for difficult changes and fosters solidarity among the vulnerable. *Liberation* entails both escape from unjust, unwarranted affliction and release into new life and wholeness as created, redeemed, and loved people of God. (Miller-McLemore, 1999, p. 80)

If the personal is political, then the care of persons is political as well, and so too is our theorizing about care: "Pastoral care from a liberation perspective is about breaking silences, urging prophetic action, and liberating the oppressed. Pastoral theology is the critical reflection on this activity" (Miller-McLemore, 1999, p. 91). The work of feminist pastoral theologians and feminist pastoral caregivers (as outlined by the tasks of resisting, empowering, nurturing, and liberating) is thus necessarily political. If such work does not challenge existing patriarchal structures, then it risks unwitting collusion with them. The care of the oppressed entails resistance to oppression. Given this resistance, and the struggle for survival implicit within resistance, we now turn our attention to another movement to do pastoral theology "from below," womanist pastoral theology.

Womanist Pastoral Theology: Carroll Watkins Ali

Carroll Watkins Ali builds on and expands Seward Hiltner's functions of pastoral care beyond healing, sustaining, and guiding. Throughout her text *Survival and Liberation: Pastoral Theology in African American Context* (1999), she convincingly argues that a Hiltnerian method is not sufficient for poor African American women and the communities they represent. Watkins Ali affirms shepherding as central for pastoral theology and in doing so evokes a more holistic image of the shepherd. If the clinical pastoral paradigm emphasizes pastoral care as care of the one versus the ninety-nine, Watkins Ali (and Black and feminist pastoral theologians) press us to see that the one is always embedded within the wider flock. For Watkins Ali, then, care in the context of the African American community is attentive to Black experience, especially that of poor Black women.

In light of the cultural context of Black women and their struggle for both survival and liberation, Watkins Ali adds three community-based functions to Hiltner's classic functions: "nurturing," "empowering," and "liberating" (p. 9).[18] To nurture the community, one must have an ongoing commitment to provide care that empowers counselees to have the strength to face various struggles within their community. The function of empowering contains the insistence that the struggle for liberation and emancipation must come from the oppressed people themselves. Pastoral caregivers "[put] people in touch with their own power so that they are enabled to claim their rights, resist oppression, and take control of their own lives" (p. 121). Finally, the liberating function entails political action. It involves working together as a community to eliminate oppression. The significance of Watkins Ali's work is her insistence that, to adequately care for a community of people,

---

18. This is done to create a more robust vision of care, not to eradicate Hiltner's work.

the caregiver must address the systemic forces of oppression that keep the community down.

By way of contrast, the care of soldiers and veterans has remained "privatized" even as the discipline has largely taken on a more public and political voice. There has been work to contextualize the care of veterans within the "congregation" rather than solely as a function of pastoral caregivers (Moon, 2015). But such moves nonetheless remain tied to the pastoral rather than prophetic tasks of pastoral care (Tietje, 2018). Just as the care of Black folks necessitates the upending of systems of White supremacy, so too does the care of veterans require a wholesale reappraisal of the moral and political context of American war, the church's relationship to the American empire, and the political realities of soldiering. We affirm Wiinikka-Lydon's (2017) claim that moral injury stands as an inherent political critique. The personal trauma of war for soldiers bears witness to the larger moral and political problems at the heart of American war making. We are certainly not the first soldiers, chaplains, or scholars to beat this drum (Mahedy, 1986/2004). Nevertheless, the current discourse within pastoral theology around moral injury continues to leave public triumphalistic narratives about soldiers and the state unchallenged and in so doing reinforces the privatization of the war trauma of soldiers.

War veterans, even after they return, continue to be placed on the sacrificial altar of the nation in order to support narratives of American exceptionalism and justice. Their stories, their lives, and their bodies are sanitized behind narratives of soldiers as national heroes and saviors (Ebel, 2015). Their struggles, their suffering, and their trauma—if and when they are acknowledged—are cast out of the polis proper. Yet, the witness of theological movements "from below" is again and again that "the personal is the political." Thus, the work of pastoral care with veterans can and should be informed by the work of feminist, Black, and womanist pastoral theologians.

AN ILLUMINATING EXCEPTION: LAMOTHE'S UNCONVENTIONAL WARRIORISM

Ryan LaMothe's writing on warriorism shows up as a notable exception to the overall trend in the field regarding the privatization and depoliticization of the care of soldiers and veterans. In "Men, Warriorism, and Mourning: The Development of Unconventional Warriors," LaMothe (2017b) examines the phenomenon of warriorism in the U.S. military. This almost autoethnographic piece is situated within his recent body of work setting pastoral theology within (and against) the context of the corrosive elements of American exceptionalism. In LaMothe's analysis, then, American service members are formed as "warriors" in the military, trained to inculcate and live by the warrior ethos.[19] The warrior ethos, he argues, is undergirded by a straightforward patriotism and faith in American exceptionalism. He contends that the disillusionment of warriors in the face of the many failures and fiascos of American power around the world should be read as a kind of grief that might lead to new insight, orientation, and action. He does this through an examination of the life and work of retired Marine Corps General Smedley Butler. He traces the shift in the life of Butler from loyal soldier to the disillusioned author of *War Is a Racket* and advocate for various egalitarian and democratic movements and reforms. He names this shift as one from being a conventional warrior, one who "obeys his military commanders and political leaders," to an unconventional warrior, one who "is more critical, possessing a sense of duty toward the people and not merely the state" (2017b, p. 834).

LaMothe is not directly engaging the literature on moral injury, but it is certainly possible to bring together his analysis around the mourning of conventional warriors with Shay's account of moral injury as betrayal. LaMothe's work suggests a way for soldiers and veterans through which they might hold on to a vital center, their identity as "warrior," even as their experience of political betrayal presses toward a new "unconventional" orientation. For his part, LaMothe remains skeptical of both warriorism as such (seeing it as inextricably entangled with American exceptionalism) and the likelihood of the emergence of very many unconventional warriors.

LaMothe's work, a minority report in the field, presents a helpful addition to the liberative trajectory we have outlined. If, as we suggest, soldiering means crossing the threshold into a political space of exception, within which moral and political agency are attenuated, constrained, and in many ways oppressive, one version of a liberation reading might be that survival means making it to the end of one's enlistment contract and liberation means being able to set aside one's identity as soldier or "warrior," in LaMothe's terms. For many, this straightforward reading may be the one with which they most readily identify. LaMothe does not directly address the political conditions of soldiering, but the implications are embedded in his analysis. Even so, his work suggests an alternative—not a release, rejection, or escape, necessarily,

---

19. The U.S. Army's Warrior Ethos is "I will always place the mission first. I will never accept defeat. I will never quit. I will never leave a fallen comrade." LaMothe (2017b) contends that warriorism is a kind of masculine ideal in a warrior society. The sociological evidence suggests the connection between masculinity and war runs much deeper. Warrior society or not, men have traditionally filled the role of warrior in times of war (Goldstein, 2001).

from one's identity as a soldier but a shift, turn, or, dare we say, a kind of moral re-formation. Both in the context of LaMothe's own biography and the life of Smedley Butler this movement occurs, in large part, in the context of separation from service or retirement. While departure is not entailed by LaMothe's account (although likely implied), it does beg the question of whether it is possible for LaMothe's "unconventional warriors" to remain within the military. While the military happily employs unconventional warriors—special operations soldiers who operate with increased agency in austere environments to accomplish unconventional missions—LaMothe's disobedient "unconventional warriors" are the kinds of soldiers the military happily retrains, punishes, or separates from service. Is there, then, a place for "unconventional warriors" within the military? We think so, but not as "lone rangers" like Butler.

With these potential "unconventional warriors" within the military in mind, there are important threads from the liberative trajectory and LaMothe's account of unconventional warriors that we'd like to carry forward, bring together, and extend. The liberative trajectory opens the door for contextualizing the moral trauma of soldiers (and veterans) within the wider moral and political context of their service. It helps us imagine care unbounded from the privatized clinical pastoral context. Key figures like Wimberly, Smith, Miller-McLemore, and Watkins Ali, taken together, suggest possibilities for life-giving care to emerge, not as a means of reinforcing the status quo of soldierly agency but as a means of empowerment within those constraints and of resistance to injustice. This implicates caregivers in the need for political work for liberation. LaMothe's work suggests that this liberative work need not entail the rejection of soldiering per se (or even loyalty to one's fellow soldiers or fellow citizens) but the abusive ways it is bound up with American exceptionalism and a form of life within a permanent state of exception.

Both the liberative trajectory and LaMothe can be supported by an even more explicitly political turn. Wimberly, Smith, Miller-McLemore, Watkins Ali, and LaMothe, each in their own way, speak to the *need* for political work. We suggest a form and direction that might take. LaMothe's limitation, in particular, is that, in homing in on Butler, "unconventional warriors" are set up as exceptional figures. Butler is a general, not a lower enlisted "joe." He is a solitary figure. Politics, at least at its most basic level (the third dimension described above), is relational and grounded in relational practices. It involves conflict and conciliation around goods held in common. If "unconventional warriorism" has any chance of emerging as a form of life within the context of the military, it is not in the context of lone, high-ranking dissenters.

While all soldiers are subject to life within the state of exception, we imagine a kind of bottom-up relational politics that is attentive to the experiences of those within the military who are most subjected to the harmful dynamics of soldiering: the low-ranking, women, and soldiers of color. At present, this is largely out of bounds. While much is made about the limits on the political speech of soldiers, the more fundamental constraint of soldierly agency is the limit on association and assembly. So it is that the possibilities of relational politics are severely inhibited from the outset. While naming and unpacking these limitations is essential for any adequate description of soldierly agency, we hasten to rejoin that these "realities" are contingent and historical. As such, they are subject to political interventions. We suggest unionization, in particular.

There are no easy answers. We are not suggesting unionization as a panacea but rather lifting it up as an example of the kind of radical re-imagination we are after. The civil-military distinction (and the legal regimes enforcing the military as a state of exception) is, in large part, an attempt to banish politics (and the partisan aspects of statecraft) from the prosecution of war. We fully recognize the danger of unleashing partisan politics in the context of the American military. Unionization, we think, would open up space for soldiers to live and breathe as political animals in the context of politics as relational practices. There are real political hurdles, but recent movements are heartening. Although federal law currently prohibits the unionization of soldiers (10 U.S. Code § 976), no such prohibition exists for National Guard soldiers on State active duty. The Department of Justice recently affirmed this gap in light of several recent pushes for unionization (Monroe, 2022; Winkie, 2022). We contend that churches and their chaplains could be key partners and advocates in the effort. Chaplains, in particular, are positioned to engage directly in political work, organizing and advocating for forms of political life for themselves and for their soldiers that disrupt the legal frameworks, national civil religious narratives, formation processes, and troubling lived realities of life as a soldier. Chaplains cannot do this work alone but must be supported by robust networks of American churches.

CONCLUSION: A MODEST PROPOSAL

In this chapter, we have argued that the current pastoral theological conversation around military moral injury has not fully metabolized the political and liberative trajectory of the discipline. This larger movement within pastoral theology away from the focus on the individual needs to be brought to bear in the context of the care of veterans. If moral injury is indeed a political wound, then what is needed is nothing less than political healing. Along with Black, feminist, and womanist pastoral theologians, we argued that those who care for veterans should attend to nurturing and empowering them, as well as joining with them in resistance "from below." Care, then, includes survival in the midst of oppression and not simply accommodation to it, but it must also include participation in the struggle for liberation. While liberation for some may mean a rejection of soldiering as such or of one's own service as soldier, we argued it need not entail that and looked to LaMothe's "unconventional warrior" as a possible exemplar for continued service.

We conclude by suggesting the following elements for future pastoral theological work around the care of soldiers and veterans.

1. The care of soldiers and veterans requires the recognition that the vocation of soldiering is contested terrain within the Christian tradition and is bound up with various accounts of the relation of church/world, church/state, just war, pacifism, etc., i.e., the contested nature of politics in the first dimension and the nature and form of the polis itself.

2. The care of soldiers and veterans requires a thick description of the constrained and burdened moral and political agency of soldiers within the state of exception, to include their location within the American civil religious sacrificial economy (and the role of Christian theology), the way that soldiering and war are bound up with masculinity (Tietje, 2021), and the ways these dynamics land very differently for soldiers who live at different intersections of race, class, gender, and rank. That is to say, a description of soldiering in terms of statecraft (or politics in the second dimension) and the limitations on relational politics (the third dimension) is necessary.

3. Within this context, then, the functions of pastoral caregivers should be extended analogously to the ways that Black, feminist, and womanist pastoral theologians have suggested: survival, empowerment, resistance, liberation.

4. If these are the functions, then military and VA chaplains and church leaders cannot help but enter into the fray of both relational and statecraft politics as allies with and advocates for soldiers and veterans. There is a bond based on solidarity that chaplains develop with soldiers and veterans, even those they did not directly serve alongside.

It is by entering into *this* fray that chaplains can support soldiers and veterans (Morris, 2021).

REFERENCES

Agamben, G. (1998). *Homo sacer: Sovereign power and bare life* (D. Heller-Roazen, Trans.). Stanford University Press. (Original work published 1995).
Agamben, G. (2005). *State of exception* (K. Attell, Trans.). University of Chicago Press. (Original work published 2003).
American Psychiatric Association (1980). *Diagnostic and Statistical Manual of Mental Disorders*. 3rd ed., rev. American Psychiatric Association.
Boisen, A. (1971). *The exploration of the inner world: A study of mental disorder and religious experience*. University of Pennsylvania Press. (Original work published 1936).
Bonhoeffer, D. (1997). *Letters and papers from prison*. Touchstone.
Bretherton, L. (2019). *Christ and the common life: Political theology and the case for democracy*. Eerdmans.
Brock, R. N., & Lettini, G. (2012). *Soul repair: Recovering from moral injury after war*. Beacon.
Currier, J., Drescher, K. D., & Nieuwsma, J. (Eds.). (2021). *Addressing moral injury in clinical practice*. American Psychological Association.
Dulmus, C. N., & Hilarski, C. (2003). When stress constitutes trauma and trauma constitutes crisis: The stress-trauma-crisis continuum. *Brief Treatment and Crisis Intervention*, 3(1), 27–36.
Ebel, J. (2015). *GI messiahs: Soldiering, war, and American civil religion*. Yale University Press.
Ellacuría, I., & Sobrino, J. (Eds.). (1993). *Mysterium Liberationis: Fundamental concepts of liberation theology*. Orbis.
Fox, N. A. (2019). Aretē: We as black women. *Journal of Veteran Studies*, 4, 58–77.
Goldstein, J. (2001). *War and gender*. Cambridge University Press.
Graham, L. K. (2015). Just between us: Big thoughts on pastoral theology. *Journal of Pastoral Theology*, 25(3), 172–187.
Graham, L. K. (2017). *Moral injury: Restoring wounded souls*. Abingdon.
Gutiérrez, G. (2004). In R. Barr (Ed. & Trans.), *The power of the poor in history*. Wipf & Stock. (Original work published 1983).
Harris, M. (2010). *Gifts of virtue, Alice Walker, and womanist ethics*. Palgrave Macmillan.
Hunter, R. J., & Ramsay, N. J. (2017). How it all began and formative choices along the way: Personal reflections on the Society for Pastoral Theology. *Journal of Pastoral Theology*, 27(2), 98–109.
Jinkerson, J. (2016). Defining and assessing moral injury: A syndrome perspective. *Traumatology*, 22(2), 122–130.
Kinghorn, W. (2012). Combat trauma and moral fragmentation: A theological account of moral injury. *Journal of the Society of Christian Ethics*, 32(2), 57–74.
Kotcheff, T. (Director) (Ed.). (1982). *First blood* [Film]. Anabasis N. V. Cinema 84; Elcajo Productions.

Kotcheff, T. (Director) (Ed.). (1983). *Uncommon valor* [Film]. Brademan-Self Productions; Sunn Classic Pictures.

Kubrick, S. (Director) (Ed.). (1987). *Full metal jacket* [Film]. Warner Brothers; Natant; Stanley Kubrick Productions.

Lartey, E. Y. (2013). *Postcolonializing God: An African American theology*. SCM.

LaMothe, R. (2017a). *Care of souls, care of polis: Toward a political pastoral theology*. Cascade.

LaMothe, R. (2017b). Men, warriorism, and mourning: The development of unconventional warriors. *Pastoral Psychology, 66*, 819–836.

Lifton, R. J. (2005). *Home from the war: Learning from Vietnam veterans*. Other Press. (Original work published 1973).

Litz, B. T., Stein, N., Delaney, E., Lebowitz, L., Nash, W. P., Silva, C., & Maguen, S. (2009). Moral injury and moral repair in war veterans: A preliminary model and intervention. *Clinical Psychology Review, 29*, 695–706.

Loveland, A. (2014). *Change and conflict in the U.S. Army Chaplain Corps since 1945*. University of Tennessee Press.

Mahedy, W. P. (2004). *Out of night: The spiritual journey of Vietnam vets*. Radix. (Original work published 1986).

McGarrah Sharp, M. (2019). *Creating resistances: Pastoral care in a post-colonial world*. Brill.

Miller-McLemore, B. (1993, April 7). The human web: Reflections on the state of pastoral theology. *Christian Century, 110*, 366–369.

Miller-McLemore, B. (1999). Feminist theory in pastoral theology. In B. Miller-McLemore & B. Gill-Austern (Eds.), *Feminist and womanist pastoral theology* (pp. 77–94). Abingdon.

Miller-McLemore, B. (2018). The living human web: A twenty-five-year retrospective. *Pastoral Psychology, 67*, 305–321.

Melin, J. (2016). Desperate choices: Why black women join the U.S. military at higher rates than other racial and ethnic groups. *New England Journal of Public Policy, 28*(2), 1–14.

Monroe, R. (2022, April 26). The National Guard soldiers trying to unionize. *The New Yorker*. https:// www.newyorker.com/news/letter-from-the-southwest/the-national-guard-soldiers-trying-to-unionize.

Moon, Z. (2015). *Coming home: Ministry that matters with veterans and military families*. Chalice.

Moon, Z. (2019). *Warriors between worlds: Moral injury and identities in crisis*. Lexington.

Moon, Z. (2020). Moral injury and the role of chaplains. In B. Kelle (Ed.), *Moral injury: A guidebook for understanding and engagement* (pp. 59–69). Lexington.

Morris, J. (2020). Veteran solidarity and Antonio Gramsci: Counterhegemony as pastoral theological intervention. *Journal of Pastoral Theology, 30*(3), 207–221.

Morris, J. (2021). *Moral injury among returning veterans: From thank you for your service to a liberative solidarity*. Lexington.

Ramsay, N. J., & Doehring, C. (Eds.). (2019). *Military moral injury and spiritual care: A resource for religious leaders and professional caregivers*. Chalice.

Rogers-Vaughn, B. (2014). Blessed are those who mourn: Depression as political resistance. *Pastoral Psychology, 63*, 503–522.

Rogers-Vaughn, B. (2015). Powers and principalities: Initial reflections toward a post-capitalist pastoral theology. *Journal of Pastoral Theology, 25*(2), 71–92.

Sobrino, J. (1994). *Principles of mercy: Taking the crucified people from the cross.* Orbis.

Scott, W. (1990). PTSD in DSM-III: A case in the politics of diagnosis and disease. *Social Problems, 37*, 294–310.

Shatan, C. (1972, May 6). Post-Vietnam syndrome. *New York Times.*

Shatan, C. (1973). The grief of soldiers: Vietnam combat veterans' self-help movement. *American Journal of Orthopsychiatry, 43*, 640–653.

Shay, J. (1994). *Achilles in Vietnam: Combat trauma and the undoing of character.* Scribner.

Shay, J. (2014). Moral injury. *Psychoanalytic Psychology, 31*(2), 182–191.

Smith, A. Jr. (1982). *The relational self: Ethics and therapy from a Black church perspective.* Abingdon.

Stone, O. (Director) (Ed.). (1986). *Platoon* [Film]. Hemdale Film Corp. Cinema 84.

Tietje, A. (2018). The responsibility and limits of military chaplains as public theologians. In S. D. MisirHiralall, C. L. Fici, & G. S. Vigna (Eds.), *Religious studies scholars as public intellectuals* (pp. 91–108). Routledge.

Tietje, A. (2021). War, masculinity, and the ambiguity of care. *Pastoral Psychology, 70,* 1–15.

Watkins Ali, C. (1999). *Survival and liberation: Pastoral theology in African American context.* Chalice.

Weidersheim, K. A. (2021). Dietrich Bonhoeffer: Ideology, praxis, and his influence on the theology of liberation. *Political Theology, 23*(8), 721–738. https://doi.org/10.1080/1462317X.2021.1925438.

Wiinikka-Lydon, J. (2017). Moral injury as inherent political critique: The prophetic possibilities of a new term. *Political Theology, 18,* 219–232.

Wimberly, E. (1979). *Pastoral care in the Black church.* Abingdon.

Winkie, D. (2022, January 25). Guard troops can unionize on state active duty, DoJ says. *Army Times.* https:// www.armytimes.com/news/your-army/2022/01/25/guard-troops-can-unionize-on-state-active-duty-doj-says/.

10

William James's Depression, Vocational Despair, and Self-Murder

REGGIE ABRAHAM

William James (1842–1910) was an American psychologist and philosopher whose work has been influential in the modern pastoral theology movement. James was the elder brother of the famed novelist Henry James, the son of Swedenborgian apologist Henry James Sr., and the grandson (and namesake) of one of early America's richest entrepreneurs, William James of Albany, New York. Thanks to his father's broad social circle, William and his siblings were regularly exposed to the leading thinkers of their day, including Bronson Alcott, George Ripley, Henry David Thoreau, and—William's godfather—Ralph Waldo Emerson.

One of the most influential and enduring of William James's published works is *The Varieties of Religious Experience: A Study in Human Nature* (1902), based on his Gifford Lectures delivered at the University of Edinburgh from 1901–1902. Acclaimed by admirers and lambasted by critics, *The Varieties* has been in continuous print since its release over a century ago. A work of particular interest to pastors, chaplains, and advocates of twelve-step programs, it was a notable influence in the life of Anton Boisen, a pioneer of 20th-century clinical pastoral education. In *The Varieties*, James (1902) reflects on religious *experience* as germane to religion, which he describes as "the feeling, acts, and experiences of individual men in their solitude so far as they apprehend themselves to stand in relation to whatever they consider the divine" (p. 34). He offers several cases of individuals who found noumenal experiences to be personally meaningful or even transformative.

Perhaps the most intriguing and discussed case of the 150 or so presented by James is that of an anonymous French "correspondent" or "sufferer" (W. James, 1902, pp. 160–161). The case begins with the correspondent describing a moment of extreme and "horrible fear" for his own existence (p. 160). His distress was accompanied by the recollection of a young "epileptic patient" he had once encountered in an asylum (p. 160). The patient was a "black-haired youth with greenish skin, entirely idiotic, who used to sit all day on one of the benches . . . moving nothing but his black eyes and looking absolutely non-human" (p. 160). Although the case is relatively brief, it brings many striking themes to the reader's attention—depression, anhedonia, epilepsy, loss of agency, and loss and reunification of the divided self. The images of darkness and fear conveyed by the French correspondent are haunting and almost palpable.

It was later revealed that the case of the French correspondent was actually James's own case (H. James, 1920, p. 145). James struggled with periods of depression throughout adolescence and adulthood. He also suffered from a variety of physical illnesses, including digestive problems, difficulties with eyesight, and incapacitating back pain. In the edited volume *Letters of William James*, his son Henry III comments: "Bad health, a feeling of the purposelessness of his own particular existence, his philosophic doubts and his constant preoccupation with them, all these combined to plunge him into a state of morbid depression" (H. James, 1920, p. 145).

Added to the physical maladies and the lack of direction regarding his professional life was a matter many young men find troubling, namely, romance. Through much of 1869, James was in an emotionally intense relationship with a vivacious young woman named Minnie Temple. Unfortunately, Minnie was sick with tuberculosis, and, although there were highs points along the way, her overall prognosis was not good. Early in 1870 her health was in a steep decline, and William—by this time a trained medical doctor—knew what the illness portended for his dreams of a life with Minnie. Minnie died on March 8, 1870, and William fell into a deep and abiding darkness.

THE DARK MOODS OF WILLIAM JAMES

In the years following his French correspondent experience, James found his way to a teaching career at Harvard University. Given his effusive brilliance, it is no surprise that he soon became an internationally renowned psychologist and philosopher. It seemed that the darkness of the earlier period of his life no longer troubled him. Looking back on these years,

William's son Henry III commented: "After some years Father himself felt and knew that he was a man renewed. He had sloughed off the morbid personality of the latter sixties and early seventies" (Richardson, 2006, p. 237). Finally established in a career—an issue that had troubled him at an earlier period—the brilliant and jocular James was well liked by faculty colleagues and adored by students. In fact, his faculty colleague and department head George Herbert Palmer commented: "We found in him a masterful type of human being, developed almost to perfection" (Kazin, 1993, p. 244). Of his many winsome qualities James was perhaps best known for his kindness. According to Palmer, James was "corrupted by kindness" (Richardson, 2006, pp. 159–160).

Some of the luminaries James trained at Harvard included Theodore Roosevelt, George Santayana, W. E. B. Du Bois, and Gertrude Stein (Richardson, 2006, p. 422). The latter once exited a philosophy exam shortly after turning in her blank exam paper with a note scribbled at the top: "Dear Professor James, I am so sorry but really I do not feel a bit like an examination paper in philosophy today." The next day James responded with a note: "Dear Miss Stein, I understand perfectly how you feel. I often feel like that myself." At the end of the course, Stein received the highest grade in the class (Menand, 2002, p. 29).

For all of James's charm, warmth, and wit, it seems he was always just moments away from slipping into a gloomy despair. His dark moods had receded but were not entirely resolved. In fact, they continued to bedevil him throughout his life. A former student, John Jay Chapman, once observed, "There was, in spite of his playfulness, a deep sadness about James. You felt that he had just stepped out of this sadness in order to meet you and was to go back into it the moment you left him" (Richardson, p. 236). The staying power of James's sadness was remarkable. One cannot help but wonder about its origins. William's son Henry III believed his father's periodic distress had something to do with "his parents' household" (Richardson, 2006, p. 237). If we want to attempt to understand the dark moods of William James, it is to his life in that household that we must turn.

Looking closely at James's life in his parents' home, it is clear that James was struggling with anxiety from adolescence and possibly earlier. High anxiety in childhood and adolescence are often predictive of "future depressive and substance abuse disorders" (Peris & Rozenman, 2019, p. 305). As mentioned earlier, Henry III connected his father's periodic dark moods to the household his father grew up in. It is worth noting that William James belonged to a family of troubled people. All of his siblings suffered from mental health challenges—some more severe than others—as did his father.

In William's case, his relationship with his parents had something to do with the career confusion and depression he experienced in adolescence.

Prior to the onset of his career confusion, William James was singularly focused on art. His younger brother Henry noted that, from the ages of 5 to 13, William was *always* drawing (H. James, 1983, p. 602). Henry III wrote that his father "had one occupation to which no reference has yet been made, but to which he thought, for a while, of devoting himself wholly, namely, painting. He began to draw before he had reached his teens" (H. James, 1920, p. 22). By mid-adolescence James was quite convinced that he would be an artist. However, he suddenly—and somewhat mysteriously—jettisoned art in favor of a scientific career. Howard Feinstein, in *Becoming William James*, observes, "His painter self, the alternative ego that he stifled, did not fade away. Instead, it insistently reappeared through symptoms that plagued him for the remainder of his life" (1984/1999, p. 145).

Despite James's drastic and emphatic shift in career path from art to science, he had some hesitation—perhaps even ambivalence—about a scientific career. He enrolled in the Lawrence Scientific School at Harvard in 1861, shortly after quitting his art classes. He then shifted plans in 1864 and enrolled in Harvard Medical School. Unsure about a medical career, he took a break from medical school in 1865 to join an expedition to the Amazon with his former instructor at the Lawrence School, the famed zoologist and geologist Louis Agassiz. James became deathly ill on this trip, decided he did not want to become a field naturalist, and returned to Harvard Medical School in 1866. His medical training was interrupted again in 1867 when, due to ill health, he decided to move to Berlin for a year of recuperation. Upon his return he rejoined Harvard Medical School and finally graduated with his MD degree in 1869. After graduation he lived in his parents' home, unemployed and isolated for the better part of the next three years.

Later in life, James grieved his lost art career. In his essay "Great Men and Their Environment" (1880), James is likely referring to himself when he writes:

> Whether a young man enters business or the ministry may depend on a decision which has to be made before a certain day. He takes the place offered in the counting-house, and is *committed*. Little by little, the habits, the knowledges, of the other career, which once lay so near, cease to be reckoned even among his possibilities. At first, he may sometimes doubt whether the self he murdered in that decisive hour might not have been the better of the two; but with the years such questions themselves expire, and the old alternative *ego*, once so vivid, fades into

something less substantial than a dream. (W. James, 1898, p. 227)

George Cotkin (1994) theorizes that this murdered self "no doubt" reflects in some way James's "own substitution of science for art" as his vocation (p. 45). Cotkin expands:

> What James meant by the idea of the "self he murdered" was that when a person chooses and becomes "committed" to a career peripheral to one desired more strongly, that individual will probably experience for a period of time a sense of loss. James's desire for art, "the old alternative ego," which was "once so vivid, fades into something less substantial than a dream." (Cotkin, 1994, p. 45)

James mourned his "murdered self"—his artistic self—as late as 1872, when at age 30 he wrote to his brother Henry about his regret over "not stick[ing] to painting" (Cotkin, 1994, p. 46):

> I have regretted extremely letting my drawing die out. A man needs to keep open all his channels of activity, for the day may always come when his mind needs to change its attitude for the sake of its health. I have been of late so sickened & skeptical of philosophic activity as to regret much that I did not stick to painting, and to envy those like you to whom the aesthetic relations of things were the real world. Surely they reveal a deeper part of the universal life than all the mechanical and logical abstractions do, and if I were you I would never repine that my life had got cast among them rather than elsewhere. (Perry, 1935, p. 329)

THE ARTISTIC SELF

To better understand James's case of the French correspondent and the clues it provides about James's period of depression in 1870, we would do well to travel back in his biography to 1857, when he had been accepted into the art school of Léon Cogniet in Paris. At the time he was just 15 years old (Richardson, 2006, p. 22). Admission to this prestigious art program had its beginnings at the Luxembourg Palace, where he first saw Cogniet's work—particularly a piece entitled *Marius sur les runes de Carthage* (1842). After seeing this painting, William convinced his father to let him begin art lessons with the master painter at the Paris School of Fine Arts. Given Cogniet's reputation at the time, one may assume that Henry's money alone was not enough to convince the old master to admit William as an apprentice. Although an untrained novice at this time of his life, William must have exhibited a great deal of artistic promise to win over Cogniet.

Henry Sr. was not very pleased with his son's interest in art (Capps, 2013, p. 143). He had deep-seated opinions about human production of art, especially "professional" art, i.e., art made by people trying to make a living from their craft, warning it lacked the "spirit" of spontaneity and exuberance of art created for its own sake. While Henry Sr. claimed to admire the aesthetic man or "Artist" in a broad and vague sense, he "scorned any particular manifestation" of an artist in a particular sense (Croce, 1995, p. 78). Henry Sr. wrote, "'When I speak of the aesthetic man or Artist, I do not mean the man of any specific function, as the poet [or] painter.'" Croce added that Henry Sr.'s ideal artist was "the worker in any field who performed from natural inspiration rather than from 'necessity or duty'" (Croce, 1995, p. 78). William was confused by his father's views. On the one hand, he was irresistibly drawn to art and was developing his skill at it. On the other hand, he struggled with his father's displeasure about his interest in the field and found it difficult to get a clear answer from his father about his resistance to it.

William's education was a matter of perennial concern for Henry Sr., and the adolescent's entry into art training set into motion a series of geographical moves for the family. Henry Sr. moved the family from Paris to the far less cosmopolitan Newport, Rhode Island, where William, at age 17, would begin a study of painting with the notable American landscape artist William Morris Hunt. During 1858–1859, William and Henry Jr. attended school at the Berkeley Institute, but on weekends they studied with Hunt. The incongruity of a move from Paris to, of all places, Newport, Rhode Island—hardly an art capital of the world—to further William's art training was not lost on his younger brother Henry, who later recalled:

> The particular ground for our defection, which I obscurely pronounced mistaken, was that since William was to embrace the artistic career—and freedom for this experiment had been after all, as I repeat that it was always in like cases to be, not in the least grudgingly granted him—our return to America would place him in prompt and happy relation to William Hunt, then the most distinguished of our painters as well as one of the most original and delightful of men, and who had cordially assured us that he would welcome such a pupil. This was judged among us at large, other consideration aiding, a sound basis of action; but never surely had so odd a motive operated for a break with the spell of Paris. (James, 1983, p. 274)

In another comment on the scene, Henry Jr. (1914) writes: "I alone of the family perhaps made bold not to say quite directly or literally that we went home to learn to paint. People stared or laughed when we said it, and I disliked their thinking us so simple" (p. 62). It seems obvious that Henry Sr. hoped to break the spell of Cogniet's art studio on William by taking him back to the United States and, perhaps, setting him up with someone he believed would be a less charismatic and revered instructor. However, Henry Jr. offers a secondary reason for the family's abrupt departure from Paris: a change in his father's attitude towards Europe. Henry Sr. had gradually ceased to "like" Europe and had come to the point where he felt "utter isolation" there due to the lack of appreciation for his theological and philosophical ideas (Dupree, 1983, p. 274). Henry Jr. reports that his father was "scantly heeded" by the Europeans (Dupree, 1983, p. 274).

THE MURDERED SELF

Much to the chagrin of Henry Sr., young William's career path as an artist was starting to take shape under the tutelage of his new teacher, William Hunt. Feinstein (1984/1999) interprets Henry Sr.'s discomfort as follows:

> The closeness to Hunt threatened to give his son a mentor who would turn his life in a direction other than the one Henry had planned. If William did not become a scientist and succeed where he himself had failed, Henry James would be left to wrestle more directly with the memory of his deceased father, William of Albany, and his own barely quieted demons. (p. 123)

The shadow of his strict and demanding father still haunted Henry Sr., and William was his path to deliverance from the harsh judgments of that father—the father who was so disappointed in Henry Sr., even from the grave.

The relationship between Henry Sr. and William of Albany is only one thread in the narrative. There are others. For example, in "James and the French Tradition," Barbara Loerzer (2014) discusses Henry Sr.'s resistance to his son's chosen career path from the perspective of religious commitments (pp. 66–73). As a Swedenborgian theologian, Henry Sr. was concerned about the "spiritual dangers" that art posed to his young son. But what these spiritual dangers might be were never clearly laid out by Henry Sr. William himself had repeatedly asked his father for clear answers to his questions about these spiritual dangers. Loerzer opines that Henry's reservations had to do with the Swedenborgian view that nature, with its "preliminary" status, tends to "hinder the development of divine creation" (p. 67). In other words, by focusing on landscapes one might miss the divine message rendered in the act of creation.

Added to this was Henry Sr.'s suspicions of Hunt's philosophy of art, which drew from European aesthetics, particularly from the Barbizon School that focused on atmosphere and light. Barbizon artists depicted realistic views of landscapes and nature in their paintings. The scenes were *earthy*, devoid of theological value (Loerzer, 2014, p. 68). Henry Sr, after all, was focused on the spirit. One critic of the time praised Hunt's work as bringing into the American context the "fervor and warmth of French art," which provided an "antidote" to Puritan, i.e., American, views of nature (Loerzer, 2014, p. 67). Henry feared that Hunt would stir the baser passions in William's thought, taking him away from the spiritual focus that was of such importance to Henry and that he hoped would be his legacy through his son. Art as a career path—learned from a tutor so conversant with the base, sensual forms of the Europeans—might turn William from the better and more wholesome path that Henry envisioned for him. This was, perhaps, later confirmed in a significant incident in Hunt's studio when Henry Jr. happened to come across his elder brother sketching the nude figure of their cousin, Gus Barker. William mysteriously dropped out of art school shortly after this incident and enrolled instead in the Lawrence Scientific School at Harvard.

MOTHER AND MELANCHOLIA

The circumstances surrounding the nude sketch of Gus Barker and the possible controversy stirred up by it might have more to do with William's mother, Mary James, than with his father, Henry Sr. Likewise, it is possible that William's relationship with his mother—a relationship fraught with conflict—had more to do with his "murdered self" and jettisoned art career than his relationship with his father. One of the chief areas of conflict between William and his mother was on the matter of financial expenditures. Worry about money—and a career as a way to earn enough money—would haunt William through much of his adolescence and young adulthood. When considering the nature of depression in William's life, we must consider the role of Mary James, described by biographer Robert W. Richardson (2006) as "the emotional and workday center of the family, the rock that made it all possible" (p. 34).

Some pastoral theologians believe that the nature of William's relationship with his mother contributed to his religious melancholia. William lost the undivided attention of his mother upon the birth of his younger brother

Henry. This is not to say that William was unloved by his mother, but it seems clear that Henry was her favorite child. William, meanwhile, seems to have been the favorite of his father, Henry Sr., and his maternal aunt, Kate, who lived with the James family. This latter relationship probably further strained the relationship between William and his mother.

Henry James Sr. was considered an indulgent parent who often entertained his children's whims and fancies. He could also be a manipulative and insistent parent. My comments on Henry's role in moving William away from art to science are based on the views of numerous James biographers, but I am most influenced in this by Howard Feinstein, author of *Becoming William James*. Nevertheless, I do recognize that people are complex, as are their motivations and decision-making processes. As is often the case when discussing the motivations of people, there is usually more than one narrative to be considered.

In the case of William James, art was a very important pursuit in his early life as he was taking his first steps towards forming a professional identity. I have already noted his brother Henry's observation that, from a young age, William was always drawing. William's attraction to drawing—and later painting—was so strong that the turn away from art to science was a drastic move that seems to have had profound psychological implications going forward from this momentous decision. In fact, we have already seen evidence, in William's previously noted letter to his brother, that William thought of his prior "artistic self" as a "murdered self"—a point I consider below by means of Donald Capps's *Men, Religion, and Melancholia*.

Some James biographers attribute William's sudden career turn and extended period of career confusion to the influence of Henry Sr. (Feinstein, 1984/1999, pp. 122–145; Richardson, 2006, p. 58; Simon, 1998, pp. 86–88). I do not disagree with this assessment. However, although that is the dominant narrative, I also believe it is only half the story. In these accounts, biographers tend to overlook any role in William's decision played by his mother. Donald Capps in *Men, Religion, and Melancholia* and Robert C. Dykstra in *Finding Ourselves Lost* have raised the question of Mary James's influential role in turning William from art to science, as well as the depressive episode associated with that life-altering move. Capps is influenced by Erik Erikson's belief that melancholy has "teeth" (Capps, 1997, p. 60). If so, who did William, given his melancholy, want to "bite" with those teeth? Capps views the French correspondent case with the intent to explore "suspicions Erikson's view raises about the role of the mother-son relationship in James's fear for his own sanity" (p. 60). Capps follows this with his working theory that "(1) Mary James had a hand in the murder of the self James imagined he could be" and "(2) she was the key player in his fear that he might become a self whom he truly dreaded becoming but knew to be a genuine possibility" (p. 60).

Capps (1997) presents four authors—William James, Rudolf Otto, Carl Jung, and Erik Erikson—who experienced the psychological (not physical) loss of their mothers at a very young age. While their losses in this regard were not unique, their experiences were also not the usual experiences of children who experience a similar loss of their mothers' unconditional attention or primary affection as they grow and mature (p. 4). Capps speculates that these four boys—young James, Otto, Jung, and Erikson—experienced traumas associated with loss of their mothers that were perhaps more severe than those of other boys in similar straits. The severity of their traumatic loss of mother disposed them to melancholia, on the one hand, and to a degree of receptivity to religion, on the other. Thus, melancholia and religious interest, for Capps, go hand in hand.

A boy of this type experiences "two losses" (p. 4). Although his mother may be present in the boy's life—in Capps's model, the loss of the mother is not a physical loss through death or departure—he has lost his prior *intimacy* with his mother, "the mother who held him close and made no effort to help him achieve the separation" (p. 4). Added to this is the second loss of "*himself* [emphasis added], the boy who lived in the aura of her unmitigated love and experienced himself as her beloved son. In the process of separation, this self-image proves untenable and altogether too simplistic" (p. 4). In this process of separation—a separation the boy did not desire or instigate—he finds himself necessarily becoming a *new* boy, one who now must strive to regain his mother's love. What once was taken for granted now must be earned because maternal love is no longer freely available or unconditionally granted. "If the separation is fraught with unusual anxiety, both the loss of his original mother and the loss of his original self will create a disposition toward melancholia" (p. 4).

Capps (1997), following Erikson, believes that young adulthood is the period of life when one "returns to one's origins, and especially a revisiting of the separation process, in search of grounds for trust and reassurance. At this time, the fact of his disposition to melancholia may become evident to the young man, whether or not he uses the actual word" (pp. 4–5). Revisiting one's childhood memories and sensations, now with the tools of maturity and life experience at his disposal, the individual starts to bring previously unconnected pieces of emotion, motivation, and personality together. Young adulthood is the time—perhaps the first time—in which the newly minted adult and the perpetually present inner child can become acquainted with one another. The adult now has the tools and experience to take inventory of his life and formulate a narrative, all the while conversing with his childhood self. In doing so,

> He discovers within himself an unexplainable sadness, exacerbated, but not fully accounted for, by broken relationships, difficulties in finding what he wants to do with his life, and so on. He also discovers within himself *a silent rage* [emphasis added] he did not know was there and he has great difficulty understanding its source, because the frustrations he encounters in his struggle to come into his own do not seem to warrant such depth of feeling, such negative affect. However, the way in which he now relates to his mother, if she is still living, is a clue to its source, as he has feelings toward her that are disproportionate to her actual provocations. Such feelings are rooted, I suggest, in the early separation process, when he lost her unconditional love and experienced the unbridgeable gulf that separated him from the child he was before the separation. Now a similar two-pronged separation occurs once again as he moves into adulthood. (p. 5).

Capps also notes that the texts he is concerned with in *Men, Religion, and Melancholy* are written by older adult men. This certainly is true of William James, who wrote at age 60 about an event—the French correspondent crisis—that had occurred when he was 28 years old. But the mature age of the authors does not indicate an "objective, disinterested, 'scientific' attitude in the writing of their texts" (p. 5). Even as mature adults, the questions and concerns of young adulthood—even childhood—are still quite live for them, particularly because they are struggling with "grievances relating to the commitments they made in young adulthood, especially commitments that were religious or quasi-religious in nature" (p. 6).

Overall, Capps's theory regarding William James's melancholy is deeply influenced by his reading of Freud's "Mourning and Melancholia" (1963). His argument is based on two interrelated points: "The first is that each author is struggling with the relationship between religion and psychopathology but, more specifically, the psychopathology they know as *melancholy* (and you and I probably know as *chronic depression*)" (Capps, 1997, p. 3). He then offers his second point, that "melancholy may be traced, ultimately, to the author's relationship with his own mother. The sadness, despair, and rage characteristic of melancholy have an object . . . the author's mother" (p. 3).

Melancholy is described in various ways by Capps in *Men, Religion, and Melancholia*. Borrowing from William Styron, he describes it is a "pain that crushes the soul," an "anxiety and incipient dread" hidden away in the "dungeons of the spirit" (1997, p. 29). Drawing on the *Diagnostic and Statistical Manual of Mental Disorders* (4th ed.; American Psychiatric Association, 1994), he describes melancholia as "a special feature of a major depressive episode that occurs in the course of a major depressive episode" (p. 29). Melancholy has proven to be a difficult psychopathology to "define with any degree of precision, because it seems to vary so much from person to person" (p. 8). Although an old word, melancholy is a remarkably current disorder that Capps (1997) ties to "the adult's experience of forsakenness" that occurs in his separation from his mother (p. 8). It is in this moment that the child experiences himself as a "dispirited soul" and feels "bereft" in his heart (p. 8).

Such feelings of loss are further exacerbated when the agent of childhood cruelty is the boy's mother, resulting in the sense of "forsakenness" taking on the bearings of "religious melancholy" in its "deeper dimensions of rage, fury, and even hate" (p. 9). Capps (1997) continues with an observation about the depth of feelings associated with severe melancholia:

> What makes melancholy somewhat unique among the "depressive disorders" is that it manifests—or, more commonly, hides—a deep sense of bitterness, the feeling that one has been mistreated or treated unjustly, as, for example, in the case of Job, a man who bitterly complains not only that he has been forsaken by God but also that God had no right to do this to him, as he was God's most loyal supporter and defender. I submit, therefore, that a mother's cruelty is an important variable in the formation of a melancholic personality. To experience separation from one's mother is one thing; sadness and longing will surely result. But to experience the withdrawal of her love in an especially cruel or unfeeling manner is another. Severe melancholia is the predictable outcome. (p. 9)

Capps believes that, in *The Varieties of Religious Experience*, William James did not expand on the role of his mother (or his father, for that matter) either because he was not very self-analytical (Myers, 1986, p. 49) or—Capps's own view—because James was too reserved to speak ill of his parents, "especially his mother" (Capps, p. 60). Furthermore, in the context of his Gifford Lectures, James was sensitive to the fact that he was invited to give a lecture series and not to share his life story and traumas with the audience. Capps says, "To engage in any more personal disclosure than he has already done would be self-indulgent, an affront to his audience, who came for something else" (p. 60).

THE INFLUENCE OF MARY JAMES

William's relationship with his mother was not entirely positive. Certainly, he was closer to his father than to his mother. It seems clear that William was Henry Sr.'s favorite child and that Henry Jr. was Mary's favorite. The age difference between William and Henry was a mere 15 months; William had a very short window in which to enjoy his mother's unfettered attention before he had to make way for his brother. In the correspondence between the mother and her two older sons, we can clearly see Mary's bias in favor of Henry. For example, she was very strict about William's spending money but was indulgent with Henry (Feinstein, 1984/1999, pp. 158–163). She was also "impatient" with William's "frequent expressions of weakness and anxiety" but appreciative of Henry's "patient, non-complaining posture" (Capps, p. 62). In Mary's view, Henry's temperament was signified by his "angelic patience" while William was always "talking about himself" (Capps, p. 62). She described Henry as the son

> who never caused trouble in the nursery, who always entered into his mother's domestic anxieties. The father thought she loved him "more than all her other progeny," and she herself once addressed [Henry Jr.] in a letter as "the dearest" of her absent boys—though at once adding, "because the farthest away, perhaps." Another time, as if seeing herself in him, she exclaimed: "You dear reasonable over-conscientious soul!" (Habegger, 2001, p. 493)

In *The Varieties*, William—who for the sake of anonymity assumes the identity of a French asylum patient—describes his mother as a "very cheerful person" (W. James, 1902, p. 161). His mother was "healthy-minded" and therefore constitutionally incapable of appreciating William's "horrible pain and suffering" (Capps, p. 60). This is another way of saying that Mary would have been unable to understand—and, so, to sympathize—with William's predicament. For Mary James, it was very important to present a good face to the world. No one in the James household should be perceived as sick or dysfunctional. All must be well. Capps (1997) brings this point to the fore by turning to the witness of William's sister, Alice James:

> In her commentary on James's essay "The Hidden Self," published in 1890, in which James refers to the "abandoned" self, Alice recalls that when she was having her attacks, "the only difference between me and the insane was that I had not only all the horrors and suffering of insanity but the duties of doctor, nurse, and straitjacket imposed on me, too." What she means

> is that it reflected a refusal to acknowledge that something was desperately wrong with the James family. (p. 62)

However, perhaps to upend this unspoken demand that nothing should be wrong with the James family, it seems that everyone in the household was emotionally and physically distraught, frequently and drastically. Sickness was a way the James children could wrangle financial advantages from their parents, allowing them the freedom to travel and enjoy certain excesses (see Feinstein, 1984/1999, pp. 192–195).

Capps illustrates the mother's attitude by referring to a time when William was in Germany and one of his friends suggested to Mary James that her son had gone overseas because of a family disagreement. Mary was not pleased to hear this and wrote William an "indignant" letter complaining about his friend's audacious remark (Capps, p. 62).

> In this letter, Mary James's snide and wounded tone expresses her indignation at the possibility of a "rupture" within the James family, or at the possibility that people might imagine such a rupture had occurred. Thus, she indirectly echoes her husband's belief that "domestic discord" is the most "frightful of all discords" and reveals her sense of responsibility not only for maintaining harmony but *for reminding her children of their responsibility as well*. (Capps, p. 62)

Maternal pressure on the children forced them to "put on a happy face"—as we might say today—despite the host of physical and psychological maladies that assailed each member of the James family.

Drawing on Richard W. B. Lewis's *The James's: A Family Narrative* (1991), Capps (1997) traces the origins of this family dysfunction to the sibling rivalry between Mary and her sister Catherine. Henry Sr. had been friends with Hugh Walsh, brother to Mary and Catherine, when he was a student at Princeton Theological Seminary. After both men had dropped out of the seminary, Henry frequently visited the Walsh household in New York City, where he first met Mary and Catherine. Both women were considered "spinsters," and neither was thought of as particularly attractive. Henry, who had a leg amputated as a result of a childhood accident, was still considered an eligible bachelor. He was a witty conversationalist, hailed from a noteworthy Presbyterian family, was independently wealthy, and was by some accounts good-looking (or, at the very least, a clotheshorse). Capps notes that the James family dysfunctions can be traced to

> the fact that Henry Senior had considered marrying both Walsh sisters, finally settling on Mary, who was the older. Yet the

> younger sister, Catherine (Aunt Kate), accompanied the young James family to England, serving as the nurse for little William and Henry. For his part, William seemed to take especially well to Aunt Kate, as he was her favorite of the two boys. By contrast, Henry Junior felt a special bond with his mother. (p. 63)

It is not difficult to imagine the complexities spawned by sibling rivalries that took this shape from the boys' early childhoods and on into adulthood. Although there is no evidence to question his fidelity to his wife, it surely must not have helped the situation that Henry Sr.—ever the provocateur—was publishing tracts questioning traditional marriage and advocating Charles Fourier's ideas on free love and polyamorous marriages (Habegger, 1989, pp. 29–30).

William was often in the care of his Aunt Kate while his mother was preoccupied with Henry Jr., and

> this emotional separation from his mother occurred when William was developing a will of his own (that is, two to three years old). In an emotional sense, he was talking about himself when in his lecture "The Dilemma of Determinism" he said that some mothers *do* strangle their firstborns. And no doubt Aunt Kate, the spurned sister, would not have protested if her sister's firstborn had a desire to "bite" his mother back for having spurned *him* in favor of her beloved second-born son. (Capps, 1997, p. 63)

Capps also notes that one of Henry Jr.'s earliest short stories, "The Romance of Certain Old Clothes," was about an "incestuous triangle involving a rivalry between sisters" (p. 64). Aunt Kate married and left the James household when William was around age 13. However, she returned three years later when her marriage broke up. She largely remained with the James family from that point on.

Mary James was fiercely protective and supportive of her husband. She was also a stronger personality than her sister. She was a formidable figure—the *most* formidable figure—in her household. By comparison, Henry Sr. was a weak man and "no match it seems for his wife, who as Kaplan points out 'remained stolidly, uncomplainingly healthy' when her five children and husband succumbed to various illnesses" (Capps, 1997, p. 64). Henry could be loud and verbose, but he was merely "a great noisemaker, an actor who could be heard in the back row," while Mary was "dominant to her children and her husband, 'by the mere force of her complete availability'" (p. 64). Capps, quoting Leon Edel, suggests that "if" the James children "used their illnesses to manipulate their parents, this was in retaliation against their mother's own manipulations" (p. 64).

The complexities of the James's domestic life—the triangle between Henry Sr., Mary, and Aunt Kate—surely influenced the various illnesses exhibited by the James children. The James children's lives were clearly complicated by a somewhat unstable father, an overbearing mother, an alternate mother figure, and a strangely itinerant lifestyle that took them from house to house—even hotel room to hotel room—across Europe and the American Northeast. One can only imagine the impact of such itinerancy upon them in relation to their education, ability to make and keep friends, and sense of having a place to call home.

TURNING AWAY FROM WILLIAM

At a very young age, William experienced the emotional loss of his mother. Perhaps this was unintentional on Mary's part, but the effect was that William experienced the loss of his mother's affection early in his childhood. Although she remained physically in close proximity to him, Mary had turned away from him in favor of his brother Henry Jr. This turn away from one to another characterized her relationship with her two elder sons for the remainder of her life. Perhaps this is best exemplified in the way she dispersed money to William and Henry. She regularly restricted William while indulging Henry, all the while communicating to William her anxieties about money. As time went on, Mary's anxiety about money was internalized by William, who was anxious about finances throughout his adult life. That anxiety, I believe, played an important role in many of his physical maladies and struck the core of his self-worth as he failed to find a profession and obsessed about his earning potential.

Much of my inspiration for this study of William James and bodily descriptors—in the form of my attention to the French correspondent who describes a "black-haired youth" with "greenish skin" and to William James's many physical discomforts and maladies—has been inspired by conversations I have had over the years with my doctoral adviser. The pastoral effect of these conversations is that I have grown in my appreciation for the role of the body in my ministerial work as a preacher, a caregiver, and a pastoral counselor—as well as in my appreciation of God's care and concern for the whole person.

As a Pentecostal Christian, I have been aware of a certain incongruity—or perhaps contradiction—in the approach to the "body" within my church community. On the one hand, in my tradition there is the strong tendency towards bifurcation between body and spirit. There is a propensity to read quite literally some of the Pauline statements exalting the spirit and denigrating the flesh. The result is a "spirit *versus* flesh" dogma that impacts views on personal morality and church culture. On the other hand, there is a great emphasis on—and I would say valuation of—the human body. The body is one of the main subjects of the Pentecostal sermon, especially in regard to physical healing. The body is also the locus of the Holy Spirit's operation. The Pentecostal tradition emphasizes the physicality of religious experience. Pentecostals may swing, sway, or dance in worship. Some people "quake" when they feel the power of the Holy Spirit upon them, and others speak out loud in "tongues."

Of course, while I was growing up in this community, I never noticed this incongruency between the low value placed on the body and the simultaneous nearly absolute focus on the body—and thus its high valuation—as the locus of the work of the Holy Spirit. Somehow, God's Spirit loved and wanted to be close to the human body. It was only as an adult that I came to recognize this odd, conflicted approach to the body in my religious tradition. Through Robert C. Dykstra's work in *Finding Ourselves Lost* (2018) I came to a growing appreciation for the human body before a loving and accepting God. In doing so, I recognized that, indeed, the work of God is not to be neatly separated between body, soul, and spirit. God's concern is with the whole being and not merely with its parts. If the spirit is ill, the body will be implicated and affected in its malaise—and vice versa. If pastoral caregivers are concerned with the soul, they are thereby concerned with the body and spirit as well. As Dykstra (2018) says, "bodily healings" cannot be "segregated from those of heart and mind" (p. 51).

Dykstra shares an incident from his childhood that has been particularly thought-provoking for him. When he was 11 years old, he attended a Christian summer camp where he experienced an "emotional confirmation of the faith in which [he] had been raised" (2018, pp. 94–95). It seems to me that Dykstra's memories of the camp emphasize a sense of an embodied relationship with Jesus, faith not only as a matter of the spirit, mind, or emotion but as a matter of the body. Dykstra says, "Memories of that camp have occasioned in me a sense of joy being ascribed to feeling *embraced* [emphasis added] there by Jesus, a religious awakening with outsized implications for my life. This aspect of what occurred continues to remain meaningful to me" (p. 94).

Dykstra describes a friendship he established with one of the boys at the camp, the "alpha-male camper" in the group. The new friend invited Dykstra to sit with him on his top bunk during evening story times:

> Everyone heard him say this. I could not believe I had been chosen. I could not believe he was allowed to choose. I could not believe that our counselors would let me listen to the story from someone else's bunk. But then, after a moment's hesitation, I believed. I scrambled up to his bed, instantly increasing my social capital among the cabin boys but also, more important, finding in this new friendship an unaccustomed surge of self-confidence that would propel me through the rest of that week. (p. 94)

The use of spatiality in the story instantly attracted my attention; belief is followed by elevation. Dykstra, who arrived late to the camp and so had to settle for a lower bunk, ascended to the top bunk at his newfound friend's invitation during story time. This spatial ascendancy was also a social ascendancy as the new friend was the alpha-male in the group and son of the camp director. But Dykstra also implies that this friendship impacted his religious experience at the Christian camp. In some ways, this friendship brought him closer to his faith, his experience of Jesus. While for many years thereafter he characterized this camp as the place where as an adolescent he felt a spiritual or emotional confirmation of his faith, he eventually came to muse that it may have been this newly established and very much embodied friendship that precipitated this connection to the divine. The religious experience and the embodied friendship became conflated in an experience of God's love for him.

While Dykstra is clearly not speaking of depression, I found myself considering his story through the lens of James's biography and in relation to major depressive disorder. One of the tendencies of people experiencing a depressive episode is disconnection from others. Meaningful friendship and connection with another person can be an uplifting experience in a variety of ways—socially, emotionally, and spiritually; the value of a friend must not be underestimated. In times of trouble, a good friend can be the difference between life and death. William James was, throughout his life, a social and jovial person—or, at least, he seemed that way in public. There were many times, however, when he would disengage from people and sit in silence during a depressive episode.

One of the most jarring images of the French correspondent case is that of the patient with epilepsy, seemingly sitting alone and isolated from others, the "shape" that William recognized and feared in himself. What Dykstra's story and James's case of the French correspondent reify is the idea that in human relationships there is an important correspondence between space, body posture, and connection. In the former story we witnessed a friendship established between two adolescent boys and, in the latter, the isolation of a boy who sits alone in darkness.

In childhood, Mary James's separation from William was not only an emotional turning away but also a physical and spatial turning away. While my perspective on this is paternal rather than maternal, on numerous occasions I have noted my own physical postures of turning away at times from my older child to attend to the needs of my younger child. To some degree this is a natural tendency as younger children are somewhat more vulnerable than their older siblings. My older child is only now starting to become aware of this difference in vulnerability; previously, she was only aware of the fact that she had once commanded but then had to relinquish my undivided attention. No amount of rationalizing can convince her that she has received double the attention that her younger sibling is receiving. Instead, she only feels the sting of the lost parental gaze. From conversations with friends who have raised—or are currently raising—more than one child, I have come to the conclusion that the scenes playing out in my house are not outside the norms of child-rearing elsewhere.

William James's case is beyond the norms, however. Dykstra draws from a variety of sources to demonstrate the obvious bias of Mary James against her eldest son in favor of Henry Jr. (Dykstra, p. 79). William's relationship with his mother fostered in him some deep-seated anxieties about his "prospects"—i.e., his career possibilities and his earning potential. As one example of the latter:

> Mary was not as sympathetic to her eldest son as she was to Harry. While she had scrutinized every dollar that William spent during his European trip, she urged her "dear reasonable overconscientious" Henry to "[t]ake the fullest liberty and enjoyment your tastes and inclinations crave, and we will promise heartily to foot the bill." What William needed, she believed, was just the opposite: not self-indulgence, but regular habits of moderate exercise and benign diversion. (Simon, 1998, p. 38)

Later, when his brother Henry was starting to earn money as a writer, William was still vocationally floundering and financially dependent, which only served to confirm Mary's assessment of her older son. William was too much like his father, unable to make any money.

The James family, though wealthy, went through periods of financial stress, if not distress. Money was always a point of concern. Henry had a household of five children, Mary, and Aunt Kate, as well as a number of servants, to provide for, and no earned income. Henry's finances were based on dispersals from William of Albany's trust. Although Henry had tried to make investments along the way, his moneymaking skills were abysmal, and he always ended up losing money (Simon, 1998, p. 38). From childhood, Henry Sr. had been undisciplined about money, a characteristic he could not quite tame, however much he periodically tried. When he thought he had gone too far with expenditures, he would quickly and drastically tighten the family budget, later loosening the strings again on a whim. Henry Sr. often needed as much parental supervision as the children did, and Mary took on that parental role.

It became clear to the children that they could not expect much of an inheritance from their father. The family funds supported their comfortable lifestyle, but they could not expect support once they were on their own. Meanwhile, although Henry Sr. disbursed the funds for travel and various purchases, Mary was the financial manager of household resources. Feinstein (1984/1999) notes that William was greatly concerned about money and that Mary raised the issue with him quite early in life (p. 159). As Mary conveyed to William her own anxieties about family finances, William took on those anxieties, personalized them, and amplified them. These worries contributed to his breakdown, as evidenced in the "French correspondent's" noting that he was worried about his "prospects"—a subject William had written about to his cousin Kitty not long before his crisis. In this correspondence, William explained "frankly that medicine attracted him because of the pressure he felt to earn a living. 'After all, the great problem of life seems to be how to keep body and soul together, and I *have* to consider lucre'" (p. 158). Feinstein (1984/1999) says,

> Two themes recur again and again in his correspondence from the Scientific School, a growing preoccupation with insanity and a mounting sense of the urgency of earning money. He maintained his usual jocular surface but his humor barely covered his fear that he, like his father, might break down. The concern about money was initially his parents' worry, but he soon made it his own. This anxiety added to the discomfort caused by the scientific direction he had taken. Why his parents, particularly his mother, became so worried about the money William was spending is unclear. (p. 155)

Later, people who knew the adult William would note his constant concern about money—how much he was being paid and his fears of being cheated or taken advantage of. In the opening pages of her biography of James, Linda Simon presents William on a quest to Syracuse to collect rent from buildings that his family had inherited. "He traveled to Syracuse at least once a year, often more; and whenever he went, he had money on his mind" (Simon, 1998, p. 1). James Jackson Putnam (1910), founder of the Department of Neurology at Harvard Medical School, recalled that James said "jokingly, one day, that when he met a new person he asked him first his age and then his income, and this was almost literally true." The images of the warm-hearted, generous-spirited Harvard scholar and the money-driven New York landlord do not seem to coalesce. Both images, however, represent William James.

Just as Mary constrained William's access to family finances, she may also have played a significant role in his drastic decision to abandon his artistic ambitions. Dykstra suggests that William's sudden decision to turn from art to science may have been occasioned by the incident, mentioned previously, of Henry Jr. happening upon the 18-year-old William and his fellow art student John La Farge sketching the athletic figure of Gus Barker—a cousin of the James boys whom Linda Simon describes as one of the "family's orphans"—who was visiting Newport on a break from Harvard (Simon, 1998, p. 48). The scandal of the incident was that Gus was completely nude, a fact that greatly unsettled Henry Jr. Dykstra (2018), referring to Henry's autobiographical statement on the incident, says,

> He was stunned to find "the beautiful young manly form of our cousin Gus Barker," an affable and athletic eighteen-year-old redhead visiting in Newport during a Harvard vacation, "perched on a pedestal and divested of every garment" as William and La Farge sketched him. This was Henry's first exposure to a life model, and he recounts that the sight of their cousin standing imperturbably naked on the pedestal had the instant effect of disabusing Henry of any artistic ambitions he had harbored by way of emulating William. (p. 79)

It is probable that Henry Jr. promptly conveyed this incident to his mother. Beholding the naked Gus Barker and William's excellent sketch of him led Henry Jr. to voluntarily "pocket" his pencil and may have forced William's hand in "self-murder." Dykstra observes that "daring to behold and portray the naked body of another young man . . . may have come to cost young William his dreams but also . . . to conjure his nightmares" (p. 79). Curiously, despite the extreme discomfort Henry Jr. experienced in this event, "He would retain and preserve for decades William's life drawing of their cousin Gus, who would die at twenty-one as a Union cavalry captain in the Civil War" (p. 78).

Henry Sr. was a deeply religious man, and, although he was no longer a Presbyterian, some biographers opine that he had never really left his Calvinistic roots. He already feared that studying painting—especially from a teacher identified with the Barbizon school—would undermine William's morality. Despite his talk about open marriages and his love of controversy and debate, Henry Sr. in many ways had the constitution of a conservative, 19th-century American Protestant. In their prior European stay, Henry Sr. had warned his sons to avoid any boys at school who would encourage them to compromise their mental and physical chastity. Habegger implies that this warning included directions against masturbation: "No doubt Henry Sr. had warned him against the grim practice he had darkly alluded to in the Second Epistle of James to the Tribune—'that horrible self-pollution . . . which is fast turning our young people into puling hypochondriacs.' Perhaps he also touched on the youthful depravities that turned colleges into 'hotbeds of corruption'" (2001, p. 415).

According to Habegger, this advice was given by Henry Sr. to William, Henry Jr., and their younger brother Garth when the boys were left alone for the first time (in Germany) while the rest of the family visited Paris. William was 18 at the time. Habegger connects this to advice the adult William would give to his own son, who was going to boarding school for the first time. William told his son that some boys use bad language and that, if he wanted to, he could use bad language as well. However, he was to be vigilant against bad behavior:

> Now that you are at Brown and Nicholses, exposed to all sorts of bad boys older than yourself, I ought to give you a word of moral advice. . . . If any boys try to make you *do* anything dirty, though, either to your own person, or to their persons, it is another matter, and you must both preach [against] and smite them. For that leads to an awful habit, and a terrible disease when one is older. (p. 415)

One can only imagine that Henry Sr. would have had a vitriolic reaction upon hearing from Mary what Henry Jr. likely confided in her about the life drawing of Gus in Hunt's studio. William's withdrawal from Hunt's art school was probably engineered by Mary, the "hovering" figure in the background, who would have "held grave reservations about William's chosen art form and, specifically in response to Henry's report, moral trepidation centering on William's susceptibility to homoeroticism" (Dykstra, p. 79).

Henry Sr. tried to manipulate his family through a variety of means, and by this point he had attempted to convince his children that he was very sick and would die soon. Whether this, too, had any effect on William's turn to science is unknown. However, something happened in the James household that dramatically changed the course of William's life. On October 1, 1860, Henry Sr. wrote to Edmund and Mary Tweedy, his sister's relatives who were touring London, asking them to bring a "special dissecting microscope" for William: "Willy needs it & will be much obliged'" (Habegger, 2001, p. 420). Although it would be many years before William would find his professional calling, through a rather awkward series of events William's professional path was becoming set. Drawing on Dykstra's observation, we see that as William's artistic dreams were dashed, he would endure a nightmare in darkness before finding a light and the path forward to a productive life (pp. 78–81).

CONCLUSION

There are many reasons why a person may struggle with depression. Depression may not be about just one thing—disagreements with one's father or the death of a loved one, for example. Depression develops as the result of many precipitating factors—physiological factors, relational factors, environmental factors. Biographers have noted that William suffered a host of physical ailments, including vision problems, neurasthenia, digestive disorders, and severe back pain. Perhaps these were not psychosomatic illnesses but actual physical ailments resulting from inflammation. Perhaps James was genuinely ill and his illnesses contributed to "sickness behavior"—that is, depression.

In the constellation of possibilities, we should note that beyond his physical ailments, William also experienced frustration over his abandoned art career. Although he gave in to parental pressure and pursued a career in the sciences, his heart was not entirely in the work at Lawrence Scientific School or Harvard Medical School. William's native intelligence enabled him to be successful from an academic point of view, but he failed to find fulfillment in his scientific pursuits. While he did complete his MD degree at Harvard, he felt ill suited for the medical profession and disconnected from patient care. William's experience as the "French correspondent" occurred shortly after he graduated medical school. Commencement was not a time of celebration for him but rather a period of great internal struggle, followed by an extended period of private pain.

It is likely that Mary James had a deep influence on her son William's depressive struggle. A host of problems—family system and financial issues, personality differences, personal preferences—kept Mary from wholeheartedly embracing her eldest son. William's frustration related to this diminished relationship with his primary caregiver extended into his young adulthood. In fact, when it came to the matter of William's jettisoned art career, Mary may have been the major force behind that fateful decision.

REFERENCES

American Psychiatric Association. (1994). *Diagnostic and statistical manual of mental disorders* (4th ed.). American Psychiatric Association.

Capps, D. (1997). *Men, religion, and melancholia: James, Otto, Jung, and Erikson.* Yale University Press.

Capps, D. (2013). *At home in the world: A study in psychoanalysis, religion, and art.* Cascade.

Cotkin, G. (1994). *William James, public philosopher.* University of Illinois Press.

Croce, P. J. (1995). *Science and religion in the era of William James, vol. 1: Eclipse of certainty, 1820-1880.* University of North Carolina Press.

Dykstra, R. C. (2018). *Finding ourselves lost: Ministry in the age of overwhelm.* Cascade.

Feinstein, H. M. (1999). *Becoming William James.* Cornell University Press. (Original work published 1984).

Habegger, A. (1989). *Henry James and the "woman business."* Cambridge University Press.

Habegger, A. (2001). *The father: A life of Henry James, Senior.* University of Massachusetts Press.

James, H., Jr. (1914). *Notes of a son and a brother.* Scribner.

James, H., Jr. (1920). *The letters of William James.* Atlantic Monthly Press.

James, H., Jr. (1983). *Henry James: Autobiography* (F. W. Dupree, Ed.). Princeton University Press.

James, W. (1902). *The varieties of religious experience: A study in human nature.* Longmans, Green.

James, W. (1898). Great men and their environment. In *The will to believe and other essays* (216-254). Longmans, Green.

Kazin, A. (1993). William James: To be born again. *Princeton University Library Chronicle, 54*(2/3), 244-258.

Lewis, R. W. B. (1991). *The Jameses: A family narrative.* Farrar, Straus, and Giroux.

Loerzer, B. (2014). William James, the French tradition, and the incomplete transposition of the spiritual into the aesthetic. In M. Halliwell & J. D. S. Rasmussen (Eds.), *William James and the transatlantic conversation: Pragmatism, pluralism, and philosophy of religion* (pp. 65-80). Oxford University Press.

Menand, L. (2002). *American studies.* Farrar, Straus & Giroux.

Myers, G. E. (1986). *William James: His life and thought.* Yale University Press.

Peris, T. S., & Rozenman, M. (2019). Assessment of pediatric anxiety. In S. N. Compton, M. A. Villabo, & H. Kristensen (Eds.), *Pediatric anxiety disorders* (pp. 302-317). Academic Press/Elsevier.

Perry, R. B. (1935). *The thought and character of William James, Vol. 1.* Little, Brown.

Putnam, J. J. (1910, December). William James. *The Atlantic.* https://www.theatlantic.com/magazine/archive/1910/12/william-james/644825/

Richardson, R. D. (2006). *William James: In the maelstrom of American modernism.* Mariner/Houghton Mifflin.

Simon, L. (1998). *Genuine reality: A life of William James.* University of Chicago Press.

11

An Eriksonian Psycho-Social Response to Confucius on the Development of Virtue in Boys and Men

HYON-UK SHIN

For more than six hundred years, Confucius has both influenced every aspect of Koreans' lives as one of the paragons of what it means to be a noble man in China. Today, Confucius's teachings provoke profound ambivalence among the older generation of Korean males. On the one hand, his social ideology summarized as Confucianism has dominated the overall mindset of Koreans and is the solid frame of reference that implicitly or explicitly regulates every aspect of life in Korea. As a result, for some Korean males Confucius is the preeminent role model, the one who almost perfectly realized the ideal of an ethical and moral human character in the midst of the secular world. For others, he is simply a historical figure who made Korean society rigid, conventional, and even feudal thanks to his seemingly grand social ideology. Because of that, he has become outmoded. In particular, the long-dormant contemporary antipathy against the hierarchical social system that is deeply rooted in Confucianism has been intensifying among those who have long been estranged from the Confucian mainstream as regards social, cultural, economic, and political affairs.

Given the pervasiveness of the influence of Confucius, the light and shade that this historical figure has cast upon the androcentric, patriarchal society of Korea has been directly or indirectly responsible for the overall developmental course of Korean males, particularly those born from around the early 1970s up to Generation Y (no later than the early 1980s). Historically speaking, Confucius's teachings were particularly significant to

AN ERIKSONIAN PSYCHO-SOCIAL RESPONSE TO CONFUCIUS

Korean noblemen and the gentry in Korea, given that their formal education grounded in Confucian principles was a practical and effective means of perpetuating or increasing their status under the rigid caste system of feudal society. This mindset of the people in the leadership class, after all, hugely influenced Korean society in giving high priority to education as well as in determining the philosophy, direction, and means for educating children, especially boys. How in particular has Confucius, or his teachings, influenced the development of male individuals in Korea? Which aspects of education are permeated by Confucian principles?

In light of Confucianism's pervasive influence on Korean society, this chapter examines the influence and implications of the Confucian worldview and teachings on the entire life cycle of older male Korean individuals, meaning those born before the emergence of Generation Y (no later than the early 1980s). In particular, I investigate the social and psychological implications of the life cycle model as evidenced in Confucius's statements about his own life and compare these implications with the implications of a life cycle model from the psychoanalytic tradition. To this end, this chapter first examines the Confucian text *The Analects*, discussing how the ideological structure of Confucianism has permeated the minds of both the older generation of Korean males as well as boys from the new generation and how *The Analects* has operated as a significant but ultimately oppressive frame of reference at every stage of these older males' psychosocial development as well as in forming their personal and social identities. Along with this text, I briefly review the childhood and youth of Confucius to examine the correlation between his life and his teachings. Second, I consider the Confucian understanding of the human life cycle by comparing it briefly with Erik H. Erikson's discourse on the stages of psychosocial development. I also review the list of virtues that Erikson suggests in the context of his proposed psychosocial development stages, imagining it as a counterproposal to the Confucian framing of the life cycle that emphasizes edification in virtues via enhanced cognition and strengthened will. Finally, the chapter briefly examines the possible contribution of the psychoanalytic framework of human development to the Korean understanding of the human life cycle that is so steeped in Confucian thought.

AN EXEMPLARY LIFE CYCLE: CONFUCIUS'S DEVELOPMENTAL STAGES

Conventionally, the life of Confucius that is succinctly described in *The Analects* has been interpreted literally, without considering his personal history and its context. The interpretation of his life has been focused solely on the wisdom that he developed with age. Because of this, the wisdom he acquired has generally been taken as a universal and objective goal that every male in Korea should aspire to attain during his lifetime. Thanks to this narrow focus, there has been little consideration of the psychosocial variables that might have influenced his views on life rather significantly, of his actual life journey, and of what he attained in each decade of his life after adolescence. Yet, given that an individual's thought is not independent of his or her life experiences, it is helpful to review his personal life experiences as well as the psychosocial contexts that were the seedbeds for those experiences. In particular, to understand fully Confucius's description of his own life in terms of the life cycle, it is crucial to review Confucius's personal experiences and their contexts during his childhood and youth.

There is significant difficulty in doing this, however, for historical materials that examine or shed light on the life of Confucius and his family are very limited in quantity and quality. The only historical records currently available are a series of historical records (史記, shǐjì) by one of the Han dynasty officials, Sima Qian (司馬遷) (1993). Sima Qian's description of Confucius's life, however, is very limited, fragmented, and vague, making the task all the more difficult. Adding to these qualitative and quantitative limitations is the problem that these texts contain many unverifiable hypotheses, myths, and legends regarding Confucius's life, family, and contemporaries. To some degree, this chapter therefore inevitably depends on assumptions and speculations that are based both on the historical record and on rational and commonsensical inferences from the overall context of Confucius's time.

A Brief History of Confucius

Confucius was born in or around 551 BCE. His father, Kong He (孔紇), known also as Shuliang He (叔梁紇), was an officer who twice led the armies of the state of Lu in 563 and 556 BCE. In contrast, historical facts regarding Confucius's mother, Yan Zhengzai (顏徵在), cannot be verified. Some scholars of Confucius assert that she was a shaman. Others say that she was a well-educated woman from a scholarly family. In any case, when Confucius's parents married, his mother and father were 15 and 66 years old, respectively. Before Kong He married Yan Zhengzai, he had already had nine daughters by his first wife and one son by his second wife, a son who, because of his disabilities, was not able to succeed him. Thus, Yan Zhengzai likely became Kong He's third wife simply to produce a male heir. According to historical sources, some time after they offered a devout prayer for a son and heir at a sacred hill named Ni, their prayer was answered (Bao 2013). They had sexual intercourse in a suburban field, in accordance with the midspring state custom of wishing for bountiful harvests, national prosperity, and the welfare of the people. Yan Zhengzai conceived and gave birth to a son named Confucius, who would carry on Kong He's family line.

However, it seems that after Yan Zhengzai gave birth to their son, Kong He did not take good care of her. In addition, their marriage did not last long. Kong He died when Confucius was only 3 years old. After his father's death, and because of the economic difficulties and the familial emotional harassment she endured, Yan Zhengzai left the family circle of Kong He's nine daughters, the son with disabilities, and his second wife and moved to Qufu, the capital of the vassal state of Lu in the Zhou dynasty. That there are so few historical materials means that little is known for sure about Confucius's childhood and youth, but the story commonly told is that Confucius had a humiliating youth because of his and his mother's severe poverty. To help his mother, who held low-paid jobs such as seamstress, cleaner, and cook, Confucius also had to seek employment. Yet, he was resourceful. While enduring abject poverty and humiliating circumstances, he developed his skills in etiquette, music, archery, horsemanship, calligraphy, and mathematics, all skills necessary to go into public office in those days. He also sought out eminent masters and teachers to learn rituals, music, and the lute, which were entrance requirements for government jobs.

When Confucius was only 17, Yan Zhengzai passed away due to hard work and a chronic illness, and at 19 Confucius married a woman named Quiguan. After that, by traveling around several neighboring states for more than 50 years, he founded his own school of Ju (Confucianism), and took between 72 and 77 disciples. At the age of 73, Confucius died in Qufu, an area to which he and his mother had moved when he was a young child.

CONFUCIUS'S LIFE DESCRIBED IN *THE ANALECTS*

A description of Confucius's life is found in *The Analects* (論語, *lúnyǔ*) (2014). Instead of giving a lengthy explanation of his life, Confucius succinctly describes his entire life by decades from ages 15 to 70, as follows:

> The Master said, "At fifteen I set my heart on learning. At thirty, I found my balance through the rites. At forty, I was free from doubts [about myself]. At fifty, I understood what Heaven intended me to do. At sixty, I was attuned to what I heard. At seventy, I followed what my heart desired without overstepping

the line [子曰: 五十有五而志于學, 三十而立, 四十而不惑, 五十而知天命, 六十而耳順, 七十而從心所欲, 不踰矩]." (p. 13)

Confucius's description of his life journey is mostly focused on the postadolescent years and the four decades after he turned 15. Rather than a typical life cycle that normally illustrates the biopsychosocial development of individuals, at first glance it seems that Confucius merely describes changes in his way of thinking or what he realized or learned, developed, or achieved throughout his life.

This autobiographical illustration of Confucius's life cycle is in stark contrast to the typical psychoanalytic framework of human development that is mainly concerned with the period of pre-adulthood and subdivides it into several developmental stages. His brief description instead reveals the course of Confucius's cognitive maturity as well as his spiritual journey. If Confucius's description of his own life is interpreted literally without considering the background contexts in the critical developmental period before adolescence, there is a risk that his self-description will be interpreted and understood as a dogmatic guideline or universal understanding of how to live and of what life should be. For this reason, it is necessary to reexamine, through his personal experience before adulthood, what Confucius's description of his own life may imply.

UNDERSTANDING CONFUCIUS'S EARLY LIFE

Very few facts are known regarding Confucius's personality due to the very limited historical materials available regarding his life. Because of this, any attempt to understand Confucius psychologically is like a jigsaw puzzle missing a few pieces, which inevitably requires a certain degree of imagination and speculation to put it together. Yet, despite the lack of historical materials, several psychosocial variables can and should be considered in his personal history during the pre-adult period. As briefly reviewed above, a few episodes in his early developmental period reveal meaningful and important clues for understanding his teachings psychobiographically.

Lost Object and the Idealized Father

The fact that Confucius lost his father when he was only 3 years old, or at the beginning of the phallic stage, and left his family circle right after his father's death suggests he likely had a developmental issue related to the Oedipal stage. It appears that Kong He had shown deep affection to his son because

Confucius was the only viable son and heir and had been hard to produce. A series of traumatic experiences, specifically Kong He's sudden death and the drastic change of family environment, might have increased the probability of an Oedipal complex in Confucius, who might have become strongly attached emotionally to his father yet whose death deprived Confucius of the developmental opportunity to identify himself with his father. Indeed, he did not even know where his father had been buried; for no discernable reason, his mother did not tell him, and because of this Confucius was never able to perform any ancestral rites for his father (Bao 2013).

For Confucius, the absence of his father to shape his morality and personal sense of ethics implies the absence of the necessary object to idealize, identify with, and internalize during the Oedipal period of his development. This also implies that the boy developed an imaginary, idealized father image as an inner object, one that was not tested by actual experiences as he grew older. It appears that this unrealistic father image that was not filtered by reality greatly influenced the formation of Confucius's ego ideal or super-ego, for it seems to have been excessively rigid and normative.

It is not clear what role (if any) Confucius's mother, Yan Zhengzai, played while Confucius was struggling with his father's absence. There are no reliable historical clues or records that might help us to infer whether Confucius's mother played any role (as a substitute or complementary figure for Confucius's father), specifically a mirroring or idealizing role. Consequently, it has long been conjectured rather superficially that Yan Zhengzai could or perhaps even must have been a good mother to Confucius simply because she bore and raised one of the greatest philosophers of ancient China. This historical fact, however, is not sufficient to infer that she was tender and caring toward Confucius. Rather, given her situation of abject poverty and Confucius's strict upbringing, she might have found it difficult to provide Confucius with a mirroring or idealizing function or to respond empathetically to Confucius in a stable, safe, and facilitating environment, which Donald Winnicott (1965) deems necessary for proper development.

As regards the object loss and the process of idealization, it is worth pondering Kohut's (1995) argument that the Oedipal phase is a critical period in an individual's narcissistic disturbance:

> In the specific case of the traumatic loss of the idealized parent imago (loss of the idealized self-object or disappointment in it) up to and including the oedipal phase, the results are disturbances in specific narcissistic sectors of the personality. Under optimal circumstances the child experiences gradual disappointment in the idealized object—or, expressed differently: the

child's evaluation of the idealized object becomes increasingly realistic—which leads to a withdrawal of the narcissistic cathexes from the imago of the idealized self-object and to their gradual (or, in the oedipal period, massive but phase-appropriate) internalization, i.e., to the acquisition of permanent psychological structures which continue, endopsychically, the functions which the idealized self-object had previously fulfilled. If the child suffers the traumatic loss of the idealized object, however, or a traumatic (severe and sudden, or not phase-appropriate) disappointment in it, then optimal internalization does not take place. The child does not acquire the needed internal structure, his psyche remains fixated on an archaic self-object, and personality will throughout life be dependent on certain objects in what seems to be an intense form of object hunger. (p. 45)

For Confucius, the death of his father around the Oedipal stage of his childhood might imply that he was deprived of the critical opportunity to experience and have an idealized object, and this might have led to his failure to internalize the idealized object optimally.

As Kohut suggests, because Confucius did not have the opportunity to form the necessary inner structure, he suffered from object hunger and, to satisfy this hunger for an idealized object, searched from the age of 17 to his early 30s for renowned teachers in various academic fields. For example, he studied rituals under legendary Daoist Master Laozi (老子) of Zhou. Chang Hong (長弘) and Xiang(襄) were his music and lute teachers, respectively (Stanford Encyclopedia of Philosophy 2013). Other than these teachers, according to Sima Qian, he also studied under several teachers—Ju Baiyu (遽白玉) of Cao Wei, Yan Pingzhong (晏平仲) of Qi, Lao Laizi (老萊子) of Chu, Zichan (子產) of Zheng, and Meng Gong Chuo (孟公綽) of Lu—who were Confucius's contemporaries (Sima 1993; Bao 2013). Yet there are no historical records that state unequivocally who among these many teachers was the most influential and significant figure to Confucius, what his relationship with each of them was like, and which one of them played not only the role of mentor but of parent to him. Though it is widely alleged that Confucius reverently and earnestly served the legendary figure Laozi (老子), there is no actual evidence of this. Though historical records mention that Confucius deliberately sought out and studied under several renowned teachers to satisfy his thirst for knowledge, it appears that this continuous search for teachers also reflects an aspect of his inner hunger for the lost idealized object that most people find in their parent(s).

Here, Freud offers a valuable insight. He suggests that the image of father corresponds to the degree of influence that teachers and authorities have on a boy during the Oedipal phase (1924). And as substitute fathers, teachers play a critical role in forming a boy's ego ideal (1914):

> We can now understand our relation to our schoolmasters. These men, not all of whom were in fact fathers themselves, became our substitute fathers.... We transferred on to them the respect and expectations attaching to the omniscient father of our childhood, and we then began to treat them as we treated our fathers at home. We confronted them with the ambivalence that we had acquired in our own families and with its help we struggled with them as we had been in the habit of struggling with our fathers. (p. 244)

The implication of this for Confucius is that the substitute fathers were eminent teachers or masters who were strongly reminiscent of his father or, in Kohut's terms, the lost idealized object. For Confucius, renowned teachers in the fields in which he was interested were the perfect father substitutes who would satisfy his object hunger.

Mother's Education: Crossing Over the Boundary

Adding to Confucius's struggle with the Oedipal issue due to the lost idealized object (his father), it appears that Confucius's mother, Yan Zhengzai, also had a huge influence on Confucius's psychological development. First, the way that Yan Zhengzai raised Confucius does not seem to accord with what is necessary to satisfy each developmental stage. After the sudden death of Confucius's father, Kong He, the only person who could educate Confucius was his mother. Though there are still disputes regarding Yan Zhengzai's role, historical records generally show that Confucius's mother was active and strict in teaching Confucius socially preferred knowledge and studies, namely, the six arts: rites (禮, lǐ), music (樂, lè), archery (射, shè), charioteering (御, yù), calligraphy (書, shū), and mathematics (數, shù). Learning this complex socially preferred knowledge at an early age would have been an enormous burden emotionally and cognitively to Confucius. His mother, it seems, put more emphasis on teaching him ancestral rites than the other arts when she educated Confucius at home. For example, according to ancient historian Sima Qian, Confucius's mother bought utensils used in ancestral rites and let him play with them when he was a child (Bao 2013; Sima 1993; Stanford Encyclopedia of Philosophy 2013). Normally, utensils used in ancestral rites are not considered appropriate playthings for a child; typically, during nonceremonial times they would be kept in a special place and be carefully handled. After all, they are objects differentiated for special use, objects through which descendants in this world communicate with and contact ancestors in the next world. Perhaps historian Sima Qian's words should not be interpreted literally. Rather than meaning Yan Zhengzai gave her little child the ritual utensils as playthings, perhaps we should interpret the historian as saying that when Confucius was a little boy, his mother was already training her son to become accustomed to a series of complex and strict rites and that as a result of his familiarity with them he became able to manipulate the utensils for rites as easily as he played with toys. Likewise, when Sima mentions that when Confucius was only about five he used to play house by organizing ritual vessels and performing ceremonies (孔子爲兒嬉戲, 常陳俎豆, 設禮容) (Sima 1993; Stanford Encyclopedia of Philosophy 2013), perhaps we should understand this as meaning that his mother trained Confucius from a young age to perform complex rites proficiently.

The fact that Yan Zhengzai taught her son these rites is significant. In those days, rites were a socially preferred knowledge that every cultured and intellectual person should study, practice, and learn, even more so anyone who aspired to political office. Perhaps his mother was more concerned that her son attain public office than she was in supporting his age-appropriate emotional and cognitive needs. Regardless of whether Yan Zhengzai was a descendent of scholarly families or a female shaman, she seems to have given priority to education as the only ladder by which her son's—and her family's—social status could be enhanced. Such an interpretation suggests that her stern parenting style might occasionally have violated certain boundaries and affected Confucius's personality. Nancy McWilliams's (2011) psychoanalytic explanation of the influence of a strict upbringing on the formation of an individual's personality is worth pondering here:

> One route by which individuals emerge with obsessive and compulsive psychologies involves parental figures who set high standards of behavior and expect early conformity to them. Such caregivers tend to be strict and consistent in rewarding good behavior and punishing malfeasance. When they are basically loving, they produce emotionally advantaged children whose defenses lead them in directions that vindicate their parents' scrupulous devotion . . . When caregivers are unreasonably exacting, or prematurely demanding, or condemnatory not only of unacceptable behavior but also of accompanying feelings, thoughts, and fantasies, their children's obsessive and compulsive adaptations can be more problematic . . . From an object relations perspective, what is notable about obsessive and

compulsive people is the centrality of issues of *control* in their families of origin (emphasis in original, pp. 296–297).

Perhaps her strict parenting did lead to her son's seemingly obsessive-compulsive personality, which later made Confucius scrutinize deeply such themes as rules, regulations, duties, orders, and formalities, themes that pervade his system of thought, rites, and Confucianism as a whole. It appears that it was his lifework to construct a seamless and grand ideological, or even religious, system that encompasses and regulates individuals, families, societies, and even states.

Economic Vulnerability and Emotional Attachment

The economic vulnerability that burdened Yan Zhengzai as a young single mother also appears to have strongly influenced Confucius's psychological development. As previously noted, Confucius lost his father when he was only 3 years old. Right after his father's death, Confucius and his mother left her husband's family circle and moved to the neighboring city of Qufu. From that point on, because of their abject poverty mother and son had to struggle without assistance from family and friends. To earn a livelihood, Yan Zhengzai not only had to work hard but took random odd jobs and worked at whatever hour of day or night was required. Surely that would have prevented her from caring for her little son. Not only that, but because of her strict parenting style it appears that she was not sensitive enough to satisfy Confucius's emotional needs at his early developmental stages. Though a mother's caring role is particularly crucial for a little boy who has lost his father at an early age in order that he might cope with his Oedipal phase, it is highly probable that Confucius not only did not have that caring presence, given her physical absence at work and her emotional distance due to her parenting style, but also that he could not find a substitute object to fulfill his emotional needs and compensate for his mother's emotional absence. In this regard, Yan Zhengzai was another lost object to Confucius, in addition to his father.

His Mother's Double Dependence on Confucius

Regarding his role in the relationship with his mother, it is probable that as Confucius grew, his role as a surrogate husband to his mother might have increased and intensified. On the one hand, in terms of the family economy, it appears that it was unavoidable that Yan Zhengzai be dependent on Confucius to some degree—such as for income. Because Confucius did anything he could to earn a little money to help the family survive, other than the basic education given him at home by Yan Zhengzai, he did not receive a formal education until he was 15 years old.

Since Yan Zhengzai lost her husband when she was only 18 years old, it is likely that the emotional dependence of the young widow on her son increased at the very time that Confucius was growing into adolescence. Here, it is probable that in addition to the emotional indifference of Kong He to Yan Zhengzai during their three brief years of married life, the 51-year (or two-generation) age difference between Yan Zhengzai and her husband, which was larger than that of the 16 years between her and Confucius, might have engendered her emotional dependence on or attachment to her son. Moreover, considering the social prejudice, discrimination, and contempt to which a single mother without family and relatives was subject by the patriarchal and androcentric sociocultural environment of ancient China, it is also highly likely that whenever Yan Zhengzai felt stressed by her isolation, poverty, and loneliness, she would have regarded Confucius as the only figure on whom she could depend. In this respect, Yan Zhengzai's emotional and economic dependence on her son seems rather inevitable.

Moreover, the fact that his mother did not divulge where his father had been buried gives us some idea of how much she was emotionally dependent on her son as a surrogate husband. In addition, due to her husband's early and sudden death, Yan Zhengzai would likely have been emotionally vulnerable, insufficiently empathetic to Confucius's emotional needs, and not mutual in her relationship with her son. This might have been the central obstacle to Confucius becoming emotionally differentiated from his mother at the appropriate time in his psychological development. Compared to others of the same age, this likely was a significant emotional burden that Confucius could not consciously recognize. Because of this double economic and emotional burden, he likely experienced a different developmental path than his peers. He might have repressed feelings and desires common among his peers.

Conquering Melancholy: Rites as a Substitute for the Idealized Mother

I suggest therefore that because of his father's death very early in his life as well as his mother's strict parenting style and physical absence, Confucius was deprived of the basic developmental opportunity to idealize his father and to receive empathetic caring from his mother. In addition, the seemingly emotionally distant relationship with his mother after his father's death around the time at which Confucius would likely have encountered his Oedipal phase reveals an important psychological theme of melancholy and suggests a possible impulse for Confucius's lifelong delving into rules and regulations. Donald Capps's (1997) view on melancholy and its subliminal influence on an individual's religiosity gives an important insight into the plausible correlation between Confucius's early object relations and his lifelong interest in order, including order embodied in rites. As an example, Capps shows that Martin Luther's experience in his early years of melancholia due to the loss of his mother suggests that his emphasis on Scripture might have been a sublimational tactic.

> [A] religious object may both aid the mourning process and take the place of the lost object . . . Luther remains unconscious of the connection between the 'matrix' of the scriptures and his mother's ways of teaching him how to experience the world around him . . . In a very real and tangible sense, the scriptures are the lost object. Unlike the mother who was the cause of disappointment, anger, and despair, they are the perfect mother, the son's ideal mother. No wonder, then, that Luther insisted on their adequacy for a saving faith—sola scriptura . . . Thus, if for Freud it was the dream that promised restoration to the lost object, for Luther it was the scriptures. For Luther, the key to keeping his melancholy from overwhelming him throughout his life was the availability of the scriptures, to which he could always repair for solace and reassurance. (pp. 175–176).

Luther delving into Scripture parallels Confucius delving into the rules, regulations, and orders of human society that were then embodied in the concrete rites of ancient China. It appears that, for Confucius, delving into the rites was an attempt to restore and idealize the lost object, Yan Zhengzai. For him, the rites were like an idealized mother who, as his frame of reference, could give him meaning and direction of life in that they embodied and taught him the pivotal human values or virtues—such as benevolence (仁, rén), righteousness (義, yì), propriety (禮, lǐ), wisdom (智, zhì), and sincerity (信, xìn). The rites were the ritualistic means by which he prevented his melancholy from overwhelming him. It appears that immersing himself in the rites consoled and reassured him. It provided him with a safe inner space.

This strong emphasis on rites and rituals for the sake of easing his melancholy can perhaps be explained by the social, political, and historical times in which Confucius lived. The period was one of warring Chinese states contesting values and ideologies among and between them. In the middle of this period, as a moral thinker as well as a political philosopher from the small and weak state of Lu, Confucius became keenly aware of the need for a coherent and solid principle to steady individuals in tumultuous times. The principles he formulated included not only individual ethics and social and political ideology but also had religious implications.

IMPLICATIONS OF *THE ANALECTS*

As noted above, Confucius's view on and understanding of human development is likely closely related to his personal history and the sociopolitical needs of his day. Obviously, the framework of developmental stages he mentioned in *The Analects* (論語, *lúnyǔ*) is the result of how he lived as well as of his aims throughout his life. However, it is more accurate to say that the developmental stages he achieved in each decade of his life were the result of his strenuous efforts to attain an idealized and desirable human character known for its benevolence, righteousness, propriety, wisdom, and sincerity and were embodied in rites rather than were simply the natural consequence of a holistic process of maturation that reflected harmony and balance among human emotion, reason, and will. In this regard, Confucius's explanation of particular aspects of human character he attained at each particular decade of his life should be interpreted and understood not as a typology of human development but as a personal retrospective account of an individual's life.

Confucius's implicit emphasis on human reason and will in attaining the developmental goals of every decade of his life after adulthood reflects his understanding of human nature as neither fundamentally good nor fundamentally evil but rather as neutral. He writes in *The Analects* (2014), "People are similar by nature; they become distinct through practice [性相近也 習相遠也]" (p. 281). By virtue of what he experienced and learned during his lifetime, Confucius understood all humans as organic beings who can and should be developed through unceasing edification and endeavor.

Though he regarded human nature as innately homogeneous, Confucius notes that what contributes to differences among humans is how much and what an individual learns and practices. In the very beginning of *The Analects*, he summarizes this view with a single question: "Is it not a pleasure to learn [xue] and, when it is timely, to practice what you have learned [學而時習之 不亦說乎]?" (p. 1) That Confucius emphasizes the role of acquisition (of skills, etc.) in shaping human nature implies that those who fail to achieve the developmental goals required at each phase of the life cycle are insincere losers who do not diligently study, learn, and practice what is required to be the noble person defined in Confucius's teachings and thoughts. This implies that the frame of what is called Confucius's life cycle is innately normative rather than descriptive. Strictly speaking, rather than a phenomenological description of human development that considers all the biological, psychological, and social aspects, his is a normative frame that aims at persuading, educating, or even enlightening individuals.

This normative perspective shown by what an individual should achieve during his lifetime is one of the main stances to which Confucius holds fast in his life and his teachings. Confucius recognizes that the character that a man should attain over the course of his life cycle exactly defines the role that every other man should play in every sphere to which he belongs. Asked by Duke Jing of Qi what are the essentials of governing, Confucius explained a man's role as follows:

> "Let the ruler be a ruler, the subject be a subject, a father be a father, a son be a son." The Duke said, "Right! If indeed the ruler is not a ruler, a subject is not a subject, a father is not a father, a son is not a son, even though there is plenty of grain, will I be able to eat it [齊景公問政於孔子. 孔子對曰: 君君 臣臣 父父 子子. 公曰: 善哉! 信如君不君 臣不臣 父不父 子不子, 雖有粟 吾得而食諸]?" (p. 186)

This dialogue, known as the "duty of rectifying names" (正名論/名實論) refers to the prerequisites of male identity formation. The implicit premise, that one is to play the role that accords with one's station and developmental stage and task, Confucius demonstrated with the example of his own life.

If we reread Confucius's own life cycle based on this understanding, we realize that Confucius's strategy of mentioning his own life is not simply a description of an individual's life but a means of didactic persuasion aimed at his disciples and followers. He is trying to persuade individuals to be assiduous in learning, studying, and practicing so that they complete each developmental task. He presents his own life as didactive and normative, as if to say: "You should set your heart on learning until you are 15. You should then be able to establish your lifework by the time you are 30, should be confident about your life at 40, should be intelligent enough to discern natural law at 50, should be solid enough to be at peace in the midst of worldly affairs at 60, and should be sagacious and serene enough to differentiate what you can do and what you cannot at 70." Yet by establishing this as the normative pattern, Confucius is implicitly ageist. It is as if he is saying, "The old person is more right and sagacious than the young," and it is this assumption that has long fostered and solidified the irreversible and rigid hierarchy between the generations in Korea.

EMOTIONAL BINDING AND MUTED INNER VOICES

Confucius's normative frame or assumptions regarding what men should be and do, which he reveals through what he achieved throughout his own life, had a huge influence on Korean society. Under the strong influence of six centuries of Confucian ideology in Korea, this seemingly personal stage of life has gradually become regarded as the normative life cycle pattern for Korean males. As a result, Korean males have valued Confucius's life as the exemplar that any male eager to be a man of virtue should emulate.

Because of the didactic, normative, educative, and guiding characteristics of Confucius's framing of the life cycle, Confucius implicitly requires concrete actions and practices from his disciples and followers. This characteristic has contributed to awakening and increasing human sensitivity to the needs of morality and industry. Yet the other side of this frame, because it gives preference to the cognitive and volitional aspect in attaining each developmental task, is that it fails to consider the emotional domain that also contributes to human development. Besides, the failure to attain each developmental goal implicitly or explicitly implies an individual's immaturity, or even lack of virtue, in that the developmental tasks were suggested and taught by Confucius as goals that an individual can attain through constant and diligent study and practice. As a result, the individual who fails to attain each developmental goal inevitably comes to feel shame or inferiority; he is regarded as a man who does not accord with the essential values of any group to which he belongs, such as a family, society, or nation.

Confucius's framing of the life cycle later became the prototype for children's education in China and Korea. A series of textbooks that reflect Confucius's thought minutely define what adults should teach as well as what children should learn and observe through speech and action at particular points in their lives in order to be the ideal persons or the noble men that Confucius suggested with his own life. Among these texts, *Lesser Learning* (小學, *xiaoxue*) (2016), also known as *Elementary Learning*, is a representative textbook that lists everything that male children and men should do, learn, and practice each year of their lives until they become 70 years old. The purpose of these teachings is clear: to raise persons who exhibit these Confucian ideals. Yet the life cycle frameworks in these textbooks have in common certain limitations, particularly that they do not give convincing reasons or explanations for why persons should do these things. It appears that adults are simply to force themselves to uncritically and blindly accept and accomplish the listed teachings. As a result, what children or men should do during their lives to be persons who fit the Confucian ideal became strict and oppressive regulations rather than edifying guidelines.

Because of its regulatory and doctrinaire character, Confucius's life cycle framing lacks any serious consideration of why the inner achievements that he himself reached in each particular decade of his life since adulthood are significant—and a model for others. Instead, Confucius overemphasizes enlightened human reason as alone having the capacity to coordinate in an organic and orderly fashion an individual, a family, a society, and a state with a single and coherent principle—Confucianism. Further, Confucianism sees the human mind not simply as a generative or formative object that individuals should care for and nurture but as an immature and rough object that needs to be trained, disciplined, and polished by seniors or elders. By not paying attention to the direct and indirect factors and conditions that influence and induce the sound growth of human cognition, emotion, and will before adulthood, Confucianism tends to enforce or impose strict and rigid norms and regulations, even on children. For example, he expects children to learn, chant, and memorize a series of Confucian teachings, yet this to my mind results merely in the pupil's perception that knowledge and life are not integrated but split.

By such desensitization to their actual and genuine emotions, children grow to be "old young"; their will and cognition are tamed to conform to Confucian norms and values. Such taming leads to a severe imbalance or disharmony between emotion and cognition-behavior. Children are pushed to be cognitively developed as well as volitionally determined and tenacious while they are still emotionally undeveloped. Instead of paying much attention to their desires, needs, and will in various experiences of life, such children interpret themselves only through the Confucian frame of reference that gives high priority to the will and cognition of the human being. Later, this gap between the ideal human character of Confucianism and the character shaped by the concrete human experiences of reality becomes a latent cause of identity confusion in children.

Confucius's life cycle framing neither derives from nor leads to a discourse on the biological, social, and psychological grounds that correspond to each developmental stage. Confucius simply pairs an individual's age with a series of pivotal tasks—such as the value of benevolence and the benign administration of an individual, a family, a society, and a nation—required to turn his thoughts and ideals into reality. Though his lofty ideals are important and valuable, there is a risk that they could ideologically or dogmatically manipulate individuals by indoctrinating the priority of community over the value of an individual. In such a forced social atmosphere, an individual's sacrifice for the community to which he belongs becomes deliberately encouraged, demagogically justified, and uncritically taken for granted. Meanwhile, in dealing with the concrete problems of human reality, an individual comes to be reared and educated to be the man of convergent thinking who tries to seek only one optimal solution in human relations and issues. This reflects the social rigidity in which only one principle or answer that meets the general social consensus is allowed and in which any divergent thinking is not socially accepted but is regarded as a socially harmful or dangerous way of thinking that causes and intensifies social confusion and finally disrupts, or even destroys, the social order.

CULTIVATING VIRTUE: ERIKSON'S COMFORT TO BOYS AND MEN

Confucius's framing of the life cycle is a phenomenological examination of human development as well as a type of normative persuasion regarding what men should be. The virtues Confucius mentions in his life cycle are different from the virtues that can be nurtured or developed on the basis of an individual's biological, psychological, and social development. He does not consider the virtues that can and should be cultivated before young adulthood. His frame is, in a sense, quite ideological in that the virtues he mentions in *The Analects* have an implicit intention of edifying, first, his disciples and followers and, second, later generations. In this sense, Confucius's discourse on virtues is clearly distinguished from the work of Erik H. Erikson (1980, 1982, 1985, 1994), who emphasizes the psychosocial aspects of the virtues that, as an innate ability or strength, can be nurtured and cultivated throughout an individual's life as the basic inner strengths needed for an individual to stand in the face of life's adversities.

Erikson mentions that psychosocially an individual develops eight virtues over the course of life—hope, will, purpose, competence, fidelity, love, care, and wisdom—virtues that he calls basic strengths. For Erikson, these basic strengths are accumulative resources that enable an individual to cope well with the challenging realities of life. According to Capps (2002), these virtues indicate the moral dimension of life cycle theory. Capps (1987) mentions that, as inherent strengths, "the virtues are persisting attitudes or dispositions, not single actions or behaviors, and that the virtues are moral and spiritual as well as psychological" (p. 76). Rather than seeing a virtue as an inherent strength, however, Confucius understands a virtue as an acquired second nature that can be indoctrinated into an individual's mind initially from outside through elaborate education and training; it then becomes embodied and engrained in that person through ceaseless effort and practice. This seemingly distinct difference hints that Erikson's view on virtue is an alternative or complement to Confucius's view on virtue described by the normative and didactic frame of the life cycle.

Erikson's view on virtue premises that through human relations with significant others an individual can cultivate and actualize virtues that they have as inherent virtues but also those they have only as potential strengths. Regarding this, Capps (1987) adds:

> Erik Erikson's list of virtues . . . are presented in developmental sequence and thus relate to the various stages of the life cycle . . . These virtues are "natural" in the sense that they are inherent strengths that all humans potentially possess. They are not accessible only to a few, to a moral or spiritual elite. But they are also "God given," because they are part of a preestablished ground plan, appearing at their appointed time through no human design or effort. We do not create virtues; they are created in and for us. But we can cultivate them and help them become a more effective force in our lives. (pp. 19–20)

Virtues are not developmental tasks that can be attained simply by education and discipline led by a few elderly and wise persons who are in a senior or superior position. Rather, virtues are the result of the normal developmental process that can be naturally nurtured and embodied through sound and reciprocal relationships with significant others during a specific developmental phase. Because the virtues are initially the fruits of emotional fertility, the cognitive understanding as well as volitional resolution that the Confucian framing of the life cycle implicitly emphasizes is not the sufficient condition but the necessary condition for cultivating the virtue of an individual's life cycle. Due to its excessive emphasis on the cognitive and volitional aspects of virtues in an individual's life cycle, the Confucian framing of the life cycle does not comprehensively examine the pre-adult period that additionally requires elaborate investigations into the emotional aspects in the formation of an individual's virtue. Under the established and pervasive influence of Confucianism, therefore, education for cultivating virtues in Korea has long proceeded not by means of reciprocal and amicable relationships in students' concrete and actual lives but through conceptually cursory and inanimate pedagogy and mainly by means of printed texts in the public-school classrooms. Erikson's framework suggests that cultivating virtue does not come mainly from such a normative and persuasive education as that of Korea but from a series of good enough experiences of relationship with significant others along with their life cycle.

In his discussions of how to develop individuals' virtues, Confucius delves obsessively into the themes of study and practice. The Confucian ideals reflected in his framing of the life cycle even have a religious implication. Because of this, Confucianism itself has long been regarded as one of the four major religions in Korea. In light of its religious character, it has not welcomed or allowed any critical and rational questioning or alternative views. This religious aspect of Confucian teaching has a dogmatic character for the followers of this discipline, especially boys and male adults. Regarding this, Capps's (1995) thought on the religious abuse of children is meaningful:

> Religious ideas in childhood are intrinsically traumatic, and therefore, among adults, religious ideas continue to be accompanied by such dissociative features as repression, compartmentalization, withdrawal of affect, and lack of confidence in one's own perceptions and judgments. (pp. 53–54)

Regarding the seemingly religious ideas that innately torment children, Erikson implicitly suggests that cultivating virtue through the experience of amicable relationships is a way of giving comfort to boys who have long been normatively oppressed by the so-called Confucian ideals that have a religious character. Erikson's discourse on virtue by means of the life cycle frame also implicitly indicates that caring for boys and men in Korea means lowering the unrealistic and rigid standards of Confucian ideals to a more realistic level as well as nurturing males' emotional strength through "good enough" relationships with significant others. Although the Confucianism of Korea that continues to push males by taking Confucius's life as the only and ideal path should be reconceived, Erikson reminds us that Confucius's framing of the life cycle is merely one of many exemplary possible life paths.

CONCLUSION

For more than six hundred years until the late 1980s, the philosophical, ethical, and political leverage of Confucius on boys and male adults in Korea has been enormous and unprecedented, and his influence on intellectuals and leaders in Korea remains unsurpassed. Even these days, in what is called the era of information and technology, his ideas about the edification of humans remain pervasive in Korea's social value systems. Much of school and family education is based on Confucianism and fosters individuals to adopt the ways and ideals of Confucius. Among his major teachings, it is the example of Confucius's own life cycle that has been and remains the pivotal frame of reference in cultivating virtues deemed necessary for Korean males if they are to be responsible members of their family, society, or state.

Precisely for this reason, however, Confucianism occasionally has been misused as an ideological means either for maintaining public or social order or for protecting the hierarchical benefits of the ruling class. Confucius's framing of the life cycle, which was initially suggested by Confucius himself looking back over his own life, is an exemplary case of this misuse. Because of this, by regarding Confucius's life as an irreplaceable frame of reference, boys and men in Korea have long been consciously or unconsciously wrestling with an illusion of idealized manhood or masculinity in order to cultivate Confucian virtues. Rather than creating a frame of reference that embodies Confucian ideals, it is more appropriate to say that Confucius modeled his framing of the life cycle on his own personal narrative, which was colored by his own peculiar experiences of life. This implies that there is an innate limitation in expanding his personal story to become the universal story that can be applied to every boy and man. Because we have not paid enough attention to this point, it is true that, under the pretext of cultivating virtues, Confucius's framing of the life cycle, as well as his other teachings, has long been misused as the implicit or explicit means of oppressing, or even manipulating, Korean males. And, indeed, boys and men in Korea have long blindly declared Confucius's life to be the ideal to be emulated. Yet their repetition of this idea has often been hollow for them for it has not been imbued with their own voices and experiences. A way of countering this is to restore and nurture their emotional sensibilities that have long been consciously or unconsciously neglected or oppressed by the myth of the ideal path of human development suggested by Confucius's own life.

At this point, the role of pastoral caregivers becomes clear. Paul Tillich (2005) implicitly mentions that the role of caregivers is to strive for reconciliation, meaning reconciliation of the sufferers' struggling forces—i.e., reconciling their genuine forces with each other and in doing so freeing them for thought and action. Working for reconciliation, according to Tillich, means helping individuals to accept themselves as they are, which enables them to look at themselves with honesty and clarity and to grasp and cope with the abnormal and oppressive mechanisms that continue to distress them (p. 40). In this regard, the role of pastoral care is to help boys and men, who for centuries have been lost in the maze of Confucian ideals, reconcile with their authentic selves. It is to let them know that an individual's virtue is shaped not by an imposed normative frame—even though it has been passed on from generation to generation—but by a series of autonomous, meaningful, and constructive relations with others. This pastoral role also entails helping them to recover and listen attentively to their genuine inner voices that have long been neglected, regulated, oppressed, or muted by Confucian mores. And finally, the caregiving role is to empower boys and men to throw off the shackles of frustration, helplessness, and inferiority that are caused by the excessive emphasis on the edification of human virtues by means of enhanced cognition and strengthened will.

REFERENCES

Bao, P. S. (2013). *Confucius biography*. China Youth Press.
Capps, D. (2000). *Deadly sins and saving virtues*. Wipf & Stock. (Original work published 1987).
Capps, D. (1995). *The child's song: The religious abuse of children*. Westminster John Knox.
Capps, D. (1997). *Men, religion, and melancholia: James, Otto, Jung, and Erikson*. Yale University Press.
Capps, D. (2002). *Life cycle theory and pastoral care*. Wipf & Stock. (Original work published 1983).
Confucius. (2014). *The analects*. Penguin.
Erikson, E. (1980). *Identity and the life cycle*. Norton. (Original work published 1959).
Erikson, E. (1982). *The life cycle completed*. Norton.
Erikson, E. (1985). *Childhood and society*. Norton. (Original work published 1950).
Erikson, E. (1994). *Insight and responsibility*. Norton. (Original work published 1966).
Freud, S. (1914). Some reflections on schoolboy psychology. In J. Strachey (Ed. & Trans.), *The standard edition of the complete psychological works of Sigmund Freud* (Vol. 13). Hogarth.
Freud, S. (1924). The economic problem in masochism. In J. Strackey (Ed. & Trans.), *The standard edition of the complete psychological works of Sigmund Freud* (Vol. 19). Hogarth.
Kohut, H. (1995). *The analysis of the self: A systematic approach to the psychoanalytic treatment of narcissistic personality disorders*. International University Press. (Original work published 1971).
McWilliams, N. (2011). *Psychoanalytic diagnosis: Understanding personality structure in the clinical process*. Guilford.
Sima, Q. (1993). *Records of the grand historian: Han dynasty I & II*. Columbia University Press.
Stanford Encyclopedia of Philosophy. (2013). Confucius. Retrieved from http://plato.stanford.edu/entries/confucius/#ConLif.
Tillich, P. (2005). *The new being*. University of Nebraska Press. (Original work published 1950).
Winnicott, D. W. (1965). *The maturational processes and the facilitating environment*. Karnac.
Zhu, X., & Hsiao, H. (2016). *Lesser learning*. Hongik.

12

Aspects of Men's Sorrow
Reflection on Phenomenological Writings About Grief

PHIL C. ZYLLA

INTRODUCTION

This chapter is about the grief of men. This is a highly complex matter given the multiple scenarios that might be explored. Although gendered aspects of grieving have been the subject of much research, studies focused on men and grief are sparse. This chapter interacts with recent studies of men's experiences of grief by focusing on written accounts of grief. In particular, I draw from understandings of the personal experiences of grief in the autobiographical accounts of three mourners: C. S. Lewis's memoir (1963) written after the death of his wife Joy, Henri Nouwen's (1980, 1982) writings regarding the death of his mother, and Nicholas Wolterstorff's (1987) reflections on the tragic death of his son Eric in a mountain-climbing accident. The expression of their extended accounts of grief gives form to many aspects of the grief of men.

Although I do not limit the focus of this chapter to middle-aged or older men, there is a common age group represented in these accounts. Henri Nouwen was 46 when his mother died and he wrote *In Memoriam* and *A Letter of Consolation*. Nicholas Wolterstorff was 51 when Eric died and he penned the poignant *Lament for a Son*. The final volume, *A Grief Observed*, was written by C. S. Lewis at the age of 62 at the death of his beloved wife Joy Davidman Gresham. Each of these accounts is a genuine expression of the experience of grief as articulated by these writers. Commenting on the essays by middle-aged men within his edited volume *In a Dark Wood*, Steven Harvey (1996) articulates some of the perspective that comes from this particular age group in their writings. He observes, "These middle-aged writers simply cannot muster much interest in public causes and are unwilling to measure themselves against the lofty standards of youthful ideals, preferring, instead, to stand as tall as they can in the mere reality of their own homes" (p. 7).

The autobiographical accounts discussed in this chapter were all written as private journals. Lewis penned his thoughts about the death of his wife in used notebooks that he found around his empty house, and when he did decide to publish his thoughts, he used a pseudonym. Wolterstorff (1987) commented on the journal notes he made at the death of his son, "Though it is intensely personal, I decided to publish it in the hope that some of those who sit beside us on the mourning bench for children would find my words giving voice to their own honoring and grieving" (p. 5). Similarly, Nouwen (1982) says of *A Letter of Consolation*, "After some thought and much encouragement from friends, I felt that it would be good to take the letter out of the privacy of my life and that of my father and offer it to those who know the same darkness and are searching for the same light" (p. 10). For the same reasons, though he hesitated for a long time, Nouwen (1980) also decided to publish the story of his mother's death, *In Memoriam* (1982).

Nouwen, Wolterstorff, and Lewis all had the vocation of being writers. Their contribution to the literature of grief was beckoned by the life situation that they found themselves in. They were thrown into it. In a sense, they continued their vocation, but their vocation was not an escape but rather a gift. It is often thought that men do not express their sorrow. In her important research on men's grief, however, Judith A. Cook (1988) found that "men's own accounts of bereavement reveal that expressiveness and disclosure of feelings for men may be characterized as something that occurs in a solitary context, [and] the nature of male mourning may thus be highly private" (p. 305). She learned that one important response to grief in men is the capacity to sit quietly and alone with one's sorrow in order to express it. Those who have the gift of writing are able to sensitively articulate their own experiences of sorrow, such as we have in these autobiographical accounts. Their reflections and skilled writing yield potent insights into the study of men's grief.

In their pioneering research on men's grief, Spaten et al. (2011) outline the procedure for their phenomenological investigation into the experiences of loss of three men: Martin (32), who lost his pregnant girlfriend to leukemia; Jens (54), who lost his wife to cancer and was left with two small children; and Claus (41), who also lost his wife to cancer and was left alone with their son. The transcribed qualitative semi-structured interviews focused on "asking the participants to describe their experience of losing their partner" (p. 5), and the follow-up questions were similarly descriptive, "asking about aspects of experience including physical and emotional responses, social support, and the process of coming to terms with their loss" (p. 5). The authors then used Max van Manen's techniques for examining the transcribed interviews, thus producing "a thematic description of the life-worlds of these men as they relate to their experience of bereavement" (p. 5). This chapter will employ two of the three techniques employed by Spaten et al. (2011) and described by van Manen (1990). These include "the holistic reading approach" and "the selective reading approach" (van Manen 1990, p. 93). In the *holistic reading approach*, the texts of autobiographical accounts of grief are attended to as a whole with the guiding question, "What sententious phrase may capture the fundamental meaning or main significance of the text as a whole?" (p. 93). The *selective reading* of the text involves reading the text several times and asking, "What statement(s) or phrase(s) seem particularly essential or revealing about the phenomenon or experience being described?" (p. 93).[1]

Some justification is required to adapt this method of phenomenological research to the analysis of autobiographical accounts of grief. In his later work, Max van Manen (2014) identifies essential features of what he terms "phenomenological writing" (p. 357). Three elements stand out in his explanation. First, phenomenological writing begins with "a peculiar attitude and attentiveness to the things of the world," an attitude that captures, from the writer's perspective, a sense of "awe or perplexity" (p. 360). When a writer begins from the midst of life and shifts to "that writerly space where meanings resonate and reverberate with reflective being" (p. 363), they have essentially attained the posture of phenomenological writing. Such writing evokes transcendent thinking in the reader, and "the space opened by the text becomes charged with signification that is, in effect, more real than real" (p. 362). Secondly, phenomenological writing, in van Manen's perspective, goes beyond "lived experience" as it is commonly defined. "Writing is much less 'writing down' the results of phenomenological analysis of the data

---

1. Van Manen (1990) offers a third step in the assessment of data that he calls the *detailed reading approach*. In this step, the text is reviewed with a focus on specific sentences or sentence clusters with the question, "What does this sentence or sentence cluster reveal about the phenomenon or experience being described?" (p. 93). However, including this step would require a more extensive paper and thus will be reserved for a future development of this study.

given in consciousness or experience... because the data are not unequivocally 'given' at all" (p. 368). The writing demands that we content ourselves with the inaccessibility of experiences and move into "this writerly space where there reigns the ultimate uncomprehensibility of things, the unfathomable infiniteness of their being, the uncanny rumble of existence itself" and where we "sense the fragility of our own existence" (p. 370). Finally, in van Manen's structure of phenomenological writing, every now and then the writer finds "an updraft and suddenly soar[s], reaching the perspective of a gaze. Phenomenologically speaking, this could be described as really 'seeing' something." (p. 373).

I argue in this chapter that the personal and autobiographical accounts of these three writers qualify on all three points. The probing of the deeply personal reveals the universal. The quest for understanding the inner emotional experience of grief, in all its hiddenness, calls for the deep attention and provocative reflection that are embodied in these writings. Furthermore, the creative "seeing" allows these authors to articulate aspects of their experiences of the "uncanny rumble in existence" as they know it.

HOLISTIC READING OF GRIEF IN AUTOBIOGRAPHIES

This first section explores the experiences of grief articulated by our authors by selecting a key phrase that may convey the meaning of the text as a whole. Van Manen's (1990) key question here for a phenomenological analysis is, "What sententious phrase may capture the fundamental meaning or main significance of the text as a whole?" (p. 93). In reviewing these books several times, I have isolated a key phrase for each author:

> C. S. Lewis: "The vast emptiness astonishes me." (1963, p. 67)
> Nicholas Wolterstorff: "How deep do souls go?" (1987, p. 49)
> Henri Nouwen: "She would not be home." (1980, p. 48)

Emptiness is a theme in the grief of men. Each author articulates something of this emptiness that accompanies grief. For Lewis, it is a "vast emptiness" much akin to Wolterstorff's deep soul ache and the knowledge for Nouwen that home is no longer the place where his mother is to be found—the family home is empty. There are elements in these statements of surprise and even astonishment. Wolterstorff (1987) experiences the sudden death of his son as an ache that moves "down, and down, deep down into my soul, deep beyond all telling" (p. 49). For Nouwen, the concept of home signals a place of belonging and intimacy that is elusive. In his reflection on Rembrandt's *The Return of the Prodigal Son*, Nouwen (1992) says of the returning son, "the way home is long and arduous" (p. 51). He was close to his mother, and her death cost him that place of belonging where he could truly be himself. Knowing that "she would not be home" filled him with dread as he and his father walk up to the door of their family home, "one of the most difficult and saddest moments of the week" (1980, p. 48). Lewis (1963) makes the unusual observation, "Death only reveals the vacuity that was always there." (p. 32).

How do men experience emptiness or vacuity in the losses they have endured? The experience of mourning itself is eclipsed by the vast emptiness that comes with men's experiences of loss. In their study of men's grief, Spaten et al. (2011) found that "mourning was encountered and overwhelmed by a feeling of emptiness. Claus described a similar experience of overwhelming feelings of grief and emptiness when he returned to the house after the death of his wife Tanja. He stated, 'Everything is completely different when she is not here'" (p. 6).

The common characterization of grief as expressive sorrow or outward crying and/or demonstration of inner anguish may not capture this inner experience of emptiness represented by men's experiences. In his psychoanalytic study of the religious sensibilities of men, Donald Capps (2013) offers the perspective that men are predisposed to a pervading sense of sadness, sober musing, and pensiveness that he calls melancholy. In particular, he focuses "on men's desire to be at home in the world" (p. xi), and in a poignant interpretation of Norman Rockwell's *Shuffleton's Barbershop* he articulates what is so important about "home." The young boy looks through the "lonely windows" of the barbershop to see the inner place of merriment. The painting conjures up memories of mother preparing the meal in the back room and the enjoyment of company of important friends and family, but the boy is left on the outside looking in. Capps gives his impression of the importance of this scene for the experience of men's emptiness:

> If men are exiles in the world—no longer at home in their original maternal environment—they are condemned, as it were, to find for themselves a place to be at home in the world in some other or imaginary environment. Some men have recovered a sense of being at home in the homes they have cocreated with spouses or significant others. Others have recovered a sense of being at home in other physical settings, especially ones in which men congregate together. The local tavern or bar is one such place. The barbershop is another. But what gives *Shuffleton's Barbershop* a distinctly melancholy tone and force is the

> fact that the painter—and viewer—are on the outside looking in. (p. 88)

The autobiographical account of this melancholic perspective emerges in Nouwen's reflections. For him, the death of his mother is "a crucial experience" (1982, p. 39), but the meaning he now places on this is his perspective from the window. Because of death he is now again on the outside looking in—longing for home. In a revealing passage, Nouwen (1980) conveys the importance of this as an experience related to his mother's death:

> From her I had come to feel an unqualified acceptance which had little to do with my being good or bad, successful or unsuccessful, close by or far away. In her I had come to sense a love that was free from demands and manipulations, a love that gave me a sense of belonging that could be found nowhere else. It is hard to express exactly what I was sensing, but the word "belonging" comes closest to it. (p. 34)

Men experience grief as a displacement in the lifeworld. The familiar elements are there, but the loss has taken something away, leaving an emptiness. This was poignantly demonstrated in a research study done of young men who had lost a friend to accidental injury (Creighton et al. 2013). To explore how participants grieved the accidental death of a male friend, the study reflected on both their narratives of the events leading up to their friend's death and an analysis of photos that they took subsequently that might "illustrate their grief and post-loss activities" (p. 37). One of the thematic findings of this study of young men's grief was "emptiness and stoicism" (p. 37). The authors state, "Many men described feeling empty or hollow in the time immediately following their friend's death. Embedded in these narratives were expressions of shock and uncertainty about how to react; in this respect, men's emptiness emerged both as a by-product of their male friend's death and an inability to be action oriented in their immediate response" (p. 37). The story is recounted of Damien and a few close friends who were on their way from a pre-party to a school-sponsored grade 12 graduation event. The researchers describe the events leading up to Damien's friend's death:

> Neither wanting to pay for a taxi or drive intoxicated, the friends opted to hitch a ride in the back of a van. When the van stopped, Damien's friend jumped out to run across the street to the event. In his haste, he did not see the bus intersecting his path. The teenager was struck and killed in front of Damien and his twin sister as well as the other young party goers across the street.

Damien recalled being taken home in a taxi at midnight following hours of courthouse interviews, his friend's sister screaming hysterically beside him. (p. 38)

Damien was invited to take pictures that might reveal his feelings and activities after this tragic event. He returned with a photograph of an empty bucket lying on the brick patterned sidewalk. He explains, "The only thing that I could think of was an empty bucket because that is how I felt; just so empty and hollow inside and I just didn't really know what was going on" (p. 38).

Men's predisposition to sadness and melancholy is rooted in their sense of being a stranger in the world. Experiences of loss deepen this aching sense of not belonging or being home—an experience that is communicated as "emptiness." Creighton et al. (2013) suggest that this experience also includes a feeling of "vulnerability." Their research suggests "that manly virtues of strength, decisiveness and self-regulation were disabled by sudden losses, in ways that left men unable to publicly align with such masculine ideals.... To counter vulnerabilities men tended to remain solitary and stoic in order to reinstate some control as to what could be seen and potentially judged by others" (p. 38).

SELECTIVE READINGS OF GRIEF IN AUTOBIOGRAPHIES

In this section I shift to Max van Manen's second stage of analysis, the 'selective reading' of these autobiographies of grief and sorrow.[2] The key question in van Manen's approach here is, "What statement(s) or phrase(s) seem particularly essential or revealing about the phenomenon or experience being described?" (van Manen 1990, p. 93). I have culled eight core themes[3] from the essential or revealing statements and phrases identified in this selective reading of these grief narratives. The themes identified include

2. Abbreviations: GO = C. S. Lewis's *A Grief Observed* (1963); LS = Nicholas Wolterstorff's *Lament for a Son* (1987); M = Henri Nouwen's *In Memoriam* (1980); LC = Henri Nouwen's *A Letter of Consolation* (1982)

3. This section follows van Manen's (2014) approach to "thematic draft writing" (p. 377). He states, "Themes are succinct phrasings that are discerned in the activity of theme analysis of the concrete or experiential material. These phrasings correspond to the variant and invariant themes of the reduction. Theme statements are generally converted into narrative passages. Increasingly, the writing needs to focus on essential and possibly originary thematic insights of the reduction. . . . Eidetic phrasings that appear to get at the heart or essence of the phenomenon may function as headings, side headings, and leading lines." (p. 377).

abruptness, helplessness, absence, sadness, despair, resistance, confusion/doubt, and loneliness.

An Abrupt Ending

"Something is over." (LS, p. 46)

"I suddenly felt a deep, inner sadness." (M, p. 48)

"... the struggle began. We were not prepared for it." (M, p. 22)

"The death of a loved one is ... an event, and it continues to affect us for the rest of our lives" (Arizmendi and O'Connor 2015, p. 58). For Wolterstorff, his son's mountain-climbing accident was experienced as an ending that came all too abruptly. "He was cut down at the peak of vitality and promise," says Wolterstorff (LS, p. 24). His life and their relationship were "snapped off" (p. 24) unexpectedly. In writing about the last days of his mother's struggle, Nouwen notes, "We were not prepared for it" (M, p. 22). So, suddenly, abruptly—life changes. The death of a loved one begins a chapter that one is not quite ready for, and "something is over" (LS, p. 46).

Helplessness

"One only meets each hour or moment that comes." (GO, p. 13)

"Instead of rowing, I float." (LS, p. 51)

"I know now about helplessness." (LS, p. 72)

"We had to relearn life." (LC, p. 14)

"The test comes when everything that is dear to us slips away." (M, p. 30)

One of the prominent features of men's experience of grief is the unforeseen powerlessness and helplessness that accompanies the experience of loss. In her study of men who had lost a child to cancer, Cook (1988) found that many of the men tried to shield others in their life from the impact of the loss even though they themselves felt it profoundly. She writes, "These men explained that they felt internal pressure from within themselves to be stoic and supportive, rather than social pressure from other people ('You want to be strong [and] you know you have to be strong')" (p. 301). This pressure to be strong is challenged by the experience of being helpless. When the death is faced up to, "everything that is dear ... slips away" (M, p. 30), and we have "to relearn life" (LC, p. 14). For Nouwen and his father, this is a new beginning that has elemental relearning attached to it. Wolterstorff also indicates a relearning—now he "floats" instead of "rowing" (LS, p. 51). Whereas before his son's death he had the power to control life somewhat, now he knows "about helplessness" (LS, p. 72). Lewis has been reduced to a moment-by-moment, hour-by-hour perspective. The powerful imagination that created worlds in his writings is now reduced by grief to an immediate world of loss and helplessness.

Absence

"The less I mourn her the nearer I seem to her." (GO, p. 66)

"She smiled, but not at me." (GO, p. 89)

"Did you ever know, dear, how much you took away with you when you left?" (GO, p. 70)

"The gardeners are gone, the neighborhood children are gone, only the wind in the oaks abides." (LS, p. 100)

"We felt for a moment as if we were in someone else's house." (M, p. 49)

"As I returned, it was her absence that pervaded my feelings." (M, p. 57)

These men also experienced in grief a deep sense of the absence of the loved one. Lewis, in one of the tender moments of his memoir, writes, "Did you ever know, dear, how much you took away when you left?" (GO, p. 70). He tries to name his losses, but they are too great. He tries to hold on to her, but she slips away; "she smiled, but not at me" (GO, p. 89). When Wolterstorff returns to the graveside of his son a year after the burial, he notices a vacancy, an absence: "The gardeners are gone, the neighborhood children are gone, only the wind in the oak abides" (LS, p. 100). Nouwen experiences his mother's absence both at the time of her death when he and his father "felt for a moment as if we were in someone else's house" (M, p. 49) and then again when he returns to the United States after the funeral. At that time, a kind of "homelessness" emerges in his inner being; "as I returned, it was her absence that pervaded my feelings" (M, p. 57). These lived experiences of loss were met not by memories or powerful symbols of ongoing connection but by absence. This common experience of a sense of absence is captured poignantly by the character, Ross, in his reflections on returning home from the cemetery:

The house seemed invariable alien and empty. How could it ever be warm again, a home again? We were abandoned to our grief. We may have tried hard to look after the house, to tend the fire, cook the meals and weed the garden. Going through the gestures of ordinary day-to-day life, but when did we contribute to life again for life's sake and not for death's sake? It all took time. . . . We drew the curtains and went to bed, exhausted with meetings and sorrow and the numerous things which had to be done. (Gersie 1991, p. 51)

Sadness

"How am I to sing in this desolate land?" (LS, p. 61)

"Is there not broken music?" (LS, p. 52)

"I suddenly felt a deep, inner sadness." (M, p. 48)

"Sorrow is an unwelcome companion." (M, p. 14)

"Tonight all the hells of young grief have opened again." (GO, p. 66)

The emotion of sadness is an important indicator in grief. However, the experiences of sadness indicated here are, with one exception, quite subdued, quiet, inner, and soft. Wolterstorff, filled with aching sadness, refers to the "broken music" (LS, p. 52). If there is any chance he can sing again, it will be a desolate, broken song. How else could it be with such a loss? Nouwen was awakened by his "inner sadness" (M, p. 48). It came over him suddenly and unexpectedly in the most ordinary moment. He expected his mother to be there at the front door, to hear his stories and to keep track of his successes as she had always done. Not this time; now he and his father would be left without her consolations, and they would have to settle for their "unwelcome companion, sorrow" (M, p. 14). One of the only deeply emotional outbursts of sadness in these accounts is Lewis's "hells of young grief" (GO, p. 66) that burst out at a time when he is expecting life to be getting back to normal.

Despair

"What chokes every prayer and every hope is the memory of all the prayers of H." (GO, p. 34)

"Our worst fears [about God] are true." (GO, p. 37)

> "I thought I trusted the rope until it mattered to me whether it would bear me. Now it matters, and I find I didn't." (GO, p. 43)
>
> "The suffering of the world has worked its way inside me." (LS, p. 72)
>
> "I buried myself that warm June day." (LS, p. 42)

Dennis Klass (2013) makes the case for revisiting therapeutic bereavement theories that seem to be biased toward optimism (p. 597). He states, "We have used different labels for less-than-optimal grief—pathological, unresolved, prolonged, chronic, complicated, and so on. A large portion of the phenomena included in those diagnoses is deep sadness, emptiness, nothingness, or depression, as well as associated behaviors" (p. 598). Klass wants to recover a sense of the sorrow and solace that are part of the ongoing experience of grief itself. Over time, it may not go away, but it may "transmute to a more tender sense of the world's fragility" (p. 601). Those who are still mourning the loss of a loved one may experience the quality of their grief changing with time, but still, they may "not laugh as deeply" (p. 601) as others.

Our authors, though all theologians and spiritual writers, do not modify their anxiety about death. They are able to live with the questions that the death has brought into their world. They allow "the suffering of the world to work its way" (LS, p. 72) inside of them and into their writing. Lewis despairs about the God he thought he knew and says that, because of this terrible loss, "our worst fears [about God] are true" (GO, p. 37). Hope itself is snuffed out because when he thinks about the sincere prayer of his wife before she died, he cannot fathom that God was listening. Why bother now with such prayer—"the rope" he thought he trusted "has broken" (GO, p. 43). Wolterstorff, in his grief as a father, also admits the despair this event brought into his life: "I buried myself that warm June day" (LS, p. 42). As it turns out, these admissions of the fragility of life and the anxiety that is produced by death leads to a kind of solace. Klass (2013) puts it this way: "If we understand that the continuing sorrow is a form of nondebilitating [sic] depression, and if mild depression is a good predictor of the future, then it would seem that the thoughts and feelings in sorrow have truth value. That is, grief's sorrow sees the world rightly" (p. 607).

Resistance/Spirituality

> "It's like a chuckle in the darkness." (GO, p. 83)

> "The sense that some shattering and disarming simplicity is the real answer." (GO, p. 83)
>
> "I shall try to keep the wound from healing." (LS, p. 63)
>
> "Mourners are aching visionaries." (LS, p. 86)
>
> "A new confrontation with death is taking place." (LC, p. 39)
>
> "Love is stronger than death." (LC, p. 93)

These spiritual writers are in touch with the counterpoint that spiritual resilience requires resistance. Rather than acquiesce to the power of death, they are in touch with the transcendent aspects of life. Wolterstorff, though he is devastated at the loss of his son, chooses to join the "mourners" who live as "aching visionaries" (LS, p. 86). To do this he must resist allowing his wound to heal. One is reminded of the prophetic lament, "Your wound is as deep as the sea. Who can heal you?" (Lam 2:13 NIV). Nouwen is convinced that "love is stronger than death" and that this new reality expressed in the death of his mother is something that must be confronted. Lewis attends to clues about the spiritual that don't equate to his lived experience so far—something new is afoot, "like a chuckle in the darkness" (GO, p. 83). He cannot see it or fully comprehend it, but perhaps, he thinks, he is trying too hard to understand death. He has "the sense that some shattering and disarming simplicity is the real answer" (GO, p. 83). These authors are able to live with deep ambiguity and strain. They are able to touch the core of their anxiety and be moved beyond it to something not quite in their grasp.

Loneliness

> "Grief isolates." (LS, p. 56)
>
> "How will things be and feel when she is no longer part of my life?" (M, p. 33)

The reorientation that comes with loss is part of the experience that these men are able to express. Grief is powerfully isolating. Others cannot access the experience, and therefore an attending loneliness is inevitable. Sometimes it is the ordinary and mundane things that bring attention to the sorrow. Emily Fragos's (2015) poem "The Sadness of Clothes" captures this in several powerful lines, "You explain death to the clothes like that dream. You tell them how much you miss the spouse . . . Words have that kind of power; you remind the clothes that remain in the drawer, arms stubbornly folded across the chest. He is gone and no one can tell us where" (n.p.).

Nouwen begins to process the new situation by asking, "How will things be and feel when she is no longer part of my life?" (M, p. 33). It is only at his mother's death that he realizes the power of her presence. She embodies acceptance and a place of belonging. He is losing that now. What will this be like? The loneliness he begins to feel is like a new dawn—something that has been since his birth is no longer. What does this mean? Although men may not demonstrate strong emotions in loss and may suppress or contain the powerful emotions of grief, these recognitions begin to take root—grief isolates.

Confusion/Doubt

> "There is spread over everything a vague sense of wrongness, of something amiss." (GO, p. 40)
>
> "When I lay these questions before God I get no answer." (GO, p. 80)
>
> "What do I do with this basket of regrets?" (LS, p. 64)
>
> "My wound is an unanswered question." (LS, p. 68)
>
> "What then is this agony?" (M, p. 30)

Grief, according to the reflections of these authors, is also disorienting and confusing. The experience itself puts a grey hue over everything: "there is spread over everything a vague sense of wrongness, of something amiss" (GO, p. 40). When death breaks the bonds of love and trust, there are many unresolved issues, regrets over things not done or things left unsaid. "What do I do with this basket of regrets?" asks Wolterstorff (LS, p. 64). Many questions emerge from death, but answers are difficult. Therefore, the wound becomes "an unanswered question" (LS, p. 68), and even if we ask God about these questions, "I get no answer" (GO, p. 80). These writers have penned many books with eloquence and clarity. However, now, in the face of their own distress and carrying the weight of unanswered sorrow, they are mute sufferers. Their words, as powerful as any others, are not potent here in the face of the death of a loved one. Their mother, their son, their wife is gone, and this is a bewildering place from which to live one's faith.

This exploration of the phenomenological writings of these three men has yielded a canvas of perspective on the meaning of death in men's experience. These grief themes form a tapestry of men's experiences that include abruptness, helplessness, absence, sadness, despair, resistance, confusion/doubt, and loneliness as common elements. I turn now to reflect on gender roles and men's grief, mourning strategies employed by men in sorrow, and the eventual transformation of grief into consolation.

GENDER ROLES AND GRIEF

Research shows that men are more likely than women to avoid emotional expression in response to a loss or to be less willing to talk about their loss (Cook 1988; Littlewood 1992; Staudacher 1991). However, the autobiographical accounts of grieving men I have selected offer further insight into how we might think about gender roles in grief. Both Lewis and Nouwen remark on the integrative function of grief in relation to the masculine and feminine aspects of one's life. In an extended reflection on the grief associated with losing his wife, Lewis indicates a change that has taken place in him because of their marriage. He recognizes a fusion of the masculine and feminine that emerged from their married life and that he only sees now that she is gone. Lewis (1963) explains,

> There is, hidden or flaunted, a sword between the sexes till an entire marriage reconciles them. It is arrogance in us to call frankness, fairness, and chivalry 'masculine' when we see them in a woman; it is arrogance in them, to describe a man's sensitiveness or tact or tenderness as "feminine" ... Marriage heals this. Jointly the two become fully human. "In the image of God create He them." Thus, by a paradox, this carnival of sexuality leads us out beyond our sexes. (p. 58)

Nouwen, writing to his father over their mutual grief, notices that his father has begun to respond to him differently since the death of his mother. Nouwen (1982) writes,

> The more I think about this, the more I realize that mother's death caused you to step forward in a way you could not before. Maybe there is even more to say than that. Maybe I have to say that you have found in yourself the capacity to be not only a father, but a mother as well. You have found in yourself that same gift of compassion that brought mother so much love and so much suffering. (p. 23)

This shift in his father's orientation is noticeable and marked. Nouwen suggests to his father that the loss of his wife has resulted in a transformation within him. The differences between the feminine and masculine are slightly altered by the loss experienced. Nouwen (1982) states, "I even sense that the memory of mother, and the way she lived her life with you, makes you consciously desire to let her qualities remain visible for your children and your friends—visible in you" (p. 25).

The lifeworld of grieving men takes new form with the loss of their loved one. There is a rupture in their lived world but also continuity. This forces an internal creative response of taking on parts of the loved one within one's own self and expressing the features of that person—even if it means changing their own sense of self. In their study of men's grief, Spaten et al. (2011) reflect on the experiences of men who find their lifeworld disrupted yet continuous with what they have known:

> [Claus] "Everything is completely different when she is not here." However, at the same time, he had to take care of their son, and this forced him to continue to engage in life, allowing no possibility for withdrawal. Like Claus, Jens also has children and their physical presence meant that there was some sense of continuity for Jens. However, this continuity was experienced in a dramatically changed world, a world where "Suddenly it is I who must be both father and mother for the children." (p. 8)

What does it mean for a man to experience the loss of a mother or a sister or a spouse? If the experiences of these men can be trusted, part of what it means is a refashioning of one's inner life to reveal the qualities of the lost one in their own self. Although this may not change their fundamental make-up, it allows *aspects of the one who died* to be brought to life or animated within their own personality. Nouwen (1982) goes on to say to his father, "You are not imitating mother. You are not saying, 'I will do things the way mother used to do them.' That would be artificial and certainly not an honor to her. No, *you are becoming more yourself* [emphasis added], you are exploring those areas of life that always were a part of you but remained somewhat dormant in mother's presence" (p. 26). Presumably what this means is that Nouwen's father is expressing the feminine aspects that endure within him as a legacy of his relationship with Nouwen's mother.

The cultural representation that grief should be endured without crying is challenged by Wolterstorff (1987) in his autobiographical reflections on the loss of his son. He signals the importance of breaking the stereotypes about men withholding tears and not crying when he asks, "Why celebrate stoic tearlessness? Why insist on never outwarding the inward when that inward is bleeding? Does enduring while crying not require as much strength as never crying? Must we always mask our suffering? May we not sometimes allow people to see and enter it? I mean, may *men* not do this? . . . I have been assaulted, and in the assault wounded, grievously wounded . . . I shall look at the world through tears. Perhaps I shall see things that dry-eyed I could not see" (p. 26).

EMBODIED REMEMBERING

Much of the literature on grieving focuses on the physical aspects of grief and the manifestations of the somatic. Worden (1982), for example, reports the physical sensations commonly reported by the bereaved: (a) experiences of hollowness or tightness; (b) oversensitivity to noise; (c) a sense of depersonalization; (d) breathlessness and sighing; (e) muscular weakness; (f) fatigue and lack of energy; and (g) dry mouth (p. 23). One way of understanding this could be to expand the physicality of men's grief to include embodied remembering. The emotional sadness that accompanies the loss of a loved one is difficult to get in touch with. However, the physicality of grief and sadness is taken up by the body and expressed in a new orientation of the self in the world. This new orientation is expressed in the body—the memory of the loved one now animated and conveyed in certain physical gestures, a frame of mind, and other fundamental features of the loved one. Johnstone (2012) undertakes a Husserlian phenomenological analysis of firsthand experience of emotions (p. 179). In this schema, emotions have several essential features: "they involve the whole organism; they each imbue the lived body with their own particular dynamic of kinesthetic and hedonic shifts; they display two distinct forms of intentionality, affective and cognitive; they arise involuntarily, but become emotions fully only when subsequently espoused" (p. 180). Of interest here is the emotion of *sadness*. In experiences of grief, sadness "seeps into the very fabric of one's surrounding world" (p. 181) and "clothes" other events in this feeling.

Wolterstorff (1987) describes the embodied desolation he felt that was fueled by the loss of his son. "Now he's gone, lost, ripped loose from love; and the ache of loss sinks down, and down, deep down into my soul, deep beyond all telling. How deep do souls go?" (p. 49). The grief had worked its way into the depths of his being. The sadness was not sporadic emotional response but rather was woven into his embodied existence—making the fabric of his life one that evoked sadness as part of who he now was. In a similar episode, Nouwen (1980) describes what he calls "one of the most difficult and saddest moments" (p. 48) of the week surrounding his mother's death.

> When we turned into the road leading to our house, I suddenly felt a deep, inner sadness. Tears came to my eyes and I did not dare to look at my father. We both understood. She would not be home. She would not open the door and embrace us. She would not ask how the day had been. She would not invite us to the table and pour tea in our cups. I felt an anxious tension when my father drove into the garage and we walked up to the

door. Upon entering the house it was suddenly clear to us: it had become an empty house. (p. 48)

Nouwen combines "deep inner sadness" with "anxious tension." Embodied grief in this account is both internal and external. The physicality of approaching the front door combines with the internal sentiment of sadness that Nouwen is carrying within his body. There is a realization of the new horizon of a different life—one without his mother's comforting presence. There is also an aching gloom that has fastened itself to the inner spirit. Such is the experience of grief carried in the human frame of mourners.

GRIEF MOURNING STRATEGIES FOR MEN

Cook (1988) argues that much of the literature on grieving parents is based on research that has tended to focus on mothers rather than fathers (p. 290). Cook's research involves a qualitative study of 55 fathers who had lost a child to cancer within the previous five years. Cook identifies four major "mourning strategies" that allowed the grieving fathers a way of "handling upsetting feelings without disclosing them to other people" (p. 294). These include (1) thinking about something else, (2) reason/reflection, (3) doing something else, and (4) solitary reflectiveness (p. 294). Interacting with these findings, I now turn to a review of the selected autobiographical accounts to link these mourning strategies with the articulations of grief I found in those three volumes.

Thinking About Something Else

In Cook's (1988) study, typically the fathers accomplished cognitive "blocking" by "deliberately thinking about practical, concrete details of their day-to-day lives" (p. 295). One father in Cook's study says, "The way that I get through the low spots, I just kind of like to think about something else that I'm looking forward to. It gives you a lift" (p. 295).

In reflecting on the period of mourning that he was going through after the loss of his wife, Lewis recognizes that he employs the strategy of thinking about something else during his normal course of work and conversation. However, he recognizes that these are often, for him, difficult times. He discloses,

> It's not true that I'm always thinking of H. Work and conversation make that impossible. But the times when I'm not are perhaps my worst. For then, though I have forgotten the reason,

> there is spread over everything a vague sense of wrongness, or something amiss. Like in those dreams where nothing terrible occurs—nothing that would sound even remarkable if you told it at breakfast-time—but the atmosphere, the taste, of the whole thing is deadly . . . I hear a clock strike and some quality it always had before has gone out of the sound. What's wrong with the world to make it so flat, shabby, worn-out looking? Then I remember. (p. 40)

However, for Lewis this mourning strategy of "cognitive blocking" backfires. Although he is somewhat preoccupied with the daily activities of his life, Lewis notices a flatness to the world—a drabness. Then, he remembers her death and is awakened to the seriousness of his loss. Trying not to think about it only makes the world grey. Likewise, Wolterstorff describes his dedicated efforts to take his mind off Eric's death by appreciating the things that he always enjoyed.

> Let me try again. All these things I recognize. I remember delighting in them—trees, art, house, music, pink morning sky, work well done, flowers, books. I still delight in them. I'm still grateful. But the zest is gone. The passion cooled, the striving quieted, the longing stilled. My attachment is loosened. No longer do I set my heart on them. I can do without them. They don't matter. (p. 51)

As a mourning strategy, thinking about something else seems to have only minimal effect. Men may use this tactic to deflect the deep sense of loss and the intense interior experiences of grief, but these accounts seem to modify this strategy. Perhaps thinking about something else ought to be modified to a new way of remembering, as suggested by Nouwen (1980): "I am back at work now: teaching, reading, writing, laughing and getting angry. It all seems the same as five weeks ago. But things are not the same. Mother has died and it was for my own good that she left. I speak less and less about her, even my thoughts are less involved with her—yet I have not forgotten her" (p. 61).

Reason and Reflection

Cook (1988) determined that men used a second strategy to manage their grief. This involved a rational reflection on the situation that caused the death of their child and a rather intentional focusing on the details of "painful memories and failures rather than blocking them from consciousness"

(p. 297). Cook offers that this is unique to men's grieving and that it has not been present in studies of female bereavement.

There is much evidence of this strategy in the accounts of our three grieving authors. Wolterstorff (1987) reflects on the situation that caused his son's death. "Each death is as unique as each life. Each has its own stamp. Inscape. The tree in Hopkins's garden had an inscape, but so did the felling of the tree. And one child's death differs from another not in the intensity of the pain it causes but in the quality. To see a young life wither and die is as painful as to see it snapped off" (p. 24). Putting into words the extraordinary pain of learning of his son's death awakens a sensitivity in him. He is reminded that a friend's son had committed suicide. He reasoned, "I thought for a time that such a death must be easier to bear than the death of one with zest for life. He wanted to die. When I talked to the father, I saw that I was wrong" (p. 25).

A contemplative Nouwen (1980) offers this reflection on his mother's death:

> In a society which is much more inclined to help you hide your pain than to grow through it, it is necessary to make a very conscious effort to mourn. The days when those in grief wore dark clothes and abstained from public life for many months are gone. But I felt that without a very explicit discipline, I might be tempted to return to "normal" and so forget my mother even against my will . . . The deeper I entered into my own grief, the more I became aware that something new was about to be born, something that I had not known before. (p. 59)

Men who shared how this strategy of reflection and reason about grief helped them said "that they had learned to accept the inevitability of the death by approaching it in a rational, logical manner" (Cook 1988, p. 296). However, the reality of death itself requires description. Death is a taboo subject. In his reflections, Lewis (1963) vividly describes aspects of his personal experience of grief.

> No one ever told me that grief felt so like fear. I am not afraid, but the sensation is like being afraid. The same fluttering in the stomach, the same restlessness, the yawning. I keep on swallowing. At other times it feels like being mildly drunk, or concussed. There is a sort of invisible blanket between the world and me. I find it hard to take in what anyone says. Or perhaps, hard to want to take it in. It is so uninteresting. Yet I want the others to be about me. I dread the moments when the house is empty. (p. 1)

Doing Something Else

Repeatedly, in Cook's study, men deflected the pain of the grief by doing other things. For many, the workplace was a place they could forget about their child's death and escape uneasy feelings through intense involvements. One father states, "Work was an escape. When I was at work I could put this part out of my mind because I had to concentrate on what I was doing" (p. 298). There were, however, multiple other activities that fathers engaged in. These activities were of two orders: one was distracting themselves from their own mourning, and the other was allowing their child's death to serve as a catalyst. This latter group of fathers became deeply engaged in community involvements that were derived from the meaning of their child's death. Such fathers offered service at a Ronald McDonald residence for parents, joined community grief support groups, or volunteered at a pediatric wing in a hospital. All these activities were, in Cook's (1988) view, motivated by "men's desire to take an active stance, a desire which had been thwarted during the illness by the helplessness that most parents reported at watching their child suffer and die" (p. 299).

These two responses of doing something else describe the range of emotional responses to grief in men. Whereas some will pull away and withdraw from sorrow by engaging in activities that will drown out their pain, others will be enflamed with new courage to face the world with an inner capacity to serve others despite the awful pain they have had to endure. Lewis (1963) articulates the path of engagement in life and fresh impetus when he describes how his grief motivates him, saying, "For me at any rate the program is plain. I will turn to her as often as possible in gladness. I will even salute her with a laugh. The less I mourn her the nearer I seem to her" (p. 66). This is not to suggest that men should simply transform their grief and endure; rather, it is a reminder that although grief can be dark and heavy and unbearable, there may come a time when the mourners become "aching visionaries" who catch "a glimpse of God's new day" (Wolterstorff 1987, p. 86).

Solitary Expressiveness

The men in Cook's study disclosed that they experienced periods of deep emotional expression and crying, but these periods of expressive grief were private and solitary experiences. Partly because of the internal pressure to "be strong" for others who were affected by the loss and partly because of social scripting, these men found it difficult to cry in public settings.

However, they did admit the need for an outlet for their emotion that they would take once they could find a private place where it was safe for them to do so.

Cook (1988) reflects, "Many men spoke about the requirement that they be alone in order to deal with their feelings. Repeatedly, when fathers did describe situations involving emotional expression, they were in solitary settings such as downstairs in the basement, outside in the garage, or driving alone in the car" (p. 290).

TRANSFORMING GRIEF

Grief is a complex, multifaceted process, and the mourning strategies above can aid in the amelioration of the inner strain of sorrow for men. However, sorrow can also be transformative. Grief can open our eyes and be revelatory. In this respect, each of the autobiographies discussed here, while taking seriously the sadness and pain that loss brings, offers a transformative vision of grief.

The sensitive reflection by Wolterstorff (1987) gives us a hint of ways that sorrow can fuel our compassion. He says, "The suffering of the world has worked its way deeper inside of me. I never knew that sorrow could be like this. Six months before, I had gone to the funeral of the twenty-three-year-old son of friends. I tried to imagine the quality of their grief. I know now that I failed miserably" (p. 72). Sorrow is transformed as it works its way into our being and transforms our actions; there is a solidarity in grief with others who are grieving. The "suffering of the world" works its way deeper within.

Lewis changes how we think about grief recovery when he carefully describes the shift from heavy, dark grief to a lighter affect and an appreciation of the memory of his wife. He shares his experience:

> Something quite unexpected has happened. It came this morning early. For various reasons, not in themselves at all mysterious, my heart was lighter than it had been for many weeks ... Indeed, it was something (almost) better than memory; an instantaneous, unanswerable impression. To say it was like a meeting would be going too far. Yet there was that in it which tempts one to use those words. It was as if the lifting of the sorrow removed a barrier. (p. 52)

This reflection on grief is a reminder that the affect will eventually change to a "lighter" one. Although sadness and a sense of loss remain, the orientation to life shifts with time. Lewis came to terms with his loss by acknowledging a sense of his departed wife's "presence" with him. As one of his biographers states, "Lewis reached the point where he practiced her absence, rather than go on pleading for her presence, in a world scoured clean of her" (Loades 1989, p. 274). His consolation in grief also became, in this way, transformative. As Klass puts it, "Sorrow remains and into that sorrow comes solace" (2013, p. 614).

Nouwen (1980), in his own way, also offers a revisioning of the meaning of sorrow. Citing the important axiom of Carl Rogers that "what is most personal is most universal" (p. 10), he describes his own experience as a son who has lost his mother to death.

> My mother died. This event cannot claim any uniqueness. It is among the most common of human experiences. There are few sons and daughters who have not experienced or will not experience the death of their mother, suddenly or slowly, far away or close by. Still, I want to reflect on this event because, although it is not unusual, exceptional or extraordinary, it remains in many ways unknown and unfathomed. It is indeed in the usual, normal and ordinary events that we touch the mystery of human life . . . It slowly dawned on me that she who had followed every decision I made, had discussed every trip I took, had read every article and book I wrote, and had considered my life as important as hers, was no longer. Little by little I became aware that mother, although far away, had always been part of my wanderings, and that indeed I had viewed the world through the eyes of her to whom I could tell my story. (pp. 10, 56)

This tender reflection is a "slow dawning" of the new situation he was in. The absence of his mother awakened Nouwen to the importance of her role in his life. The loss was integrated into his ongoing story, and the tasks that lay ahead, for him, required fresh courage and the embrace of "the mystery of human life" (1980, p. 10).

CONCLUSION

Recent literature on men's approaches to grieving has helped us to understand more specifically how men experience mourning and sorrow. This study accentuates the internal experiences of grief in men by examining the phenomenological writings of Henri Nouwen, C. S. Lewis, and Nicholas Wolterstorff. The selective reading of these memoirs of grief yields insight into eight common experiences of all three authors: abruptness, helplessness, absence, sadness, despair, resistance, confusion/doubt, and loneliness. Their exploration gives a thick description to male mourning and offers a beginning point for further research into male grieving. Although gender stereotypes continue to reflect the resistance of men to public crying, this study reveals that men internalize their grief and find ways to express it privately. The chapter argues that men embody grief in a way that changes their outlook, and this needs further exploration. Finally, grief is transformed into action, and one way that men may employ to resolve their ongoing sorrow is to transform it into constructive patterns of integration. Although this may be limited to middle-aged men who demonstrate some maturity, it was also reflected in limited ways by younger age groups.

REFERENCES

Arizmendi, B. J., & O'Connor, M.-F. (2015). What is "normal" in grief? *Australian Critical Care, 28*, 58–62. doi:10.1016/j.aucc.2015.01.005.

Capps, D. (2013). *At home in the world: A study in psychoanalysis, religion, and art.* Cascade.

Cook, J. A. (1988). Dad's double binds: Rethinking father's bereavement from a men's studies perspective. *Journal of Contemporary Ethnography, 17*(3), 285–308.

Creighton, G., Oliffe, J., Butterwick, S., & Saewyc, E. (2013). After the death of a friend: Young men's grief and masculine identities. *Social Science and Medicine, 84*, 35–43.

Fragos, E. (2015). The sadness of clothes. Academy of American Poets. https://www.poets.org/poetsorg/poem/sadness-clothes. Copyright 2015 by Emily Fragos. Originally published in Poem-a-Day on July 21, 2015, by the Academy of American Poets.

Gersie, A. (1991). *Storymaking in bereavement: Dragons fight in the meadow.* Jessica Kingsley.

Harvey, S. (Ed.). (1996). *In a dark wood: Personal essays by men on middle age.* University of Georgia Press.

Johnstone, A. A. (2012). The deep bodily roots of emotion. *Husserl Studies, 28*, 179–200. doi:10.1007/s10743-012-9107-4.

Klass, D. (2013). Sorrow and solace: Neglected areas in bereavement research. *Death Studies, 37*, 597–616. doi:10.1080/07481187.2012.673535.

Lewis, C. S. (1963). *A grief observed.* Seabury.

Littlewood, J. (1992). *Aspects of grief.* Routledge.

Loades, A. (1989). The grief of C. S. Lewis. *Theology Today, 46*(3), 269–276.

Nouwen, H. J. M. (1980). *In memoriam.* Ave Maria.

Nouwen, H. J. M. (1982). *A letter of consolation.* HarperCollins.

Nouwen, H. J. M. (1992). *The return of the prodigal son.* Doubleday.

Spaten, O. M., Byrialsen, M. N., & Langdridge, D. (2011). Men's grief, meaning and growth: A phenomenological investigation into the experience of loss. *Indo-Pacific Journal of Phenomenology, 11*(2), 1–15. doi:10.2989/IPJP.2011.11.2.4.1163.

Staudacher, C. (1991). *Men and grief.* New Harbinger.

van Manen, M. (1990). *Researching lived experience: Human science for an action sensitive pedagogy.* Althouse.

van Manen, M. (2014). *Phenomenology of practice: Meaning-giving methods in phenomenological research and writing.* Left Coast.

Wolterstorff, N. (1987). *Lament for a son.* Eerdmans.

Worden, J. W. (1982). *Grief counseling and grief therapy.* Springer.

Index

Abraham, Reggie, xxi, 236–59
Addams, Jane, 101–3
Addiction, to pornography, 123
Adhesive idealization, 199–202
Adolescence. *see also* Children
   Black males, 104–6
   Confucius, early life, 264
   gender creative, 61
   A Monster Calls (Ness), 52
   pornography, effect on, 125
   religious conversion, 16
   treated seriously, 32–33
   warrior ethos and, 194–95, 196
   William James, early life, 237, 238–39
African Americans, negative experiences, 81–82, 221–25
Alienation, 148–49
Ambivalence, emotional, 33, 46, 48, 49, 52, 53
American Beauty (movie), 154
Anxiety, 5, 98, 107–8, 111, 135, 136, 194, 201, 238
Arjona, Rubén, xx–xxi, 158–87
Association, psychological theory of, 17–18, 21
Autobiography, accounts of grief, 282–84

Baden-Powell, Robert, 131–32
Baldwin, David, 83–85
Baldwin, James, 80–97
   adopting Delaney's way of looking, 93–95
   Beauford Delaney, first meeting, 87–88
   first experiences, negative, 81–82

   friendship with Delaney, 92
   Go Tell It on the Mountain, 83–84
   ideal father, 85
   life in Harlem, 86–87
   love for Delaney, 96
   portraits by Delaney, 92
   reflections on God, 87
   self-worth, restored, 82
   stepfather, relationship with, 83–85
   ugliness, theme in life, 82–85, 87, 88, 95
Baudelaire children (characters), 2–4, 10, 11, 14–15, 20–22
Benjamin, Walter, 146, 147
Bibliotherapy, 2–6, 10–13, 21–24, 30–53
Black male bodies
   associated with sin, 106–7
   objectification of, 101–3, 105–6, 114
   splitting (individual or group), 103–4, 107, 108–10
   transference, demonic, 110–14
   unconscious criminalization of, 101–3
Black pastors, 221–25
Blood, Benjamin P., 25
Boy Scouts, 131–32
Boys
   Black, interviews with, assessment, 117–18
   Black, negative portrayals of, 99
   Black, self-experiences of, 114–17
   dreams and, 40
   Korean, effect of Confucianism on, 274–75, 277–79
British Sexual Fantasy Project, 138

INDEX

Butler, Smedley, 195, 197, 199, 200, 202–9, 229, 230

Capps, Donald, 236
  influenced by Erikson, 245
  on Jesus, 43, 51
  on life of William James, 244–51
  on Martin Luther's melancholia, 271
  on masculinity, 196
  on melancholy, 244–47, 271, 285–86
  Men, Religion, and Melancholia, 244, 246–47
  men, religious sensibilities, 285–86
  mothers, psychological loss of, 245
  on mystical or conversion moments, 1
  on religious abuse, 278
  six degrees of transmission, 24–28
  on virtues, 276
  virtues, 276–78
  young adulthood, 245–46
Caregivers, pastoral, 61, 78, 117–18, 218n9, 227–28, 230, 232, 279–80
Carlin, Nathan, xxi, 30–54, 189, 204–5
Children
  bibliotherapy, 2–6, 10–13, 21–24, 30–53
  Black boys, 99, 114–17
  confronting death, 2
  Confucianism, 261, 274, 275, 278
  Confucius, death of father, 264, 265, 266, 270–71
  gender creative, 58, 61
  masturbation and, 131
  Nouwen, death of mother, 285, 289, 299
  pornography, effect on, 125
  religious conversion, 16, 20, 28
  self-diagnosis, 5–6
  Wishes Don't Make Things Come True (Rogers), 30, 52
Christian, Jules, 131
Clemens, Samuel Langhorne. *see* Twain, Mark
Cognitive blocking, 297–98

Condensation, 41, 45
Confucianism
  influence on Korean society, 260–61
  limits of, 279
  virtues, contrasted with Eriksonian psychosocial development, 276–78
Confucius
  developmental stages of, 261–64
  importance of rites and rituals, 271–72
  Kong He (father of), 262–63
  life cycle model, 261–63, 273–79
  life described (*The Analects*), 263–64
  life of, 262–64
  melancholy, 271–72
  Oedipal stage, absent father, 264–67
  psychoanalysis and, 261
  role as surrogate husband, 269–70
  virtue, cultivating of, 276–78
  Yan Zhengzai (mother of), 262–63, 267–69
Congregations, gender-creative persons, 69–70
Conor (character). *see also A Monster Calls* (Ness)
  psychoanalytic reading, 43, 45–46, 48–49, 50–51
  self-hatred, 50, 51
  wishes, mother's death, 52–53
Counselors, view of sexual fantasies, 144–45
Criminalization, Black male bodies, 103

Dark Rapture (Delaney), 92
De Shazer, Steve, 26–27
Death
  bibliotherapy, 2–6, 10–13, 21–24, 30–53
  confronting, 2
  A Monster Calls, 33, 53
  narratives on, 281–303
  of a parent, 2, 5, 52, 53, 264, 265, 266, 270–71, 285, 286, 289, 299

phenomenological writings on,
  281–304
Delaney, Beauford, 80–97
  art as freedom, 82
  early life, 88–92
  friendship with Baldwin, 92
  James Baldwin, first meeting, 87–88
  mental illness, 91
  painting career, 91–92
  portraits of Baldwin, 92
  way of looking, 93–95
Demonic transference, 110–14
Depression. *see* Melancholy
Despair, 290–91
Diagnostic and Statistical Manual for Mental Disorders (DSM-5), 149–51
Disorders
  masturbating to images, 124
  masturbation as a, 150–53
  melancholy, 8, 247, 253, 270–74
  Post-Traumatic Stress Disorder (PTSD), 213, 216, 217
  sexual, 124, 149–53
Displacement, 41, 110, 111
Divided self, 7–9, 14, 17–18, 237
Doehring, Carrie, 215
Dowd, Siobhan, 32
Dreams, 33, 40–42, 43, 45, 48, 52
DSM-5. *see Diagnostic and Statistical Manual for Mental Disorders*
Du Bois, W. E. B., 98
Dykstra, Robert C.
  chapter by, 1–29
  on counseling, 182
  David Marsten, therapy sessions recounted, 2–4
  with Donald Capps, xviii
  Finding Ourselves Lost, 244, 252–53
  Images of Pastoral Care: Classic Readings, 57–58, 76
  interview with David Marsten, 6–7
  on Mary James, 254
  personal life, 5, 252–53
  on sexuality, 164–66
  on William James, 256, 258

Ego, 48, 49

Ehrensaft, Diane, xx, 58, 61
Eine klinisch-forensische Studie (von Krafft-Ebing), 140
Emotions, 145, 182, 213, 275, 296
Empathy, inadequacy of, 99, 117–18
Erikson, Eric H., 162, 194, 200, 245, 261, 276–78
Eye (as "the organ of tactility")
  to desire someone else, 146, 147
  engaged in touch, 148
  for pornography and masturbation, 148
  replacement for sexual fantasy, 144–45

Fanon, Franz, 95, 101
Father
  absent, 264–67
  bond with son, 1–3, 22–24
  Confucius, Kong He as, 262–63
  James Baldwin, stepfather of, 83–85
  Nicholas Wolterstorff, as a, 281–82, 287–94, 295, 299
  Smedley Butler on father figures, 197n9
  teacher as substitute for, 266–67
  Williams James, Henry James Sr. as, 240–43, 254–57
Father-son bond, 22
Finding Ourselves Lost (Dykstra), 244, 252–53
Ford, Richard, 46
Freud, Sigmund
  dream work, 41–42
  "On Dreams," 33, 40–42, 48, 52
  on fatherhood, 266–67
  Interpretation of Dreams, 40, 48
  on love, 180
  on masturbation, 131, 136, 140–41
  on melancholia, 50
  "Mourning and Melancholia," 50, 246
  on sexual fantasy, 140–41
  Three Essays On The History Of Sexuality, 140
  types of dreams, 42
Friendship, 175–77, 184–86, 252–53

Gender, continua of, 56
Gender creative, definition, 58n6
Gender diversity, 56–79
Gender-creative persons
    2015 U.S. Transgender Survey, 58–61
    emergence of, 60
    percentage of population, 56–57
    resilience strategies, 61–75
Gibson, Danjuma G., xx, 98–119
Go Tell It on the Mountain (Baldwin), 83–84
God, acceptance of, 53
Gospel Of John, 184–85
Graham, Larry, 214, 215
Grief
    abrupt ending narrative, 288
    absence, 289–90
    autobiographical accounts of, 282–84
    bibliotherapy, 2–6, 10–13, 21–24, 30–53
    confusion/doubt, 293–94
    Danny (case study), 2–6, 8–24, 27–28
    despair, 290–91
    as displacement, 286
    embodied remembering, 296–97
    emptiness, 284–85
    helplessness, 288–89
    loneliness, 292–93
    male gender roles, 294–95
    A Monster Calls, 33, 53
    mourning strategies, men, 297–301
    narratives, 287–94
    phenomenological research on, 283–84
    resistance/spirituality, 291–92
    sadness, 290, 296, 297
    transforming, 301–2
Grief Observed, A (Lewis), xxii, 281
Group-dynamic themes, 108
Group-level racial delusion, 103–5

Hamman, Jaco J., xx, 120–57
Handler, David, 2–3
Harlem, life in, 85–86
Helplessness, 288–89, 302
Hinds, Jay-Paul, xx, 80–97
Homosocial love, 175–82
Hypersexuality, 149–53

Id, 48, 49
Idealization, process of, 264–66
Images, mental or external, 148
Images of Pastoral Care: Classic Readings (Dykstra), 57–58, 76
In Memoriam (Nouwen), xxii, 281, 282
Interpretation of Dreams (Freud), 40, 48
Isolation
    feeling of, 5
    by gender-creative persons, 61, 74
    pornographic images leading to, 128, 148–49

James, Henry, Jr., 236, 240–41, 250
James, Henry, Sr., 240–43, 254–55, 256–57
James, Mary, 243–44, 248–51, 254, 256, 258
James, S. E., 58–61
James, William, 236–59
    art career, 239–43, 244, 256
    Benjamin P. Blood effect on, 25
    depression, 237, 243–44, 245–47, 253, 254
    divided self, 7–9, 14, 237
    early life, 237–42
    Henry James, Sr. (father), relationship with, 240–43
    lectures on conversion, 16–17
    Mary James (mother), relationship with, 243–44, 248–51, 254, 256, 258
    melancholy, 8
    religious conversion, 28
    on the subconscious mind, 18–21
    transcendence, 25
    The Varieties of Religious Experience: A Study in Human Nature, 236
Jesus, 46, 51, 76–78, 184, 185, 252–53
Jung, Carl, 245

INDEX

Kafka, Martin, 150
Kahr, Brett
  disordered masturbation, criteria for, 151–53
  pornography and masturbation, 144–45
  Sex and the Psyche, 138–45
  on sexual fantasy, 124, 138–45
  sexual fantasy and masturbation, 143–44
  sexual fantasy and shame, 139–40
  sexual fantasy, as normal behavior, 141–42
  sexual fantasy, purpose of, 142–43
Kinsey, Alfred Charles, 120, 132, 133, 141
Kohut, Heinz, 24, 103n1, 114, 265–66, 267
Kong He (Confucius' Father), 262–63, 264–67, 270
Korea, 274–75, 277–79
Kübler-Ross, Elisabeth, 53

Lament For A Son (Wolterstorff), xxii, 281
LaMothe, Ryan, xx–xxi, 188–211, 228–30
Laqueur, Thomas, 129, 132–36
Letter Of Consolation, A (Nouwen), xxii, 281, 282
Lewis, C. S.
  on death of wife, 281–82
  grief, on reason and reflection, 299
  grief and cognitive blocking, 297–98
  grief as emptiness, 284
  grief narrative, 287–94
  A Grief Observed, xxii
  on grief recovery, 301–2
Life cycle model, Confucian, 261–63, 273, 274, 275, 276–78, 279
Litz, Brett, 213, 215, 217
Loneliness, 128, 292–93
Luther, Martin, 271
Lynching, 101, 102–4

Manning, Jill, 125–26
Marsten, David, 1–28
individualized nature of religion, 20–21
  on narrative therapy, 7, 14, 27
  religious conversion, 16, 20–21
  Robert Dykstra interview with, 6–7
  therapy sessions, 2–4
Marten, John, 130, 132, 133
Masten, Ann S., 62
Masturbation
  addiction to, Jude (case history), 123–29
  anxiety about, 135
  Christian monks on, 130
  confusion from, 124
  dangers of, 120–21, 122
  as disordered, 150–53
  fantasy and, 133–34, 137
  guilt from, 124, 135–36
  history of, 129–38
  Marten on, 130, 132, 133
  medical views on, 129–35
  neurosis from, 136
  pastoral theological evaluations, 129
  pornography, effect of, 123, 144–45
  as a practice, 154–55
  practices, driven by the eye, 124–25
  religious and philosophical views, 136
  sexual fantasy and, 143–44
  studies, history of, 120–23
  taboo, promoted by bourgeoisie, 130, 132
  Tissot on, 120–22, 123, 129–30, 131, 137, 140, 149
  Western attitudes towards, 129–31
Masturbation: The History of a Great Terror (Stengers and Van Neck), 129–32
Masturbatory paradox, 124, 139–40, 144
McWilliams, Nancy, 200–201, 268–69
Media portrayal, black male bodies, 107–10
Melancholy, 8, 245–47, 270–74. *see also* Depression

Men
  Black, objectification of, 101–3, 105, 107, 164
  experience grief as displacement, 286–87
  grief mourning strategies, 297–301
  Korean, effect of Confucianism on, 274–75, 277–79
Men, Religion, and Melancholia (Capps), 244, 246–47
Miller-McLemore, Bonnie, 225–27
Mimesis and Alterity (Taussig), 146–49
Mimetic desire, 146–49
Mind, healing power of, 13–14
Monster Calls, A (Ness)
  dream interpretation, Freud, 40–42
  first story, summary, 43–44
  hallucination, 50
  Jesus as savior, 46
  Oedipal stage, 45–46
  plot summary, 33–40
  prodigal son, parable, 48–49
  psychoanalytic reading, 33, 42–43, 45–46, 48–49, 50–51
  second story, summary, 47
  theological reading of, 33
  third story, summary, 49–50
Moon, Zachary, 215
Moral injury
  care, depoliticized, 214–17
  care, privatizing, 218
  care, repoliticalization of, 217–28
  pastoral theology and, 213–35
Morris, Joshua, xxi, 212–35
Mother
  death of, 5, 11, 281–82, 284–85, 286, 294, 299, 302
  deceased, as co-therapist, 11–13
  dying, in *A Monster Calls*, 30–53
  effect on Confucius, 262–63, 267–69, 270–72
  effect on William James, 248–51
Mourning, 188–211
  grief, strategies for men, 297–301
  warrior ethos and, 191–200, 202, 204, 208, 209
  warriorism and, 203–9

"Mourning and Melancholia" (Freud), 50, 246
Mystical moment, 24–28
Mystical moment, method of, 24–28

Narrative therapy, 1–28
  conversation, power of, 5
  ethics and power, 14–15
  fictionalized personal letters, 10–11, 13–14, 21–22
  on grief, 287–94
  sessions, 2–4, 10–13, 21–22
Ness, Patrick, 32–33
Nouwen, Henri
  on death of mother, 281–82
  embodied remembering, 296–97
  grief, on reason and reflection, 299
  grief as emptiness, 284–85
  grief narrative, 287–94
  on grief recovery, 302
  A Letter of Consolation, xxii, 281, 282
  on male gender roles, 294–95
  on melancholy, 286
Numbness, 7, 12–13, 15, 16, 21

Objectivization, Black male bodies, 101–3, 105–6
Oedipal complex, 45, 51–52, 83, 142, 264–67, 269, 271
"On Dreams" (Freud), 33, 40–42, 48, 52
Oppression, in LGBTQ communities, 67–69
Otto, Rudolf, 245

Parables, 48–49, 76–78
Pastoral counseling
  Black men, 82, 221–25
  on countertransference feelings, 181
  as a friend, 175–77, 184–86
  gender creative persons, 75–78
  on homosocial love, 175–83
  Mexican men, 158–87
  practice of, 75–76, 78
  supporting resilience strategies, 75–76

INDEX

therapeutic relationships, 179–83
Pastoral theologians
  affirmative strategies, gender-creative persons, 78
  counseling relationships, 168
  on masturbation, 129, 154, 155
  on moral injury, 212, 213–17, 218, 220–28, 232
  practice by, 75–78
  religious view of masturbation, 154–55
  repositioning biblical verses, 71
  on William James, 243
Pastoral theology
  Black liberation, 221–25
  feminist, 225–27
  gender diversity and, 57–58
  moral injury and, 212–33
  sources of, 220–28
  William James as progenitor, 7–9
  womanist, 227–28
Pentecostalism, 251–52
Phenomenology
  Confucius, 273, 276
  emotions, 296
  research, on grief, 283–84
  resilience practices, 62
  writing as method, 281–304
Phillips, Adam, 51–52, 176
Pornography
  addiction, Jude (case study), 126–29
  addiction, neuroscience of, 127–28
  defense against loneliness and isolation, 128
  definition of, 123
  images and sexual fantasy, 123, 145, 174–75
  impact on children, 125
  internet, 124–28, 154
  masturbation and, 123, 144–45
  negative effects of, 125–26
  violent images of, 153
Positive role models, gender-creative persons, 73–75
Post-Traumatic Stress Disorder (PTSD), 213, 216, 217
Psychoanalysis
  fairytales, 51–52
  on masturbation, 143–44
  A Monster Calls, summary and analysis of, 30–53
  strict upbringing effecting personality, 268–69
  unconscious prejudice, black males, 99
Psychological loss, 245–46
Psychological transformation, 24–28
Psychopathia Sexualis (Van Kaan), 140
Psychotherapy, gender-affirmative model, 61
PTSD. *see* Post-Traumatic Stress Disorder (PTSD)
Public spaces
  Black boys' experience in, 114, 115, 117
  and Black male bodies, objectivization and criminalization of, 99, 100, 101–3, 104, 106, 107
  demonic transference, 110–11, 113
  racial delusion in, 106–10

Racial delusion, religious, 106–10
Racism, 81–82, 102–3, 221–22. *see also* racial delusion
Ramsay, Nancy, 215–16
Reciprocal hospitality, 76–78
Religious communities, 75–76, 106–7, 113–14
Religious conversion
  of Black persons, 106–7
  definition of, 17
  individualized nature of, 20–21
  from melancholy, 17
  six degrees of transmission, 24–28
  subconscious and, 19
  therapeutic transformation in, 16–21
Religious fundamentalism, 198–99
Resilience, gender-creative, 61–63
Resilience strategies
  awareness of oppression, 67–69
  cultivating hope, 70–71
  embrace self-worth, 66–67
  engaging in social activism, 71–73

as a positive role model, 73–75
self-generation definition of self,
    63–66
supportive community, 69–70
Resistance, 226–27, 232, 291–92
Rites (Confucian), 270–72
Rogers, Fred, 30–32
Rorty, Amélie, 94, 96
Rousseau, Jean-Jacques, 131, 135
Rubano, Craig A., xx, 56–79

Sadness, 290, 296, 297
Schaeffer, J. A., 110–13
Self, defining as gender-creative,
    63–66
*Series of Unfortunate Events, Book
    the Ninth, A; The Carnivorous
    Carnival* (Handler), 2–3, 10–11
Sex and the Psyche (Kahr), 138–45
Sexual Behavior in the Human Male
    (Kinsey), 120, 132, 133, 141
Sexual fantasy, 138–45
    definition of, 123
    dependent on visual stimulation
        (the eye), 145
    eye as dominant organ, 149
    Freud on, 140–41
    images and, 123, 148
    leading to orgasm, 140
    masturbation and, 143–44
    as normal behavior, 141–42
    as normative experience, 140
    pornographic images and, 123
    purpose of, 142–43
    shame and, 139–40
    source of pleasure and shame, 139
    varieties of, 142
    views of therapists and counselors,
        144–45
Shay, Jonathan, 213–14, 229
Shin, Hyon-Uk, xxi, 260–80
Sick soul, 7–9, 17
Sin, black male bodies, associated
    with, 106–7
Singh, Anneliese A, 61–63
Six degrees of transmission, 24–28
Smith, Archie, 223–25

Social activism, by gender-creative
    persons, 71–73
Society for Pastoral Theology, 216
Soldiers
    moral injury and, 212–13, 214,
        218–20, 221, 223
    pastoral recommendations, 231–33
    Smedley Butler on, 229–30
    warriorism and, 228–30
Solitary expressiveness, in grief,
    300–301
*Solitary Sex: A Cultural History Of
    Masturbation* (Laqueur), 129,
    132–36
Spiritual resilience, 75, 292
Splitting (individual or group), 103–4,
    107, 108–10
Stengers, Jean, 129–32
Stress, 115, 127, 128, 151
Subconscious mind, 18–21
Superego, 48, 49, 265

Taussig, Michael, 146–49
Taylor, Clyde R., 95
Teenagers. *see* Adolescence
Tender conscience, 9, 21
The Analects (Confucius), 261
    Confucius' life, 263–64
    implications, 272–74
Therapeutic transformation, religious
    conversion and, 16–21
Therapists, view of sexual fantasies,
    144–45
*Three Essays On The History Of
    Sexuality* (Freud), 140
Tietje, Adam, xxi, 212–35
Tillich, Paul, 113–14, 279
Tissot, Samuel-August, 120–22, 123,
    129–30, 137, 140, 149
Tolbert, Mary Ann, 48–49
Townes, E. M., 112, 113, 114
Transference, characteristics of,
    110–14
Transgender people, 56–78
Transgender violence, 58–60
Transmission, six degrees of, 24–28
Trauma
    cultural, 86, 95, 108

INDEX

loss of loved one, 247, 265–66
Post-Traumatic Stress Disorder (PTSD), 61, 213, 216, 217, 228
sexual, 125, 137, 144, 145
Twain, Mark, 121–23

Ugliness, 82–85, 87, 88, 95
Unconscious
   basis for splitting, 104, 108
   criminalization, of black males, 98, 99, 101–3, 108
   dreams, 42
   Freudian paradigm, 110
   homoerotic desire, 182
   optical, 147–48
   sexual fantasy, 141–42, 145, 147
   transference, 110–11
U.S. Transgender Survey (James), 58–61

Valor, xxii
Van Driel, Mels, 129, 136–38
Van Kaan, Heinrich, 140
Van Manen, Max, 283–84, 287
Van Neck, Anne, 129–32
Varieties of Religious Experience, The: A Study in Human Nature (James), 1, 7–9, 236
Veterans
   moral injury and, 208, 212–18
   pastoral recommendations, 220–21, 223, 228, 229, 230, 231–33
Vietnam, 212, 213, 215–17
Violence
   emotional, 101, 110
   intracultural, 99–100
   lynching, 101, 102–4
   military, at war, 190
   pornographic images of, 153
   reactionary, towards Black men, 103–4
   sexual, 127, 142, 153
   societal, 101–3
   transgender, 58–60
Virtues, 197, 222n14, 261, 276–78
Visual symbols, 41–42
Von Krafft-Ebing, Richard, 140, 154
Vulnerability, xxii, 269, 287

Warrior ethos, 189–200, 202, 204, 208, 209
Warriorism
   characteristics of, 189–90, 198–203
   moral injury and, 228–30
   mourning and, 203–9
   warrior ethos and, 191–200, 202, 204, 208, 209
Watkins Ali, Carroll, 227–28
Watzlawick, Paul, 26
Welldon, Estela, 151
Wells-Barnett, Ida B., 101, 103–4
Wilson, Gary, 127–28
Wimberly, Edward, 221–25
Wishes, 49, 52, 53, 141, 142, 143
Wishes Don't Make Things Come True (Rogers), 30–32
With The Hand: A Cultural History Of Masturbation (Van Driel), 129, 136–38
Wittgenstein, Ludwig, 25–26
Wolterstorff, Nicholas
   on death of son, 281–82
   embodied remembering, 296
   grief, on reason and reflection, 299
   grief as emptiness, 284
   grief narrative, 287–94
   Lament For A Son, xxii, 281
   on male gender roles, 295
   on suffering, 301
Woods, John, 124–28, 148, 149, 153, 154

Yan Zhengzai (mother of Confucius), 263, 265, 267–71
Yew tree, 43–44
Yew tree monster (character), 33–40
Young men, pastoral counseling of, 162–63, 165–66, 168–77, 179–85

Zylla, Phil C., xxi–xxii, 281–304

www.ingramcontent.com/pod-product-compliance
Lightning Source LLC
Chambersburg PA
CBHW052146300426
44115CB00011B/1543